# NOW IS THE TIME!

# NOW IS THE TIME!

## Detroit Black Politics and Grassroots Activism

**Todd C. Shaw**

Duke University Press • *Durham & London* • 2009

Printed in the United States
of America on acid-free paper ♾
Designed by Amy Ruth Buchanan
Typeset in Minion by Tseng
Information Systems, Inc.
Library of Congress Cataloging-in-
Publication Data appear on the
last printed page of this book.

*To Mom, Dad, and*
*Grandmother Catherine*
*for all of your wondrous*
*love and lessons*

# Contents

## Acknowledgments

It is ironic that I entitled this book *Now Is the Time!* Given the amount of time it took me to complete it, my family suggested as equally fitting: *No Time like the Present!* All joking aside, my journey of completion has been so winding that I cannot possibly name all of the people who served as guideposts. To the best of my recollection, however, I name many of the people and groups who, if had I not had their help in clearing my path, I doubt seriously I would have made it through.

My editors and reviewers deserve a lion's share of the credit for this book's clarity, while I assume the blame for any of its lingering murkiness. At Duke University Press, I am truly indebted to my former editor, Raphael Allen, because he first placed great faith in this project and demonstrated great patience with me even as the work tarried. Equally important has been my current editor, Courtney Berger. As combined with the epiphanies of my anonymous reviewers (many thanks), Courtney's on-point editorial insights and guidance are most responsible for making this book much better than it would have otherwise been.

There are many Detroit activists, organization leaders, government officials, and scholars who generously shared their time to respond to my sometimes inarticulate or uninformed questions. But without their wealth of insights, primary sources, and leads in locating others, the narratives I present in this book would be lopsided, at best. I extend a very special thanks to Ted Phillips, Annie Sanders (Kaleema Sumareh), Doug Smith, and Ruth Williams, who are or were at one time with the United Community Housing Coalition or PLAN, as well as to Marilyn Mullane of Michigan Legal Services; Beverly Manick and Karen McCleod of the Cass Corridor Neighborhood Development Corporation and SOS; and, most especially, to the heroic Marian Kramer, Yvette Linebarger, Wayne Pippin, and Maureen Taylor of the Michigan Welfare Rights Organization, Michigan Up and Out of Poverty, and the Detroit / Wayne County Union of the Homeless. To this day, many of the above have kept up the "good fight" to make those in power accountable to the grassroots.

I am also grateful to the very helpful staffs of the former Detroit City Planning Commission and the Planning Department, particularly John Lowe; to archivists and librarians at the Archive of Labor History and Urban Affairs at the Walter P. Reuther Library, Wayne State University (WSU), the Detroit Public Library's Burton Historical Collection, and the University of Michigan's Bentley Historical Library. I also thank current and former WSU faculty members in the Department of Political Science, including Timothy Bledsoe, Ronald Brown, Richard Elling, Errol Henderson, Mary Herring, Lyke Thompson, and Harold Wolman (especially as they made their unit a welcoming place for my postdoctoral research); the rich details and reams of documents provided by Tom Nutt-Powell, J. Scott Rogers, and Curtis Smith of Capital Needs Unlimited and Housing Solutions; as well as other Detroit citizens too numerous to mention but who generously shared their expertise and contacts with me.

Several people currently or formerly at the University of Michigan, Ann Arbor, started me down a fruitful path of inquiry during my doctoral work, which resulted in this book. Among them were John Ballard, Barry Checkoway, and Harold Johnson in the School of Social Work; Kate Warner in the School of Urban Planning; and Jim Chaffers of the School of Art and Architecture. Members of my dissertation committee displayed infinite patience for my "half-baked ideas" and genuine encouragement when I was "on to something." Genuine thanks go to my co-chairs, Michael Dawson and Hanes Walton Jr., for they made me truly appreciate the study of African American politics, as well as my other committee members, Rick Hall and Earl Lewis. There were others who did not serve on my committee but greatly contributed to my thinking: Nancy Burns, Mary Corcoran, and Steve Rosenstone in political science, as well as Robin Kelley in history.

Of course, it is also very important to pay homage to those who subsidized the work and helped to pay the bills. I thank the University of Michigan's Department of Political Science for a Gerald R. Ford dissertation research grant; the Social Science Research Council for a very generous dissertation fellowship through its Research on Urban Poverty grant; and the Department of Political Science, University of Illinois, Urbana-Champaign (UIUC), particularly under Peter Nardulli, for the office space and the superb resources necessary to complete the dissertation phase. Moreover, my thanks to the Ford Foundation and the National Science Foundation's Minority Postdoctoral Fellowship, which helped me to gather vital data and buy additional time as I began to sketch the post-dissertation outline of this work.

A number of faculty colleagues, many of whom are also good friends, served as readers at various stages of the project, including Robert Brown, Cathy Cohen, Christian Davenport, Jeffrey Edwards, Frederick Harris (especially through his African American politics conference at the University of Rochester), Richard Iton, Kimberly Jones, K. C. Morrison, Michael Owens, Dianne Pinderhughes, Michael Preston, Robert Smith, and Lester K. Spence. At my current academic home, the University of South Carolina, Columbia (USCC), under Harvey Starr and later Daniel Sabia, my thanks go to my political-science colleagues Ann Bowman, David Darmofal, Jill Frank, Mark Tompkins, Kenny Whitby, Laura Woliver, and Christopher Zorn. Among my African-American Studies colleagues and others throughout the university, my thanks go to the following for their helpful feedback and questions during various research presentations: Glenda Coleman, David Crockett, Bobby Donaldson, Nancy Glenn, Daniel Littlefield (of the Institute for African-American Research), Val Littlefield, David Simmons, Kimberly Simmons, Terrance Weik, and Qiana Whitted. I appreciate the constant support of Andrew Billingsley, Cleveland Sellers, and Patricia Sullivan.

In addition, a small legion of brilliant and industrious graduate students and other research professionals went above the call of duty, and often the proper compensation, to make sure I got my numbers and facts straight. They include David Dormofal and Dorian Warren at UIUC; as well as A. J. Bargothi, Christopher Buckowsky, Athena King, Chenhong Li, Lucas McMillan, Mekell Mikell, and Dheeraj Thumma at USC. Also at USC, the assistance of Kevin Remington and Lynn Shirley in the Geography Department's Geographic Information Systems laboratory were invaluable as I analyzed the contexts of grassroots activism.

Finally, my heart is full because of a rich circle of personal support. The love, laughter, and prayers of my immediate and extended Shaw family have been my greatest source of earthly strength: my father (James), mother (Ruby), brothers (Rodney, Van, and Dean), and sisters-in-law (Beth and Kelly), as well as my nieces, nephew, aunts, and cousins. Likewise, I am grateful for the loving counsel of my pastor, Bishop Tonyia Rawls, First Lady Gwendolyn Rawls, and my church family at Unity Fellowship Church Charlotte, all of whom literally helped me *keep the faith* as I *ran this race*. With regard to friends I have not yet mentioned, there are many souls who traveled this long distance with me and deserve my thanks, including Ona Alston-Dosunmu, Juan Battle, Yvonne Brooks, Jeffrey Cabusao, Robert Castro, Antoine Clark, Vincent Danner, Karen DeGannes, Mark Ellis, Regina Freer, Cynthia Henderson, Catrina Johnson, Roderick Linzie, William Neal, Randy Rogers, Dwaun Sellers, Jocelyn Sergeant, Pilgrim Spikes, Hopeton Stewart, and Gerald Walker. I must underscore how invaluable my brother and colleague, Robert A. Brown (brotherman!), has been to my work, livelihood, and spirit. Along with Robin Soler, he has been my truest and most faithful friend.

.................................

An earlier version of chapter 3 appeared in Ollie Johnson and Karen Stanford, *Black Political Organizations in the Post-Civil Rights Movement Era* (Rutgers University Press, 2002). Portions of chapter 6 appeared previously as "Race, Regime and Redevelopment: Opportunities for Community Coalitions in Detroit, 1985–1993," *National Political Science Review* 9 (2003), and "Race and Representation in Detroit's Community Development Coalitions," *Annals of the American Academy of Political and Social Science* 594 (2004).

# INTRODUCTION

## The Right Tactic, Time, and Place

**[Public housing residents] decided that: "*Now is the time* that we're going to start doing something, and we're going to start to fight for the rights of people who live in public housing."**
**—Ruth Williams, co-chair, Preserve Low-Income and Affordable Housing Now! (PLAN), 1994**

### WHAT TIME IS IT?

Black creative genius takes many forms. Commonly it is at work when talented African Americans produce a desirable outcome using the right tool, at the right moment, in the right setting. For instance, a host of conditions influenced the playing of the jazz virtuoso Charlie "Bird" Parker: his choice of saxophone, the time of the performance, his state of mind, the mood of the venue. As his song "Now's the Time" suggests, Bird knew just when and how to use these conditions to create masterful improvisations.[1] In a similar vein, I examine the political imagination of black grassroots activists in the city of Detroit, Michigan. I study their unique choices in tactics, timing, and places as they mobilize to hold public officials accountable to the needs of low-income citizens. Famous for Berry Gordy's Motown recording company as well as industrially prominent as the "Motor City," Detroit provides an ideal case study for understanding the creativity of black grassroots activism in the post–Civil Rights Movement era. Amid stark urban poverty, this city's rich history of labor activism, civil-rights activism, and strong black political empowerment, especially under Mayor Coleman A. Young, has compelled black grassroots organizers to be innovative as they pressure government to meet basic needs such as high-quality and affordable housing.[2]

Consequently, this book's main refrain is that black grassroots activists and their allies must select the right *tactic*, *time*, and *place* for activism to be effective in demanding political accountability to the needs of the poor. While the conditions underlying black grassroots activism are fascinating, my main interest is when and how this activism induces accountability. I want to know not simply when activists make noise, but when they are heard and occasionally heeded by those in government. Grassroots activism is not my shorthand term for protest; it includes the broad repertoire of collective actions lower-income activists take to demand government accountability—from mobilizing the vote against jaded incumbents (normal politics) to standing in front of bulldozers (extra-normal politics.) Not every moment is ripe for protest; nor can every conflict be resolved by citizens politely waiting for politicians to hold public hearings. The acute activist properly reads the signs of the time and chooses. Accountability means that public officials at least take responsibility for government actions that have or may have adverse effects on their constituents, but ideally accountability should be part of a broader ethic of public officials responding to and promoting citizens' preferences and needs.[3]

In between the activism and accountability relationship are the intervening factors of *utility*, or the right tactic; *timing*, or the right moment; and *context*, or the right setting. They are among the factors political-process theorists consider vital in explaining the success of social movements. Such theorists believe that political opportunity structures (POS) explain which arrangements of ideals and institutions are most likely to produce effective political dissidence.[4] I borrow from POS theory to present an Effective Black Activism Model (EBAM), in which the vision and agency of activists—not predetermined political structures—are the starting points for determining whether mobilization leads to responsiveness.[5] Through this model, I hypothesize when grassroots activists who perceive the utility, timing, and context of black grassroots activism can most effectively apply pressure to black and other public officials, despite the barriers of race, class, gender, and regime.

First of all, attention to utility permits activists to (1) forge oppositional alliances with insiders that challenge a (black) regime's dominance (*disruptive coalitions*); and (2) use various forms of political action flexible enough to overcome the power of entrenched incumbency (*adaptive tactics*). Second, attention to timing permits activists to (1) join a larger movement and strike when a regime is vulnerable (*activist cycles*); and (2) exploit any beneficial changes in the "rules of the game"—for example, court injunctions, laws, and regulations (*strategic advantages*). Finally, attention to context permits activists to (1) project group identities and goals that bridge ideological and social and class divisions (*collective identity and framing*); and (2) use organizational assets to overcome the costs of mobilization—for example, arrests, jail time, and loss of income (*group resources and networks*).

Because it is unreasonable to assume that grassroots campaigns must have all six sub-factors on their side to be effective, I contend that the necessary, if not always sufficient, conditions are the three "As" of strong *allies*, *advantages*, and *adaptive tactics*. Utility and context conditions favor activism when activists are connected to instrumental allies. Timing favors activism in those instances when strategic advantages benefit activists and most affect regime stability. And utility conditions favor activism when adaptive tactics empower insurgents with a political veto over a regime's plans. From roughly 1933, when the federal government began to shape public-housing and urban economic-development policies, to 2005, when Kwame Kilpatrick, Detroit's third black mayor, agreed to place the city's public housing under a limited federal receivership, this book explores black activists' claims that black and other public officials have neglected low-income-housing needs and that it is thus time for counter-action.

My model permits us to read various settings, moments, and tactics to determine whether *Now Is the Time*. To be sure, I discuss several instances when grassroots campaigns were quite successful because they had strong allies, advantages, and adaptive tactics—for example, the Save Our Spirit community-development campaign and the Parkside Homes HOPE VI Project. But, I also present several counterfactuals when advocates lacked strong alliances (e.g., the Herman Gardens HOPE VI project), strategic advantages (e.g., the Brewster-Douglass anti-demolition campaign), or adaptive tactics (e.g., public-housing versus community-development activism overall). Thus, those in power were much less accountable to ordinary citizens. To not understand fully when conditions are ripest for grassroots activism is to fundamentally misread the currents of black politics in this post–Civil Rights Movement era. We risk implying to younger generations that all opportunities for effective black grassroots activism have long since passed, especially if that activism assumes the form of protest—for example, anti–Iraq War protests or the Jena Six campaign.[6]

## EXPANDING BLACK POLITICS AND BLACK ACTIVISM

My larger intellectual project is to expand and more strongly link our conceptions of African American politics and black grassroots activism. During the 1960s, blacks led or helped to lead a spate of social-justice causes, including civil rights, black power and black community control, antipoverty programs and welfare rights, the women's movement, workers' rights and militant unionism, anti–urban renewal campaigns, and affordable housing and tenant rights.[7] Each outpouring of citizen dissent contributed to a turbulent season, however brief, when the American political system was compelled to make limited policy concessions to quell dissent. Yet several contemporary students of African American politics, especially Adolph Reed and Robert Smith, assert that this storm of black activism has largely dissipated due to the *hyper-institutionalization* of black politics, in which electoral politics has supplanted grassroots activism, as well as the *demobilization* of black nongovernmental organizations. With the mid-1970s advent of a new and prolific generation of black elected leaders able to tug at the levers of power from within government, tactics such as marches, sit-ins, pickets, squatting, blockades, and street theater assumed more symbolic than instrumental purposes. Contributing to campaigns, voting, and holding office became the modus operandi of black political power. To paraphrase Bayard Rustin, African American politics shifted from grassroots *protest* to governmental *politics*.[8]

Inspired by fusionist approaches to black grassroots activism such as those of James Jennings and J. Phillip Thompson III, my study is unique. It empirically tests and revises the hyper-institutionalization and demobilization theses by viewing black insurgency as integrally linked to, as opposed to alienated from, institutional politics. In fact, my model helps to discern when black activism can challenge or possibly even expand the normal boundaries of black and electoral politics. Utility matters, for, like Jennings and Thompson, I broadly define the parameters of black grassroots activism and thus envision insurgent electoral politics as one pole on a dynamic continuum, with protest at the other end. It simply depends on which set of tactics (or strategy) is best suited for a specific policy goal. A key delineation between the various forms of grassroots activism I study is whether a group is relatively advantaged by its membership in an urban interest-group system (e.g., community-development organizations), and thus principally relies on institutional lobbying, or a group is more insurgent (e.g., public-housing activists) and more often must resort to protest.[9] True to the cycles of protest literature, timing matters, for there have been noticeable points of post–Civil Rights Movement insurgency in Detroit and other cities that experienced decades of black political empowerment. The 1970s certainly witnessed an overall decline in black insurgency. But the analysis I present in this book confirms that the early and mid-1980s were periods of renewed black activism, partly in response to federal and local government retrenchment.[10] Finally, context matters because it suggests those locales where black activists are most likely to make headway against the barriers of race, class, gender, and regime. As I explain later, context indicates those locales, such as Detroit, where African American politics is occasionally expanded to include not only issues of racial but also those of economic redistribution and where black women's leadership helps to define a city's economic interests as larger than those of the central business district.[11]

## THE REGIMES OF RACE, CLASS, AND GENDER

How can race, class, gender, and regime impede the opportunities for effective grassroots activism? Often, the political context or the temperament of a local administration encourages or complicates public accountability to the poor. Clarence Stone and others define a classic *urban regime* as an informal but efficacious growth coalition composed of a city's public officials, civic leaders, and capitalist stakeholders. I broaden use of the term "regime" to include the ideologies and political mechanisms necessary to justify a top-down growth agenda, whether or not it has the full capacity to be an urban regime. All urban regimes are undergirded by particular configurations of race, class, and gender, but not all regimes are the same or the same over time.[12]

The key chapters of this book focus on grassroots activism in Detroit during the administration of Mayor Coleman A. Young (1973–93). As Marion Orr and Gerry Stoker conclude, Young did not have a functioning urban regime by the end of his term. But his choosing to exert enormous energy to create one, even though he failed, is politically significant. As both the longest-serving and first black mayor of Detroit, Young was a charismatic, racially proud, and powerful leader whose fascinating biography as a militant labor activist and as a state senator and Democratic Party stalwart make him an exemplar of the first generation of black mayors to transition from the era of protest to politics. Like other black mayors of the period, Young came to power at an unfortunate moment in the 1970s—during the "urban crisis"—when most American cities were saddled with staggering economic troubles and social ills. Thus, the reins of local power and his ability to publicly effect change were severely curtailed. Regrettably, as his incumbency lengthened, various challenges also eroded his administration's ability, and sometimes willingness, to meet the most pressing needs of its poorest citizens.[13]

Worsening bouts of business disinvestment, global competition, poverty, racial tensions, and white population flight frustrated many of Young's best efforts to resurrect Detroit's past industrial and commercial prosperity. But the political heavy-handedness his political machine used to pursue its top-down growth agenda also slowly aroused a vocal opposition from grassroots organizations fearful that their constituents were adversely affected by cuts in public services and unfairly dislocated by economic redevelopment. By the latter half of this tenure, Young and his supporters had so rigidly framed black politics that they interpreted even moderate black-led resistance to his administration's economic and housing policies as inimical to black group interests. When black electoral challengers and black-led community groups openly questioned the city's fiscal priorities, the mayor often castigated them as troublemakers and racial turncoats. The latter was a particularly damning charge within Detroit's racially polarized politics.[14]

Given the persistent inequalities of race in Detroit and elsewhere, it is no wonder that racial solidarity and antiracism are the pre-eminent ethics of African American politics and thus foment group consciousness and feelings of a common fate. Nevertheless, economic redistribution is a vital corollary to antiracism, as shown by various twentieth-century calls for racial justice and full employment, such as the March on Washington for Jobs and Justice in 1963, and the Black Radical Congress's antiracist, antipoverty agenda.[15] It is equally true that widening black class differences and divergent ideological interpretations can spark community debates as to whether a black elected leader such as Young is responsive to the black poor. Another highly relevant ethic within black politics—the equal empowerment of black women—is often inadequately addressed or entirely overlooked by a male-dominated black leadership, for like class, gender can be trumped by race.[16] Still, gender implicitly matters within black grassroots politics, for a great majority of the Detroit struggles I studied were led by black women, reflecting a broader trend. Gender as experienced by women is an indispensable part of their multiple identity and "standpoint." It inspires a certain style of collective leadership and builds group cohesion, even if its inequities are not one of the overt grievances women activists cite.[17]

During contentious policy debates when varying interpretations of the antiracism and antipoverty ethics compete, and the problems posed by gender inequity are disregarded, the needs of the black poor may be neglected by some of the very same black elected officials who pledge to advance the well-being of *all* African Americans. Protest is a tool of last resort for black grassroots activists to be heard over the public clamor, but such insurgency poses a paradox. Those most in need of being heard over the din of public debate have, by definition, the fewest resources to vocalize and defend their needs. So my Effective Black Activism Model helps tackles the thorny question: Under what conditions and at what points can black grassroots activists, in predominantly black cities, voice effective opposition to anti-redistributive policy? Whereas as the EBAM most directly applies to African American urban politics, its broader formulation can be generalized to a host of other situations where leftist insurgents seek to challenge a post-insurgency or new liberal regime—for example, South African HIV/AIDS activists confronting the lethargy of the Mbeki government; anti-NAFTA or anti-globalization advocates challenging the Clinton administration; or Russian true believers in "*perestroika*" criticizing the administration of Boris Yeltsin.[18]

## LOW-INCOME HOUSING IN DETROIT

Before I discuss this book's methods and outline, it is important to explain why my policy focus is on low- and moderate-income housing—housing rehabilitation or community development, public housing, and services to the homeless. Few other multifaceted areas of public policy are more fundamental to the security and well-being of families and individuals than government subsidies for or the provision of high-quality, affordable housing. Likewise, few other policy areas have been more politically contentious because of the conflicting interests that have vied for control over housing locations, construction, maintenance, and demolition.[19] For the entire history of the federal government's role in granting cities and local agencies monies to construct public housing or to subsidize rents and home repair, there has been a problematic linkage between affordable housing and economic development. Born of a compromise between real-estate interests and home builders, the fate of public and other subsidized housing has often been determined more by the imperatives of downtown and suburban developers than the needs of its primary stakeholders—that is, public-housing tenants, homeless citizens, and home-repair clients. Over the past three decades, the trajectory of federal and thus local policy has been a greater reliance on market solutions while the federal government has attempted literally to "get out of the housing business." In the early 1980s, the Reagan administration's "New Federalism" combined political devolution with fiscal retrenchment and proposed the deepest of all of its social spending cuts in the areas of housing and community development. In the 1990s, the "new liberalism" of the Clinton administration merged liberal ideals with the conservatism of the previous Reagan–Bush era. The resulting Empowerment Zone and HOPE VI initiatives stressed neighborhood revitalization through public–private partnerships and the building of often privately managed "mixed-income" public-housing communities. The second Bush administration harked back to elements of Reaganism by proposing an "Ownership Society."[20]

Again, I have selected Detroit as my principal case. As the largest city in the

United States (just under 1 million residents) with a majority African American population (now 82 percent) and a pronounced history of working-class activism, it represents a critical case for examining the victories, setbacks, and contradictions of contemporary black politics and efforts at grassroots democracy. Although there are a number of fine works on the contemporary politics of race and class in Detroit, my book bridges the scholarly gaps between longitudinal studies of community-based advocacy, post-1960s African American politics, urban public policy, and social movement theory. Without ever assuming that I speak on behalf of Detroit's grassroots advocates or their constituents, I ponder the profound wisdom they generously shared with me and revise some of the academic conclusions about why and when activism and protest matter.[21]

## METHODS

Mindful of what Marco Giugni calls "the problem of causality, that is, how to establish a causal link between a given movement and an observed change," I measure or infer the effects between activism and accountability in four broad ways. First, I collect data on the actions of several actors other than the movement activists, thus controlling for alternative influences on policy changes. Second, I observe "broad social-change variables" such as black racial ideology, the class structure, or housing markets as they affect policy outcomes. Third, I set up a comparative research design by contrasting the case of Detroit against the cases of other black-led cities—Atlanta, Newark, and Washington, D.C.—thus accounting for changes in varying contexts. And fourth, I take longitudinal measures of insurgency and policy responses to understand not only when "a given movement's actions ha[ve] led to change, but also . . . situations in which no outcome can be observed."[22] Among the qualitative methods I use are guided personal interviews with sixty-two primary actors in the low-income housing arena, participant observation, the historical method using archival data, and interpretative analyses of government documents and secondary sources, including a basic coding of newspaper articles. On average, the sixty-two guided interviews were an hour long and conducted between April 1994 and April 1998, as well as in July 2006. Some subjects were interviewed more than once (see appendix 1).[23] Overall, these interviews gave substantive meaning to my narrative and allowed me to understand the accounts and perceptions of important actors as well as their linkages.[24] My quantitative methods include the analysis of survey, budget, census, geographic, and electoral data ranging from simple cross-tabulations to multivariate techniques.

## OUTLINE AND CONCLUSION

This book is divided into three parts, under which come an introduction, seven chapters, and an epilogue. Part I contains my framework chapter 1. Part II presents my meticulous analysis of the Detroit case, between 1933 and 1993, and describes black grassroots housing activism prior to and during Young's tenure. In chapter 2, I use historical sources to demonstrate how the utility, timing, and context of grassroots housing activism found the most fertile soil and progressive outcomes during the Great Depression and in the 1960s. Chapter 3 extends this history and explores the contextual dimension of African American politics under Young, especially as his supporters and he attempted to define the contours of black politics and suppress black opposition to his top-down development regime. Chapter 4 illustrates the utility and timing dimensions of the problem. Against the backdrop of Detroit's affordable-housing crisis of the 1970s and 1980s, the Reagan administration's fiscal retrenchment and lax federal oversight, coupled with the Young administration's mismanagement of public housing, chapter 4 presents attitudinal and behavioral data to argue why and how the mid-1980s became a period of renewed grassroots activism, especially with regard to housing.

Chapters 5 and 6 are the linchpins of the book in which I demonstrate the EBAM's full range of insights about the need for allies, advantages, and adaptive tactics. These two chapters test the counterfactual question: What occurs if we hold the context and timing dimensions relatively constant and vary the utility dimension, as was true of the differing types of tactics Detroit community developers employed versus the tactics public housing advocates employed? Chapter 5 explores community development activism by focusing on the predominantly white but often black-led coalition Save Our Spirit (SOS). Through ample interpretative and quantitative evidence, I argue that SOS negotiated the Young administration's precarious framing of racial politics and its top-down community development agenda. SOS built strong alliances with the City Council, benefited from strategic advantages, and successfully lobbied so that community-based projects received higher block-grant allocations. While protest was a secondary complement to SOS's strategy, chapter 6 shows how protest became the primary strategy for public-housing and anti-homelessness activists as they fought to save their complexes from the Young regime's demolition plans. In that chapter, the Brewster–Douglass protest cycle of the late 1980s is compared to the more successful Parkside and Jeffries Homes protest cycle of the early 1990s. Leaders of the latter cycle had learned from past lessons and more clearly profited from strategic advantages. But both predominantly black campaigns were largely confined to protest tactics and had weaker alliances than did the majority-white SOS.

Part III entails two final chapters that extend beyond the tenure of Mayor Young and look beyond the Detroit context. Chapter 7 analytically complements chapters 5 and 6. Whereas those chapters hold timing and context constant and vary the utility factor, chapter 7 varies the contextual dimension and holds the utility and timing factors constant. I tell a story of missed and mixed opportunities regarding the Empowerment Zone program but principally the HOPE VI tenant-involvement and community revitalization program. By the end of two terms (1993–2001), Dennis Archer, Detroit's second black mayor, had led the city through a period of unprecedented economic growth and downtown construction, but his "new liberal" regime fundamentally disappointed many grassroots advocates. I contrast my findings for Detroit with those for three other cities that had HOPE VI projects and at least thirty years of black political empowerment—Atlanta, Newark, and Washington, D.C. I explain how, as public-housing activism tactically shifted from protest to programming, some advocates greatly improved their public-housing neighborhoods without encouraging gentrification. Some benefited from stronger community alliances, stronger strategic advantages, and innovative revitalization plans because they did not suffer displacement at the hands of black urban regimes. In the epilogue, I summarize the visions of black grassroots activism as rooted in democratic faith and deep democracy and speculate about the political fortunes of black grassroots activism in black-led majority cities such as Detroit, which now has experienced a third, troubled, black mayor, Kwame Kilpatrick.

All of my analysis is guided by my belief in a fully participatory citizenship. In the introductory chapter of *The City and the Grassroots*, Manuel Castells asserts: "If urban research is to respond to the questions of our time—the urban crisis, the role of the state, and the challenge of urban protest—we need to integrate our analyses of structure and process, or crisis and change. *Our purpose is to cautiously construct a new theory of urban change that can light the path to a new city.*"[25] I am cautious in setting the goal for this book, but my belief in the right of lower-income citizens to be agents and not objects of public policy is why I link my epilogue's conclusions to broader questions of democratic faith and deep democracy. In the next chapter, I provide new clarity on the circumstances that allow black activists to determine whether the time and place are right to pressure the old city to address persistent grievances.

# PART I

*From Black Politics to Grassroots Protest*

# 1

## Making Black Activism Matter

**[Homeless] people started telling us, "This is the first time I have an opportunity to get arrested for something that is decent—for a house, for a home, for something decent. I don't care."**
**—Marian Kramer, president, National Welfare Rights Union, 1994, commenting on the dangers of sit-ins in vacant public-housing units in Detroit**

### POLITICS IS NOT ENOUGH

In their book *Protest Is Not Enough*, Rufus Browning, Dale Marshall, and David Tabb explore black and Latino political incorporation in ten California cities in the 1970s and 1980s. They conclude, "Although demand-protest yields some measurable gain in responsiveness from city governments, the [political] incorporation of the [minority] groups yield much more."[1] There is nothing particularly controversial about this conclusion. In fact, it reflects a strong pragmatism about the limits of protest politics. What is questionable, however, is the timing of their claim. Once we pass the initial phase of minority incorporation in several major cities such as Detroit and Atlanta, how do we assess whether local government is responsive to African Americans, especially the poor? How, if at all, can contemporary grassroots leaders and groups pressure black elected officials to not become jaundiced incumbents who are oblivious to vital community needs?

In this chapter, I present my theory of how effective black grassroots activism in this post-Civil Rights Movement era can prompt public accountability to black low-income communities despite the barriers of race, class, gender, and regime. But those who seek to shake up the powers that be in government must calculate which form of political action is the right tactic, at the right time, and in the right place. Thus, they have strategic choices to make—sit-ins, lobbying for funds, electoral politics, and so on. To invert the claim of Browning and his colleagues that "protest is not enough," I respond that a contemporary politics divorced from a broadly defined grassroots activism is equally inadequate for empowering the black poor. My Effective Black Activism Model (EBAM) asserts that activism induces accountability when black and other advocates consider its utility, timing, and context. Thus, at the very least, they recruit powerful allies, or *disruptive coalitions and group networks*; exploit game rules, or *strategic advantages*; and employ flexible political actions, or *adaptive tactics*. Protest has strategic value in inducing accountability within black politics, but my task is to explain why it is only one strategy in the grassroots activist's repertoire. Later in this chapter, I also explain why critics such as Robert Smith and Adolph Reed believe that an unintended consequence of the enormous political gains African Americans derived from the Civil Rights Movement has been the hyper-institutionalization of black politics and the demobilization of grassroots activism.[2] Using what I label a fusionist approach, I explain the theoretical linkages between my chief independent variable, *accountability*, and my key dependent variable, *grassroots activism*. Then I present, and later disassemble, my model to specify when and how grassroots activism matters in inducing political accountability to the black poor.

## THE LINKS BETWEEN ACCOUNTABILITY, GRASSROOTS ACTIVISM, AND PROTEST

### Political Accountability and Responsiveness

*Political accountability* is a process whereby a public official explains policy stances or governmental actions to a constituent group and takes responsibility for the detrimental or potentially detrimental outcomes of such policy stances or governmental actions. I measure political accountability by examining public officials' reactions and explanatory statements—budget vetoes, press conferences, statements at public hearings—especially when these officials or their colleagues are the targets of dissent. The community-organizing tradition interprets the notion of accountability not as a mere protocol of public input or accurate bookkeeping but, instead, as a broad ethic of public officials answering to citizens. For instance, during municipal elections in Detroit in 1989, neighborhood activists banded together to write a "PEOPLE's Platform" as a guideline to assess mayoral and City Council candidates and declared, "Accountability and accessibility are vital elements of good leadership. It is time for the elected leadership to remember to whom they are answerable."[3] I agree with Hannah Pitkin's criticism that, within the representation puzzle, the actions of an official who merely "accounts for" past wrongs (formalistic representation) lack the gravitas of one who "acts for" or on behalf of constituents (substantive representation.) Urban policing and public education are just two arenas in which accountability has a highly contested meaning.[4] Still, accountability is a vital starting point. If a black mayor or black school-board member cannot *at least* explain a government's actions and take responsibility for outcomes that jeopardize constituents' well-being—for example, Philadelphia's Mayor Wilson Goode apologizing for the police bombing of a neighborhood to subdue a black militant group—then it is difficult to imagine how she can more proactively represent the same constituents' interests.[5]

*Responsiveness* is a process whereby a public official promotes, as well as favorably responds to, the demands, preferences, or expectations of a constituent group. I measure responsiveness by examining public officials' policy initiatives and symbolic acts of solidarity with grassroots constituencies: initial budget votes, policy proposals, speeches at rallies, and so on. Not as a reaction or afterthought but as part of her active intent, a public official must pursue policies that embrace the demands of citizens to be considered responsive. For example, the initial election of Mayor Harold Washington in Chicago by a highly energized black community encouraged him to redirect funds toward black and other low-income neighborhoods.[6] Put differently, accountability is reactive because it is explanatory behavior usually initiated *after* a precipitating event, and responsiveness is proactive because it is representative behavior usually initiated *before* a precipitating event. Ultimately, to conclude that a politician or bureaucrat is truly being attentive, accountability and responsiveness must be part of a string of continuous actions rather than isolated or compulsory behavior.

## Grassroots Activism and Protest

Having defined the representation side of the problem, I now turn to the mobilization side. *Grassroots activism*, or community organizing, is a form of political action that assumes ordinary citizens can confront maldistributions of power by organizing as communities of geographic or ascriptive identity (race, class, gender) and thus use their indigenous creativity, leadership, and resources.[7] While protest has often been mistaken as synonymous with grassroots activism, it is only one strategy within this activism's dynamic range. Our principal question is: What tactic best suits the ends of empowering the disadvantaged at a given moment? Michael Owens challenges the view that the breadth of black grassroots activism is simply delimited by the poles of protest or electoral politics. Observant of black churches engaged in community development, he interjects programming as a halfway point where black public–private collaborations build community capacity, leverage community influence, and serve the needy. According to Sekou Franklin, *black grassroots activism* involves black-led attempts to organize and mobilize disadvantaged communities, whether these black activists are in mono-racial, multiracial / multiethnic, or single-issue groups.[8] The local social movement field debates whether a group consensus of organizing around economic or material interests too often glosses over equally important cleavages and identities—race, gender, sexual orientation—and whether the provision of programmatic services such as housing, job training, or youth programs, requires a group to cooperate with government and business at the expense of politically confronting them. To determine whether leaders are most inclined to pursue collaborative or confrontational approaches to activism, we must know whether they are part of an urban interest-group system.[9]

Although I am interested in understanding the broad range of actions grassroots organizations use to advocate their causes, protest is a unique form of political action, a unique strategy, because it seeks to voice opposition publicly by disturbing business as usual. *Protest*, or insurgency, is the range of confrontational and often disruptive political actions that grassroots groups use to assert their interests in various arenas to challenge other interests that are more dominant and entrenched. Peter Eisinger says that protest includes various "collective manifestations, disruptive in nature, designed to provide 'relatively powerless people' with bargaining leverage in the political process."[10] It often has a symbolic or theatrical value, but it is most instrumental when it trespasses on the property of those in power and provokes them to negotiate with the trespassers. Event-history analysis is useful in measuring occurrences of protest as reported in newspapers or organizational records.[11]

Neglected or unrecognized claims such as those of homeless advocates may use insurgency to reinforce the advocacy of public officials who are their allies, to convert other public officials into allies, or to compel indifferent or obstinate public officials to heed their demands. Among others, Leonard Moore has examined how reformist black politicians such as Mayor Carl Stokes of Cleveland relied on local grassroots activists to make noise to create pressure for new agendas of racial and economic reform. My thinking coincides with Michael Lipsky's assumption that protest is a "political resource" because it can potentially attract the attention of reference publics from whom politicians derive their legitimacy. And as E. E. Schattschneider's work has long reminded us, it is the less powerful who need to draw attention to their plight by starting a fight or by "socializing conflict."[12]

## The Potential and the Limits of Protest

All of the above suggests that sometimes protest may make a difference, but in the contemporary black urban context, when does it make a difference? Recall that the efficacy of protest depends on its disruptive potential, which is an assumption I borrow from Frances Fox Piven and Richard Cloward. In their book *Poor People's Movements*, they define disruption as "simply the application of a negative sanction, the withdrawal of a crucial contribution on which others depend, and it is therefore a natural resource for exerting power over others."[13] Moments of societal transition or crisis—the Great Depression; shifts in Southern agricultural production; tension in urban ghettoes—provide opportunities for this disruption to have leverage in making demands on the power structure. However, Piven and Cloward assert that the black poor will have difficulties in using disruption: "Influence depends, first of all, on whether or not the contribution withheld is crucial to others; second, on whether or not those who have been affected by the disruption have resources to be conceded; and third, on whether the obstructionist group can protect itself adequately from reprisals. *Once these criteria are stated, it becomes evident that the poor are usually in the least strategic position to benefit from defiance.*"[14] Poor people may retaliate through actions that James Scott and Robin Kelley call "infrapolitics," or various non-collective acts of resistance, such as confronting a public-housing manager or drawing political graffiti on a wall. Still, when compared with individual dissidence, collective action is a more visible form of resistance that requires communal discourse.[15] Piven and Cloward likely overstated their case when they assumed that permanent organizations are incapable of sustaining protest, but we must appreciate their warning that contentious politics eventually affect an organization's viability and longevity.[16]

Critics have fairly pointed out several clear limitations to protest, not the least of which is that disruption has repercussions and can make negotiation quite difficult.[17] But it is also true that, on occasion, confrontation is not only useful but necessary. Conflict practitioners and theorists—from John Lewis of the United Mine Workers to Dianne Nash of the Student Non-Violent Coordinating Committee (SNCC)—have argued that agitation is required when it compels those in power to negotiate or suffer political instability. It is for this very reason that Frederick Douglass's axiom has cogently warned generations of black activists: "Power concedes nothing without demand. It never did and it never will."[18] To be effective, activists have to pick and choose their battles and their weapons based on the vulnerabilities of the regime, the temperament of the times, and the specific arena of combat.

## THE EFFECTIVE BLACK ACTIVISM MODEL

### Political Opportunities and the Activist Standpoint

Because opportunities for activism to compel accountability partly depend on the specific disposition and stability of the targeted government, I borrow from the political opportunity structures (POS) literature. Unlike some of the POS literature, I am interested not simply in which conditions foster activism but, rather, in when such political actions have an impact on government and public policies. It is difficult, however, to consider whether activism can make a difference if it occurs in political systems that are closed and thus zealously repress, discourage, or inhibit public dissent. So the POS literature is a useful starting point in constructing the EBAM. Peter Eisinger introduced the concept of POS to examine the institutional factors that affected whether a large subsample of American cities witnessed protest behavior in the late 1960s. He discovered that black protest most often occurred within systems that had either a mixture of open and closed features or mayor-council forms of government, sizable overall populations, or large numbers of black elected officials.[19] All of the above aptly describe Detroit. After comparing the works of several prominent POS theorists, Doug McAdam and colleagues discerned that the variables theorists most commonly cited as significant were whether a political system is open or closed, the stability or instability of elite governing coalitions, the presence or absence of elite allies for insurgents, and a state's capacity and propensity for repression.[20] Each of these variables is integrated into features of my model.

Although Eisinger's and McAdam's conclusions are useful, they provide grist for critics who complain that POS theory is entirely too structuralist and gives inordinate weight to static factors such as government institutions at the expense of dynamic factors such as ideology and public norms. Jeff Goodwin and James Jasper are concerned that POS is unimaginative and displaces the agency of activists.[21] Taken to its logical extreme, the structuralism of POS implies that insurgents can protest only as much as state institutions allow. Mindful of these criticisms, including the healthy self-critique of some POS adherents,[22] I place the perceptions and imaginations of activists at the center of my model. In this respect, my model is a "signal model" because I choose

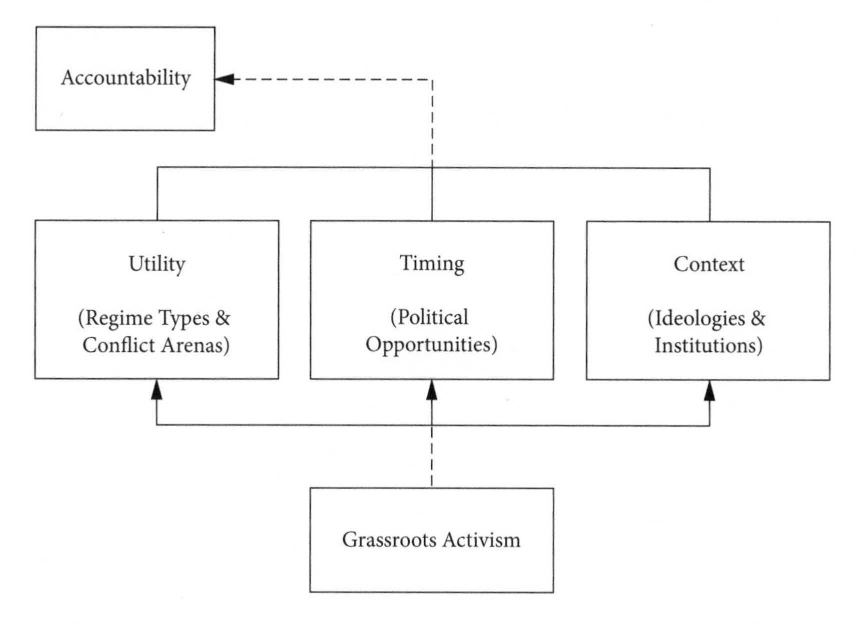


**Figure 1.** The Effective Activism Model

to understand the chances for effective grassroots insurgency from the vantage point of leaders and groups.[23] To avoid the thought puzzle—"Does a protest opportunity exist if no activist sees it?"—I choose to focus on the range of possibilities activists perceive and, for whatever reason, are or are not able to act on.

## Utility, Timing, and Context

My model's specific contribution to the POS literature is that it further conceptualizes activists' perceptions. Figure 1 illustrates my general assumption that in between the accountability and activism relationship are the intervening factors of utility (the right tool), timing (the right moment), and context (the right place). I also assume these three factors are highly interrelated. In fact, many of their sub-factors belong in more than one box, but I keep my model as simple as possible. Later I explain the general "Effective Activism Model" and how it constitutes the primary and secondary levels of my theory—or a meta-model—on which I can hang a more detailed tertiary level of theory and later apply it to the African American experience. The dotted arrows of these models reflect that there is no guarantee of a desired outcome.

*Utility* involves the range of tactics or the strategy grassroots activists should employ to prompt optimal government accountability. Again, sometimes protest works, and sometimes it appears less effective. For example, millions of demonstrators worldwide could not compel the Bush administration to reject its plans to invade Iraq.[24] Nested within the dimension of utility are the sub-variables of *regime type*, or whether a specific governing arrangement is more likely to repress, permit, or encourage effective dissent, as well as the *conflict arena*, or whether activists voice their grievances in public forums most likely to yield the desired relief. There is wide variance as to how well urban regimes incorporate grassroots participation in development agendas, and this is why urbanists have derived several regime typologies, ranging from progressive (e.g., Chicago under Harold Washington) to conservative (e.g., New York under Rudolph Giuliani). As Schattschneider reminds us, arenas of conflict vary as to the most effective weapon or tool actors are expected to wield, and, of course, different arenas imply different targets. For example, an orderly community demonstration during a Detroit City Council hearing was a tactic best suited to the policy arena, because the City Council was pressured to increase Mayor Young's budget allocations to neighborhood groups. The target was the City Council. Group mobilization for a ballot initiative that reduced the council majority needed to override a mayoral budget veto was a tactic best suited to the electoral arena. The target was the public.[25]

*Timing* is simply those temporal considerations—whether they are singular instances, points in a sequence, or periods—that determine the efficacy of activism, which in turn often coincides with the various seasons of a political system: budget deliberations, elections, administrative transitions. *Political opportunities* are relevant to this factor because they capture the specific moments when regimes must take note of grassroots demands. We might also call these moments "windows of policy opportunity." In fact, Piven and Cloward believe that protest action is most likely to occur and be effective during periods when a regime undergoes transition or suffers from economic and political instability, as was the case during the Great Depression of the 1930s and the Civil Rights Movement of the 1960s. Federal and local governments, as well as businesses, could restore order in the midst of economic and political turmoil only by making some concessions to workers, unemployed people, and racial minorities.[26]

Finally, *context* is the geographic setting and, thus, social climate for grassroots action. *Ideology* and *institutions* fall under its purview, for political ideas as well as societal hierarchies are shaped by and reciprocally help to shape the place or environment for action and accountability. Hanes Walton Jr. and other black political scholars have argued that the "contextual variable" mat-

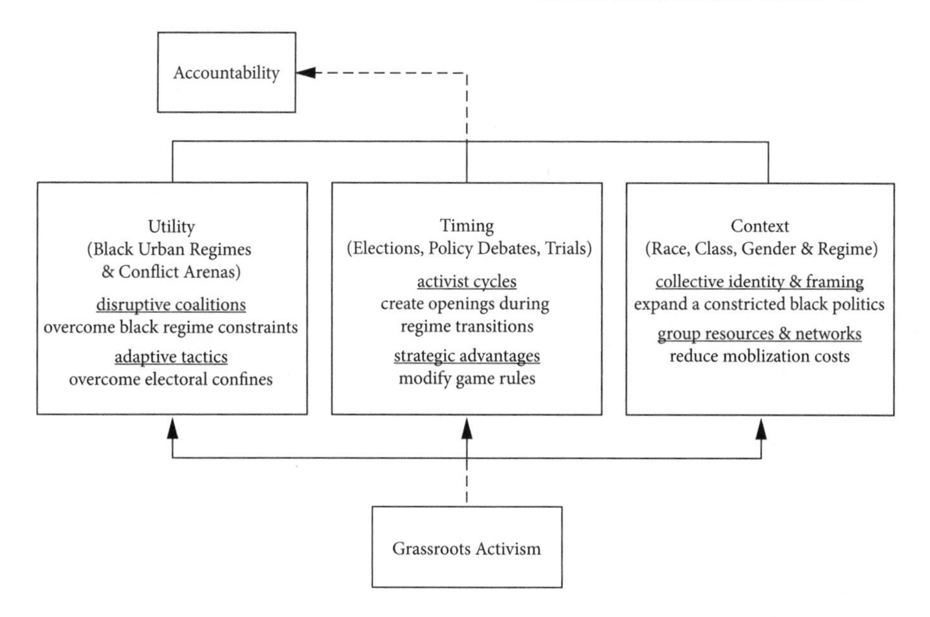


**Figure 2.** The Effective Black Activism Model (EBAM)

ters, for it helps explain differential black experiences with American racism. For example, the de facto racial discrimination of the North differed from the de jure racial segregation of the Jim Crow South. Students of the Civil Rights Movement such as Charles Payne recognize that local variances in black economic autonomy partly explain why civil-rights activists in Mississippi enjoyed less success in highly repressed Delta counties such as Greenwood than they did in more independent downstate communities such as McComb. White supremacy as an ideology and social structure varied across locales and differently affected the opportunities for efficacious protest.[27]

Toward the end of applying the general model to the black urban experience, I present Figure 2, or the Effective Black Activism Model. Each of this model's third-level sub-variables comes under the utility, timing, and context factors. For emphasis, each sub-variable is underlined within the large, central boxes—*disruptive coalitions*, *adaptive tactics*, *activist cycles*, *strategic advantages*, *collective identity and framing*, and *group resources and networks*. Later in this chapter, I further explain how these contingent solutions overcome the *constraints of black urban regimes*, *confines of electoral arenas*, *construction of black politics*, and *costs of mobilization*.

### Utility: Disruptive Coalitions and Adaptive Tactics

Looking at the center-left box in Figure 2, the *black urban regime* and *conflict arena* sub-factors are under the utility factor, which all shape the indispensable need for organizers to form *disruptive coalitions* or to employ *adaptive tactics*. Based on the previously cited assumptions of Piven and Cloward, I define a *disruptive coalition* as an oppositional alliance between grassroots activists and politically or civically influential people that attracts public attention and confounds the regime's normal operation. Such a formation is particularly useful against the *constraints of the black urban regime*. Such a regime is an informal growth coalition between dominant black politicians, civic leaders, and corporate interests. A regime's agenda does not always prevail if activists can recruit sympathetic insider critics and other public-opinion shapers to their side, thus upsetting—or, at least, deferring—the regime's plans.[28]

*Adaptive tactics* capture a group's ability and willingness to use whatever political action is best suited to a specific arena of conflict. While Charles Tilly first labeled the activist toolkit the "repertoire of collective action," political scientists have long conceived of political action as a continuum. Contemporary students of social movements have observed that groups ranging from workfare protesters to anti-free-trade globalists have expanded their "repertoires of contention" and derived new protest innovations, especially with the emergence of the Internet. Peter Bearman found that a group's "structural position" in a movement has an impact on its protest repertoire.[29] I simply contend that, for the efforts of grassroots activists not to be frustrated by the *confines of the electoral arena*, where democratic systems produce powerful incumbents such as Mayor Young who are less threatened by the ultimate sanction of nonelection, activists have to be creative and flexible in the range of weapons they use to hit their targets.[30]

### Timing: Activist Cycles and Strategic Advantages

With the central box of Figure 2, the timing sub-factors *elections*, *policy debates*, and *court trials* are those routine political moments I identify as framing grassroots activists cycles and strategic advantages. This is a straightforward proposition because these sub-factors by definition create openings for new regimes, new priorities, and new legal interpretations.[31] *Activist cycles* are those *Zeitgeist* moments when grassroots leaders discern whether their mobilization coincides with a swelling tide of activism that has put those in government on the defensive. Similar to "cycles of protest," David Snow and Robert Benford define such moments as "sequences of escalating collective action that are of greater frequency and intensity than normal, that spread throughout various sections and regions of society, and that involve both new techniques of protest and new forms of organization."[32] Deborah Minkoff's investigation of the relationship between the Civil Rights and women's movements confirms that the breadth and length of one cycle of protest affects subsequent cycles. Likewise, my observations about the cycles of Detroit public-housing activism confirm that a movement's capacity to exploit *regime transitions*, such as the movement from the Young administration to the Archer administration, is partly a function of that movement's magnitude and longevity.[33]

Often, grassroots activism directed at government involves ordinary citizens denouncing what they see as unfair ballot outcomes, policy decisions, or court orders. However, *strategic advantages* are those occasional instances when the "rules of the games" change in the favor of ordinary citizens. At times, activists win, and a government is compelled to heed their concerns because the electorate, a legislative body, or a judge decides that a government's actions are in violation of established preferences or rights. A prime example of this is when in the late 1960s, especially with the cases of *Shapiro v. Thompson* and *Goldberg v. Kelly*, the U.S. Supreme Court took an expansive view of public welfare and veered close to recognizing welfare as a right with constitutional protections. Detroit has its own history of activist municipal judges who have been willing to veto the actions of the police or the mayor if seen in contradiction to the interests of minorities and the poor.[34]

### Context: Collective Identity and Framing, Group Resources and Networks

At the extreme right of Figure 2 are the contextual factors *race*, *class*, *gender*, and *regime*, which provide the environment for *collective identity and framing*, as well as for *group resources and networks*. By collective identity, Debra Friedman and Doug McAdam mean a group or "individual announcement of affiliation, or connection with others. To partake of a collective identity is to reconstitute the individual self around a new and valued identity."[35] Identities such as anti-apartheid, anti-abortion, or antipoverty led to the corresponding phrases and scripts of "one person—one vote," "protect the unborn," or "up and out of poverty." According to Snow and Benford, "framing" means that activists use language that helps to "assign blame for the problem they are attempting to ameliorate."[36] It is the process of using ideas to justify the cause of a self-defined group and thus any subsequent collective action. When broadly constructed, frames can bridge social divisions by appealing to common ideals such as the sanctity of life, a belief in democratic citizenship, or the embrace of women's equality.[37] Collective identity and framing enable activists to foment a multiple consciousness, according to black feminists, based on an equal determination to fight racism, poverty, and gender inequality.[38] Hence, as Figure 2 indicates, activists can temporarily expand any narrow construction of *black politics* where politicians define accountability to black constituencies only according to racial criteria—for example, more African Americans in executive positions at the housing department—but relegate issues of poverty and gender equity by, for example, neglecting the needs of public-housing tenants, many of whom are women.

Resource mobilization theory asserts that *group resources and networks* involve the range of organizational mechanics and affiliations required for insurgent recruitment, planning, and direct action. An excellent illustration of this concept is Belinda Robnett's description of black women's "micromobilization," for they were untitled but vital intermediaries between ordinary citizens and the formal male leaders of the Civil Rights Movement. Similarly, Daniel Cress and David Snow found that homeless union activists in cities such as Detroit and Oakland, California, garner a range of moral, material, informational, and human resources to produce instrumental activism. Unlike Piven's and Cloward's prediction, self-selected external patrons and allies may enhance rather than co-opt homeless insurgency.[39] On the collective level, preexisting organizational networks as well as friendship and neighbor networks, what Alberto Melucci calls the "pre-political" formations "rooted in everyday life," can serve as launching pads for activism and buffers to soften regimes' reprisals.[40] Overall, any formidable *costs* associated with *mobilization*—such as individual time, travel costs, jail time, or public ridicule—can be subsidized if a group taps extant resources and networks.[41]

Finally, I measure *accountability* (at the top left in Figure 2) by understanding the pattern of direct, public responses public officials make or do not make to the demands of activists, such as statements at public hearings or votes on funding requests. But it is very important to stress that local governments in the 1980s and 1990s had a number of severe constraints on what they could yield to activists. Elected leaders in large impoverished cities with majority-black populations such as Detroit and Newark grappled with enormous fiscal constraints—depopulation, declining tax revenues, stagnant business growth—as well as political constraints, such as state and county governmental authority and metropolitan fragmentation, which made it difficult for them to concede much to the grassroots.[42] Nonetheless, the relevant question is: What choices did these public officials make among their very limited menu of options and why? In the next section, I demonstrate the improvements my model makes to leading theories of black grassroots activism and black politics in the post-Civil Rights Movement era, beginning with the pivotal thinking of Bayard Rustin.

## BLACK GRASSROOTS ACTIVISM IN THE POST-CIVIL RIGHTS MOVEMENT ERA

### Rustin's Thesis

By several accounts, Bayard Rustin (1912–87), who was a brilliant civil-rights strategist and openly gay human-rights advocate, helped set the tone for black mass expectations after the protest phase of the Civil Rights Movement. At the height of the movement, he wrote the influential essay "From Protest to Politics."[43] He believed, in the wake of the 1964 Civil Rights Act and the landslide Democratic victory of Lyndon B. Johnson, that it was time for the movement to shift from the direct-action tactics of the Southern protest phase to electoral mobilization and coalition building, "A conscious bid for *political power* is being made, and in the course of that effort a tactical shift is being effected: direct-action techniques are being subordinated to a strategy calling for the building of community institutions or power bases."[44] Three years after he praised SNCC's voter-registration efforts, he quibbled with Martin Luther King Jr.'s "Poor People's Campaign." Although Rustin fundamentally supported the struggle of economic justice, he argued that King's plan to militate for an expansion in public welfare and for the creation of full employment programs by marching on Washington, D.C., was not strategic, only antagonized lawmakers, and literally was bogged down in the rainy mire of the national plaza.[45]

Without the benefit of hindsight and given all of the sacrifices civil-rights activists made to expand the black franchise, it is quite understandable why Rustin turned to formal, institutional politics as a new means to cultivate black political power. Nonetheless, his call for black community control separate from protest now sits at a contested juncture. The African American community, which has never been a political or economic monolith, has in this post-Civil Rights Movement era experienced increased class divisions and policy disagreements as it has moved away from grassroots participation. Ironically, both outcomes are a function of the movement's success in greatly expanding educational, business, and housing opportunities for the black middle and upper working classes, though the poor have experienced minimal progress. Research consistently discovers new cross-cutting policy cleavages among

African American communities, whether driven by class, gender, religiosity, sexual orientation, or other factors. Black civic activism has declined, according to Frederick Harris and his co-authors; thus, black elected officials, who often are in cities with enormous political and fiscal constraints, are left to make choices among the divergent policy preferences of black constituencies.[46] When black and other housing activists conduct protests against black-led administrations, such as the protests over the razing of homeless shelters to build Atlanta's Olympics venues in 1996, a form of activism once used to place black politicians in City Hall may now be necessary to beat on their doors.[47] So it is an issue not of politics *over* protest per se, but of politics *and* protest.

## Three Counter Theses

Contrary to Rustin's thesis, students of black politics have provided interesting counter-theses for why effective black activism has taken a different intensity and form in the post-Civil Rights Movement era. In a provocatively entitled book *We Have No Leaders: African Americans in the Post-Civil Rights Era*, Robert Smith articulates the *hyper-institutionalization* thesis. Implicitly refuting the incorporation argument, Smith asserts that "the strategy or methods employed by blacks to press their demands in the post-civil rights era have been wholly systemic—voting, elections, and efforts at multiethnic coalition formation. . . . [P]rotests in the post-civil rights era have become institutionalized and those that have occurred in the last twenty-five years have been largely symbolic or ceremonial."[48] Most at issue, in Smith's view, is the black political establishment's preoccupation with meeting black demands through institutional remedies while their "Black agenda" has hovered around essentially the same economic and civil-rights policy demands since the mid-1970s. Smith's purpose is to demonstrate the incongruity between the incremental legislative and electoral strategies black leaders and opinion shapers have pursued versus the real need African American communities, especially the poor, have for transformative change.

Whereas Smith's thesis is rooted in a Black Nationalist perspective, Adolph Reed provides a neo-Marxist analysis and polemic that argues the *demobilization* view. In a republished essay entitled "Sources of Demobilization in the New Black Political Regime," Reed contends that the decline in "progressive Black mobilization" is due to the limits of the political incorporation approach, the problematic rhetoric of the underclass discourse, and the black left's failure to more critically conceptualize race and stratification within the American system.[49] He first outlines the post-1965 voting-rights transformation that resulted in the election of record numbers of black officials, who at the municipal level rewarded middle-class constituencies and professionals by placing them in charge of municipal bureaucracies such as "housing authorities, welfare departments, and school systems." The rise of these black urban administrations "short-circuits critiques" of municipal-agency performance because these bureaucracies are shielded by "the racially inflected language most familiar to black insurgency."[50] Black elected officials who use the language of black empowerment, in Reed's view, can reduce the consideration of what constitutes black accountability to race-based symbolism and co-opt several black civic leaders.

In stark contrast to both Reed and Smith is the *fusionist* argument of James Jennings. Entitled *The Politics of Black Empowerment: The Transformation of Black Activism in Urban America*, Jennings's book reaches a decidedly more optimistic set of conclusions about the efficacy and intensity of contemporary black grassroots activism. Similar to Smith, Jennings has a regard for Black Nationalism but believes that a significant counteroffensive gained ground in the 1980s in which community control and autonomy were combined with economic populism. What Jennings deems a new black empowerment activism requires substantive power beyond mere incorporation goals. "It is no longer accurate" he writes, "to describe Black leadership and activism along a divided continuum of activism and electoral activity. . . . Presuming that electoral activism is a totally different category from protest activity obscures the vision of how the former has become part of the latter."[51]

The more recent *Double Trouble: Black Mayors, Black Communities, and the Call for a Deep Democracy*, by J. Phillip Thompson III, is also an in-depth analysis of African American mayors, grassroots activism, and coalition politics. By examining various black-led cities such as New York and Chicago, Thompson, as a fusionist and a "deep pluralist," analyzes a problem he calls "the dirty little secret of black politics": All too often, black mayors resort to a tacit demobilization of the black poor in favor of the less demanding black middle class. Again, these mayors confront myriad fiscal and political constraints in urban governance, including limited federal and state allocations and metropolitan competition, and thus can return few benefits to a mobilized black poor; nor do these mayors wish for involved activists to disturb their pro-growth agendas by demanding redistribution. Thompson asserts, "The lack of a strategy of grassroots black civic empowerment to shore up elected black mayors has weakened black political participation and, in consequence, has weakened black mayors in their struggles with white-led legislatures and suburbs, and federal officials"[52]—thus, the "double trouble."[53]

## Reconsidering the Timing and Utility of Black Activism

Among these three theses, my work is a fusionist approach and greatly benefits from the studies by Jennings and Thompson. My model, however, is more predictive and dynamic in its approach to black grassroots activism than any of the aforementioned. While Reed, Smith, and Jennings posit that there are shifting environs or contexts for contemporary black insurgency, they fail to consider this activism's seasonality in a more sophisticated way. Of these theorists, Thompson pays the greatest attention to questions of timing and context, but he does not test his interesting propositions using the multi-method technique I employ. Each scholar needs to more precisely consider whether this activism varied not just according to condition, but also according to time, according to period. Did it ebb and flow in nonlinear patterns, and if it did, why and by how much?

By the account of Frederick Harris, Valeria Sinclair-Chapman, and Brian McKenzie, black political participation and civic engagement was not on the decline in the 1970s until the mid-1980s, after experiencing a peak in the late 1970s.[54] Figure 3 validates this claim. According to data collected by Susan Olzak and Elizabeth West, which I analyze, there was a precipitous drop-off

**Figure 3.** Newspaper coverage of protest in 318 American cities, 1955–1992. *Source*: Susan Olzak and Elizabeth West, *Ethnic Collective Action in Contemporary Urban U.S.: Project Description and Coding Manual* (Palo Alto, Calif.: Stanford University, 1995), Ethnic Collective Action data set.

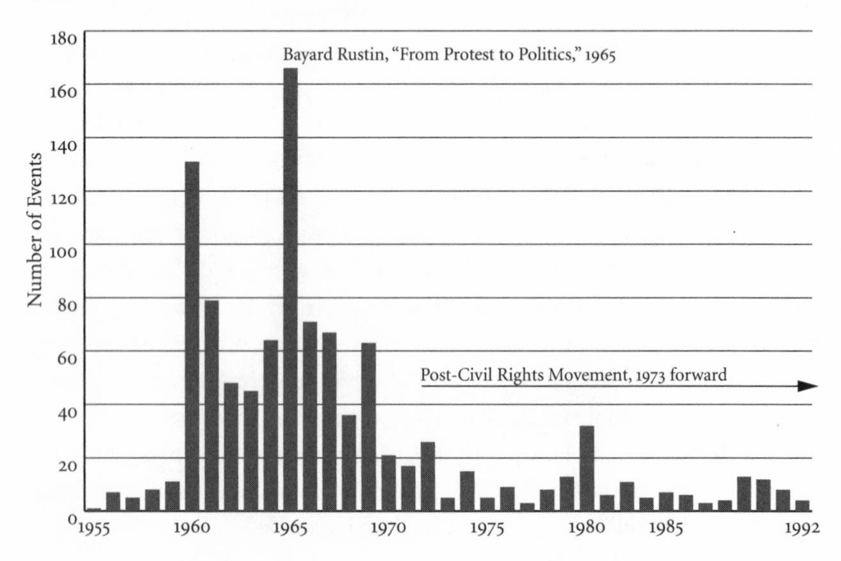

in the late 1960s in the number of black protest events the *New York Times* recorded in 318 cities. As the story goes, some civil-rights, Black Power, and community-control activists moved from "the streets to the suites" and took posts in new, black-led administrations such as that of Carl Stokes in Cleveland or of Richard Hatcher in Gary, Indiana. To be sure, Reed and Smith are absolutely right. The baseline number of protest events in Figure 3 was smaller by the late 1970s; thus, there is good reason to suspect demobilization and hyper-institutionalization. But in the post-Civil Rights Movement era of 1973 until about 1993, the city of Detroit witnessed two black mayoral administrations, six mayoral and City Council elections, several recessions and fiscal crises, and a multitude of other racial, economic, and political shocks.[55] Such changes in the political and economic context of Detroit and other cities helped foment new waves of black grassroots activism. Thus, demobilization and hyper-institutionalization were not a fait accompli.

Consequently, timing or periodicity is important in understanding how opportunities for effective black grassroots activism contracted and expanded. Akin to Sidney Tarrow's thinking about "protest cycles," I contend that *activist cycles* are highly useful indicators of when a black-led movement's leaders should mobilize. When these leaders are not alone, then "now is the time" to join those heaping demands on an already beleaguered regime. Like Figure 3, my work verifies that there were renewed, though small, waves of activism in cities like Detroit in the early and late 1980s. *Strategic advantages* send leaders cues that are very easy to decipher precisely because these leaders are already monitoring to see whether the rules of the game have changed in their favor.[56]

My model also responds to Smith's utilitarian concern that post-Civil Rights Movement black protest has become a largely symbolic and ineffectual exercise. Although the social movement literature concludes that nonviolent protests have become routine, research consistently confirms that most Americans, including African Americans, consider it the rarest form of political action. Specific to Detroit in the 1980s, Barry Checkoway and Marc Zimmerman discovered that even highly engaged neighborhood organizations were much more likely to report testifying at a public hearing (92 percent) than mobilizing a demonstration (32 percent.) These findings parallel the responses a representative sample of black Detroiters gave in the 1989 Detroit Area Study.[57] Even when black-led public demonstrations have elements of symbolism—for example, the Million Man March in 1995 or the protest over the South Carolina State House flying the Confederate flag in 2000—such protests can still be quite political, for they challenge public framings like black men as "irresponsible" or racist Jim Crow icons as harmless symbols of "Southern heritage."[58]

Having emphasized how activist cycles and strategic advantages improve our understanding of timely and effective black grassroots activism, the rest of this chapter details why collective identity and framing, disruptive coalitions, and adaptive tactics, as well as group resources and networks, help activists to navigate contextual barriers.

## Reconsidering the Context of Race, Class, Gender, and Regime

Regime transitions and changed game rules are opportunities. Specific barriers to black grassroots activism are the constraints of the black urban regime, the narrow construction of black politics, the confines of electoral politics, and the costs of grassroots mobilization. To reiterate, these barriers are shaped by the larger context of race, class, gender, and regime. Later I explain why framing and collective identity processes permit grassroots activists to bridge key divisions within black politics so as to attract instrumental allies and broaden community support. Moreover, this is a problem of black class divisions, gender differences, and the determination of black group interests.

### • *Black Class Divisions, Gender, and Black Group Interests*

In the sections that follow, I describe what is required to form urban black-led movements that either are class-elastic or show class solidarity with the poor. Again, the principles of racial justice and economic redistribution form an ethical core within contemporary African American politics. But as evident from the black middle-class gentrification of certain low-income neighborhoods in Atlanta and Harlem, these principles can and do form a cross-cutting cleavage. In the post–Civil Rights Movement era, this cleavage is further driven by increasing quality-of-life disparities between the black upper and lower classes.[59] Having said this, there are opportunities for "multi-class" campaigns to emerge between black middle-class and poor citizens if there is a threat to a common place identification (e.g., a neighborhood) or an issue is tinged with economic injustice (e.g., the failure to evacuate the black poor during Hurricane Katrina) that, for some African Americans, class solidarity is also an expression of racial solidarity. It is, however, a delicate balance. The studies by Steven Gregory, Kesha Moore, and Mary Pattillo-McCoy wonderfully illustrate instances in which African American communities in New York, Philadelphia, and Chicago organized and identified across class lines in the interests of their larger neighborhoods, despite persistent class tensions.[60] What further makes such inter-class affiliations possible is the great diversity within the black middle, working, and lower classes. As Thomas Boston adeptly theorizes, people within these classes have such wide variances in their class locations, class statuses, and class identities that, on occasion, it is possible for a new Harvard Law School graduate such as Barack Obama to be attracted to working-class-community organizing.[61]

Gender inequities can also increase the prospects for solidarity as well as division. Works by black feminists such as Patricia Hill Collins and critical race theorists such as Patricia Williams lend vital insights, for the collective identities I examine in this book are mostly processes of "intersectionality" or "multiple consciousness."[62] When issues trigger the shared, often spiritual dimensions of black women's "standpoints"—for example, fighting sexism and sexual violence, concern for the whole community's welfare—that is also when female grassroots leaders are likely to frame these issues as uniquely relevant to poor black women and a broader sisterhood. After all, the welfare-rights leader Johnnie Tillmon reminded all her sisters that "every woman is one man away from poverty."[63] Without naïvely assuming that all black women share an undifferentiated gender experience, a cross section of women activists are at the forefront of contemporary urban activism, especially in Detroit. Among others, the environmental justice movement literature provides excellent studies of how women activists call for gender justice and a sisterhood across all lines, though both are difficult to achieve.[64]

Moreover, I observe when black grassroots communities and their allies act collectively as though they have common interests—*black group interests*, as Michael Dawson calls them—and I consider the many barriers that impede the realization of such instances. In the final analysis, I do not argue that black elected officials in Detroit and elsewhere should only be accountable to how low-income communities envisioned Detroit's renaissance. I simply question whether, during difficult policy debates, black poor and moderate-income Detroiters were fully invited into deliberations that affected their lives as citizens, or whether they were excluded like subjects. The former is the essence of deep democracy.[65]

• *Overcoming the Black Urban Regime*

My previous rationale for theorizing that disruptive coalitions have the capacity to temporarily overcome the constraints of the black urban regime relies on the POS literature's assumptions that insider–outsider alliances destabilize regimes. While traditional urban regime theory is sympathetic to questions of citizen decision making and equity, much of it trains its analytical attention on elite interactions. Thus, it often overlooks the subtler dynamics of ideology and community institutions that can either legitimize or, on occasion, challenge these elite interactions. Drawing from the work of Clarence Stone and others, Karen Mossberger and Gerry Stoker conclude that an urban regime exists only if a city's public and private actors "*with access to institutional resources*" have the ability to set the city's development agenda and, through cooperation, produce tangible outcomes.[66]

Black urban regimes vary in style, if not in substance, from the archetypal regime. Reed asserts that black urban regimes are not "led by inept, uncaring or mean-spirited elitists," for black elected officials are often stronger advocates of economic redistribution than their white counterparts. To the contrary, Reed points out: "The central contradiction facing the black regime [is that] it is caught between the expectations of its principally black electoral constituency, which implies downward redistribution, and those of its [white corporate] governing coalition, which . . . [calls for] upward redistribution."[67] Robert Brown's work provides empirical verification for Reed's claim. From the 1970s to the early 1990s, cities with greater numbers of black elected officials were more attentive to the needs of low-income constituents than their white-led counterparts, especially in the areas of housing and community development.[68] But Reed also believes that the racial symbolism of black politicians (black appointments to commissions; modest grants to black nonprofits) allows these officials to command their black constituents' loyalty or quiescence while also making these officials "especially attractive partner[s] in the progrowth coalition."[69] The black urban regime often swings in between the poles of conservatism and progressivism. For these very reasons, my model assumes there are diverse actors within a regime. Thus, disruptive coalitions are those rare moments when it is in the interests of outspoken insiders (such as city councilors) to align with outsiders (such as defiant community activists) to veto or delay regime priorities. Opportune changes in the game rules, or what I call strategic advantages, simply reinforce the power of such alliances.[70]

• *Expanding Black Politics*

As part of my enterprise of expanding black politics, I previously suggested that black middle-class alliances with the black poor may be more likely if viewed as a form of racial solidarity. According to Cathy Cohen, the problem is that sentiments of black common fate are too often "qualified." Black leaders use perceived "consensus issues" of race and racism to define group interests and investments of indigenous resources, as well as the advocacy of public policy, even if such practices exclude marginal or "less respectable" groups such as the poor, people living with HIV/AIDS, or lesbians and gays.[71] Black studies scholars who agree with Cohen's view believe that an inordinate reliance on racial criteria causes black citizens to be uncritically loyal to black leaders and thus not to criticize them or "air their dirty laundry," even when these leaders should be held accountable for their actions. One controversial example is voters in Washington, D.C., reelecting Mayor Marion Barry despite his prosecution for using crack cocaine. The so-called race card becomes a source of political capital.[72]

Nonetheless, I theorize there are at least two ways activists can use the processes of collective identity formation and framing to expand black politics. Robnett reminds us that "frame bridging . . . involves providing those already predisposed to one's cause with information sufficient to induce them to join the movement."[73] First, activists can more specifically engage in a process called "frame amplification," in which activists' goals and group identities are made to resonate with the broader black politics ethic of racial justice as reinforced by other forms of justice. A popular quote of Martin Luther King Jr. is: "Injustice anywhere is a threat to justice everywhere."[74] Second, activists can engage in the more difficult project of "transformative politics" or "frame transformation" in which they call on leaders to recognize the contradiction of professing a holistic belief in racial justice if they ignore the needs of the black poor, black women, black lesbians and gays, and other marginal groups. Frame amplification, or calls for racial and economic justice, in a city like Detroit is a less difficult process than transformation, precisely because these ethics already resonate in a predominantly black city with a strong history of labor-union identification and activism. But there are no guarantees. Even when black activists helped lead "homeless unions" to oppose the Young administration's plans to demolish public housing, they reported receiving little to no support from mainstream black or labor leaders.[75]

• *Acting beyond the Electoral Arena*

Just as the black middle class and poor are not monolithic, neither are the larger political systems of urban regimes. As elite governing coalitions, regimes can be powerful enough to dominate a city's political system and elevate the importance of a specific arena—civic, legal, corporate, or other. This does not mean, however, that a regime is the same as a city's entire political system. Thus, advocates may be able to circumvent regimes and operate within various arenas or "spheres of activity" to influence the political system and its outcomes. Barbara Ferman concludes, "Groups seeking incorporation essentially have three choices: they can use the logic of the dominant arena to make their case . . . ; they can seek to change the underlying logic of the dominant arena

. . . ; or they can shift operations to another arena if the first two options are not viable."[76] Of course, in democratic systems the electoral arena has the most powerful sanction available to citizens who want to hold their elected officials accountable: the vote. The problem is that the power of incumbency, especially in urban politics, may foreclose this arena to grassroots advocates. Relative to black politics and Detroit, between 1974 and 2006 majorities of black voters so strongly supported mayoral incumbents—Young, Archer, and Fitzpatrick—that none of these mayors lost reelection bids. Many city councilors also retained their seats. As Richard Wood stated, based on Gamson's work, "[American] movements whose goal is the *displacement of elites* systematically fail."[77]

Therefore, adaptive tactics, as I call them, are the strategic and tactical choices black low-income advocates must make—support ballot initiatives, press lawsuits, picket City Council offices—to get around any electoral confines and still affect policy outcomes. Informed by the "repertoires of contention" literature, my thinking is that the more black-led activists innovate in their strategies and tactics, within limits, the more likely they are to find a policy opportunity to exploit. It will be evident from my discussion in subsequent chapters that veterans and descendants of the Civil Rights and Black Power movements, who led Detroit grassroots movements in the 1980s and 1990s, had a long history of tactical innovation. After all, it was in Detroit that Malcolm X delivered his famous "Message to the Grass Roots" and then, six months later, called on blacks activists everywhere to make a basic strategic choice—the "Ballot or the Bullet"—to advance black freedom.[78]

• *Reducing Mobilization Costs*

Although my work focuses on the outcomes of activism, it is apparent that activists have to navigate a minefield of problems, both internal and external, to mobilize the resource-poor. So it is important to know what contemporary black urban activists can do to instrumentally organize and network with other groups to overcome the costs of mobilization. The works of Marshall Ganz and Richard Wood are instructive in answering this last question, for beyond political opportunities and tactical repertoires, they consider a group's "strategic capacity." By this, they mean "the product of two sets of factors, grouped under 'leadership' and 'organization.'"[79] Leadership includes the ability of groups to benefit from the activist biographies, political lessons, and movement ties of leaders, whereas organization entails the internal and external mechanisms for group deliberation, accountability, and ally and resource accumulation. Borrowing from Michael Chwe, who believes that a mixture of strong and weak ties is critical to a movement's success, they assert that weak ties among movement organizations are better if the threshold for movement actions is high. They also assert that leadership talent and money from multiple constituencies strengthens a movement's chances for success.[80]

To understand how group networks and resources overcome mobilization costs, I posit that black-led grassroots groups with a diversity of ties to external institutions, as well as weak but diverse ties to peer organizations, have a greater capacity to mobilize despite threats of political reprisal. In my chapter on community development activism, I discuss the successes of SOS, a highly ad hoc coalition that broadly lobbied for increased allocations to *all* neighborhood groups over central business district projects. Its requirements for membership were as minimal as a neighborhood leader appearing at a City Council meeting wearing an SOS button or carrying an SOS sign. Because SOS and the public-housing organization PLAN drew from the leadership experiences and resources of organizations and networks as well as from the national low-income network and public-housing tenant and homeless organizations, they were able to weather the storms of reprisal from the Young administration at least long enough to reap modest successes.[81]

## CONCLUSION

I believe the EBAM is both logical and dynamic. As a fusionist approach to post-Civil Rights Movement black grassroots activism, the EBAM theorizes the connections between an effective activism and public accountability to the black poor. Protest cannot guarantee a desired result, but it is sometimes critical in broadcasting the concerns of the marginalized to the ears of unresponsive or inattentive politicians and in legitimating the declarations of responsive politicians. Utility, timing, and context are fundamental to understanding the opportunities for effective black grassroots activism. Under these respective factors are disruptive coalitions, adaptive tactics, activist cycles, strategic advantages, and collective identity and framing, as well as group resources and networks, which overcome the constraints and dynamics of black regimes, electoral confines, game rules, narrowly defined black politics, and mobilization costs.

Of the pro-activism variables, I believe that allies, advantages, and adaptive tactics are the necessary conditions for circumventing accountability's barriers. While my model certainly places activist genius at its center, the POS literature stresses the need for activists to have at least a few government and movement allies, system advantages, and tactical breakthroughs so their efforts constitute more than an unheard shout in the dark. Some black grassroots activists in

Detroit who demanded affordable housing were disappointed when, despite enormous efforts, their demands were not fully heeded. But an even greater tragedy would be for us to ignore why their raised voices mattered more in some periods than in others. The next chapter lays out the historical proof for this assertion.

# PART II

*Black Grassroots Activism and Accountability in Detroit, 1933–1993*

# 2

## Where are the People?

*Early Black Housing Poverty and Grassroots Activism*

**It's always been whenever black people moved from one area . . . they moved into second-hand housing. You know; something that the white man done moved out of.**

**—James Cartwright, Parkside Homes resident, 1995**

### MORE THAN JUST BYSTANDERS

Urban lore maintains that the thousands of abandoned buildings and weed-strewn lots that now pockmark Detroit's cityscape are mute testimony to the helplessness of ordinary citizens as their city's economy and housing stock have deteriorated.[1] But in this chapter I go beyond the lore to demonstrate that these citizens are not mere bystanders to this decline. One journalistic account that greatly neglects historical context is Ze'ev Chafets's *Devil's Night: And Other True Stories of Detroit*. To provide evidence that deteriorating race relations and stillborn neighborhood revitalization still afflict Detroit decades after its 1967 riot, Chafet spins lurid tales of crime and urban anomie in the city. Most memorable is the Halloween eve ritual of youthful pranksters torching their own neighborhoods.[2] On the other side of the spectrum, Thomas Sugrue's acclaimed *The Origins of the Urban Crisis* is a historically adroit analysis that concentrates on structural factors. He meticulously demonstrates that Detroit's urban crisis began decades before the 1967 riot with the post–Second World War period's complex mixture of racial and economic contradictions—government-sanctioned residential discrimination, broken union and liberal alliances, and the black middle class's indifference to the housing needs of lower-income families.[3] Beth Bates, Timothy Bates, and Grace Boggs note in their otherwise complimentary review of Sugrue's book, "For all of Sugrue's appreciation of the role both structure and agency play in historical analysis, we feel more attention to grass-roots activism within the black community would rescue African Americans from the role of passive participants."[4] Analogous to contemporary descriptions of Detroit as eerily vacant, the critical question these reviewers poses to Sugrue's analysis is: "Where are the people?" In short, what role does black grassroots activism and protest play? In her more recent *Whose Detroit?* Heather Thompson nicely addresses Sugrue's omission by examining the grassroots ideological coalitions and cleavages among Detroit's radicals, liberals, and conservatives as each wrestled for control of a postwar and post–Great Society city.[5]

Since the historical analyses by Sugrue and other scholars have so skillfully mapped the racial and economic fault lines confronting black Detroiters who sought affordable and high-quality housing, little is gained if I simply rehash their conclusions. Instead, I integrate insights from the social movement and black politics literature to explain the opportunities for effective black grassroots activism in the pre-1973 period, before the election of Mayor Coleman Young. If, indeed the Effective Black Activism Model is accurate and successful protest depends on whether it is the right tool (utility), at the right time (timing), in the right place (context), then it is necessary to concentrate on the openings created by new allies, advantages, and tactics. From a historical standpoint, this chapter provides the context in which Rustin first concluded that African Americans in Detroit and elsewhere must move "from protest to politics." This chapter suggests why some grassroots activists, despite Rustin's plea, still considered protest and other forms of activism a necessary complement to institutional politics.

## THE CONTEXT AND REGIMES OF RACE AND HOUSING

### Detroit's Postwar Housing Crisis

First, let us examine the top-down contextual factors that structured and limited the housing opportunities of postwar black Detroit. Active labor recruitment by Ford Motor Company, the black church, and the Detroit Urban League fueled successive waves of pre- and post–Second World War black migration into the city. Between 1940 and 1950, the black population doubled from 150,000 to 300,000 and thus made up 16 percent of Detroit's nearly 2 million in population and 67 percent of its total growth (see Table 1). The 1940s was a period of intense racial animosity, which included both legal and extralegal methods to confine the African American community to overcrowded and unhealthy slums. Such practices were in the interests of unscrupulous white and black landlords and of white homeowners fearful of integration. A third of all

**Table 1.** Detroit black population and housing growth, 1900–2000

| Year | Total population | Black population | Black total (%) | Black total increase (%) | Black home-owners (%) | Ratio of Black owners to black renters | Ratio of Black owners to white owners |
|---|---|---|---|---|---|---|---|
| 1900 | 285,704 | 4,111 | 1.4 | — | 16.1 | .208 | .162 |
| 1910 | 465,766 | 5,741 | 1.2 | 1 | — | — | — |
| 1920 | 993,672 | 40,838 | 4.1 | 7 | — | — | — |
| 1930 | 1,568,662 | 120,066 | 7.7 | 14 | 15.0 | .185 | .344 |
| 1940 | 1,623,452 | 149,119 | 9.2 | 53 | 14.7 | .172 | .355 |
| 1950 | 1,849,568 | 300,506 | 16.2 | 67 | 33.6 | .506 | .591 |
| 1960 | 1,670,144 | 482,229 | 28.9 | 102 | 39.0 | .639 | .603 |
| 1970 | 1,511,482 | 660,428 | 43.7 | 112 | — | — | — |
| 1980 | 1,203,369 | 758,468 | 63.0 | 32 | 53.1 | 1.132 | .810 |
| 1990 | 1,027,974 | 777,916 | 75.7 | 11 | — | — | — |
| 2000 | 951,270 | 775,772 | 81.5 | 3 | 53.4 | 1.147 | .812 |

*Source*: Census of the Population, Detroit.

black Detroiters resided on two main streets, Hastings and St. Antoine, which were east of Woodward Avenue or the main north–south meridian. By 1950, 95 percent of the 47,000 residents who resided in this corridor were African American.[6]

Paradise Valley and its "Black Bottom" counterpart became the epicenters of overcrowding and fear of its explosive consequences.[7] Since the federal government had declared a moratorium on any housing expenditures not related to war production, an enormous backlog of unmet needs amassed that the postwar building boom met in extremely selective and racially prejudicial ways. To stem the roaring tide of some 70,000 under-housed blacks after the war, the Detroit Housing Commission only built 1,800 new units and recorded the construction of 200 private units. From 1943 to 1945, a mere 6 percent, or 2,100, of the 37,000 black families who applied for wartime housing were granted leases. Despite the impassioned pleas of black leaders and sympathetic white housing advocates, little progress was made. Forty-three percent of all returning black veterans reported sharing rented rooms, trailers, or tourist cabins.[8] Table 1 also reveals that in the 1940s, blacks had only a little more than a third of the rate of homeownership as whites. By the 1950s, this had increased to almost 60 percent.

## Housing Discrimination and Black Class Divisions

Consequently, what were the outcomes of housing as segregated by race? From the 1940s and 1950s on, white homeowners, real-estate interests, and government appraisers used mechanisms to reserve the lion's share of Detroit's meager housing resources for white families. The rise of white neighborhood improvement associations is a story of how white homeowners resisted what they saw as black encroachment on their right to protect property values and to preserve racial homogeneity. Roughly 85 percent of all of Detroit's residential property was covered by racially restrictive covenants by the 1940s. White homeowners banded together and agreed not to rent or sell to African Americans, although "blockbusting" occurred when real-estate speculators stoked whites' fears of new black neighbors and profited from hasty home sales.[9]

When whites perceived that realtors, the courts, or other public officials were unwilling to protect their neighborhoods' racial sanctity, they often turned to mob violence. Echoing the infamous case of Dr. H. Ossian Sweet who in 1925 violently defended his home in a white neighborhood, there were more than 200 recorded incidents of verbal harassment, rock throwing, cross burning, and arson between 1945 and 1965.[10] All of this must be understood in the context that the racial violence of Detroit's riots in 1943 and 1967 was on an unprecedented scale. Powerful federal collaborators such as the Home Owners Loan Corporation and the Federal Housing Administration (FHA) exacerbated racial inequities by practicing "redlining," which summarily rated black neighborhoods as too risky for federal mortgage insurance and subsidized home loans. Because of this process, 50 percent of all Detroit homes were declared ineligible for FHA loans, including homes in black middle-class neighborhoods that were literally walled off from their white neighbors.[11]

So how did the black class structure present African Americans with varying options? Middle-class and working-class blacks had at least two general options not open to low-income blacks. In the 1940s, middle-class professionals confronted the extreme racial hostility vented toward them by successfully locating homes in communities surrounded by indifferent white neighbors. The well-paid working class bided their time until the 1950s and 1960s to occupy neighborhoods newly vacated by whites fleeing to suburban or nearly suburban areas.[12] Map 1 indicates the location of several of Detroit's historic black neighborhoods.

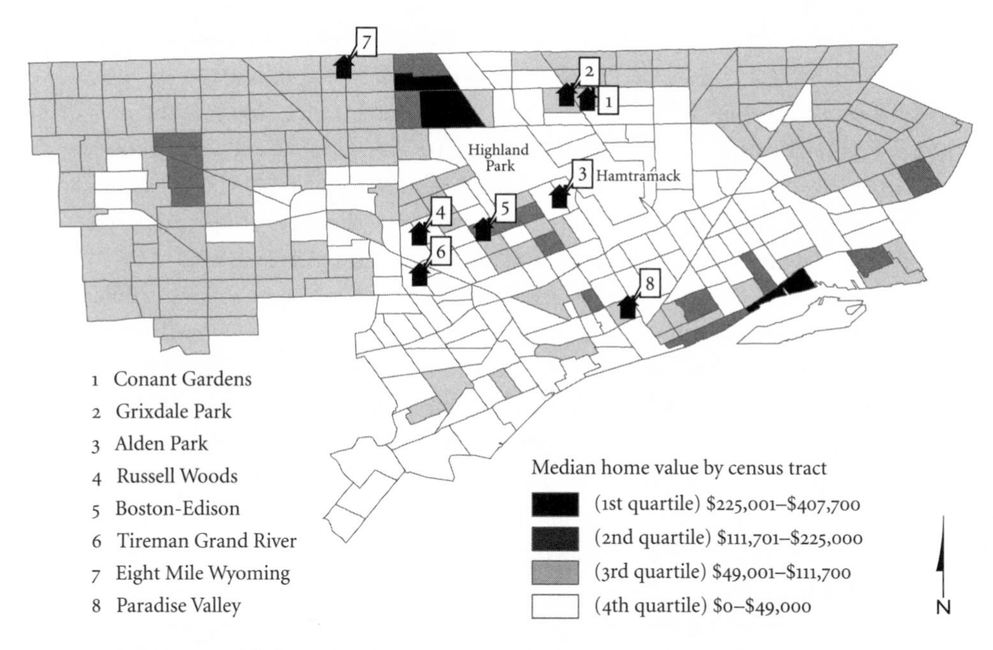


**Map 1.** Detroit black median housing value and historic black neighborhoods, 1990.

Composed predominantly of middle-class professionals, Conant Gardens (or number 1 on Map 1) was the city's most exclusive black neighborhood in the 1940s. As early as 1950, residents of this neighborhood had the highest level of education of any black Detroiters, and two of the three census tracts that constituted the area ranked first and second in median income for all city tracts with more than 500 blacks. But Conant Garden leaders clearly drew lines of class and race. The neighborhood association was so eager to protect the community's class status and property values that in the 1940s it protested the nearby construction of the Sojourner Truth public housing complex, even when it was occupied by fellow African Americans.[13] With regard to race, the community held such a strong community identity that it enacted restrictive covenants to exclude whites. Other neighborhoods similar to Conant Gardens—Grixdale Park, Arden Park, Russell Woods, and the "Millionaires' row" of Boston-Edison (or numbers 2–5 on Map 1)—were also harbingers of a small black bourgeoisie who, like their white contemporaries, migrated to the periphery of the city or eventually to upper-income suburbs such as Bloomfield Hills. The exodus of affluent blacks is quite evident from Map 1, for many of these once exclusive neighborhoods sat in the midst of or near housing poverty by the 1990s.[14]

As in other public-housing battles in Midwestern cities, such as Cleveland and Chicago, middle-class blacks in Conant Gardens continued to serve as prospective allies for whites who opposed public housing. In 1966, the predominantly white Krainz Woods Community Council sponsored an advertisement in Detroit's major black newspaper. Krainz Woods solicited black Conant Gardens homeowners to attend a meeting at a local church to protest proposed scattered-site housing and open occupancy, because, they reasoned, "That's why they [Conant Garden residents] moved there—so their children could live in a stable neighborhood in the *proper way*."[15] Not only did such black class opposition hamper the city's efforts to site federally subsidized scattered-site housing, from an ideological standpoint it tacitly reinforced a class ethic of home ownership among the well-paid black working class, who differentiated themselves from the poor.[16] The housing activist Annie Sanders (Kaleema Sumareh) explained the prevailing prejudice: "Public housing is not native to the culture of African American people in this city. We are homeowners. *Individual* homeowners. And we have never liked the projects as a community. It was more stigmatized here, I think, because if you wanted and you saved, you could buy a house in Detroit. If you were *any* kind of person; if you had *anything* going on," it was assumed, "you could buy a house."[17] Other advocates I interviewed corroborated this assertion and the social isolation that public-housing residents confronted between the 1970s and 1990s. By 2000 (see Table 1), black homeowners outpaced black renters by a ratio of nearly 1.2 to 1 and nearly matched the rate of white homeownership. Racial discrimination was clearly the main culprit in explaining this isolation, but this section suggests that black class schisms made it more difficult to mobilize a community consensus in defense of the black poor.

## THE REGIMES OF PUBLIC HOUSING AND URBAN RENEWAL

### The Cross Purposes of Public Housing and Slum Clearance

Next I consider how antagonism in the 1980s between the Detroit advocates of low-income housing and the promoters of downtown development was due to a decades-old conflict between the urban regime and public-housing supporters. In November 1933, the Detroit Housing Commission (DHC) was created as a quasi-state and municipal agency to administer $3.2 million in slum clearance and low-income housing funds. After a five-member commission was appointed, Josephine Gomon, a strong New Dealer and former executive secretary to the New Deal mayor Frank Murphy, was appointed its

**Table 2.** Detroit's major public housing projects, 1937–1952

| Name of complex | Number of units | Initial racial designation | Year completed |
|---|---|---|---|
| Brewster Homes | 703 | Black | September 1938 |
| Brewster Addition[a] | 240 | Black | July 1941 |
| Charles Terrace Homes | 428 | White | October 1941 |
| Douglas Homes[b] | 1,006 | Black | September 1951 |
| Herman Garden Homes | 2,106 | White | May 1943 |
| Jeffries Homes | 2,170 | White | November 1952 |
| Parkside Homes | 737 | White | September 1938 |
| Parkside Annex[a] | 355 | White | September 1941 |
| Smith Homes | 210 | White | January 1943 |
| Sojourner Truth Homes | 200 | Black | March 1942 |
| *Total* | *8,155* | | |

*Sources*: Detroit Housing Commission, *Tenth Annual Report* (Detroit, 1944), 57; Detroit Housing Commission, *The Detroit Housing Commission: Our City's Local Public Agency* (Detroit, 1957), 20.

[a] The total for the entire complex is the sum of the number in the addition number plus the number in the main development.

[b] This is the second complex for what became Brewster-Douglass Homes.

first director-secretary. Until 1974, all five DHC members were appointed by the mayor to serve two-year terms without monetary compensation. Between 1938 and 1955, Detroit spent about $70 million to construct seven major sites: Brewster-Douglass, Parkside, Sojourner Truth, Charles Terrace, Herman Gardens, John W. Smith, and Jeffries (see Table 2). In sharp contrast, the DHC spent $40 million on a single high-income development in downtown Detroit. For the sake of appeasing more affluent citizens and business interests, public housing in Detroit and in the United States has a conflicting, bureaucratic linkage with efforts to redevelop the inner city and spur economic growth. These cross-purposes remained when, a generation later, the federal housing agency was renamed the Department of the Housing and Urban Development in the fall of 1965 and the Community Development Block Grant program was established nine years later, in 1974.[18]

## Race, Public Housing, and Detroit's Urban Renewal Regimes

Although African Americans confronted an extreme housing shortage, the undeniable animus whites had toward racial integration greatly curtailed housing options for blacks. When first established, the DHC condoned an official policy of racially segregating public housing. It was a policy the DHC followed well into the 1940s, contrary to the antidiscrimination rulings that civil-rights advocates pursued in the courts. Gomon and subsequent racial moderates, including some black leaders, acquiesced to this segregation as a pragmatic means to protect Brewster Homes and other exclusively black-programmed developments from white occupancy and gentrification. Nonetheless, the entire period of the late 1930s until the early 1950s was characterized by myriad, vigorous protests by white improvement associations as they swayed or forced the City Council to reject the DHC's public-housing recommendations. In the early 1950s, Arthur Kornhauser found that as many as 68 percent of whites favored some form of racial or residential segregation, and many cited the Jim Crow South as an exemplar of race relations.[19] Again, the most infamous of these struggles to preserve black occupancy was the Sojourner Truth Homes controversy of 1942. Among other white officials, Mayor Edward Jeffries succumbed to white neighborhoods' fears of black tenants. He and his supporters charged that an electoral challenger, Richard Frankensteen, who was pro–public housing and aligned with the United Auto Workers (UAW), was pro-communist and antiwhite. Those in favor of black occupancy eventually won, although a series of violent exchanges ensued.[20] This victory merely stoked the anger of white conservatives, who demanded and got a moratorium on public-housing construction, and the man most pivotal in ensuring that Detroit's urban regime prevailed over public housing was Mayor Albert Cobo.

Once elected in 1950, Mayor Cobo made no effort to conceal his hostility toward public housing and launched the most aggressive downtown redevelopment agenda in the city's history. Armed with President Harry Truman's 1949 Housing Act (and its Title I slum-clearance or urban-renewal provisions), Cobo began his term by forcing out DHC commissioners and staff members sympathetic to public housing and replacing them with business elites and leaders from white homeowner associations.[21] An organizational shift within DHC also resulted in personnel transfers from the public housing unit to the newly created and well-staffed Redevelopment Division. Cobo's pro-development cabal systematically deleted ten of twelve redevelopment sites from a slum clearance plan.[22]

Consequently, the DHC displayed a fairly callous position toward the African Americans it displaced from the upscale Gratiot / Lafayette Park housing project. Of the approximately 6,000 persons evacuated from the area in 1956, about 38 percent were unaccounted for due to the DHC's strict interpretation of relocation statutes. The housing market for blacks remained so tight throughout this period that a 1950 survey of sixteen apartment buildings comprising 11,000 units turned up exactly three vacancies![23] When various critics complained about the DHC's callousness toward relocatees, they were either stalled or were given the curt response of DHC Director Harry Durbin: "We can't clear slums without hardship."[24] Of course, this was no consolation to the relocating families, since the nearly $13 million Gratiot and Lafayette Park Project produced 3,000 middle- to upper-income high-rise, townhouse, or cooperative apartments, none of which these low-income families could afford.[25] This dislocation was akin to how federal highway subsidies were used to raze other African American communities, including the Oakland-Hastings expressway and the bulldozing of north Hastings Street; the John C. Lodge Freeway and the displacement of 2,000 buildings; the Edsel Ford Freeway and destruction of the black West Side, as well as the heart of Paradise Valley; and I-75 and the razing of the rest of Hastings Street, including the vibrant business life of "Black Bottom" or Paradise Valley (see number 8 on Map 1).[26]

Between 1949 and 1971, a total of twenty-seven urban-renewal projects were initiated, for a total of $263 million. Despite these glittering improvements to the city's facade and in its public services, the black poor were most often uprooted and provided with inadequate relief. By 1963, the combined displacement effect of Detroit's urban-renewal projects had moved 43,000 persons from their homes, and 70 percent of them were black. It was no wonder that urban renewal in Detroit and elsewhere was cynically dubbed "Negro Removal."[27] Suffice it to say that the heavy-handedness of the Cobo regime and other urban regimes became both the bane and the motivation for grassroots activists to find new, oppositional ways to assert their communities' interests.

## EARLY BLACK POLITICS AND HOUSING ACTIVISM CYCLES

### The Early Structure of Black Politics

While I maintain that racial justice and economic redistribution, vaguely defined, are key ethics within African American politics, widely divergent black ideological interpretations of the group's racial, class, and often gender interests complicate group consensus. Such was true of early black electoral politics in Michigan and Detroit since some black leaders served as collaborators with and others served as challengers to the dominant white political regime. In fact, pre–Second World War black politics in Detroit were very dependent on a church-based clientage system where for more than twenty years, beginning in the 1920s, the automobile magnate Henry Ford used influential black ministers as intermediaries with black labor recruitment and social control.

Prior to the 1950s, Detroit's at-large electoral system and white racial hostilities effectively diluted the black vote so that only one black, S. C. Watson in 1882, had ever served on the City Council.[28] Wilbur Rich notes that the black minister patron–client politics of Henry Ford "inhibited the development of an independent black leadership and the entry of blacks into the official Democratic party."[29] In 1931, Charles Roxborough, a Republican, was elected to the Michigan State Senate as part of the Ford machine. But a year later, a small cadre of black political entrepreneurs, including the future state senator Charles Diggs Sr. and the attorney Harold Bledsoe, began to engineer the defection of black Detroiters from the party of Lincoln. They were successful partly because the old Ford machine failed to incorporate the more assertive politics of the new black elite that became part of President Franklin D. Roosevelt's New Deal coalition—labor, white ethnics, minorities, and so on. Drawn by the economic liberalism of Mayor Frank Murphy and Roosevelt's New Deal, black voters were also widely attracted to the prospect of electing Diggs, a funeral director and civic leader, to the State Senate and to realign en masse with the Democrats after 1936. In 1940, Reverend Horace White was elected as a state representative, which put him in line for appointment to Mayor Edward Jeffries's housing commission.[30] By the end of the 1950s, black Detroiters had sent three black state senators and eight state representatives to the State Capitol and had one seat on the City Council. Throughout the period, black members of the state legislature, such as senators Charles Diggs Sr. and Charles Diggs Jr., as well as Coleman Young, were vital sponsors of housing legislation aimed at low- and moderate-income households.

## Early Low-Income Housing Activism

One proof that opportunities for effective activism existed was the different alliances in the 1930s and early 1940s among radicals, black renters, and elected officials. Another is that organizers used a plethora of interesting tactics—from rent strikes to petitions—to disrupt business as usual. Activists made only limited gains, however, because strategic advantages such as tenant-rights laws were missing. During the Great Depression, communist organizers, who had gained a civil-rights reputation for anti-lynching activism, actively pursued economic justice in Detroit and elsewhere by setting up tenant leagues and unemployment councils among blacks and whites. In 1931, the DHC relocated about 1,000 families to build the Brewster Homes in Paradise Valley. On several occasions, black families squatted or refused to move, for they distrusted the DHC's pledges of improved housing. To recruit the disenchanted relocatees of the threatened black neighborhood, communist organizers established a Hasting-Ferry Street unemployment council. A black UAW worker, Joseph Billups, became a prominent black communist. While Louis Blount, president of the National Association for Colored People (NAACP), led a peaceful delegation of thirty-six black organizations to request that the DHC fulfill its original pledges, unemployment councils held eviction counter-protests and espoused a confrontational approach with private landlords. They made courageous but only piecemeal strides.[31]

Beyond this radical agitation, black tenants also organized within all-black organizations to demand that unscrupulous landlords be challenged. In November 1937, more than sixty black families joined the Rent and Consumer League and refused to pay their rent until their demands were met. Four years later, their activism was followed by Louis R. Taylor and the United Tenant Association, which encouraged tenants to form picket lines, engage in legal suits, and use rent strikes as a means of holding landlords accountable. In one demonstration in 1941, striking black tenants pressured a particularly egregious landlord to reduce rents from $5 to $2.50 a month. These protest efforts outside the arenas of political power complemented the efforts of the few blacks inside such corridors, including Diggs and the Coordinating Committee on Housing and the City Council's Fair Rent Committee, on which Diggs and Taylor sat. At best, their successes were modest, which prompted Reverend Horace White to initiate a Rent Day protest to lobby the Roosevelt administration for more federal housing.[32] Although unable to spur large-scale reform, this activism of the 1930s and 1940s set the tone for insurgency in the 1960s.

## THE ALLIES, ADVANTAGES, AND TACTICS OF GRASSROOTS HOUSING ACTIVISM

The context, timing, and utility factors of collective identity and framing, group resources and networks, strategic advantages, disruptive coalitions, and adaptive tactics differentially advanced the cause of black-led grassroots movements interested in fair and affordable housing in the 1950s and 1960s. Of these factors, I consider activist alliances, advantages, and tactics the strongest determinants of effective activism. True to previous periods, gender joined race and class as a salient determinant in these struggles for "respectability," because black women often occupied the front lines against top-down regimes.[33]

A cluster of movements made up Detroit's low-income-housing advocacy network by the early 1970s: tenant rights, anti-urban renewal and early community development, welfare rights / antipoverty, and public housing. I first explain briefly how the civil rights–labor coalition's call for fair housing lost out to black radicalism's more influential call for community control. This debate helped define the breadth and trajectory of subsequent grassroots activism and protest.

## The Civil Rights–Labor Coalition, Black Radicalism, and Fair Housing

On no other issue was the coalition among civil-rights organizations, black politicians, and labor unions more apparent but also more strained than on the fair-housing issue. While the infamous Mayor Orville Hubbard of Dearborn, Michigan, railed against whites' being required to "live with niggers," Detroit groups such as Reverend C. L. Franklin's Detroit Council on Human Relations and suburban groups such as the Greater Detroit Committee for Fair Housing mobilized for local fair-housing ordinances. Intense advocacy for fair housing did not win in Detroit until the late 1960s and the 1968 Housing Act—thus, the emergence of new strategic advantages—but Detroit still became the nation's most residentially segregated metropolitan area.[34] A sea change in ideological framing occurred where black support for liberal integrationism and racial fairness in home buying, which mostly benefited higher-income families, was supplanted by radicals' and black nationalists' calls for "community control" and affordable housing, which mostly benefited low and moderate income families. In fact, Reverend Albert Cleage Jr., who as Bishop Jaramogi Abebe Agyeman later founded the Shrine of the Black Madonna and the Pan African Orthodox Christian Church, reasoned that open occupancy would "only panic white people."[35] Thus, the illusion of residential integration would give way to the reality of white flight. Instead, the nationalist answer was to control the resources, housing, and governance of the black community. It was a position Malcolm X stridently defended at a conference in Detroit in 1963, when he derided the so-called house Negro civil-rights leadership's preoccupation with living "near his [white] master."[36] It was Black Nationalism's denouncement of moderate housing goals that helped a younger generation of black militants to more deeply contemplate how to challenge economic and racial oppression. By the late 1960s, independent black unionism had merged with revolutionary nationalism, and the result was radical black workers' parties, especially the League of Revolutionary Black Workers and the Black Panther Party.[37] As I will explain later, "the league" was preceded by and helped to maintain a radical network that directly supported the rights of public-housing tenants, among others.

## Tenant Rights Activism: CORE and the UTCA

Headquartered in Harlem and led by Jesse Gray's Community Council on Housing, which led historic rent strikes, the 1960s tenant-rights and anti-slumlord movement extended on the framing of the Civil Rights Movement. As opposed to Southern hamlets, Northern ghettos became the primary context for battle. Youthful activists in Detroit's Congress of Racial Equality (CORE) chapter and the NAACP threw themselves into the fight for tenants' rights and built an effective network of grassroots allies that included the Northern Student Movement, the Adult Community Movement for Equality, the West Central Organization (WCO), the Neighborhood Legal Service (NLS), and the Commission on Community Relations (CCR). CORE's national secretary, James Farmer, framed the problem at a Detroit rally this way, "March, picket and be willing to go to jail if necessary, [because] you are now part of the civil rights movement as much as those who marched from Selma to Montgomery."[38] While racial justice in the low-income rental market was the key frame that activists stressed to build a collective identity, gender was significant, for black women, as I explain, were indispensable leaders and participants.[39]

Conditions in many Detroit rental buildings were deplorable and were only aggravated by the city's lax building-code inspection system. A mother receiving Aid to Dependent Families (ADC) once joked it was so bad that "we used to pay $70 a month, but we're sharing with rats and roaches, so now we pay $75."[40] One of the tactics CORE used to combat slumlords was to picket urban-renewal projects that implicated the use of government funds and implicitly drew government officials into the fight. Among the most egregious of slumlords was the Goodman Brothers Real Estate firm. In spring of 1965, members of CORE, the NAACP, and the Seward Street Tenant Action Council picketed the construction site of the luxury St. Regis Hotel co-owned by the Goodman Brothers and carried signs reading, "St. Regis Built With Slum and Tax Money" and "Govt. and Slums equals St. Regis." Delores Whiteside, a Goodman Brothers tenant, joined the protesters while her little boy carried a placard stating, "Roaches Are My Playmates." They protested the firm's eviction of Whiteside and four other residents in retaliation for their activism.[41] About a week later, CORE activists sponsored a "chain-in" at the St. Regis site and physically shackled themselves to its entrance. Six members of the Tenant Action

Council participated. This protest benefited from timing, for it prompted local press coverage of slum conditions right when President Lyndon Johnson proposed a War on Poverty. The state legislature and the city responded with modest steps by requiring greater accountability from landlords, including liens on properties where a landlord's negligence endangered newborns, and halting vendors' payments of welfare recipients' rent to landlords who violated city building codes.[42]

Modest victories such as these emerged partly because the activists formed disruptive coalitions, employed diverse tactics, and gained strategic advantages from the activities of black public officials, the courts, and service agencies. By the fall of 1966, city inspectors had cited another owner, Russell Harrison, with 205 violations. Still Harrison flagrantly disregarded a court order and shut off the electricity and gas to forcibly evict thirty-three tenants. When Arthella Peoples, a member of a CORE-sponsored tenants' union, was asked about her participation in a subsequent outdoor vigil, she chuckled, "It will probably be warmer out there than in my apartment."[43] After a flurry of judicial findings against Harrison, he fled. Once alerted to the problem, Congressman Charles Diggs Jr. took matters into his own hands. Cheered by a vigil, he entered the darkened building and broke into the utility closet to restore power. Wayne County Judge John Swainson ordered a bench warrant for Harrison's arrest and told the sheriff to restore the gas. Dismayed by Harrison's brazen actions, the City Council passed an ordinance making it illegal to shut off utilities to induce an eviction. By 1967, the NLS had won its lawsuit against Goodman Brothers for the real-estate company's retaliatory harassment and eviction of five Seward Street tenants.[44]

On the heels of these victories, the United Tenants for Collective Action (UTCA) emerged. The UTCA was founded in July 1967 by the charismatic Fred Lyles. Mike Smith of Community Legal Services (CLS) and Ron Reosti of the NSL believed that Lyles became UTCA's president because he broadened the framing of the campaign from his individual distress (a respiratory illness from poor ventilation) to the racial and economic injustices confronting all Detroit tenants. The UTCA was also assisted in its development by the West Central Organization, the Trade Union Leadership Council, and, later, the League of Revolutionary Black Workers. Like other UTCA leaders who suffered harassment, Lyles paid an extreme cost for his activism when an assassin's bullet, probably fired by police agents and intended for the League's leader, General Baker, made him a quadriplegic.[45]

Nonetheless, the UTCA challenged the Goodman Brothers' retaliatory and illegal evictions. In 1968, Albert Goodman was forced to negotiate because, after a six-month rent strike, the UTCA and its NLS lawyers used new tenant-rights laws and secured an injunction preventing rent collection. State senator Coleman Young sponsored a bevy of reforms, including a public-housing Board of Tenant Affairs (Michigan Public Act 344), urban-renewal citizen districts, and tougher penalties for slumlords. As a result, Goodman agreed to turn over the management of seventeen of his buildings to the UTCA and received only a quarter of the rent revenues once repairs were made. Lyle expanded the campaign against slumlords in October 1968 to include 500 residents throughout Detroit and applied pressure by picketing the homes and businesses of offending landlords while placing tenants' rent in escrow. Although there was legal wrangling about the legality of this action, leaders of the strike claimed a victory because landlords were forced to negotiate the resumption of rent payments. A subsequent UTCA partnership and foray into "black capitalism" produced the first black-led nonprofit housing corporation, Marvel Unlimited, and the $3 million purchase of twenty-one apartment buildings. Unfortunately, this did not pan out, partly because arsonists destroyed some of the units.[46] Nonetheless, CORE and the UTCA succeeded to the degree that they combined new strategic advantages and influential allies with creative and instrumental tactics.

## Housing and Anti-Urban Renewal Activism: Saul Alinsky and the WCO

Another group that pushed the city administration to ensure safe and affordable housing while challenging the urban-renewal regime was the WCO. Whereas CORE and the UTCA were mostly black-led groups, the WCO was a multiracial group in which blacks made up a third of its leaders, including its eventual executive director, John Watson. Its founders sought counsel from the renowned community organizer Saul Alinsky and his Industrial Areas Foundation. Alinsky had strong ties to clergy in Detroit who espoused religious social action, especially Catholic Monsignor Clement Kern, and to civil-rights and labor leaders. Among these clergy was the WCO's first president, Reverend Richard Venus, the young, white pastor of the Fourteenth Avenue Methodist Church, who declared, "Our job . . . is to build power. It is to channel the discontent that exists in slums into constructive change."[47] Venus reflected Alinsky's non-ideological pragmatism that promoted reform through neighborhood-based militancy. Local capacity building and autonomy were Alinsky's chief aims; thus, he preferred citywide coalitions or networks among pre-existing civic groups. In 1965, the WCO was founded by sixty neighborhood groups. Likely in deference to Detroit's labor history, it framed itself as a "People's Union." Housing was at the center of its "good government" demands. It took pride in its decentralization and racial and gender parity, as well as its focus on community control.[48]

While the WCO's use of confrontational tactics was very effective in publicizing housing and economic inequalities, they also exposed various ideological, racial, and class fissures. For example, the WCO demanded the demolition of 1920 West Alexandrine Street, a vacant house in which three black boys died tragically in a fire. On July 1, 1965, the WCO and its "Peoples Community Action" coalition of some 150 blacks and whites demonstrated in front of the City-County Building led by the black state representative James Del Rio and Reverend Venus. Protesters carried signs and small caskets for dramatic effect, then entered City Hall to directly express their grievances to the council. Del Rio's backing of the outspoken WCO stood in contrast to the criticisms of Council Members Mel Ravitz, a white liberal, and Nicholas Hood, a black moderate. Del Rio directly challenged Ravitz's claim that the city had spent $2 million on demolition: "Well, you are not moving ahead fast enough . . . the people want action!" Mayor Jerome Cavanaugh attempted to defuse the situation by promising to better patrol vacant neighborhood lots, and the council invited the WCO to return to a subsequent meeting.[49] Unsatisfied with this response, the WCO increased pressure on the insurance company that owned the building by picketing a radio station owned by the company's vice-president, Dr. Haley Bell, an African American. Although Venus was quick to claim that the protest was not racial, the image of a black businessman as a slumlord stood in stark class contrast to the image of a poor black mother publicly grieving her children with a sign reading, "2 of My Children Died There—I want 1920 Alexandrine Down." By the end of July, the remnants of the structure had been razed and cleared.[50]

About a year later, the WCO directly confronted Mayor Cavanaugh's urban-renewal regime by opposing plans to expand Wayne State University's campus, known as "University City" and "Research Park." It was preceded by the Medical Center plan, where a black ministerial coalition, the Detroit Fellowship of Urban Renewal Churches, opposed the massive $300 million, eight-year plan that affected 10,000 mostly black residents, as well as their churches and surrounding properties. Although the fellowship was unable to convince the city to build low-income housing in the area, the churches that won the concession of remaining on their properties and developing their own housing included Friendship Baptist and Plymouth United Church of Christ—the latter's pastor was Councilman Hood.[51]

With the University Park's plan to relocate 3,000 families, however, the WCO preferred the tactic of protest to public–private negotiation. Ethel Watkins, chair of the WCO's Urban Renewal Committee, declared in classic Alinsky language: "We are going to stop this mess right now. It certainly isn't *the American way* to [run] thousands of people out of their homes with federal money to create socialism for the rich. If this is Wayne State University's idea of democratic education we can use less of it."[52] Through mass leafleting; demonstrations; the occupation of abandoned houses; noisy public hearings; challenges to Mayor Cavanaugh, the City Council, and housing officials; and even the presentation of a live skunk to Wayne States's trustees, the WCO characterized its campaign as a confrontational effort, "to change the rules for urban renewal."[53] By my definition, they sought a strategic advantage. The WCO demanded accountability from federal and local officials by insisting on changes in federal urban-renewal regulations, a transfer of urban-renewal projects from under the DHC, and the firing of the DHC's director, Robert Knox. The WCO had two meetings in the late 1960s with Governor George Romney and convinced him to support greater citizen participation in Detroit's urban-renewal programs.

Council Member Hood, however, upbraided the WCO and its clergy allies for demanding Knox's resignation but failing to do anything to pragmatically increase the city's supply of affordable housing, as he claimed he and some members of the black clergy had done.[54] Hood's disagreement with the WCO's approach presaged the racial divides that existed among low-income-housing advocates in the 1980s, where some black church-based housing corporations disdained the confrontational politics of multiracial low-income housing activists. As its imaginative and incessant protest tactics exploited strong strategic advantages, the WCO was successful because it bridged certain divides of race and class to create fairly strong alliances and disruptive coalitions. It ceased to exist by the early 1970s but had laid the basis for future generations of antipoverty advocates, such as Marian Kramer, a vital "bridge leader" in Detroit. Kramer's activist biography connects various movements together, including civil rights, community control, public-housing rights, black radicalism via the League (she is a co-founder of the League, and General Baker is her spouse), and most especially welfare rights and antipoverty.[55]

## Welfare Rights and Antipoverty Activism

Inflamed by passions for racial, gender, and economic justice, many black women activists made a linkage between antipoverty and affordable-housing activism. After all, transfer payments or rent subsidies determined monthly rent payments; thus, public-housing developments became logical sites for welfare-rights organizing. A network of Welfare Rights Organizations (WROs) in Detroit and elsewhere facilitated activist intersections between antipoverty, pro–public housing, and tenant-rights campaigns. A united front was desirable due to several shared grievances—insufficient benefit levels and budget allocations for recipients, paternalistic and insensitive bureaucracies, and inadequate involvement of recipients despite claims to encourage the "maximum feasible participation" of the poor. Difficulties aside, activists exploited the new policy and ideological opportunities of Johnson's War on Poverty or Community Action Programs (CAP), which in Detroit was the Total Action Against Poverty (TAP) and later Model Cities. Although TAP was short-lived and mired in conflicts, some 130,000 low-income Detroiters, most of whom were black, were provided services such as landlord / tenant counseling, and these programs trained an entire generation of antipoverty and housing activists.[56]

The many activist welfare mothers who helped found the National Welfare Rights Organization (NWRO)—Johnnie Tillmon, Beulah Sanders, Annie Smart, among them—did not come to the movement as empty slates. They brought invaluable lived experiences and often previous involvement in other groups such as CAP or the Black Panther Party. The NWRO's core principles of combating poverty, racism, and sexism through the empowerment of welfare recipients and the establishment of a right to livable benefit levels were most directly shaped by these lived experiences and involvements. Undergirding all welfare-rights activism was a broad framing of women's economic vulnerability. To reiterate, Tillmon said all women were "one man away from poverty" and, by extension, homelessness.[57]

Such ideals sparked a new collective identity among low-income African Americans and had them confront the personal humiliation, embarrassing scrutiny, and public stigma often heaped on public-aid recipients and public-housing tenants when labeled the undeserving poor. Yvette Linebarger, a veteran activist, described how she rebelled against the onerous stereotype that "if you were on ADC . . . you didn't have any rights. . . . People always viewed you as being a liar. A nobody." Her consciousness was pricked when a neighbor in her Brewster-Douglass complex prodded her to join a WRO called the Westside Mothers. It made her realize, "This is what I've been thinking should be around all the time. You know. Knowing that you do have some rights and stuff like that. I got involved, and I guess within a year I was an officer in the organization."[58]

Linebarger's personal narrative of recruitment by a fellow public-housing tenant echoes the larger reality of the connection between welfare-rights and public-housing activism. Like other large cities, Detroit had a pre-existing network of groups that preceded the NWRO's founding in 1966. The NWRO was knitted together partly due to the tireless organizing efforts of its executive director, George Wiley, and the Poverty/Research Action Center. Before the formation of Detroit's citywide coalition, the Jeffries Welfare Rights Organization, Westside Mothers, and the Federation of Aid to Dependent Children—as headed by Lena Bivens and assisted by the future City Council president Maryann Mahaffey—were all viable organizations. They were followed by or joined by groups in Brewster-Douglass Homes, Herman Gardens Homes, and Parkside Homes, among others.[59]

At its peak cycle of protest from 1966 to 1969, the NWRO mobilized a vibrant network of some 800 affiliates, in all fifty states, and incited welfare protests and lawsuits in hundreds of cities. During this same period, Detroit WROs mobilized more than two dozen campaigns and lobbied state and county officials. Initially recruited into the movement by Beulah Sanders, Kramer reflected, "We did mobilization here [in Detroit] which sprung a hell of a movement at that time."[60] Although it disbanded in the mid-1970s because of intense disagreements over its collective identity and agenda, the welfare-rights movement experienced at least limited success. Its tactical creativity as well as its alliances with radicals and some public officials disrupted business as usual and prompted reform. The intersection of race, class, and gender consciousness that welfare-right organizers incited among the black poor reinforced the type of collective identity cultivated by public-housing advocates.

## Public-Housing Activism

Congruent with my theory, the Detroit public housing strike in 1969 benefited most from strategic advantages and alliances, despite ideological and tactical differences that fractured its identity. In the end, however, its strategic advantages mattered more than did its ideological divides. Under Michigan Public Act 344, the state required the City of Detroit to establish a Board of Tenant Affairs (BTA) by October 30, 1968. Of the sixteen members, half were elected by public-housing tenants, and the other half were appointed by the mayor. By a two-thirds majority vote, the BTA could veto certain DHC decisions. Even though in December 1968 the DHC approved a rent increase to take effect on February 1, 1969, it failed to comply with the law and first establish the BTA so that tenants had democratic input. With the rent increase, the DHC did not consider that the cost of living had risen 15 percent over the 1960s while state welfare payments in 1968 were based on 1960 census figures. Such considerations precipitated conflict, and tenant groups announced rent strikes and protests in the Jeffries, Brewster-Douglass, Herman Gardens, and Parkside Homes.[61]

The strike began with the Jeffries Homes, where the outspoken Ronald Scott of the Black Panther Party headed the Jeffries Rent Strike Committee. At the time, Kramer worked with the WCO and welfare-rights groups while maintaining ties with the League and the Black Panthers. She explained, "In 1969 some people in the Jeffries projects came to my house and asked me to help organize the tenants against rent increases. On a Sunday we had a *big* meeting and we decided to do a rent strike. We forged a unity between the seniors and the youth. Ron Scott, who was in the Panthers, lived in the projects. We set up a picket line and used the young people from the Panthers and the League to help man it. We spread to Brewster."[62] Given her active involvement in the housing efforts of the WCO (and the fact that Watson of the League was also director of the WCO), Kramer shared these ideas—especially the idea of picketing landlords' homes—in the spring of 1968 during a community forum at the University of Detroit titled, "Can Rent Strikes Be Successful?"[63] This is a clear example of tactical innovation. The closest allies of the rent strike were the Black Panther Party, the WCO, Community Legal Services, the CCR, and sympathetic public officials.

While the Jeffries Strike Committee prepared for a February 1 action, the DHC announced a January 31 deadline for people interested in running for the BTA seats. Tenant organizers doubted the DHC's motives in announcing these BTA seats, as well as the claim that the strike would bankrupt the authority. In an effort to forestall such a possibility, the City Council considered subsidizing the $19 a month increase for the 8,200 families in public housing. To aid these families, Robert Knox, the housing director, proposed a means-based rent supplement between February and July 1 at the cost of $460,000. But hardship compelled an additional 400 tenants to sign up for public assistance.[64]

The strike in Jeffries proceeded and was followed by one in Brewster-Douglass. True to the other tenant-rights campaigns of the period, Black Power and grassroots populist appeals for "community control" became the movement's ideological frame. An undeniable subtext of the joint demands issued by the approximately 300 strikers was that public-housing tenants were denied the right of democratic self-governance and citizen participation. Examples of their seven demands included their insistence "(1) that [two thirds] of the commissioners on the Housing Commission be public housing tenants; (2) that 80% of the maintenance staff be tenants in the projects; (3) that all rent increases be set with the approval of the BTA," and so on.[65]

Underscoring this point, the Brewster-Douglass Strike Committee asserted that "High rent is not the only reason we are striking. We must control our own community."[66] Later, the committee amended its demands to include the removal of Knox as housing director, and the appointment of the DHC director by the commission. The CCR endorsed most of the demands of the strike committees. By the first part of June, the DHC had issued a round of eviction notices, since according to it, strike negotiations were at a standstill. With the assistance of legal-aid attorneys, strike leaders pursued the matter in court. In turn, the new BTA passed a resolution calling the rent increase illegal.[67]

The new tenant-participation and rent laws provided activists with the strategic advantages they needed to disrupt the process. When Public Act 344 defined the BTA's authority, members of the strike committee who were elected to this board had a new platform from which to air their concerns and confront public officials. One activist who especially exploited this opportunity was Ronald Scott. Black class dissension and divergent notions of black group interests were obvious from the clashes between Conrad Mallet, an African American who was housing operations superintendent, Scott, and other BTA members who aligned with Scott.

Scott and the militants accused Mallet of betraying the interests of public-housing tenants; they also charged the DHC with reneging on its promise not to pursue evictions. They in turn "summoned" Mayor Cavanaugh and Mallet to attend a meeting with state legislators. On July 1, the black state representative David Holmes, an original sponsor of Public Act 344, mediated and arranged the meeting. Tensions were so high, however, that the BTA and the DHC argued over the terms of a subsequent joint meeting.[68] The DHC's antagonism toward the BTA was apparent, for it failed to transfer documents necessary for the BTA to fulfill its duties. Wayne County Court Judge Charles Farmer then handed the rent strikers a large tactical victory. He ruled that people who had been served with eviction notices had the right to appeal their cases to the BTA. This provided the BTA with the ability to delay the process by taking its time to schedule hearings and to review these cases. All the while, the strike was costing the city more than $100,000.[69]

The next day, Scott took further advantage of the DHC's predicament by interrupting its regular meeting for twenty minutes and announcing a flurry of demands that included BTA salaries, a budget of $300,000, creation of a "youth arm," and investigations into housing-maintenance neglect. Scott exhorted, "We label this day as 'Up against the Wall, Detroit Housing Commission Day!'" William Price, chairman of the DHC, said he would accept the demands in good faith if presented in writing. A few days later, Scott further escalated the battle of words and wits when he used characteristic Black Power hyperbole:

"We need to expose the Housing Commission for what it is; an animalistic agency that sucks the blood of the people!" Henry Cleage, brother of Reverend Albert Cleage and counsel to the BTA, observed about the BTA's new exposure, "You may not know it, but this board is becoming quite famous, at least in the black community."[70]

However, this intense rhetoric created an ideological rift on the BTA. The moderate faction appointed by Mayor Cavanaugh aligned behind the chairperson, Eleanor Green, a Herman Gardens resident. Green questioned the legality of Scott's last round of demands, and she believed the Scott faction was unnecessarily contentious with the DHC. As a sign of good faith, she extended the deadline for Mallet to respond to the Scott demands. An extremely stormy BTA meeting followed her peace gesture. One observer reported that it was "punctuated by shouting and much gavel-pounding."[71] Then ideological friction boiled over into personal rancor and intrigue. Four BTA members claimed that "extremists" had threatened their lives, and Green reported that her son had intercepted a mysterious telephone call from a man named "Soapy" who asked whether she had "got the check." Invoking her history of involvement in the Civil Rights Movement and childhood in the rural South, Green indignantly professed, "If anyone wants to kill me, go ahead and do it." The impasse between the rent strikers and the DHC promised to deepen when the DHC threatened to issue a new round of 400 eviction notices.[72]

A second strategic advantage saved the day and provided each side with the incentive to negotiate. U.S. Senator Edward Brooke introduced a pivotal amendment through the 1969 Housing Act. This statute and its successors ensured that local public-housing authorities received sufficient federal subsidies so they no longer had to charge tenants monthly rents that exceeded one fourth of their income. A retreat was scheduled for January 1970 in Allen Park, Michigan, where members of the DHC and all of the members of the BTA peacefully conferred. Under the auspices of Mayor Roman Gribbs's new administration, the strike was effectively concluded on February 26, 1970, and tenants were promised necessary improvements to their developments, as well as no foreseeable increases. Mallet defined the conference as demonstrating that the DHC was "accountable to public housing tenants."[73]

## Post-Uprising Housing Advocacy

Despite the hopes and struggles of liberal reformers and grassroots militants, the factors of racism, residential segregation, housing poverty, white flight, and economic disinvestment collided in July 1967 to produce a terrible outcome. Sparked by police brutality, Detroit had the largest and most costly civil disorder of the 1960s—43 persons dead, 600 rendered homeless (most of the dead and homeless were black), and a total of $45 million in property damage. Foremost in Mayor Cavanaugh's mind when he surveyed the devastation of the Twelfth Street epicenter was the prophetic assessment of his housing director: the administration failed to put proper emphasis on housing. Prior to this explosion, Cavanaugh had been informed that Detroit needed 80,000 more units of public housing, 60 percent of it for African Americans. The riot cost Cavanaugh his reputation as an effective liberal reformer and inflicted severe and enduring pain on the city and its black community.[74]

Immediately following the uprising, a spate of governmental, corporate, and civic groups coalesced around a new urban regime committed to addressing post-uprising needs. Chief among them was the civic coalition New Detroit Inc. The Metropolitan Detroit Citizens Development Authority (MDCDA), founded by the UAW leaders Walter Reuther and Walker Cisler in 1966, received $3.4 million from New Detroit between 1968 and 1972 to assist community groups, including the UTCA, to rebuild housing. But constant bickering over community control meant that only 2,700 of a projected 25,000 new units materialized.[75] All the same, various advocates of community control avidly believed that Detroit's rebirth rested with a pragmatic "bricks and mortar" revitalization that would address immediate housing woes through multiracial activism. One such advocate was the Michigan Coalition on Housing (MCOH) headed by Chris Alton, a longtime UAW organizer and chair of the Forrest Park Planning Group. Founded in 1966, the MCOH—later, the Michigan Housing Coalition—was an umbrella group particularly active during the early 1970s and Young's first mayoral term. Before the community development movement fully took root in Detroit, the MCOH was a pioneer that grappled with the unprecedented and eviscerating losses Detroit suffered in its affordable-housing market. In 1972, the MCOH help establish the very important National People's Action on Housing in Chicago led by Gale Cincotta and Shel Trapp. The MCOH and its allies helped nurture the first generation of Detroit community developers and, thus, the post-uprising grassroots housing network.[76]

## CONCLUSION

In this chapter, I have conducted a historical overview of the period between the 1930s and the late 1960s and have reinforced the scholarly conclusion that federal authorities, city officials, land developers, realtors, and white homeowner associations colluded in the denial of fair and affordable housing for black Detroiters. What is unique about my work, however, is that I go beyond this understanding to discuss opportunities for effective black grassroots responses to these inequalities. To be sure, persistent racial inequalities in the housing market motivated this activism. However, protest was most effective in inducing accountability to the poorly housed when it was the right tactic (it exploited a regime vulnerability); in the right place or context (ideology, social structure, and the dynamics of black politics cohered to create strong alliances); and at the right time (moments of political instability required new reforms and strategic advantages).

How did utility matter? The 1930s and 1960s witnessed the emergence of liberal mayoral regimes, which in turn encouraged liberals and leftists to openly and loudly express their discontent with policies that disadvantaged poorly housed citizens. Protest was the right tool because those in City Hall were more sympathetic to the grievances of the protesters than their successors or predecessors. Whether the chosen arena of conflict was the market or public policy, activists of the 1930s and 1960s adapted their tactics—from the petition to the rent strike—and created disruptive coalitions when businesses and politicians were more likely to make concessions due to system crises such as the economy and the Great Depression or the political system and the Civil Rights and Black Power movements.

Very related to utility was context, which included the dimensions of ideology, the black social structure, and the status of black politics. As I theorize, framing, the structure of black social relations, and politics mattered because the crisis atmosphere of the 1930s and the 1960s were energized by a wider diversity of ideologies than were the more conservative and ideologically restricted 1940s and 1950s. Moreover, these frames and their ideological consensuses mattered in the cementing of networks and alliances. Although race and racism were the primary determinants of black housing opportunities, widening black class fissures and economic segregation complicated group consensus. As the number of black elected officials grew, grassroots activists potentially had more allies within government. When coupled with increasing class divisions, however, this led to more internecine conflicts about how best to serve black housing needs.

Finally, timing mattered because these conditions meant that the 1930s and 1960s witnessed more radical or diverse cycles of protests. The concessions that those in power made to insurgency—from tepid rent control to the participation of public-housing tenants in the governance process—only provided additional strategic advantages to activists. As the logic goes, these eras presented activists with windows of opportunity to voice their cases because they could draw on resonant framings of problems in black housing, changing party realignments or comparatively greater numbers of black allies within government, liberal middle-class advocates, and more liberal city regimes.

Let me be clear: I am not arguing that insignificant levels of activism occurred in the 1940s and 1950s, for there were the protests around occupancy of the Sojourner Truth Homes and the fair-housing movement. It is very important to remember that activism takes various forms. I simply focus on the role protest played and conclude that, from a comparative standpoint, black protest had greater political leverage in the 1930s and 1960s. These eras promoted a broader diversity of answers to black housing poverty than the more retrenched, intervening decades. New allies, advantages, and tactics cohered in these more fertile periods to create unique moments for effective grassroots activism precisely when political regimes and local economies were already under enormous strains. Next, I discuss how Mayor Coleman Young and other African Americans assuming leadership of the city further complicated the dynamics between race, redistribution, and grassroots activism.

# 3

## Trading Activism

*The Young Regime and the Context of Black Politics*

**I think we traded the activism of the 1960s for a certain kind of political activism in the traditional political process and began to stake all out indicators of success based upon who we could elect and how successful we could be in that process.**
**—Adam Shakoor, former deputy mayor of Detroit and former member of the League of Revolutionary Black Workers, 1994**

### "ACCOUNTABILITY TO THE BLACK COMMUNITY"

Elected as Detroit's first black mayor in 1973, Coleman Young was returned to office four times between 1977 and 1993. Thus, he served longer than any chief executive in Detroit's history ever has or probably ever will. This chapter discusses the barriers effective black grassroots activism confronted in the 1970s and 1980s as Mayor Coleman Young and his regime narrowly framed Detroit black politics. Young's political charisma, street savvy, and significant strides in making city government more racially inclusive earned him high regard among black Detroiters.[1] It is ironic that at times he and his supporters were heavy-handed in using race and racism as touchstones to deflect criticism that too often his regime's pro-growth agenda was not accountable to the black working class and poor.

In 1972 Young and part of the Michigan delegation angrily stormed out of the National Black Political Convention (NBPC) held in Gary, Indiana, because they felt that convention leaders also narrowly construed the obligations of race and unity. This walkout was a categorical rejection of the convention's agenda, which Young and others felt was hastily considered and racially separatist. Assembled under the banner "Black Unity without Uniformity," the NBPC's roughly 6,000 delegates overcame fractious divides to pass several resolutions, including a "Model Pledge for Black Candidates" that asked black candidates and officeholders to promise, "I will constantly act out my accountability to manifest the interests of the Black Community."[2] Although the NBPC and its National Black Political Assembly were short-lived and lacked the endorsement of many black elected officials, they were attempts to meld black grassroots activism with black electoral power—what I consider the fusion between black institutional and insurgent politics. Coming at the climax of the Black Power Movement, however, the Young quarrel demonstrates that competing conceptions of group interests and political accountability have perennially confounded black politics.[3]

I use the Effective Black Activism Model (EBAM) as a lens to understand how the *context* of Detroit black grassroots activism and protest mattered because of the black class and ideological differences activists had to overcome, especially as Young tightly constructed black politics and increased the costs of mobilization. I secondarily argue that the utility of grassroots activism is a relevant issue, for it faces a "top-down" regime that limits arenas for voicing opposition. This was especially true as Young vigorously pursued a black urban regime and deflected calls for greater accountability because of his electoral invincibility. Whereas this chapter mainly lays out the contextual dimensions of the problem, the next chapter discusses the contingent solutions activists derived when, in the mid-1980s, they realized that the utility of and timing for new activism were right.

## THE CONTEXT OF BLACK CLASS DIVISIONS

### Detroit's Contemporary Black Class Divisions

To understand how Coleman Young was able to influence the currents of black politics in Detroit, it is important to understand the context in which he operated. Despite the historic prosperity of Detroit's black working class, the city witnessed enough black class stratification to produce radically different life chances and standards of living for those who occupied the extreme ends. Economic and spatial concentration effects were partly to blame.[4] From the angle of housing wealth, we know that before the late 1940s, racial violence, residential segregation, and housing discrimination all colluded to bar a small black bourgeoisie from residing in comparable white neighborhoods. Black middle-class enclaves such as Eight Mile and Wyoming (or Northlawn) and West Tireman and Grand Boulevard emerged. After the housing reforms of the 1950s and an accelerating white exodus, lower-middle-class and working-class blacks migrated westward from historic eastside neighborhoods. "Old Guard" families then concentrated in black elite enclaves such as Conant Gardens and Boston-Edison to live out privileged existences.[5]

On the one hand, some members of the old black aristocracy did not migrate to the suburbs, and their numbers grew in the 1970s with the onset of a new "black capitalism." Pressures on white firms to hire minorities, contract with minority firms, or franchise minority businesses in the post-Civil Rights Movement era all created greater employment and entrepreneurial opportunities for those blacks who could take advantage of them. This pattern held true in Detroit. Of the nation's twelve largest black-owned firms in the late 1990s, nine of them resided in the Detroit area, including Mel Farr's $600 million auto dealership—one of the largest black firms in the nation. These new black capitalists of the 1970s and 1980s were joined by a lower segment of new black professionals, corporate managers, and public-sector administrators, who experienced the most rapid increases of all Detroit occupational categories. Affirmative-action hiring in municipal departments and city contracting with minority firms under the Young administration also contributed to the opportunities of this new middle class.[6]

On the other hand, the numbers of black Detroiters trapped in poverty also rapidly increased in the 1970s. Between 1970 and 1990, the number of black people in Detroit with incomes below the poverty line increased from 18 percent to 32 percent. Urban renewal, substandard housing, and government-sanctioned racial and economic segregation in public housing hemmed growing numbers of working poor and unemployed people into communities that more affluent families had abandoned. Paul Jargowsky says that Detroit was one of the five cities accounting for two-thirds of the concentrated neighborhood poverty in the United States between 1970 and 1980. Furthermore, Carter Wilson calculates that by 1980, more than 50 percent of all black Detroiters lived in concentrated poverty census tracts, and 75 percent of the black poor lived in such tracts. By 1990, there was greater income inequality between various neighborhoods in Detroit than was true in cities such as Chicago, Los Angeles, or New Orleans. As the job floor fell out from under the working class, the public-assistance rolls burgeoned. Whereas public assistance recipients constituted 5 percent of Detroit's population in 1973, that percentage had mushroomed to 20 percent by 1986! Various economic downturns crippled the automobile industry and the larger economy in the 1970s, which profoundly demoralized black skilled and unskilled labor.[7]

Figure 4 provides an overview of income-defined class boundaries by presenting the black–white income distributions for Detroit individuals in 1950 versus 1980. Its class categories of poor, working class, middle class, and upper

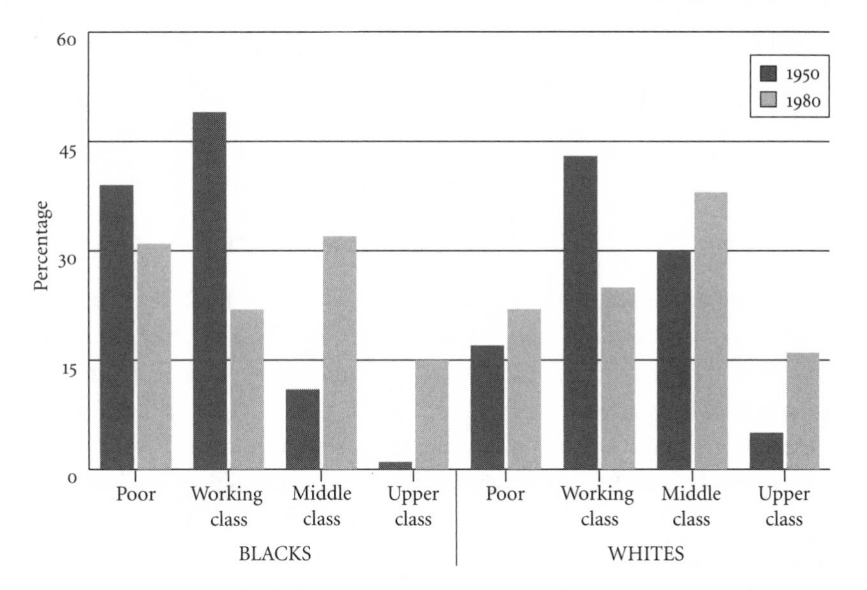


**Figure 4.** Income distributions for blacks and whites in Detroit. *Source*: Steven Ruggles et al., *Integrated Public Use Microdata Series*, version 3.0 (machine-readable database), Minnesota Population Center, 2004.

class are roughly based on Reynolds Farley's and his colleagues' categories.[8] In line with black class bifurcation in the post-Civil Rights Movement era, the black working class—the great middle—was literally squeezed upward and downward by 1980 so that the black class distribution went from a left-leaning mound in 1950 to twin peaks by 1980. This corroborates the findings of Jennifer Hochschild that between the 1940s and 1990s income inequalities between blacks widened more greatly than between whites. While these stark intra-racial class disparities are sobering, Melvin Oliver and Thomas Shapiro, as well as Dalton Conley, remind us that the wealth differences between blacks and whites is an equally, if not more, important determinant of black life chances, for Figure 4 reminds us that a greater percentage of Detroit whites were part of the middle classes and were not in poverty.[9]

Differences in educational attainment reinforce this disparity. Against a backdrop of intense debates about desegregation and how to improve Detroit's beleaguered public education system, there was progress in the number of African Americans who attained high-school diplomas and college degrees. About 70 percent of black men in their late twenties and more than 80 percent of white men in that age group had earned their high-school diplomas in 1990. Unfortunately the college attainment and enrollment gaps between blacks and whites in Detroit were among the largest in the nation.[10] Therefore, blacks' shared experiences of racial inequality can at times mediate class polarization and create moments when differing classes agree in principle with appeals for economic redistribution.

## Class and Black Attitudes toward Redistribution and Race

Briefly, understanding the complex relationships between differing class indicators and a person's ideology helps rule out simplistic assumptions such as the one that middle-class African Americans uniformly oppose redistributive programs such as public housing, thus they all supported the Young administration's subsequent demolition plans. Of course, income and educational attainment are correlated, but they tap diverse aspects of a person's socioeconomic background, especially since education often has a liberalizing effect. Also, women are very prominent as Detroit political leaders and participants, but gender differences are not apparent in every instance of Detroit black politics. When they are significant, I contemplate their meaning to understand black women's activism.[11]

Figure 5 presents the bivariate relationship between black family income and support for redistributive policies, including government guarantees of jobs and housing. Throughout this and the next chapter, I use the 1976 Detroit Area Study because it was conducted only two years into Young's first term and dealt with issues of housing—this book's key policy domain.[12] Not surprisingly, both figures show that those on the lower economic rungs are more likely than those on the higher rungs to support a federal government guarantee of jobs and housing. As many as 20 percentage points separate the lowest and highest quartiles in their support for these proposals, and a policy cleavage is apparent from the fact that there are smaller majorities who support guaranteed housing. Still, black Detroiters across the income distribution overwhelmingly supported these assertions, suggesting that redistribution was a relatively shared principle.

To further probe black class dynamics and black attitudes about economic redistribution as well as race relations, I performed multivariate analyses using the 1976 Detroit Area Study data and report these results in Table 13, appendix 2. This table includes the results when I regress a battery of independent variables, including my socioeconomic measures of family income and years of education, by support for a government guarantee of jobs, support for a government guarantee of housing, the belief blacks should have nothing to do with whites, and the belief that whites want to keep blacks down. I find that

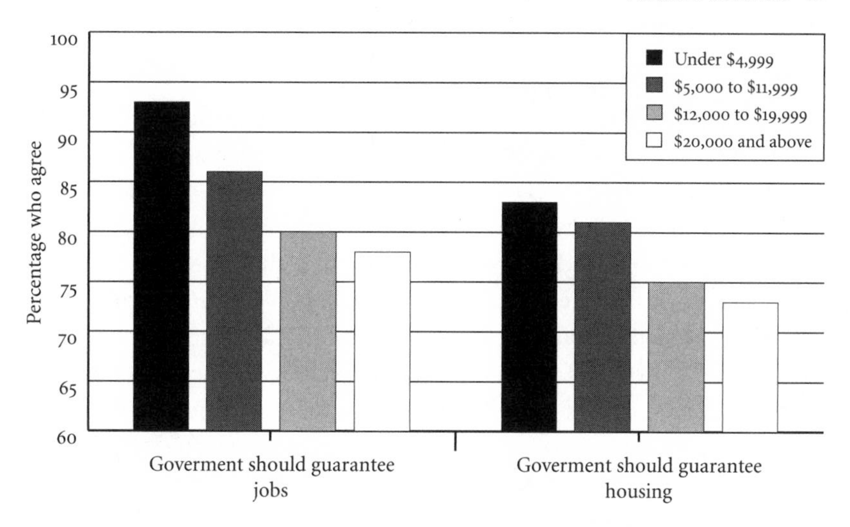


**Figure 5.** Black income quartiles and attitudes toward redistribution, 1976 Detroit Area Study. *Source*: 1976 Detroit Area Study (198 total respondents).

those black respondents who reported higher incomes were slightly less likely than their lower-income counterparts to support government job and housing guarantees, which reflects national trends.[13] Homeownership was the only other significant variable, but homeowners were five times more likely than renters to support guaranteed government jobs. During the late 1970s, Detroit's working-class homeowners suffered from housing speculation scandals and escalating rates of foreclosure due to massive job losses. So this response may be due to their feeling particularly vulnerable to the vagaries of the job market. Whereas higher-income blacks were less likely to support a government guarantee of housing, more highly educated blacks were seven times more likely to support this proposition. With renters witnessing a 23 percent loss in real income during the 1970s and all enduring a 44 percent increase in the vacancy rate, possibly a liberal cadre of educated people—for example, some teachers, social workers, college students, and legal-aid attorneys—departed with the mainstream middle class and believed public housing was one of the few viable solutions to Detroit's increasing housing crisis. In subsequent chapters, I examine the prospects and limits of a class-elastic black housing alliance.[14]

Only about 5 percent of all black respondents agreed with the statement that blacks should "have nothing to do with whites." Those blacks who were more affluent, male, older, and regular church attendees strongly opposed this statement. However, those who self-identified more as "black" than "American," resided in predominantly black neighborhoods, or owned their homes were most likely to concur. This result for all-black neighborhoods confirms the findings of Susan Welch and her colleagues that neighborhood context mattered in shaping black Detroit's racial attitudes.[15] Finally, one-third of black Detroiters were convinced that whites purposely wanted to suppress blacks. Only the black homeowner and black-identity coefficients are positive and statistically significant. Given the severity of Detroit's continued housing crisis, there is little wonder that black homeowners, who directly confronted the latent prejudices of white home sellers and realtors, harbored distinct suspicions of whites' racial motives. With the influence that Black Nationalist groups such as the Black Slate exerted within Detroit black politics and the persistent racial tensions between Detroit and its white suburbs, it is not surprising that those respondents who gravitated more toward blackness were suspicious of white America's racial intentions.[16]

In summary, the black class and ideological context that faced the newly elected Young administration was a mixture of subtle fissures and potential alliances. Regarding fissures, black class polarization bolstered inter- and intraclass schisms over redistributive policies, including public housing. Yet there was a significant black consensus that racism, if not all whites, was a persistent group threat. Into this swirling vortex stepped Coleman Young, a sharp-witted and highly adept spokesman of black political frustrations. In the process, he argued that his political agenda was in sync with Detroit black politics and grassroots interests. Adhering to the EBAM, the next sections lay out the barriers of electoral confines, black political constraints, and the black urban regime.

## RACE, YOUNG, AND THE CONFINED ELECTORAL ARENA

After his initial election, Coleman Young's public stature and political influence burgeoned and enabled him to build a dominant electoral coalition. This not only solidified strong black and adequate white support for his reelections but also rebuffed challengers. One segment of black Detroit was so fiercely proud of Young that it construed sharp criticism of his policies, including his housing and community-development policies, as conceivably racist attacks, even if they were expressed by black-led antipoverty and low-income-housing advocates. In practical terms, this meant that Young's incumbency made it difficult, though not impossible, for black grassroots activists to use the ballot box to hold him accountable. The irony is that Young first emerged as a progressive black candidate for mayor who knitted together a relatively bottom-up coalition.[17]

Background

Unlike the mild-mannered Richard Austin who was the first black to win the Democratic Party's mayoral nomination in 1969, Coleman Young was unabashedly outspoken in his 1973 candidacy. Grounded in the leftist tradition of labor organizing, and descended from the quick wits and folkways of Detroit's Black Bottom community, Young had great appeal during a historic moment when African American voters were eager for leaders able to translate growing black electoral strength into outcomes. Although his reputation as a Michigan state senator and leader in the state and national Democratic parties provided him with the political capital to make a viable bid, he came to this position through a very circuitous path.[18]

Never fully embraced by Detroit's old black bourgeoisie, Young was shaped in childhood by the working poverty of the eastside ghetto and stories of his so-called "uppity nigger" father fleeing the racial terrorism of Tuscaloosa, Alabama. Never one to surrender a battle, Young was once fired from a job at Ford's River Rogue plant because he struck a white co-worker who made a racist remark. The opportunity to serve his country during the Second World War did not assuage him, since his service was with the racially segregated Tuskegee Airmen. But he was undeterred in seeking to organize with liberal and radical whites, partly due to his political education in the barbershop of Hayward Maben, a black grassroots Marxist who invited radical white organizers to join community debates.[19] Though red-baited and purged from the UAW, which was dominated by Walter Reuther, and its Wayne County CIO affiliate in the 1940s, Young still gained a fundamental enthusiasm for leftist politics, as is evident from his executive directorship of the Michigan chapter of the leftist National Negro Congress and the National Negro Labor Congress. From the very beginning of his political career, Young was fiercely antiracist. He assumed the stature of a minor folk hero in the radio parlors of Black Bottom when, during a House Un-American Activities Committee hearing, he upbraided the committee's Dixiecrats and anticommunists for their racial paternalism.[20] Such experiences of government harassment and surveillance, when coupled with the later federal scrutiny of Young administration officials suspected of misconduct, fueled Young's unabated distrust of "the feds." A former aide once disclosed to me that Mayor Young constantly kept a television on in his office to create background noise in the event that the "damn feds . . . might be bugging me." Years later, the *Detroit News* corroborated this apprehension, for it discovered from FBI files that Young had been under surveillance.[21]

Unable to pursue his first love, political activism, from the mid- to late 1950s due to constant red-baiting, he pursued odd jobs until he was elected to the state Constitutional Convention, or "Con Con," in 1960. Young helped draft the first version of the Civil Rights Commission Act and in 1964 ran for and won a seat in the State Senate. He still had a strained relationship with the UAW but soon gained the favor of the Senate's Democratic leadership and was named party leader. In 1968, he attended the tumultuous Democratic National Convention in Chicago as the first black member of the National Committee and later was elected vice-chair. While in the legislature for ten years, he sponsored and lobbied for several progressive measures, including tenant-rights laws, the creation of public-housing tenant boards, and citizen district councils.[22] He emerged as a very attractive candidate for mayor not simply because of his no-nonsense public persona but also because of his legislative record and negotiating skills.

## Race and Detroit Mayoral Elections

Detroit's history of pernicious racial inequalities ensured that no factor mattered more in determining elections than race. But as a member of the first generation of major city black mayors, Young was initially successful because he brokered this divide. In 1973, Detroit's white police chief, John Nichols, also ran for mayor. Nichols was popular among registered white voters, but he simply did not have Young's public gravitas and political acumen. In addition, Nichols was the architect of an infamous, mostly white, crime squad called STRESS, or "Stop Robberies, Enjoy Safe Streets," which in three years had arrested four hundred suspects without warrants and killed twenty-two persons, most of whom were black. Quite naturally in this post-1967 rebellion period, police relations and crime emerged as the central campaign issue, with Nichols posing as the "law and order" candidate to excite white racial fears of black crime and Young as the proponent for a racially representative and responsive police force.[23]

Even when Nichols won the nonpartisan primary with 34 percent to Young's 21 percent of the vote, Young won the general election with 54 percent of the vote. Young's racial finesse inspired one observer to note that he could be "two totally different personalities adapting to the environment," thus "wrapping around his finger" members of the Chamber of Commerce or Detroit Economic Club, in one respect, and black Baptist congregants, in another. Over time he assembled an eclectic electoral coalition that consisted of key businesses, ecumenical alliances and mainstream black churches, the Black Slate of the Black Nationalist Shrine of the Black Madonna, and other black politicians and activists. Later, Young mended old wounds with the UAW and the TULC

(Trade Union Leadership Council). A formidable assortment of Detroit's economic elite eventually enlisted with his coalition and contributed to his campaign coffers, which by the mid-1980s had grown to $4 million.[24]

As further evidence of his racial brokerage, Young knew that his initial campaign was greatly helped by Richard Austin, then the secretary of state, and Kenneth Cockrel, a radical activist attorney, both of whom decided not to oppose him and thus split the black vote. By 1981, Young was so sure of his electoral popularity that, except for a few rhetorical barbs, he largely ignored his unknown challenger, Perry Koslowski, the president of a white-collar union, and concentrated on ballot initiatives and on unseating a political nemesis, the city clerk James Bradley. Because Young was both an incendiary commentator on racial politics and a target of prejudice from whites, his election bids invariably experienced racially split votes. For instance, in 1973 predominantly white districts gave Nichols 96 percent of their vote, on average. When the 1981 race was concluded, there was roughly a 40 percent margin of voters, some black but predominantly white, whom observers considered the "ABC," or "Anybody but Coleman," contingency.[25]

Overall turnout declined beginning in 1965, but Young was the chief beneficiary of blacks' constituting larger percentages of the voting age population—70 percent by the mid-1980s. Increasing numbers of black voters led to the election of more black officeholders; this in turn bolstered black political agency and reanimated the cycle. Cities such as Cleveland and Atlanta experienced increases in the percentage that blacks constituted of the total electorate, which emboldened black voters and encouraged black electoral empowerment. Yet along with black voter ascendancy, such numbers reinforced the entrenchment of astute black incumbents.[26]

## Young's Incumbency and the "Race Card"

Cognizant of how race played a central role in Detroit elections, Young chose to play the so-called race card and portray his African American electoral challengers as beholden to the interests of whites, as well as to the suburbs. To borrow a phrase from Cathy Cohen, he rendered them outside the "boundaries of blackness" and black group interests. While he most certainly did not manufacture the racial divide in Detroit and sought to be a tribune of black empowerment, there was still an unfortunate myopia to how he constructed Detroit black politics. Young touted symbolic racial representation as the key criterion for assessing political accountability to black Detroiters.[27] His last primary bid of 1989 best illustrates this point.

Whereas Young drew only 21 percent of the white vote but 60 percent of the black vote, his opponent Tom Barrow, who had a more dispassionate persona, drew 70 percent of the white vote and only 21 percent of the black vote. Barrow was a black businessman with moderate, neighborhood-centered views and was highly critical of Young's housing and economic-development policies. From Young's vantage point, Barrow's views and support basis justified dubbing him "the Great White Hope," just as Young had labeled his first black opponent, Council Member Ernest Brown, in 1977. In addition, the incumbent mayor derided African American reporters who were critical of his record: "You have black reporters who are turncoats who just throw themselves out to be used. In the case of the women, they are Aunt Jemimas. They ought to be exposed."[28]

The vigorous support of influential black ministers and leaders of other black groups abetted this narrow framing of race and Young's reelection bid. Two other prominent black challengers joined Barrow to vigorously oppose Young for the mayor's office in 1989: Council President Erma Henderson and Congressman John Conyers. Like Barrow, both of these candidates were critical of the political trajectory Young's administration had taken.[29] Countering with a zealous call for black voters to rally behind Young, Reverend Charles Adams of the renowned Hartford Memorial Baptist Church admonished Young's three black challengers:

> It is political suicide for Black leaders to mount a serious campaign against the mayoralty of Coleman A. Young. . . . For years, the White reactionary forces in the city and daily media have attacked and disparaged everything that Coleman Young has accomplished. . . . If we lose what now remains of [our] imperfect unity, we will have picked up our marbles and gone our splintered ways to march clean off the political map. Blacks will never govern this city again. . . . [W]e can only give mouth and muscle to the criticisms of Whites against Mayor Young at our own peril.[30]

Horace Sheffield Jr. of the Association of Black Organizations in Detroit was more reluctant than Adams to imply that any black with the temerity to oppose Young was a traitorous "Uncle Tom or an Aunt Jane," but he still asserted the reason for black voters' gratitude to Young should have been crystal clear: "Detroit was supposed to die. But it didn't and it's due singularly to Coleman Young." Sheffield echoed Adams in saying that a "powerful array of conservative and racist forces are out to unseat Mayor Young because of his notable success in moving [forward] the clock of social progress for Blacks. And we need to stop them in their bigoted tracks right now." Arthur Jefferson, a past president of the NAACP, concurred with Sheffield when he talked about a confidence he had shared with Young: "You are the victim today of a lot of white bitterness and resentment and it's primarily because you would not let the city commit suicide."[31] It was this equating of a defense of Young with the fight against racism that became the principal rationale for black support.

I examine the basis of Young's African American support from an attitudinal standpoint to assess how racial and economic appeals worked during the mayoral election year of 1989. Table 3 reports results from the 1989 Detroit Area Study, where I regressed several variables against black responses to a feeling thermometer for Coleman Young.[32] The median score for Young among black respondents was 70, which is a fairly warm "temperature" or high score. Roughly 30 percent, or almost a third, of black respondents gave Young a perfect 100, whereas only about 6 percent gave him a 0.

Of principal concern in this analysis is the interplay between racial and economic attitudes and a respondent's feelings toward Young. I expect that, as a respondent is more concerned about racism, she will be warmer toward Young, and as she is more sensitive to differences in class, she will be colder toward Young. My three "race variables" include whether a respondent believed that racial discrimination against blacks is still widespread; whites want to keep blacks down; and African Americans ought to rely on self-help as opposed to government aid to solve their problems. The last variable might measure a Black Nationalist principle of self-determination as much as it measures policy conservatism. As expected, all three of the racial variables are significant and positive. In fact, as the Young feeling thermometer increases by 1 unit, there is nearly a 17 percent increase in those who say that blacks suffer from a lot of discrimination. Thus, Young and his campaign seemingly were able to tap into black perceptions of racism and black self-empowerment to garner support for his leadership.[33]

My class variables include family income, education, working-class social identity, and poor social identity. From one standpoint, one can imagine how those with higher incomes and education might resent the working-class background, sensibilities, and abrasive political style Young brought to the mayor's office, especially if he challenged their political influence. One member of the "Old Guard" confided her view that Young was "loud and difficult from the moment he got elected in 1973. . . . He despised successful blacks just as much as he disliked the whites who had left for the suburbs."[34] Inversely, it is possible that educated dissenters to Young were composed of organic intellectuals—for example, scholars, students, community activists, and social-service providers—who believed that he had somewhat betrayed his working-class roots.

**Table 3.** Black respondents and the Coleman Young Feeling Thermometer, 1989 Detroit Area Study

| | |
|---|---|
| *Control variables* | |
| Age | .039 |
| | (.112) |
| Female | .024 |
| | (.039) |
| Length of residence | −.030 |
| | (.057) |
| Church attendance | .057 |
| | (.061) |
| Union membership | −.000 |
| | (.041) |
| *Race variables* | |
| A lot of discrimination against blacks | .168[a] |
| | (.079) |
| Whites want to keep blacks down | .126[a] |
| | (.039) |
| Black self-help | .124[a] |
| | (.048) |
| *Class variables* | |
| Family income | .094 |
| | (.076) |
| Education | −1.957[a] |
| | (.878) |
| Identifies with working class | −.094[a] |
| | (.017) |
| Identifies with poor | −.058 |
| | (.053) |
| Constant | .652[b] |
| | (.151) |
| Adjusted $R^2$ | .075 |
| Standard error or estimate | .262 |
| Total cases | 253 |

*Note:* Entries are not standardized. Ordinary Least Squares regression estimates with standard errors are in parentheses.

[a] Indicates $p < .05$.

[b] Indicates $p < .01$.

The activist biographies of people such as Kenneth Cockrel, James and Grace Boggs, or Marian Kramer, as well as the history of groups such as the Detroit Alliance for a Rational Economy or U-SNAP-BAC, speak to the presence of a self-taught or formally schooled liberal opposition willing to challenge the Young administration's approach to the needs of the working class and poor.[35] Certainly not all black educated people who critiqued Young's heavy-handed economic-development policies or neglect of public housing were committing "class suicide," but some were inspired by visions of community revitalization aimed at the working class and poor.

Interestingly, all of the class variables except income are negatively associated with the Young feeling thermometer, though income and identification with the poor are not significant. In contrast to family income, those with higher educations are colder toward Young, as are those who identify as working class. It appears that family income and education are tapping differing elements of socioeconomic status. Whereas Young's gritty political style was an outgrowth of his working-class roots, ironically those who identified as working class had less favorable feelings toward his leadership. In the context of the 1989 election year, both racial and class attitudes mattered in explaining black sentiments toward this black mayor.

## THE YOUNG REGIME AND THE CONSTRUCTION OF BLACK POLITICS

To be sure, the advantages Young enjoyed in the electoral arena reinforced his influence in the public-policy arena and thus his influence over Detroit black politics. Had Young commanded hegemonic control over black politics, however, there would be no significant grassroots opposition for me to discuss. The reality is that ordinary black Detroiters were sophisticated and embraced a seemingly contradictory but actually pragmatic ethic: support the mayor for reelection but, when necessary, disagree with his policy stances. So how much power did Young command in the policy arena?

### Race and the Young Machine

Even Young's leftist critics commonly expressed admiration for the trailblazing reforms of this first term but regretted how his administration became politically calcified. Maryann Mahaffey, Council president and a social democrat, once said, "He is what we [Detroit] needed and he *did* a good job his first term, and not too bad the second. Then it began to deteriorate with the power move. . . . [His administration became] top down instead of bottom up."[36] I begin my discussion of how Young shaped black politics by addressing the question of whether or not he had a "top-down" political machine, for the presence of a machine, through the suppression of opposition, would facilitate the establishment of a "top-down" development regime. In fact, Young freely conceded that he was an admirer of the "machine" system of governance:

> Despite the charges of bossism in Detroit—the Big Daddy image I've been carrying around in recent years—we do not and cannot have a spoils system in this city, and consequently cannot put together a political machine on any scale comparable to the old one in Chicago. I don't control tens of thousands of jobs as Daley did, and don't have the power to reward and punish as he did. I wish I did. Although it may not have been the purest form of local government, I'm not reluctant to say that I envied Daley's machine. He had the ability to do whatever he thought was necessary for his city.[37]

Wilbur Rich agreed that it was impossible for Young to have a political machine due to the diffuse nature of Detroit's political system.

Nonetheless, Young strongly influenced the dominant contours of public affairs in Detroit. Racial loyalty ensured that Detroit's first black mayor enjoyed support among important sectors of the African American community—for example, senior citizens, churchgoers, civil-rights leaders, and Black Nationalist spokespeople. After all, it was Young who reformed and completely integrated the police force, achieved affirmative action goals, aggressively defended Detroit and black political control against a hostile (white) media and the suburbs, and averted financial collapse of the city in the early 1980s.[38]

Certainly, Young was unable to build a political machine in a classic sense—a party-based, patronage-controlling hierarchy maintained by self-perpetuating elites. From the institutional side, Detroit's nonpartisan electoral system and its reform civil-service bureaucracy inhibited the rise of a classic machine organization. Detroit politics were, and remain, highly personalized and constituent-based. From the resource side, Young and his administration did not have at their disposal an appointment system on the same grand scale as did Mayor Richard J. Daley of Chicago. In fact, the devastating 1974–75 recession compelled Young to implement austerity measures by laying off 4,000 city employees for fear of a projected revenue shortfall between $25 million and $35 million. The only saving grace was a $46 million Comprehensive Employment and Training Act allocation from the Carter administration.[39] After 1978, budgeted positions in the city government were stringently cut and did not rebound until 1985. With the end of federal revenue sharing in 1987, the city lost nearly $40 million, and only state revenue sharing was an offset. John

Engler, a very conservative Republican, won the governorship of Michigan and proposed additional austerity measures. All of this occurred in the midst of huge net losses in property and income tax revenues due to a decrease of 1,500 manufacturing firms by the late 1970s and of some 200,000 manufacturing and retail jobs by the early 1980s.[40]

There are, however, two caveats to the contention that Young could not build at least his version of a black political machine. First, Detroit still had a strong-mayor form of government that permitted the mayor to have a predominant say in the budget process until 1988; he also could, and did, make myriad political appointments to departments, commissions, and other public and quasi-public agencies. The city government was the third largest employer in Detroit after Chrysler and General Motors (GM) in the early 1980s, and despite huge personnel cuts, 14 percent of all Detroiters were still city employees. This mattered to African Americans, for by the end of Young's term and into the Archer administration, roughly 70 percent of all city employees were African American. The administration was also responsible for administering and dispersing millions of dollars in public contracts and grants in pursuit of affirmative-action goals. In Young's first term alone, city contracts with minority firms rose from a mere 3 percent to 20 percent.[41]

In addition, it is implausible to suggest that Mayor Young, who always had the grit and determination to aggressively lobby for his proposals, did not couple this determination with the influence he commanded as a respected black mayor. In a racially polarized context such as Detroit, vocal black opposition to such a strong symbol of black pride is difficult. Council Member Mel Ravitz, a white liberal, explained, "Black members of the council and the black leadership of other groups in the city did not in any way want to tarnish the reputation of the first black mayor of the city of Detroit of whom they were justly proud. . . . So, members of the City Council, for the most part, who were black, are not going to be opposing Coleman. And as Coleman's legend grew and his political power grew, you would challenge him if you were black at your peril." White council members had to be equally cautious about offending a black mayor in a predominantly black city.[42]

During my interviews, there were other instances when Detroiters confirmed that blacks' ideological fears of "airing dirty laundry" added psychic costs to mobilizing against the mayor. One black grassroots activist said that he viewed Young's initial election as an "incredible" expression of black solidarity. But then, a principle of racial loyalty meant, "'We can't do anything to criticize or embarrass black people that are in office.' . . . A lot of community activism . . . particularly through the 1970s and early 1980s just became neutralized as a result. People were afraid to attack Coleman whether he was right or wrong out of respect for this 'icon' that was the mayor. It was probably at least the mid-1980s before elements of the community really became visible in criticizing and attacking Coleman Young." Osvaldo Rivera, director of Latino Family Services, also saw these politics as creating a dilemma at the time: "I think [Mayor] Coleman Young has encircled himself with a machine that's very effective, but it's stifling grassroots empowerment. . . . We're in a mixed bag. How do you criticize an administration that *needs* to be criticized, but not go overboard and blame it for things that are not of its doing? That's the dilemma that a lot of progressives are in."[43] To the degree that intermediary black leaders and institutions—ministers, labor unions, civil-rights and community leaders—supported the Young administration without objecting to its development and housing policies that dislocated the poor was the degree they lent political legitimacy to his so-called black regime.

## Race and Young's "Urban" Regime?

As noted earlier, I use the term "regime" in a global sense to mean a prevailing local order that differs from an "urban regime" or a dominant, informal, cooperative, and effective urban-development coalition. Marion Orr and Gerry Stoker have concluded that Young was ultimately unsuccessful in formulating an urban regime that meets the standard definition. When the city most needed new infusions of capital to brave a spiraling economic decline, Young only got the grudging cooperation of extant business and corporate elites. Toward the end of his tenure, he did not even bother to co-sign the "strategic plans" formulated by various civic-corporate study groups.[44] Nevertheless, Young was driven by a desire to make meaningful public and private linkages to pursue an almost singular economic mantra. "Regardless of the numbers [of jobs produced]," he once said of the controversial GM Poletown Plant, "the important thing was to keep making cars in Detroit—to preserve the Motor City's 'chief reason for existence.'"[45] Although his very laudable goal was to combat joblessness, he was determined to pursue the vision of the industrial Detroit he knew and loved despite its arguable incongruence with current market realities. It is very true that his regime had little capacity, but what also mattered—what was political—is that he expended great energy to create a urban regime in three ways.

First of all, Young made direct alliances and contacts with Detroit's insular circles of corporate and financial power. Despite his activist labor background, Young was directly involved with the Detroit Renaissance corporation during his first year in office. Led by Henry Ford II and the Detroit financier Max Fisher, Detroit Renaissance was a highly connected organization of fifty-one corporate leaders, including 250 interlocking directorates. Young helped them save the $300 million Renaissance Center—an enormous, gleaming office tower and hotel-retail complex across from City Hall. Through a city tax abatement of $700,000 a year, he later directly intervened on behalf of Al Taubman, famed developer of suburban shopping malls, to develop the Riverfront West luxury apartments. The City Council strenuously objected, for there were no assurances that the project would include subsidized housing, but to no avail. Mayor Young told me during an interview, "One thing we proved, I think, during my administration is contrary to the rule and judgment of the establishment, there is a market for middle-class housing in Detroit. Victoria Park [a middle-class development] and all that development along the Riverfront proved that. . . . These apartments [sitting in Riverfront Towers] proved that."[46]

A second way in which Mayor Young pursued an urban regime in the late 1970s was by creating several public and quasi-public corporations to "coordinate public and private development efforts through a membership roster heavily weighted toward Detroit's business and civic elite."[47] They included the Economic Growth Corporation, the Economic Development Corporation, and the Downtown Development Authority, which were each modeled on the same interlocking directorate system of Detroit Renaissance and headed and populated by many of the same personalities. These entities employed a broad set of development tools to stimulate investment, revenue, and growth. Housing and neighborhood projects were sandwiched in between and determined by larger development objectives.[48]

A third and final way the mayor attempted to build an urban regime was by organizing his staff into "loose action clusters." The aim was to allow key aides to respond quickly to and facilitate development opportunities presented by enterprising developers. Among the mayor's close circle in the early 1980s were Ronald Hewitt of the Planning Department and Emmet Moten of the Community and Economic Development Department, as well as white corporate liaisons such as Bob McCabe of the Renaissance Center and Robert Spencer of the Economic Growth Corporation. Executive aides were often shuttled in between clusters so that they were transferred to work with C&EDD, one of the economic-development corporations, a private firm, or a developer until called back to work in the Mayor's Office. In describing how economic decisions were made in the Mayor's Office at the time, Wilbur Rich says that the mayor first had to be convinced of a project's merit before it could be placed on the expedited decision track. However, despite the good intentions of this approach, it held the city hostage to the vagaries of capital and abrogated the city's leverage to argue for favorable development and tax-revenue agreements.[49]

For all of these reasons, Young likely had what Susan Fainstein calls a "conserving regime" whose objectives were to stop the city's economic hemorrhaging. Young's strategy was to return Detroit to its economic and industrial prominence based on manufacturing. I agree that the Detroit urban regime unraveled and eventually was not a consensual process with the capacity to deliver. In his last few years in office, Young was prevented by a persistent respiratory ailment from making numerous public appearances.[50] Still, he expended great energy to construct a variant of the standard urban regime, and here again, politics matters. To the degree his quasi-political machine bolstered his weak urban regime, it is likely that his *machine regime* demarcated battle lines between an elite-led vision of the city's economic renewal and the vision of groups who claimed to be more accountable to the grassroots. Before concluding, I briefly discuss one episode in which the Young administration used race, class, and regime to overpower grassroots activists. Shortly afterward many activists felt it was time they push back.

## A Final Straw: The Poletown Plant Controversy

As one of the largest cases of urban land condemnation, the Central Industrial Park, or GM's Poletown Plant project, is an exemplar of just how formidable the odds were that grassroots advocates faced in the late 1970s and early 1980s as they struggled to shift the city's housing and development priorities. Late in 1979, GM informed Detroit that it had to clear and deliver a roughly 600 square acre rectangular parcel with access to the major highways if the city wanted to be considered for a nationwide $40 billion plant-modernization program. Located in a western section of the historically Polish township Hamtramck, the Dodge Main plant and two-thirds of a bordering community became immediate prospects for this parcel.[51] Although it was called "Poletown," the community was ethnically diverse, and 40 percent of its residents were black. To meet GM's requirements for a new Cadillac plant, the city relocated 3,400 residents and razed 1,300 homes, 143 businesses, 2 schools, a hospital, and 16 churches, including a Catholic parish and several black storefront churches. GM bought the huge plot at a significant discount of $8 million, while projected costs to the government ran to $200 million. In return, the company promised to deliver 6,000 direct jobs, with a multiplier effect of 20,000 ancillary jobs. It later revised this figure downward to 3,000 direct jobs and never promised to employ Detroiters.[52] To finance this extraordinary plan, the city borrowed

$100 million from the U.S. Department of Housing and Urban Development's Section 108 program, spent $65 million of Community Development Block Grant (CDBG) funds, and granted GM a tax rebate that cost the city $60 million over twelve years. To divert that many dollars into a single project, the Young administration rescinded CDBG funding to several community groups and instead used the $3 million to pay for court and relocation costs, which negatively affected the city's fiscal state for years.[53]

What is most relevant about the Poletown case for my purposes is that it was an example of how the Young administration demobilized community opposition by using various levers of racial and economic politics. When the residents of Poletown organized the Poletown Neighborhood Council (PNC), the administration quickly appointed a Poletown Citizen District Council, which not only affirmed the administration's decisions but also interrupted the meetings and counter-mobilized against the PNC. As the ethnically diverse but still largely Polish PNC tried to rally community support, the administration recalled the lessons of urban renewal and offered renters—the predominant number of whom were black—$4,000 in relocation fees as well as $15,000 to homeowners above and beyond the sale price of their homes. Surveys indicated that two-thirds of all residents still preferred to stay. When the consumer advocate Ralph Nader joined the fight and the controversy began to attract national media coverage, Mayor Young labeled Nader and these protesters outside agitators who were racist, for, he said, no such concern had been shown toward his native Black Bottom community when it was razed forty years earlier.[54]

While there were a few black voices of opposition, some of those who spoke out said their family members were fearful for their lives. Many other African Americans supported the mayor's actions, given the city of Hamtramck's disregard for black neighborhoods at the height of the urban-renewal program. Several black storefront congregations received relocation compensation of about $50,000, which was insufficient for them to find comparable spaces. Activist organizations such as the Association of Community Organizations for Reform Now (ACORN) and the Concerned Citizens of Cass Corridor were threatened not to align with PNC if they wanted to apply for future city funding. The Catholic archdiocese gave its blessing for parish demolition. Likewise, the UAW fell into line because it was warned its opposition would mean the loss of vital jobs. Although the militant Council Member Kenneth Cockrel loudly protested, the City Council, which lacked full information, felt pressured to vote affirmatively because GM would not wait for lengthy public deliberations.[55] On several fronts, the Young regime claimed victory.

## CONCLUSION

In this chapter, I have detailed how black class and racial attitudes toward race and redistribution set the stage for Coleman Young's mayoralty. Such a narrative is very important, for it demonstrates how the race, class, and regime variables nested within the context dimension and, secondarily, the electoral and regime variables nested within the utility dimension are all part of an opportunity structure for effective black grassroots activism. Subtly competing black class sentiments about redistributive policies meant that issues of racism, not redistribution, provided broader points of consensus. Thus, race became the most exploitable political commodity available to Young as he solidified his incumbency, his political machine, and his efforts to create an urban regime. At the end of the 1970s, many black Detroiters broadly expressed sympathy toward the less fortunate. I strongly believe that the mayor also sympathized with lower-income Detroiters. But his political groundings in insurgent labor activism and liberal pragmatism gave his top-down, hard-knuckled style of politics sufficient capital to nullify grassroots critics who claimed that his economic development and housing polices displaced lower-income communities. Black ministers and civic leaders, who were concerned with symbolic racial representation and the maintenance of a black elected leadership, also vigorously defended the mayor. So there were considerable barriers to mobilizing black grassroots dissent against the mayor's machine regime. However, Young's political power was not a fait accompli. The next several chapters advance my argument that at key moments, black and other community activists concluded that enough was enough and that it was time to hold him and other public officials accountable.

# 4

## Picking Up Spears

*The Timing and Utility of Renewed Activism*

**We refused to lay down our spears. And sometimes the numbers have been greater and sometimes the numbers have been less.**
**—Marian Kramer, President, National Welfare Rights Union, 1994**

### MAKING A DIFFERENCE

Angered by conditions in several Detroit public-housing developments—Parkside, Jeffries, and Charles Terrace Homes—leaders with the short-lived Public Housing Tenant Unions helped initiate a rent strike in 1975 and asked the City Council as well as the courts for redress. Charlene Wray of the Jeffries Tenants Union articulated the intersection of racial and class inequalities: "I can't help but think that the city would respond much quicker if the people involved—the public housing tenants—weren't black and poor."[1] While tenants pressured the Detroit Housing Department (DHD) to relent on rent increases insisted on by the U.S. Department of Housing and Urban Affairs (HUD), the DHD still declared the strike illegal. Because most rents were not held in escrow as required by law, DHD evicted all tenants unable or unwilling to pay past due rents.[2] Taken in isolation, skeptics might consider such defiance as making little difference.

From a more panoramic vantage point, however, this public-housing strike was not a flash in the pan. It was part of a broader antipoverty network that included the causes of tenant rights, welfare rights, anti-hunger advocacy, homeless advocacy, community organizing, and neighborhood development. The refrain of this book is that black grassroots activism is strong enough to prompt political accountability to the poor if utility, timing, and context are on its side. But strong alliances, useful political advantages, and flexible tactics are necessary to create such opportunities. In this chapter, I argue that a new activist cycle had emerged by the mid-1980s, for Detroit's housing crisis deepened and grassroots groups perceived small openings to challenge the powerful Young administration's housing agenda. A few of Adolph Reed's and Robert Smith's propositions about the 1970s witnessing the demobilization of black grassroots activism are tested. To expand on this chapter and to serve as a prologue for my linchpin chapters 5 and 6, I discuss why the timing and utility of this renewed activism mattered as Detroit activists decided it was necessary to "pick up spears." I demonstrate that they were not alone in their opposition to city policies; nor were they foolhardy to believe that their actions alone would draw significant public attention.

## THE STRUCTURE OF DETROIT'S CONTINUED HOUSING POVERTY

### Housing Poverty and Economic Differences among Blacks

It is first important to understand what issues motivated renewed activism. The provision of high-quality and affordable housing to moderate- and low-income families was no less of a daunting task in the late 1970s than it had been decades earlier. Mayor Young once admitted, "I was taking the administration of Detroit because the white people didn't want the damn thing anymore." Like other black mayors of this period, he was inheriting a so-called Hollow Prize, or a city steadily suffering abandonment by fleeing white taxpayers and employers.[3] Massive job layoffs, white flight, high unemployment, and burgeoning poverty all created a vicious cycle of housing poverty that fueled economic decline. Both the status of the housing consumer and overall quality of the housing in Detroit greatly deteriorated between 1970 and 1977. The real income for all renters and owners declined, with renters experiencing a percentage loss almost six times the loss suffered by owners. Meanwhile, population outmigration resulted in a 106 percent increase in the number of days rental units were vacant and an 84 percent increase in the number of days homes were for sale. In turn, the total number of vacant homes increased by 66 percent, and the total number of vacant rental units increased by 47 percent. During this period, the abandonment of properties accelerated at such a brisk pace that the city, on average, demolished 6,000 dwellings per year. Astoundingly, Detroit had enough tax-reverted properties in its possession to house a town of 50,000 people![4]

Much of this abandonment was a result of a massive scandal involving homes subsidized by the Federal Housing Administration in the early 1970s, in which unscrupulous speculators profited from HUD homes through insurance fraud, arson, or the bribing of HUD inspectors to allow the sale of these homes to low-income tenants. As early as 1973, the Housing Task Force of the Detroit Commission on Community Relations (CCR) asserted, "[A] state of emergency exists. It must be declared. Some blocks have lost half their homes."[5] The controversy resulted in the indictment of 200 persons and cost taxpayers an estimated $250 million. By 1975, Detroit had nearly 17,000 HUD properties, and about half were lost to fire or to abandonment and eventual demolition. When added to Detroit's already flagging economy, this scandal was tragic because it inflicted enduring harm on the housing quality of Detroit's older neighborhoods.[6]

Between 1970 and 1990, twin racial and class processes were at work. First, black homeowners and renters experienced greater poverty than their white counterparts. For example, black renters went from a poverty rate of 40 percent to 52 percent, versus 32 percent to 38 percent among white renters. Second, the gap between the percentages of black homeowners to renters increased from 24 percent to 32 percent, whereas it increased only from 16 percent to 25 percent among whites. Also, black homeowners experienced a marginal decline (4 percent) in their median family incomes relative to the drastic losses of black renters (23 percent.) Overall, the need for affordable low-income housing increasingly outstripped the availability of units within the low-income price range. In 1985, Mayor Young touted his accomplishment of retaining 3,000 jobs in Detroit by way of the General Motors Poletown project, which razed about 1,000 homes. But there were almost twice as many families in need of low-cost housing as there were available units in the low-income price range.[7]

Table 4 shows that in 1985, the majority of construction in the Detroit area was for families making moderate and low incomes, likely due to the HUD subsidies of the early 1980s that survived budget cuts by the Reagan administration. Four years later, the reverse was true. No housing starts were built for low-income and working-class families between 1986 and 1989, and increased construction solely benefited upper-income families. Despite depressed housing conditions and sentiments among blacks that the quality of their neighborhoods and the housing stock was degenerating between 1985 and 1989, housing surveys reveal that a majority of black households in the metropolitan area also believed that city (or county) services had improved. Area homeowners were less likely to hold this view than renters, but African Americans who lived within Detroit proper felt there were greater improvements there than in the suburban ring, possibly reflecting pride in African American political control.[8]

Increasing housing disparities among black Detroiters manifested them-

**Table 4.** New housing starts in Detroit, by income, 1981–1989

| | New construction (in the previous four years) | | | |
|---|---|---|---|---|
| Family income | 1981–85 | 1986–89 | Total | % of Total |
| Below $10,000 | 2,600 | — | 2,600 | 36 |
| $10,000–$19,999 | 2,100 | — | 2,100 | 29 |
| $20,000–$29,999 | 100 | — | 100 | 1 |
| $30,000–$39,999 | 500 | 900 | 1,400 | 19 |
| $40,000 and above | 200 | 900 | 1,100 | 15 |
| *Total* | | | *7,300* | *100* |

*Source*: U.S. Bureau of the Census, *American Housing Survey*, 1989, 1991.

selves in interesting ideological differences. Table 14 in appendix 2, presents regression analyses of questions from the 1976 Detroit Area Study in which black respondents were asked whether it was important for them to have neighbors of their race; then they were asked whether it was important to have neighbors with the same income. Only 18 percent of respondents endorsed same-race neighbors, and this is consistent with the literature on blacks' preferences for racially integrated neighborhoods.[9] More highly educated African Americans preferred racially integrated neighborhoods, as did longtime Detroit residents. Those who identified more with blackness significantly endorsed having black neighbors. This is further proof of the point made by Susan Welch and colleagues that neighborhood context shapes racial attitudes and, in this case, inspires racial solidarity or Black Nationalist sentiments.[10] However, 53 percent of respondents believed that their neighborhoods should be economically homogenous. Blacks with higher incomes, as well as longtime residents, opposed neighborhoods with integrated classes, while highly educated blacks disagreed. This supports my previous assertion that class is a complex phenomenon and that, at times, education and income capture opposite impulses. These findings suggest why differing sectors of the black middle class supported low-income housing advocates as they opposed the demolition of public housing and neighborhood gentrification.[11]

### The Context of Race, Invisibility, and Homelessness

Although the situation of all black housing clients with low incomes clearly worsened and precipitated class divisions, the plight of those with little or no income was particularly perilous. Since the squatting practices of the Great Depression, homelessness remained an obvious sign of housing poverty in twentieth-century America and in Detroit. But by the mid-1980s, the issue of homelessness took on a new visibility due to media coverage and public-policy debates. Even before President Ronald Reagan's infamous remark that many people who were homeless actually "preferred" this lifestyle, homelessness was becoming a hotly contested issue.[12] This contentiousness stemmed partly from the politics of defining and counting the homeless. There were debates as to who constituted the "visible" homeless versus those who were ill-housed or housed in nonpermanent situations—that is, doubling up with families or living in transitional homes or halfway houses. National numbers ranged widely, from HUD's estimate of 250,000 to the numbers cited by advocates such as Mitch Snyder, who said there were 2 million to 3 million homeless people in the early 1980s. In Detroit, U.S. census takers discovered only 1,300 homeless persons in 1990; the Young administration asserted there were 12,000; and advocates countered with 60,000.[13]

Now as then, homeless citizens were an extremely diverse population, but they were becoming predominantly younger; more were female, had families, and were of color, especially black and Latino. About 85 percent of all homeless Detroiters were black in 1996, compared with national figures of 40 percent. While the gender and age dynamics of this changing population were open to debate, the shelter providers and care workers I interviewed said that more and more youth and women with children were using their facilities by the early 1990s. They reported that more than a fourth of all homeless people were women with children.[14] Beyond the politics of identification, numbers, and demographics was the question of causes. The theories most often proffered were the deinstitutionalization movement of many states in the late 1960s and 1970s; the destruction of skid-row and single-room-occupancy hotels; the destruction of the social-welfare safety net under Reagan; the outbreak of the crack cocaine epidemic; fluctuations in the housing market; social and economic shocks to black extended-family networks; and joblessness.[15]

To be sure, part of the larger problem is that the causes of homelessness are as diverse as the people who make up the homeless population. Specific to Detroit, and Michigan, were shocks that precipitated greater homelessness. When Republican Governor John Engler cut 90,000 persons off General Assistance in 1991, advocates estimated that the ranks of 30,000 homeless Detroiters could swell by 15 percent. Previous layoffs in the automobile industry, combined with the disappearance of affordable and decent housing, created another set of shocks that increased the number of people at soup kitchens, as well as in day and nighttime shelters.[16] Formerly homeless black Detroiters gave testimony as to how they shared in the "American dream" but found themselves laid off, behind on their bills, and thus slowly losing their grasp on economic stability once savings and alternative job options disappeared. The homeless organizer Wayne Pippin explained that, after working at a good job at a Ford plant for two years, "slowly things started happening—layoffs. After layoffs, the notice of the plant closing and moving out. . . . After that I was so distraught, I dibbled and dabbled in the drug scene for a while." Eventually, he said, "I found myself sleeping in abandoned buildings, and in cars, or anywhere I could. Until one day they told me about the shelter—COTS [Coalition on Temporary Shelter]."[17]

Pippin's story, as its reflects others, conveys how the highly disruptive processes of deindustrialization and economic disinvestment—and, likely, globalization—rendered African Americans and other stable, working-class citizens out of bounds, unstable, and unwanted trespassers. When public- and private-sector actions resulted in a sparse number of available shelter beds, an increasing lack of affordable housing, and an escalating number of abandoned homes and vacant lots, many homeless citizens in Detroit were reduced to a state of permanent trespass. As Talmadge Wright puts it, they were permanently "out of place," and in some cases, like that of Pippin, this slowly politicized them.[18]

## THE YOUNG REGIME AND PUBLIC HOUSING RETRENCHMENT

No public-policy failure angered grassroots activists more or contributed more to Detroit's affordable-housing crisis than the Young regime's neglect of public housing. In 1974, the new city charter gave Mayor Young new appointment powers and budget authority; it also radically reorganized the departments of housing, city planning, and development. The Detroit Housing Commission (DHC) was renamed the Detroit Housing Department (DHD) and was stripped of its responsibility for urban renewal and community development.[19] Five of the DHD's nine-member Board of Commissioners were appointed by the mayor, and two were appointed, respectively, by the Board of Tenant Affairs and the Coordinating Council on Community Redevelopment (CCCR). The director of the DHD reported directly to the mayor and to the department's Board of Commissioners, and the commission reported to the City Council and the mayor. The justification for this reorganization was that it gave citizens greater input into housing and development policymaking.[20] Unfortunately, it had two inherent flaws.

First, the DHD was a city department, not an independent authority like the public-housing systems of several other cities; thus, bureaucratic efficiency was compromised.[21] The DHD had to rely on the Law Department for legal representation; the Purchasing Department to procure supplies, equipment, and materials; and the Budget Department for various central accounting and payment functions. Because of this arrangement, its accounts were not properly maintained (there were two sets of books), and its investment income was diverted into a general city fund and not reserved exclusively for its needs. The DHD also had to adhere to citywide rules and regulations regarding contracts, travel, training, personnel, and union negotiations and thus could not independently determine policies and objectives suitable for its unique mission.[22] In effect, the DHD had to subsidize and depend on the efficiency of other city departments to fulfill its obligations to low-income clients and tenants. Even under the best of administrators, such a system is unwieldy.

Second, in theory and in practice the historic but problematic linkage between low-income housing and economic development was preserved. The City Planning Commission (CPC) merely became a citizen advisory body under the City Council that made recommendations about community development dollars to community groups. Under the mayor, a corresponding department to the City Planning Commission—the Planning Department—was created, along with the Community & Economic Development Department (C&EDD). The Planning Department's vague mandate was to be a liaison that gathered information so the mayor could prepare and update the Master Plan. In the twenty years of Mayor Young's tenure, however, his administration never revised a 1951 Master Plan to account for demographic, industrial, or commercial changes. Instead, it simply reacted to erratic development opportunities.[23] The C&EDD became the most important of the triumvirate, for it was the local public agency charged with administering and overseeing Community Development Block Grant (CDBG) projects and with acquiring and taking care of the city's development "land bank."[24] Housing needs were secondary to economic-development goals.

Overall, the City Council exercised only limited oversight over the DHD, but the department was often caught in the crossfire of disputes between the mayor and the City Council and thus was highly politicized. Under Detroit's reform-oriented charter, the City Council had the authority to require approval of every city contract in excess of $5,000. As one former development director complained, "[If the] Council wanted something from the Recreation Department they couldn't get, they would hold your [housing department] contract hostage."[25] The Reagan administration's policy shifts and substantial cuts to public-housing subsidies provided the Young administration with a basis for asserting that it lacked the resources to properly administer public housing.

## The Reagan Administration: Devolution through Retrenchment

Before the 1980s, the Young administration enjoyed an excellent intergovernmental relationship with the Carter White House. Young's early endorsement of Jimmy Carter boosted Carter's presidential bid and created a close bond. Not only did Young enjoy an unusual level of access to the president, but several members of his executive staff and department heads worked in the Carter administration, especially at HUD. At the height of federal aid to Detroit in 1978, Washington was contributing $400 million to the city's coffers, and several grants were made specifically to public housing.[26]

Under the Reagan administration, however, the relationship drastically changed. It was not helped by Mayor Young's off-the-cuff "prune face" remark about President Ronald Reagan. Beyond the personal antipathies, the federal government greatly lessened its commitment to provide cities and states with adequate subsidies for low-income housing. Of the many areas of social-welfare spending that Reagan cut, his cuts to low-income housing subsidies were most severe—one-third of the total. HUD's budget authorization was decreased by more than 70 percent, or by $19.2 billion, between 1981 and 1987, and the total number of newly subsidized units went from 175,000 in 1982 to a mere 35,000 in 1988. While the Carter administration's subsidies for low-income housing peaked at $32 billion in 1978 alone, the spending for Reagan's last four years was no more than $33 billion.[27]

In severely curtailing the role the federal government played in developing urban housing, the Reagan administration promoted what Edward Goetz refers to as "devolution through retrenchment." This hinged on the fiscally conservative philosophy of "New Federalism," which argued that the market could best provide for low-income housing and many other social needs.[28] Reagan's Commission on Housing, which was composed of bankers and real-estate interests but contained no housing consumer advocates, hailed "the genius of the market economy" over a meddlesome federal government attempting to meet needs for low-income housing.[29] Consistent with HUD Secretary Samuel Pierce's announcement that the federal government was basically "getting out of the housing business," the commission made several recommendations to "shut off the housing spigot" by, among other measures, eliminating nearly all funds for the construction of new public housing; reducing high vacancy rates in public housing through demolition, conversion, or the sale of public-housing buildings; increasing the amount of rent public housing authorities were permitted to charge tenants by calculating transfer payments as part of the 30 percent income ceiling; and using private-market housing vouchers as the primary federal housing subsidy.[30]

Relevant to Detroit's plight, the administration cut all operating subsidies from $1.6 billion in 1984 to just $1 billion in its proposed 1986 budget. Nationwide, public-housing authorities that already were wrestling with depleted staffs and a lack of funds for routine maintenance had to deal with even fewer resources to maintain aging properties. Furthermore, the administration proposed to cut the public-housing modernization program, or the Comprehensive Improvement Assistance Program, from $2.6 billion in 1983 to a mere $175 million in the 1986 budget. Since demolition was actively encouraged for a "thinning out" strategy—a move that had serious repercussions in Detroit and elsewhere—the administration made 3,500 vouchers available to public-housing tenants displaced by local demolition.[31] It was a repetition of urban renewal's previous efforts to relocate the inner-city poor. In the next chapter, I discuss the Reagan administration's added austerity measures with regard to the CDBG program. Suffice it to say for now that the administration reduced overall CDBG outlays from about $3.7 billion in 1981 to $3.1 billion in 1986 and no longer required cities to ensure that a majority of CDBG expenditures benefited low- to moderate-income families.[32]

## Federal Housing and Development Subsidies to Detroit

While these actions prompted the Young regime to assert that its hands were tied regarding the upkeep of public housing, the DHD fared no worse under the first term of the Reagan administration than under Carter's single term. Funding from the Carter administration reached a high of 59 percent of total DHD revenues in fiscal year 1980–81, but the highest (constant dollar) amount was in the Reagan year of 1982–83, in which HUD provided 70 percent of the department's budget. Of course, the DHD, like other departments, needed higher levels of funding overall, given the extreme deterioration of its almost 10,000 units. But the Carter administration's sizable public-housing appropriations, coupled with the Reagan administration's inability to rescind a lion's share of the funds from the Carter years, provided a cushion until the late 1980s.[33] Thus,

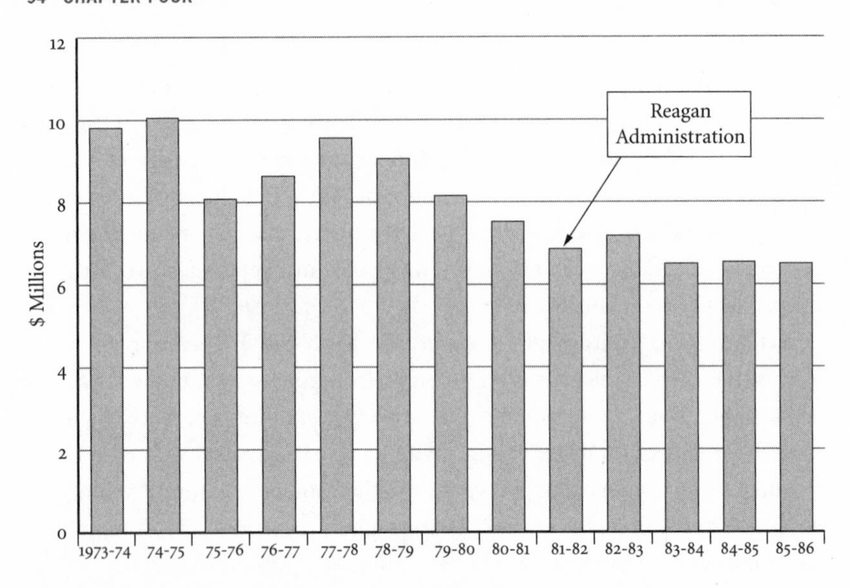


**Figure 6.** Detroit Housing Department maintenance and operation expenditures, 1973–86 (in constant 1986 dollars). *Source*: U.S. Department of Housing and Urban Development, Office of the Inspector General, Region V, reports for August 26, 1983, and March 24, 1987.

in the early 1980s Detroit officials did not suffer from an absolute paucity of federal housing subsidies.

A more relevant set of questions is: How did HUD authorize the DHD to spend federal dollars, and did the DHD spend these dollars wisely? Figure 6 maps the operations and routine maintenance funds Detroit spent between fiscal year 1973–74 (the beginning of the Young administration) and 1985–86 (the beginning of Young's fourth term). It shows that, while funds under Carter peaked in 1974–75 and 1977–78, by 1983–84 the Reagan administration was authorizing only about 60 percent of the highest Carter figure. Likewise, it shows that the Carter administration, as part of its fiscal anxiety in the late 1970s, made key reductions before the end of its term. Thus, it ironically set a precedent that the Reagan White House continued. Unfortunately, it is between 1978 and 1983 that public housing in Detroit suffered substantive decay. Although this was undeniably due to the tightening of the public-housing spigot, it was also due to the DHD's inability to maintain an efficient management system and a professional staff. Such a context was ripe for public housing to become a source of political patronage in whose mismanagement the Reagan administration colluded.

## The Politicization and Neglect of the DHD and Public Housing

According to the Young administration, there simply was no fundamental need for the city to maintain 10,000 public-housing units since by 1980 the city had lost more than half a million residents, and "our experience has proven that the majority of applicants are shopping for something cheaper or better physically."[34] While Mayor Young decried Washington's cuts in public-housing subsidies, he explained to me why he felt that a lot of Detroit's public-housing stock had outlived its usefulness: "These projects were built for another economic era. They were built when Detroit was the automobile center, and during World War II, was the Arsenal of Democracy. We had damn near two million people in Detroit at that time. Housing was a premium."[35] HUD auditors questioned this thinking, since population flight actually led to a shortage in the availability of low-rent units. But Thomas Lewis Jr., Young's longest-serving DHD director, was frustrated with HUD's unwillingness to consider the city's large vacancy rate as a sign that public housing simply was not an attractive option for low-income families, which, of course, related to its disrepair.[36]

Economic development initiatives commanded center stage of the Young administration's agenda; public housing and its professional management were marginal concerns. One mayoral staff member candidly informed me that the department and its director simply were outside Mayor Young's inner circle of advisers.[37] In the history of the nine DHD directors Mayor Young appointed between 1974 and 1993—from his first appointee, Michael Smith, forward—only one, Tom Lewis, had a background in the management of low-income housing. Henry Hagood, a local housing and commercial developer and one of the mayor's most respected directors of the C&EDD, only served as interim housing director for a brief period in the early 1990s. As a testament to the political machine's influence, Ronald Bell, the second-to-last DHD director appointed by Mayor Young, was the husband of Young's niece and had no prior training in public-housing management.[38]

Amazingly, Lewis recounted what he felt was the general disregard the administration had toward DHD in discussing his appointment as director in November 1982: "I never met with the Mayor. He never asked me what my philosophy was; what my ideas were; what my theories were. I got a call from [an aide] saying, 'Tomorrow, Tom, you're the director of public housing.' That's how it went down. I went over there with no direction, looked at the problem, and tried to solve the problem in the best way I thought I could."[39] Lewis said his vision directly countered the prevailing view of the mayor's inner circle: "I think they thought they were hiring a caretaker; a person to maintain the status quo. That was never my agenda; never my agenda. I saw [it] as an opportunity to grab the panoply of social problems that exists in the world of people who have the least amount of resources, but the greatest amount of problems, and attempt to do something about it." Despite the constraints on operating subsidies, Lewis made an extraordinary admission about what he saw as the Young administration's negligence and indifference:

> People in the administration bought into the fact that there wasn't a damn thing you could do about [public housing]. No one believed in these people [the residents]. That it was a place for people of last resort. "Let us just warehouse these people and that's it. HUD doesn't give us enough resources." Hell, when I got over there, HUD was about to take $275,000 from Parkside Homes because we hadn't spent the money. I said, "Ain't no way in hell that we should lose a dollar because we don't spend the damn money as badly as we need money."[40]

An audit of the DHD by HUD in 1983 corroborated Lewis's assertions of laxity and misadministration, but it also implicated him as part of the problem. The DHD was given a "severely troubled" designation in 1979 that it retained until 1997. Due to attenuating HUD maintenance and operating subsidies, the DHD's staff was cut by almost a fifth between 1979 and 1982. Furthermore, the DHD was subject to the decisions of the Budget Department and was not permitted to hire replacement workers. The remaining ill-equipped and, in some cases, unwilling maintenance staff simply left several repairs undone.[41] There was also an inadequate and largely nonexistent system for logging requests for maintenance work by tenants, and by January 1983, more than 8,300 orders out of a total of 10,000 were backlogged or had been written off. This led to a cycle of severe deterioration and unsightliness among the DHD's properties that, when combined with an equally inefficient tenant-occupancy system, led to a vacancy rate that eventually climbed to 42 percent. About 65 percent of vacant units were vacant for nearly a year. Although the DHD received a total of $16 million in rehabilitation funds for Herman Gardens Homes in 1976, HUD asserted, "We found no evidence that the vacant units were subsequently rehabilitated and rented. . . . In fact, [one building] of the project is slated for demolition due primarily to its irreversible deterioration."[42]

When left vacant, buildings were often subjected to vandalism and theft, as one public-housing organizer, Elizabeth Mack, poignantly explained. Although she left her unit spotless and pleaded with housing officials to board it up, "Nothing was done for . . . almost four weeks. By the time housing got down there, the furnace was gone, the basement windows were broken out, the doors were taken off. . . . The hot water heater, the stove, the refrigerator [were all gone]! There was a wall broken in between the bedroom and the kitchen that you could walk through. There's no excuse for that!"[43] In several embarrassing instances, some DHD employees were accused of having stolen and resold appliances from units or even used the granting of housing preferences as a means of extortion. At the same time, those resident managers and other employees who earnestly wanted to serve the tenants were so ill-equipped that, to make photocopies, just as one example, they had to leave their complexes and drive several miles downtown to the central office, for the DHD supplied no on-site copying machines. Added to this deplorable situation, the DHD spent $143,000 in CDBG funds for canopies on "completely vacant buildings" in Parkside Homes when other more pressing structural deficiencies—"roofs, windows, and heating systems"—were in desperate need of repair.[44] In line with the Reagan administration's objective to extract greater levels of rent from public-housing tenants, HUD field auditors were dismayed that the DHD failed to collect about $1 million in delinquent rents, especially from recipients of Aid to Families with Dependent Children (AFDC). By June 1982, the DHD had a peak, cumulative operating deficit of more than $11 million. Unfortunately, the Reagan administration's proposed cuts to AFDC were undermining the ability of these very same people to pay their rent and meet other necessities.[45]

Lewis gave what I first thought to be a peculiar answer to my question about whether the Reagan administration was overly antagonistic toward Detroit, for he considered it "one of the best Republican administrations for housing that we could have." He complimented HUD Secretary Pierce and Assistant Secretary for Public Housing and Indian Affairs Jim Ball. Shortly thereafter, I understood his positive evaluation from an anecdote he told about a tense encounter with a HUD area manager:

> I went in one meeting and the area manager came over there and told me he was going to take my funding back, and I asked him was he finished? He said, "Yes." I said, "Good. Now, let me get the fuck on out of here!" So I got up and walked out and went to call [U.S. Senator] Don Riegle; called Jim Ball. By the time that son-of-a-bitch got back to Chicago he wasn't taking a goddamn thing. I said to him, "Now, why should I sit here and deal with someone who doesn't have the power to say, 'yes'? Let me *leave*."[46]

Robert Prescott, director of the Public Housing Division of the HUD regional office in the late 1990s, explained to me, "For the local HUD people to try to be forceful with the city was a joke. I mean, they couldn't! They had no clout.

So basically they would write up the report and make their recommendations and hope that the city would read it, and they would take some action. But the local HUD office really had no power politically to try to force the city to do anything. The city was better connected than they were [laughs]."[47] In effect, the Reagan administration's decision to constrain the authority of HUD area offices, coupled with the Carter administration's friendly relations with Detroit, meant that Washington co-signed the mismanagement of public housing in Detroit until the late 1980s.

There was even a way the narrow construction of black politics complicated the meeting of needs for low-income housing. Council President Maryann Mahaffey explained to me, "The problem with HUD was that for most of the years the attitude was that 'Coleman is so powerful we can't touch him.' And I even had a meeting with the deputy director [of the HUD area office] who was African American [and he] was insistent that nothing be done to embarrass the mayor."[48] As discussed in chapter 3, here, too, antiracism served as a rationale for supporting black politicians but also shielded the administration from substantive scrutiny. One public-housing organizer criticized such myopic, racial thinking among housing officials through parody: "The reason I'm not doing my job, and the reason I can't get my staff to stop the water and paint from leaking, is because of racism; because we don't have money. And we are a proud black community—rah, rah, rah! [chuckles]"[49]

## FROM POLITICS TO PROTEST: A RENEWED GRASSROOTS INSURGENCY

Were I to end my narrative here, it would give short shrift to those black Detroiters and their allies who, despite considerable odds, led and joined vocal grassroots organizations committed to alternative visions of affordable housing and community development. And to quote the veteran antipoverty activist Marian Kramer, she and other like-minded advocates "refused to lay down our spears," even given the pride and confidence many black Detroiters had in Young's leadership.[50] This final section illustrates some of the EBAM's major propositions by suggesting that, overall, black grassroots activism in Detroit in the mid- to late 1980s occurred in the right place (context), at the right time (timing), and as the right tool (utility), with an emphasis on the latter two.

## The Protest Context for Black Grassroots Activism

Recall that my model includes ideology and group dynamics as part of the context that shapes activist opportunities. Students of black politics have debated whether increasing office holding among blacks ironically dampened their enthusiasm for active participation because blacks trusted their representatives to act and speak on their behalf or because the racial limits to political power led to cynicism. The theses of Adolph Reed and Robert Smith are variations on this question, for both scholars imply that black protest politics declined in the late 1970s in relative proportion to the number of African Americans elected to public office.[51] Using data from the 1976 and 1989 Detroit Area Studies, Table 15 in appendix 2 presents my attitudinal investigation of black Detroit and confirms that it saw protest as an instrumental form of political action, although there were clear limits to its use.

While 70 percent of black respondents agreed that voting was their only say, more educated blacks felt efficacious in not just voting but also lobbying and protesting for their policy preferences. Unlike black homeowners, black women were inclined to agree that voting was their only say. Mindful of the "activist mothering" literature and the greater civic engagement of black women, it is possible that there was a disjuncture between attitudes and behaviors—more black men were willing to say they embraced protest politics even though more black women actually showed up at the barricades. Because homeownership engenders "social capital," it is not hard to imagine that homeowners concerned about property values and neighborhood quality would be the first to contact city officials about such issues as the siting of homeless shelters, the persistence of abandoned buildings and vacant lots, and the repair of dilapidated homes.[52]

Not surprisingly, African Americans who were more highly educated, older, belonged to politically active churches, and who owned their homes reported voting in the 1988 presidential election. Because 68 percent of all black respondents reported voting, which is somewhat higher than the actual turnout, there likely was a social desirably effect to this question. But the more educated said they engaged in protest at some point, and the elderly and women were more inclined to report that they did not. Sixty-nine percent of all black respondents in 1989 believed that protest was an effective tactic, but Reed's demobilization hypothesis finds limited confirmation. Those who reported living in predominantly black neighborhoods were less likely to have engaged in protest. This partly explains why multiracial organizing was a common but still contentious feature of Detroit grassroots insurgency.[53]

Finally, and most intriguing, is the finding that black respondents who felt protest was effective were positively and significantly warmer toward Young. As a black mayor with roots in the Civil Rights Movement and the labor movement, Young was most respected by the segment of black Detroit most likely to embrace the black protest tradition, such as civil-rights leaders, Black Nationalist organizers, and community advocates. In the late 1980s, it appears, black and other grassroots activists confronted a difficult protest context in which many fellow African Americans generally supported the use of protest, but not necessarily to express opposition to Mayor Young.

## The Timing and Protest Cycles of Black Grassroots Activism, 1976–1993

Next I examine the dynamics of grassroots mobilization by coding newspaper articles that featured public protest or demonstrations in the city of Detroit. The two newspapers I used were the *Detroit News*, the Detroit daily with the largest circulation, and the *Michigan Chronicle*, Detroit's oldest African American weekly. I chose the *News* and the *Chronicle* because both have indexes that extend back to 1976 and 1977, respectively, and up to 1993. This time period covers most of Young's tenure. Although the work of Doug McAdam and many other social-movement scholars establishes the examination of newspaper articles as an effective means to quantify protest incidents, I do not consider these two newspapers a comprehensive journal of all grassroots activism. Mindful of editorial and journalistic biases, the analysis of these two newspapers captures local trends in the use of public protest in Detroit, if not all of the specific activities and angles. The media has to be a part of the process, for by definition protest seeks to gain public attention.[54]

Between the years 1976 and 1993, a total of 421 stories mentioned distinct exercises of public protest or demonstration—strikes, marches, rallies, picket lines, sit-ins, vigils, boycotts, blockades, or other attention-getting tactics—that occurred within Detroit's boundaries. Figure 7 graphs the total number of newspaper articles that mentioned protest incidents in order of year. As theorized, it appears that this coverage and, conceivably, the number of incidents were cyclical. The Carter years and the end of Young's first term, as well as the early 1980s and the beginning of the Clinton administration, witnessed a decline in the number of protest incidents recorded. But the beginning and midpoint of the Reagan years, as well as throughout the Bush years, experienced greater newspaper coverage of protests. This process of waxing and waning, ebbing and flowing, is exactly what the cycles of protest literature assumes. Veteran activists translate a movement's ideals, goals, tactics, and networks

**Figure 7.** Newspaper coverage of protest issues in Detroit, 1976–93. *Source: Detroit News*, 1976–94; *Michigan Chronicle*, 1977–93.

to neophytes, who reformulate a new phase of the struggle. Peaks and valleys emerge. Each of these peaks is a point of regime transition; thus, institutional dynamics clearly matter, as the students of political opportunity structures insist.[55] Figure 7 does not directly respond to the question of whether there were lulls in black protest activity per se. Yet given that Detroit was a predominantly black city, it lends limited evidence to James Jennings's assertion that there was a resurgence in black protest in the mid-1980s. It does not support Reed's and Smith's inference of absolute demobilization in the late 1970s, because Detroit papers registered a sharp spike at that time.

So what were these citizens protesting about? How much were housing issues at the heart of this activism? Figure 7 also graphs the number of cumulative protests that occurred relating to housing, race and racism, public welfare, economic issues, and labor issues. Though there are some points of dissimilarity, overall there seems to have been a basic periodicity to the coverage of these types of demonstrations, suggesting that housing activists were not lone voices of dissent. Instead, they were part of an organizational milieu that both complemented and likely competed against others. In an unreported analysis of these same data, I found, not surprisingly, that labor issues were the most frequent cause of protest—about 13 percent of the total. J. Phillip Thompson concludes that the health of local grassroots activism is integrally connected to the health of labor activism.[56] Education, race and racism, and debates about economic issues (principally economic development) were the fourth, fifth, and sixth most reported concerns. The high prominence of race and racism, as well as of labor and economic issues, confirm that in this predominantly black city, questions of race and redistribution had great currency. In eighth place were housing issues, which accounted for almost 6 percent of the total. By housing, I mean stories about subsidized housing, abandoned housing, and homelessness. This finding suggests that housing activism was at least a middle-range player in the broad swath of contenders that competed for newspaper headlines. Although Detroit city departments and agencies were most often the targets of protest (21 percent), only a tiny number of protests were directly targeted at Mayor Young or members of the City Council (about 2 percent each.) The grassroots activists I studied strongly disagreed with Young's policy stances, and often those of his council allies, but it was rare for them to personalize their grievances by directly attacking the mayor.[57] Indeed, Detroit witnessed a new protest cycle in the mid-1980s that housing activists joined. The mid-1980s was the *right time*, but both this and the previous section imply there were limits to activists' making Young a frequent target of their protests.

## The Utility of Black Grassroots Activism

Building on the tradition of the low-income-housing network of the late 1960s, grassroots organizers in Detroit became part of what observers considered a nationwide "new citizen's movement" in the late 1970s.[58] In the shadow of, and in response to, industrial layoffs, corporate disinvestment, and deteriorating housing conditions, community organizations and antipoverty activists mobilized alliances that were important precursors to the mid-1980s. These alliances were fairly class-elastic and black-led, although they were most often multiracial. Often racial politics were a subtext that groups had to confront, but they advocated broad mantras of economic redistribution and egalitarian fairness to the working class and poor. Below are four exemplars of the new citizen activism that gained ground in the 1980s. These activists believed there was an increasing utility to grassroots activism and provided groundwork for subsequent groups and movements.

- *Detroiters for A Rational Economy*

Kenneth Cockrel, a self-described black Marxist and leader in the defunct League of Revolutionary Black Workers, organized the Detroiters for A Rational Economy (DARE) as a multiracial coalition committed to economic redistribution. DARE opposed tax abatements to corporations; organized and successfully defeated an austere tax proposal by Young in 1978 but lost in a similar referendum in 1981; opposed widespread layoffs in the city's workforce and parallel cuts in public services; and opposed public financing for the projects of the influential Detroit Renaissance, Inc., as well as Riverfront West developers. Cockrel once noted that DARE's groundbreaking activism had a "Sisyphean nature" due to "the business of playing the opponent of this immensely popular black mayor."[59] Detroit's black political lore maintains that Cockrel may have succeeded Young as mayor had the former not died of a heart attack in 1989. A high point of DARE's insurgency was when it cemented an electoral coalition that elected Cockrel to a seat on the City Council in 1977. He won despite the objections of Young and members of Young's electoral coalition, including the UAW and the Black Slate. On the council, Cockrel was not only a consistent voice of opposition to Young's development agenda, but he also countered what he saw as the "not in my backyard (NIMBY)" elitism of middle-class neighborhoods who resisted the nearby siting of public and subsidized housing.[60] Although DARE unwound partly due to the difficulties of mounting continued challenges to a popular mayor, their questioning of the city's priorities complemented the efforts of other black-led or multiracial grassroots groups.

• *Michigan Avenue Community Organization*

Among the strongest grassroots challengers to Young was the Michigan Avenue Community Organization (MACO). Organized in 1974 as a congress of neighborhood groups and as an offshoot of the Committee for Ethnic and Neighborhood Affairs, MACO was a late-1970s version of the Alinsky-inspired West Central Organization. MACO applied the vision of Monsignor Eugene Baroni and the National Center for Urban-Ethnic Affairs to build a grassroots, multiethnic alliance that stabilized neighborhoods at risk of drastic transitions, especially with housing. MACO's service area was predominantly white (67 percent) but had significant black (25 percent) and Latino (10 percent) populations. MACO's black constituent neighborhoods faced the particular problem of vacant lots, for they made up more than a third of all properties. Under the leadership of black and white presidents, including Denise Jacobs, Virginia Davison, and Lavelle Williams, MACO had no compunction about using aggressive tactics to voice its displeasure. In describing MACO's insurgent goals and tactics, one planning document said the organization's "main purpose is to empower the poor and working people of its neighborhoods so that they can influence what happens in their community for the better. Its community leadership has repeatedly used 'direct action' tactics and strategies to successfully take on many different elements of the 'power structure' and win."[61] Among the issues for which it used direct action were the city's administration of public services, the clearance of abandoned houses and lots, and the dispersion of community development grants. Whether it was sending HUD Secretary Carla Hills an Easter basket full of charred eggs to represent the state of older neighborhood housing or floating a "money boat" up the Detroit River to protest riverfront development, MACO, in the words of one former member, was "a 900 pound gorilla" that was eager to use headline-grabbing tactics. Although a deep rift developed over MACO's community development efforts, it helped foment the community development movement in Detroit.[62]

• *Tenant Rights and Antipoverty Activists*

Along the public-housing and antipoverty front, which, indeed, was black-led, I have already mentioned the activities of the Public Housing Tenants Union. Its efforts were short-lived, yet in conjunction with tenant-advocacy groups—the United Community Housing Coalition in the late 1970s, the brief but important Detroit Tenant Unions (which raised the issue of rent control), and the Michigan Tenant Rights Coalition[63]—these tenant-rights endeavors paved the way for the late 1980s. This is also true for welfare-rights activism as it continued through the efforts of Marian Kramer and Yvette Linebarger of the Wayne County Welfare Rights Organization and the ten WROs they helped organize in Wayne County.[64] By this maintaining of the local energy once generated by the National Welfare Rights Organization, they laid the groundwork for alliances between AFDC and food-stamp clients who lived in public housing and who wanted to militate for fundamental improvements. Evidence of instrumental coalitions between advocates and public officials is found in the initiation of the Neighborhood Opportunity Fund (explained in chapter 5) and the Nuisance Abatement Ordinance.

• ACORN *and the Nuisance Abatement Ordinance*

Founded in 1978, the Detroit chapter of the Association of Community Organizations for Reform Now was a grassroots, multiethnic, and participatory organization interested in the welfare of low-income communities. It was an Alinsky-style spin-off whose national organizer, Wade Rathke, was George Wiley's deputy director at the NWRO. The national ACORN leadership began a crusade in the early 1980s to address the housing-poverty crisis by initiating a series of "squatter" or "homesteader" takeovers of properties owned by HUD in cities across the country.[65] ACORN's squatting in abandoned Detroit homes powerfully stressed the loss of so many HUD-owned homes during the 1970s scandal. Years after the scandal, Mayor Young, the City Council, Congress, and HUD struggled with how to rehabilitate and sell these properties through "urban homesteading" (Section 810) and "as-is" sale programs sponsored by Council President Erma Henderson. Most of these programs only put a dent in the problem, because they were badly managed and left some low-income householders with dwellings badly in need of repair.[66] Consequently, a Philadelphia model of squatter protests inspired Detroit activists. Between May and October 1982, Detroit ACORN, with a flyer that simply asked, "Need a House? Call ACORN," moved as many as fifty needy persons into vacant homes, most of them black women and children. Because of this campaign, Council President Henderson studied the initiatives of the Philadelphia City Council, and the Detroit City Council unanimously approved the Nuisance Abatement Ordinance (NAO) in July 1983. After that came the "Repair to Own" program. The Young administration legally resisted the first ordinance for years and was sued by several housing organizations. Court verdicts upholding these combined programs represented a legal victory, but by 1993, only 110 people out of 10,000 applicants had actually received NAO properties. Activists had good reasons to continue the fight on other fronts.[67]

## CONCLUSION

The main point of this chapter is that, by the early to mid-1980s, black grassroots and other activists believed, despite many obstacles, that it was *time* they mobilize—or *pick up their spears*—and grapple with Detroit's panoply of problems, including its housing crisis. This chapter builds on my conclusions in chapter 3. Mayor Young's popularity and ability to shape black politics in Detroit made him a formidable opponent. Thus, activists had to carefully frame their opposition against how his machine regime met housing and community development needs, for some intended policy beneficiaries were neglected, such as public-housing clients, the homeless, and homeowners in need of housing repair. In this chapter and the previous chapter, I have analyzed various types of data—census, public-opinion surveys, government expenditures, and newspaper articles—to indicate the relationship between ideas, institutions, and insurgency. I conclude that Detroit in the mid- to late 1980s was the right place, or context, for protest, for protest was a valued, if still limited, form of black political participation. It was the right time, because new cycles of protest emerged across several policy domains. And finally, protest was the right tool, for the new citizen movement used it to at least publicize, if not always to win, on issues such as tenant rights and community development. Next I examine the community development and public housing preservation movements to understand their specific obstacles and opportunities for effective activism.

# 5

## Holding Them Responsible

*Community Development Activism*

**We've never been afraid to stick our necks out, because we are what we say we are. We represent low-income people. We represent people who choose to live in a diverse community.**
**—Karen McCleod, executive director, Cass Corridor Neighborhood Development Corporation, 1994**

### SQUEAKY WHEELS

While it is clear that protest generates noise, this chapter addresses the question: "When do those in power hear this noise and affirmatively respond?" In other words, I explain which squeaky wheels get oil in the Motor City. The focus of this chapter—the Save Our Spirit (SOS) coalition—used a range of tactics to pressure the City Council to target more Community Development Block Grant (CDBG) dollars to community groups and distressed neighborhoods. For example, on May 10, 1986, fifty community-based organizations participated in a daylong, SOS festival and "Rally to Build a Monument to Neighborhoods." That year, eight of nine City Council members overturned the mayor's veto of 130 CDBG allocations to community groups, many of whom served low-income constituencies. The following year, when SOS and its allies generated even noisier protests, the mayor's veto of several allocations for community groups was sustained. So how can we tell whether protest played any role in making the mayor and City Council more accountable to low- and moderate-income citizens?[1]

Between 1985 and 1993, my analysis of Detroit's CDBG budget politics reveals, SOS was successful in forming instrumental alliances (utility and context), exploiting new policy advantages (timing), and employing a range of innovative tactics (utility). However, because SOS was part of an institutionalized if still contentious CDBG interest-group system, it often used protest in symbolic ways to complement its primary strategy of advocating through formal channels, such as the application and budget process, public hearings, and lobbying. In this respect, it greatly differed from its sister movement of public-housing and homeless activism, as I describe in the next chapter. During Young's tenure, community development advocacy was highly complicated by the divisions of race, class, and regime. SOS was a predominantly white but partly black-led alliance that firmly prodded the Detroit City Council to oppose some of the recommendations of a strong-willed and popular black mayor with his own visions of race and redistribution.[2] To examine this problem, I discuss the Young regime's efforts to spark redevelopment, the politics of the community development budget, the activism of SOS, and the outcomes of the budget-lobbying process. The outcomes of their activism bode well for better meeting the housing and other needs of impoverished communities. But there were trade-offs to their activism as it navigated various barriers. Good intentions notwithstanding, interest-group systems are imperfect representatives of low- and moderate-income communities.

## THE YOUNG REGIME AND COMMUNITY DEVELOPMENT POLITICS

### Detroit and the CDBG

Debates as to how to spend CDBG dollars in Detroit were contentious because they were among the few federal dollars available to meet the growing needs of the city's impoverished and poorly housed citizens. Under the 1974 Housing and Community Development Act, the CDBG program was conceived by the Nixon administration to streamline and devolve to cities and locales several job-training, urban-infrastructure, neighborhood-revitalization, and urban-redevelopment programs. Although all municipalities that met a basic needs threshold were eligible, an application was still required. Roughly $8 billion was authorized for the first three years of the program, but each federal administration emphasized a degree of local discretion in the expenditure of these funds. When the Reagan administration took the reins with its mantra of "New Federalism," it decided to do three things that had an immediate impact on Detroit and similar cities.

First, it reduced the overall outlays from about $3.7 billion in 1981 to $3.1 billion in 1986 and folded several more program categories into CDBG, further increasing competition among cities. Second, it no longer required cities to ensure that a majority of CDBG expenditures benefit low- to moderate-income

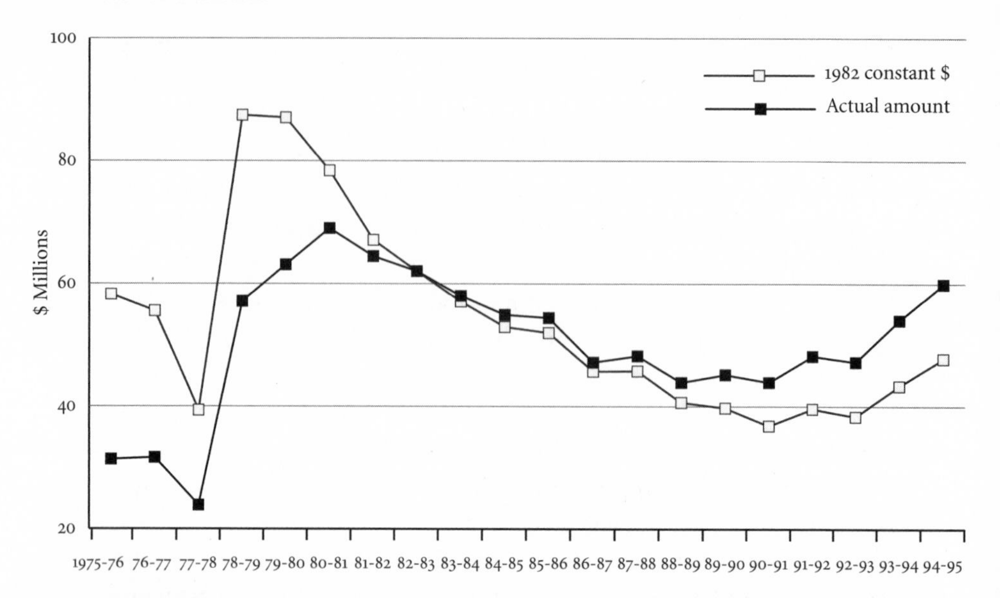


**Figure 8.** Total CDBG allocations, 1975–95. *Source*: Beverly Manick; Detroit City Planning Department, 1985–91; U.S. Department of Housing and Urban Development, Consolidated Plan, City of Detroit.

families; nor did it conduct regular HUD reviews of how much local program activities actually benefited low- to moderate-income families. Finally, despite loud protests from Congress and interest groups, it reversed the fairly assertive oversight HUD field offices did under the Carter administration and shifted most of the decision-making onus to political appointees in Washington.[3] At the end of the Carter administration in 1980–81, Detroit received roughly $69 million in CDBG dollars. By the second Reagan term in 1988–89, this figure had dropped in absolute dollars to about $43 million (see Figure 8). So undeniable resource constraints emerged in the late 1970s and throughout the 1980s that prevented Detroit and other cities from meeting the housing needs of low-income communities.

## Downtown, the Neighborhoods, and Community Development Organizations

The community development movement stepped into the void created by federal program cuts. As an outgrowth of the community-organizing movement of the 1960s and 1970s, the goal of this movement was "capacity building" or the grassroots-led planning and economic revitalization of constituent neighborhoods in partnership with for-profit developers, government grantors, foundations, and community lenders. Community development organizations (CDOs) in Detroit feared that the Young administration would use increasingly sparse CDBG funds for downtown redevelopment, despite the needs of declining neighborhoods. Many believed that adherence to the CDBG's modest low- and moderate-income benefit requirements was missing from various administrative plans: Chrysler's Jefferson automobile plant, the Riverfront West housing complex, and the middle-class-oriented Jefferson-Chalmers housing developments. Lavelle Williams of MACO angrily charged in response to the Poletown Cadillac plant, "Any big corporation that comes through and says, 'I want,' gets. Coleman Young does as he pleases. The only people he's responsible to are the corporations."[4] Council Member Mel Ravitz reiterated this downtown-versus-neighborhood theme in a March 1985 letter to his colleagues: "I am distressed, but not surprised, to note that the Mayor has, in his [CDBG] recommendations, given greater priority to downtown and economic development projects than to Detroit's neighborhoods and community organizations."[5] In his budget and veto messages, Young routinely refuted this argument: "The most persistent, outrageously false allegation is that the preponderance of [CDBG] funds are targeted for the downtown area." Yet he defended his emphasis on large-scale redevelopment: "The last time I looked, the people of this city lived in the neighborhoods. And the last time I looked the major need of this city was still jobs."[6]

No matter where the dollars were targeted, the administration believed that CDOs and other nonprofits lacked the city's capacity to implement housing rehabilitation and neighborhood revitalization. Given the city government's reputation for bureaucratic inefficiency and delay, these critics reasonably questioned this claim. The 1990 HOME program (formally the Home Investment Partnerships) of the Cranston-Gonzalez Housing Act provided cities with a new funding stream for the construction of low-income and affordable housing, roughly $9 million for Detroit in 1992–93, and required at least 15 percent of these new funds be reserved for "Community Housing Development Organizations." A basic analysis of a 1993 CDBG Grantee Performance report suggests that non-city housing developers were on par with the city in the rehabilitation of multifamily units.[7]

Nonetheless, Young expressed general disdain for community developers. "Rather than spend our block-grant money for development projects," he reasoned, "these 'poverty politicians,' as I call them, would prefer to hire community planners at $50,000 and $75,000 a throw. That's one of the best ways I know of to jettison your cash."[8] Henry Hagood, one of Young's former

Community & Economic Development Department (C&EDD) directors, tempered this view in conceding that, with CDBG and Neighborhood Opportunity Funds (NOF) moneys to community planners, "The mayor kind of viewed it as a necessary thing, but believed that it was too dispersed. That the funds should be concentrated more, and that we're 'pissing in the wind' with a lot of the money."[9] This sentiment was widely known among Detroit's community developers. In one interview, a developer independently used language similar to Hagood's to share what the mayor was rumored to have said: "Funding [CDOs] is like pissing in the sea." Another community developer shared with me her misperception that community developers in other locales had equally antagonistic relationships with their city halls, when this was not the case in cities such as Pittsburgh, Cleveland, and San Francisco. In fact, Christopher Walker concluded that, among twenty-three cities, Detroit had among the weakest partnerships between its CDOs, city leaders, and city planners. Between 1988 and 1991, the mayor wanted city agencies to administer a median of 66 percent of all CDBG housing funds, but the City Council and he agreed on a median of a little more than a third.[10]

There were neighborhood bodies and service agencies that Mayor Young firmly supported in his CDBG budget recommendations, including the Citizen District Councils (CDCs). As a state senator, Young took great pride in creating these largely mayor-appointed, advisory development councils: "I found that it was ironic that I should sponsor the [CDC] legislation and then come down here as mayor and be able through cooperation with these neighborhood groups, bring into fruition some of the things I had visualized as a state senator."[11] In each of his budgets between 1985 and 1992, Mayor Young proposed that CDCs receive somewhere between $1 million and $2 million, which sometimes constituted as much as a fourth of the total amount he proposed for dozens of other groups equal in size and programmatic scope. SOS coalition members alleged that, at its worst, this CDC funding represented political patronage where these groups were compelled to be loyal to the machine and actively counter-mobilize against its critics.[12]

## The Neighborhood Opportunity Fund

Concerned that the lion's share of CDBG funds in Detroit would not benefit struggling neighborhoods, a predecessor to the SOS, the Coalition for Block Grant Compliance, lobbied Council President Erma Henderson and other council members to directly target funds to community organizations. As a result, the council established the NOF in 1975. It was a CDBG budget category,

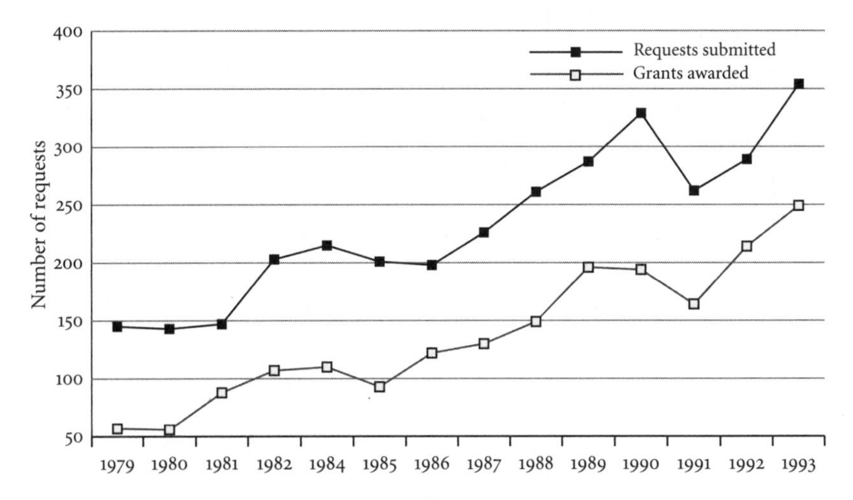


**Figure 9.** Neighborhood Opportunity Fund requests and awards, 1979–93.
*Source*: City Planning Commission, 1993.

separate from line items, whose aim was to reserve at least 10 percent of CDBG funds to community organizations engaged in home repair and the revitalization of low-income neighborhoods as well as commercial properties. By 1977, the City Council had established an eleven-member NOF Citizens Review Committee (CRC), in which citizen representatives made specific recommendations on group applications. Between 1976 and 1980, the council approved 67 percent of all CRC recommendations and only 29 percent of the mayor's recommendations. Over the span of Young's tenure in office a total of $112 million in NOF funds were allocated to community groups.[13]

Overall, the mayor viewed NOF as a form of council patronage and thus was often much less generous in his recommendations. HUD Grantee Performance Reports between 1974 and 1984 reveal the city spent almost as much for administration (23 percent) as it contributed to or spent on housing and neighborhoods combined (24 percent). An absolute majority, or 51 percent, of CDBG funds were spent for development-related purposes that might have benefited low-income communities only indirectly. According to Michael Rich's analysis of CDBG priorities, Detroit's priorities were anomalous.[14] Despite absolute declining CDBG dollars, NOF allocations increased to an all-time high by the end of Young's term in 1993. Figure 9 shows that five times as many groups requested NOF in 1993 compared with 1979, and there was a particularly steep increase beginning in 1985, the year SOS was founded. As an accountability measure, NOF's existence led many community organizations to conclude that the City Council was more responsive to their block-grant applications than was the mayor. My analysis of CDBG allocations cannot tell whether there was an electoral calculus to how City Council members dispersed these funds. But overall, the geographic dispersion of these grants was fairly broad, and the council became increasingly generous in the total number it funded.

## The CDBG Budget: The Mayor versus the City Council

Each year, the city administration initiated the CDBG budget process by submitting a "Preliminary Statement of Community Development Objectives and Projected Use of Funds" to HUD and the City Council. The budget process ran in tandem with the general budget process from early March to early June. Until it was reorganized under President George H. W. Bush, part of the city's CDBG application also entailed submitting a Housing Assistance Plan to describe how proposed spending objectives addressed specific housing needs. In its "Preliminary Statement," the administration usually stated that its chief objective was to "stimulate private investment to create new jobs and to retain and upgrade existing jobs for all City residents," while secondarily recognizing the need to rehabilitate housing or to "upgrade existing housing stock." One of the NOF's most popular funding categories was "home repair for low to moderate-income persons."[15]

While the mayor often made encouraging pronouncements in his CDBG budget communications to the City Council, each year three central questions occupied the thinking of community groups: (1) How many groups would the administration recommend for NOF grants? (2) What level of funding would they receive? and (3) Would the administration include any groups as CDBG line items? As a rule of thumb, CDBG line items received much larger sums of money—about $250,000 to $600,000—as opposed to NOF grants, which ranged somewhere between $25,000 and $80,000. The former category was the rubric under which the administration funded large-scale programs such as the Central Industrial Park (Poletown), the demolition of abandoned structures, or capital for the Economic Development Growth Corporation. On one hand, the larger each CDBG line item, the fewer the dollars that were available for each NOF grant. On the other hand, the more groups the administration included in the NOF budget, the fewer groups it felt inclined to include as CDBG items. CDOs, tenant-advocacy groups, and homeless shelters were in need of sizable block grants because their normal streams of federal and state funding were insufficient.[16]

Shortly after the tense battles of the early 1980s, the relationship between the City Council and Mayor Young began to deteriorate due to the vastly different interpretations each had of the council's authority. Tensions were further fueled by Detroit's strong-mayor system, which required more than a three-fourths majority (or seven out of nine council votes) to override a mayoral veto; this gave the mayor considerable power in the budget process. Whether the issue was budget appropriations, the Nuisance Abatement Ordinance, or council requests for department heads to make reports, Mayor Young might ignore the council's directives, claim executive privilege, or summarily rule a council decision in violation of the city charter. Relations became so frayed that even one of the mayor's supporters, Reverend David Eberhard, lamented Young's display of "an imperial mentality."[17] Young felt that the council frequently intruded on his executive authority and latter dubbed its members "an extra nine would-be goddamn mayors sitting up there in the City-County Building."[18]

Moreover, this struggle with the mayor increased extant political divides on the council. One of the mayor's most ardent backers was Reverend Nicholas Hood Sr. From 1988 to 1993, Reverend Hood was second only to Barbara-Rose Collins in the number of times he voted with the administration on its veto of CDBG allocations—76 percent versus 91 percent. Ironically, Hood's council colleagues complained that he and other Young supporters were at times overturning their own budget initiatives.[19] Reverend Hood spoke about his awareness of Detroit's housing and neighborhood needs, especially due to his experience with his own Plymouth Housing Corporation. However, he admonished groups like MACO and SOS by saying that "the only problem with them was that they didn't see the larger picture. They only saw the picture of the agencies which they represented. The council and the administration [had] to look at the larger picture." Still, Hood maintained that the council was "closer to the people" than was the administration and thus more attuned to the needs of neighborhoods.[20] In order of magnitude, those members who occasionally joined with Collins and Hood to sustain Young's CDBG budget vetoes were David Eberhard (40 percent), Gill Hill (17 percent), and Clyde Cleveland (12 percent; see Table 16, appendix 2).

Council Members Erma Henderson, Maryann Mahaffey, and Mel Ravitz, by contrast, were joined by Jack Kelly, Reverend John Peoples, Reverend Keith Butler, and Kay Everett in voting to overturn 100 percent, or nearly 100 percent, of Young's CDBG vetoes. Each time I asked respondents in the low-income-housing network whether they had any allies on the City Council, the names of Mahaffey, Ravitz, and Henderson were mentioned. Mahaffey and Ravitz were white; Henderson was black. Usually the most glowing descriptions were reserved for Mahaffey, who was a social worker by training and a social democrat by calling. One African American activist who participated in the struggle to relocate homeless people into vacant public-housing units said, "While a lot of politicians pay a lot of lip service to issues, [Mahaffey's] been one of the few people on the City Council that's really been there, and truly understands what we're fighting for." Another explained, "Maryann Mahaffey has been supportive since the beginning. . . . Whatever and whenever we do something, she's always there. Whether she speaks out 90 percent of the time, she does it just to let us know that she's there. She's been the most active." Inversely, Mayor Young used impassioned vitriol to deride those he labeled "the critics, mostly bleeding-heart liberals . . . several of whom [were] led by Maryann Mahaffey (my former campaign worker) and Mel Ravitz."[21]

Despite Young's ire, voters in Detroit thought highly of these three council members and rewarded their outspokenness by returning each of them to the City Council for an average of 25 years. Mahaffey served as president of the council between 1990 and 1998 and 2002 and 2005, which means she received the largest number of votes in Detroit's at-large council elections. The popularity she enjoyed among Detroit's majority-black electorate was a testament to her "deep roots" in the community, the racial tolerance of black voters, and her strong support of racial and economic redistribution while still leading the loyal opposition to Young's ill-advised policies.[22] The veteran black Congressman George W. Crockett Jr. of Detroit once endorsed Mahaffey's reelection by reminding black voters, "Her record, not her color, should be the yardstick by which her measure . . . is taken. If voters in Detroit vote their consciences, Maryann Mahaffey will win—and so will Detroit."[23] Moreover, the critiques Mahaffey and other council members had of Young's CBDG recommenders were informed by the views of grassroots advocates such as SOS.

## THE SOS COALITION: NAVIGATING THE BARRIERS

The SOS Coalition arose as a product of community development and neighborhood-based organizations that were affiliated with a low-income-housing advocacy network. In 1985, a total of thirty-five organizations joined in the creation of SOS and, along with Council Member Mahaffey, marched to and then held a candlelight vigil at City Hall's "Spirit of Detroit" statue. It was no coincidence that the coalition framed itself as integral to the city's livelihood—in fact, representing the very spirit of the city and of its neighborhoods.[24] With the motto "Neighborhoods Are the Spirit of Detroit," SOS called itself, "a Detroit City-Wide Coalition dedicated to equitable Block Grant spending in Detroit's older neighborhoods."[25] Its core set of organizations included the Cass Corridor Neighborhood Corporation, U-SNAP-BAC, the

United Community Housing Coalition, and the Warren / Conner Development Coalition. They and a few others took turns coordinating the coalition's activities from year to year. SOS officially was an ad hoc confederation with no elected leaders whose only requirements for membership entailed attending one of its several community meetings or showing up and expressing solidarity during a demonstration or public hearing. SOS annually presented an alternative budget, or "People's Budget," to the City Council to lobby for a general increase in the CDBG funds allocated to all neighborhoods and community groups. In fact, it explicitly stated: "Save Our Spirit does no individual lobbying for any one organization." Thus, it made no line-item recommendations.[26] Relevant to my study, SOS represents a case of black grassroots activism within a multiracial coalition. To be sure, whites made up a majority of SOS, but often African Americans and occasionally Latinos were its spokespeople and key lobbyists.

## The Context for SOS's Activism

### • *Black Politics versus Collective Identity and Framing*

SOS confronted the contextual challenge of Young's influence over black politics by framing itself as an advocate of all working-class and low-income neighborhoods, regardless of race. Mayor Young once launched the following broadside against such detractors: "Frankly, it offends the hell out of me that I'm charged by the pansy-ass liberals with ignoring the poor folks—[that is], the black folks. For God's sake, I've spent a lifetime fighting for the black man's privileges and standard of living! It's what I do."[27] Clearly, Young insisted that his policy agenda was inherently in sync with black (racial) group interests and the interests of the poor. Because SOS was predominantly white but partly black-led, it faced great difficulties in negotiating the minefield of Detroit's racial politics, especially when it directly opposed Young's policies. In most instances, SOS leaders stressed their desire never to personalize their conflict with the mayor and instead portrayed their differences as simply divergent perspectives on how best to pursue neighborhood revitalization. On June 1, 1987, SOS addressed "An Open Letter to City Council," in which it asserted:

> Apparently some City Administration officials have indicated that some of the larger "line item" groups do not represent Detroit's Black citizens, even though they are situated in Black neighborhoods. . . . Discrediting these organizations based on racial arguments misses the most important point here: Detroit citizens of all colors are working together in Detroit because

> they love Detroit, not because they are Black, or because they are White, or Hispanic, or Asian or any ethnic or racial background. We all recognize and feel, as Detroiters, the effects of racist attitudes from suburbanites and out[-of-]state people, and we must continue to fight that attitude—but this is not the place to wage that battle. This is the place and time to fight together for our older neighborhoods.[28]

Note how the latter part of this statement frame bridges, because it agrees that fighting the "racist attitudes" of those (whites) outside Detroit is an imperative for "all . . . Detroiters," but it calls for closed economic ranks to fight poverty.

Consistent with my assumptions, Young on occasion openly employed race as a means to demobilize black and white Detroiters who were critical of his development policies. In this respect, he did not ameliorate the racial divide, though he clearly was at times a champion of antiracism. One white SOS advocate believed that race was "always, always a problem. Part of the mayor's strategy was to make it racial, so part of our strategy was to make sure our spokespeople and our constituents were multiracial." The same leader confided to me the severe rebuke his organization received when it investigated the neighborhood impact of a proposed correctional facility the Young administration endorsed. As the group proceeded with its investigation and contacted the State Department of Corrections, the mayor confronted them: "Coleman was furious, *furious* that we had to do that. 'Who in the hell . . . ,' he cussed me out and it got *racial*. But that was the approach."

Both in the participant-observation research I did to follow SOS activities in the spring of 1994 and in the written copies of SOS public testimony before the City Council, I noted that at least one African American or Latino was always designated to speak on the group's behalf. In several instances this was Rosa Sims of U-SNAP-BAC, Angela Brown of the Warren / Conner Development Coalition, Lavelle Williams of MACO, or Michelle Brown of the Cass Corridor Neighborhood Development Corporation. I even noticed instances in the transcripts in which the names of prospective white spokespeople such as Reverend Ed Rowe of the Cass Community United Methodist Church were crossed out and replaced with the name of a black member. Because the main actors of SOS were CDOs, and a large number of executive directors and staff members of CDOs in Detroit and elsewhere were not black, SOS still had the difficulty of building and maintaining a coalition descriptively representative of black Detroit. Still, its characterization of its identity as a defender of the neighborhoods—all neighborhoods—helped occasionally to shift attention away from these racial politics.[29]

• *Mobilization Costs versus Group Resources and Networks*
SOS subsidized the contextual costs of mobilization through its use of group resources and networks. Among the larger costs individual SOS organizations bore was the possible retribution of the Young administration. In a memorandum to his colleagues dated June 3, 1985, Council Member Ravitz argued for the council to override the mayor's budget vetoes and added, "I am concerned that some of these [community] projects may have been vetoed because of their outspoken advocacy to Council on behalf of Detroit's neighborhoods."[30] Two years later, in June, Ravitz declared that the mayor's "vetoes were designed to suggest reasonableness by making only selective cuts and punish the neighborhood groups that are the leaders of the Save Our Spirit organization. Review which groups were cut. . . . [They were] all groups that have been active in advocating for neighborhoods for some time."[31] During the intense budget battle of 1988, one SOS supporter, whose organization had applied for CDBG funding, also joined public-housing activists to challenge the administration's demolition plans. He claimed that the mayor said to him in a meeting: "'You motherfucker, what do you think you're doing, coming in here telling me . . . !' You know, totally going off on me. And in the course of it pointing at me and saying, 'And I know where your funding is, and we are going to look into that!'" SOS leaders conceded that the possibility of such reprisals greatly hindered their efforts to recruit more black-led organizations.

Consequently, organizers decided that SOS would have no formal structure largely as a defense mechanism against political retaliation. One leader explained, "It's very loose, because with the [Young] administration the thought was that you couldn't hit a moving target. The leadership changed so that one group couldn't be singled out and their funds cut. That was the theory. Sometimes it worked; sometimes it didn't." While the loose structure of SOS allowed it to be a "moving target," the flexible and "ad hoc" arrangement also left it susceptible to the vagaries of an indeterminate membership. It handled what Mancur Olson calls the "free rider problem" in an interesting way.[32] Neighborhood organizations soon recognized they had recourse if they disagreed with what the administration recommended in the NOF or CDBG budgets. By aligning with SOS, an umbrella group with a negligible amount of hierarchy, groups claimed membership in a united front that got the City Council's attention. In the view of social-movement theorists, they were part of an instrumental collective action that was motivated by self-interests.[33] SOS "membership" was as simple as neighborhood groups walking into the auditorium of the City County building for a public hearing and agreeing to wear a red-paper SOS button or carry an SOS placard handed to them by an organizer.

## The Utility of SOS's Activism

### • *The Black Urban Regime versus the Disruptive Coalition*

As mentioned earlier, Young's machine regime influenced black politics in Detroit and convinced a segment of black-led neighborhood groups to support his community- and economic-development designs.[34] On two occasions, an SOS advocate said, he approached a few pro-mayor groups at particularly raucous public hearings and asked why they were carrying banners that declared "Support the Mayor," even when in one case the mayor had proposed they receive about half the amount the council proposed. Allegedly, the group leaders responded, "We were told to be here," or in response to a disparity in the figures, they said "Well, no, you're not showing me the right stuff." Furthermore, one study discovered that voting precincts in Detroit with greater numbers of blacks, homeowners, and homes with high average values were more likely to support the Cobo Hall expansion project, a downtown development priority of the Young administration in 1988, and thus tacitly endorse the regime.[35]

Therefore, the City Council became the political fulcrum for SOS's advocacy. Members of the council were seen and saw themselves as either more attentive or, if not more attentive, more vulnerable to neighborhood demands than the mayor. Research indicates that City Council members in at-large systems like Detroit's are attentive to economic-development issues based on the number of years they have served and the amount of media attention these issues attract. One SOS leader partly corroborated this finding: "It may have been that council could be more shamed; or council was more fearful of not being elected because there were constituencies that each council person felt that they had to appeal to; or that they were better people or better leaders. Probably a little bit of all of that."[36] Another SOS member wrote in a community newsletter: "Our strategy is simple. We don't want to fight or insult the Mayor, who apparently feels he is just doing his job. We just want to make it clear to the City Council that they have the support of many organizations across this City, and many thousands of people that they represent, so that they can do *their* jobs."[37]

SOS's ability to form a disruptive coalition with certain City Council members was due not merely to the persuasion of its arguments but also to concrete ties from mutual interests. First of all, there were SOS leaders who, for at least a short while, served on council members' staffs or had close relationships with their staffs. For instance, Angela Brown-Wilson of the Warren / Conner Development Coalition and Vicki Kovari of the Detroit Tenants' Union both served as interns with Mahaffey in the late 1970s and early 1980s and learned budget and constituent-contact practices. Council members also ensured that certain task-force and commission seats under their purview—including the City Planning Commission and the Citizen Review Committee—were filled by SOS and other neighborhood-based activist groups.[38] Second, staff members of these sympathetic council members often alerted SOS leaders of administrative actions when they were not publicized but affected the dispersion of CDBG funds. One SOS flyer asked community leaders, "DID YOU KNOW?—On July 28th, the Mayor recommended a shift [from] NOF funds committed on June 2, 1987, to [the] Demolition of Dangerous Buildings" in the amount of "$2.5 million. This amounted to a cut in all but 27 [of 130] projects or 35.8% . . . DID YOU KNOW?—*SOS was notified by several council staff persons* and was able to notify its members by phone tree in time to appear at council in protest."[39] Third, Council Members Mahaffey, Ravitz, and Henderson appeared at SOS demonstrations and publicly spoke at its gatherings. From time to time, their opinions and speeches were printed in the SOS-affiliated publication the *Exchange*. And fourth, SOS members were active participants in the election campaigns of council allies. For example, one SOS leader managed Mahaffey's 1993 campaign for council president and along with other members of the low-income-housing advocacy network, worked to secure the reelection of Mahaffey and Ravitz.[40]

• *Electoral Confines versus Adaptive Tactics*

SOS had to perform a very delicate balancing act to disagree with Young. One black SOS leader, who characterized her group as "a thorn in [Young's side] on a continuous basis," was puzzled about why black criticisms of the mayor's development agenda did not translate into a challenge of his incumbency: "For people that opposed Coleman [and] some of the decisions that he made, there were still those individuals that would vote for Coleman. And that's always been a dichotomy that's never quite made any sense to me, but it was one that was there." She noted that even some of her group's board members voted for Young.

To navigate around this electoral quandary, SOS employed a range of tactics, from formal lobbying to protest demonstrations. Despite its lack of a formal structure, SOS had two "standing" committees on which any volunteer could sit: the Budget Committee and the Political Action Committee. Each year, the Budget Committee was responsible for analyzing the administration's CDBG and NOF proposals and formulating the alternative "People's Budget" that justified the shifting of CDBG dollars away from the mayor's development and demolition priorities toward neighborhood revitalization, public services, and housing.[41] SOS's budget analysis also provided sympathetic council members with fodder to build their cases. As Ravitz once revealed: "Over the years, [SOS] regularly presented [the council] with alternative ways to spend the limited funds that we had; always from the viewpoint of the grassroots homeowners, tenants, and citizens of the city. A very valuable perspective from where I sit . . . [for] here on the 13th floor of the City-County building, I can never reach the grassroots as thoroughly as they can."[42]

The Political, or Direct, Action Committee was responsible for planning and implementing protests to gain media attention. For example, on March 13, 1987, SOS sponsored a "March for Neighborhoods" in which it held a rally and asked those assembled to participate in a postcard campaign—seven hundred postcards were delivered to council members. A year later, two hundred SOS supporters, inspired by "Hands across America," formed a human chain across Belle Isle Bridge to symbolize the link between downtown and community development. They wanted the City Council to shift $22 million of Young's proposed $48.2 million development pool for that year to neighborhood groups.[43] Throughout this period, SOS was joined by other activist groups such as MACO, which independently mobilized dozens of their members for City Council public hearings. Overall, SOS and its partners made it at least moderately difficult for unsympathetic council members to ignore the potential threat such protest might pose to their public images.[44]

## The Timing of SOS's Activism

### • *Activist Cycles and Strategic Advantages*

Finally, SOS acted at the "right time," for it contributed to a tide of grassroots activism in the mid-1980s and gained strategic advantages that shifted the ground rules in favor of community-based organizations. Electoral confines notwithstanding, SOS leaders still pondered how they could use the ballot box as an accountability mechanism. As early as the 1985 elections, they asserted, "We will publicize the names of those City Council members who voted for the [mayoral CDBG] override, and those who didn't. We intend to hold our City Council accountable for once."[45] They then promptly published how each of the nine members had voted for each organization that requested NOF or CDBG funds with the discernible pattern of Collins and Hood consistently voting "no" for the appropriations of vocal community groups and SOS affiliates.

In fact, SOS fortuitously asked questions of public accountability when the council majority chaffed at the minority that continued to sustain the mayor's vetoes. In November 1988, Council President Henderson introduced Proposal "N" for "neighborhoods." The referendum read: "Do you favor amending the

Detroit City Charter to provide for a [two-thirds] majority of Council Members serving (6 votes) to override Mayoral vetoes of the City Council's amendments to the City Budget?" Surprisingly, the body voted 8-0, and it was placed on the November ballot. It was a measure mutually beneficial to the individual and institutional motives of council members, as well as to the funding needs of SOS and other community-based organizations. Its passage gave a strategic advantage to grassroots advocates because it was a shift in the rules of the budget game. Moreover, it was proposed during the 1988 presidential election year, when the voters of Detroit did not support other candidates and measures Mayor Young strongly endorsed—that is, three incumbent members of the school board and a $25 million general obligation bond to expand Cobo Hall, the city's main convention center. Already a loose alliance of black church leaders and neighborhood groups had led the opposition to Young's ballot initiatives in favor of building casinos.[46]

In late September 1988, SOS leaders quickly mobilized grassroots proponents of Proposal N. Framing the problem as a "downtown versus neighborhood" dichotomy in the administration's budgets, they formed a multiracial coalition called Amend the Charter to Improve Our Neighborhoods (ACTION). By the very end of September, ACTION claimed to have seventy-five member organizations and was conducting "door-to-door," "church-to-church" canvassing.[47] After several months of facing fairly tepid opposition, Proposal N won with 69 percent approval. Young suffered so many defeats to his agenda in 1988 that he angrily taunted critics, "Anybody who thinks I have exposed a vulnerability is welcome to come on in and try me."[48] The Proposal N victory allowed grassroots advocates to combine the strategic flexibility of the public-policy arena with the electoral arena.

## SOS ACTIVISM AND COMMUNITY DEVELOPMENT ACCOUNTABILITY

### Data and Method

Next, I return to the central question of whether SOS not only raised its voice but was heeded by elected officials. Though in previous work I discovered that there was broad agreement between SOS proposals and the actions of the City Council,[49] the following analysis precisely examines several factors weighing on mayoral and council decisions. It is based on data compiled from the 1988–93 CDBG budget actions the mayor and City Council took at every major step of the process, for every project or program that submitted a request. This yields a total of 2,062 observations, which on average was 340 requests per year. My main dependent variables are difference measures where I subtracted the amount the mayor recommended or enacted from the amount the City Council allocated. Such measures allow me to test whether and how each branch was accountable to various interests, for I observe which attempted to rectify an outcome by proposing more funds relative to the other branch. If the resulting coefficient is positive, the City Council allocated more. If the resulting coefficient is negative, the mayor recommended more or cast a veto that was more.[50]

## Estimating Activists' Efficacy

Explicit measures of ideological framing, activist cycles, and group resources were difficult for me to include in the regression models I present. Thus, I approximate measures of these concepts and use four independent variable batteries to capture my other utility, timing, and context assumptions. Allow me to briefly explain. First, my "Context: Race, Class, and Regime" battery includes ten variables and indicates whether the mayor or the council was more likely to allocate funds to a project located in a census tract based on a range of characteristics. Through these measures I answer the question of whether the mayor or the council was more likely to serve the various constituencies or give greater priority to these racial, economic, and housing characteristics. All are direct determiners of how *context* mattered and whether political *accountability* occurred, for they tell us which branch of government believed it necessary to rectify the community-specific actions of the other.

Second, I include a "Utility: Disruptive Coalition and Adaptive Tactics" battery to gauge whether and how implicit council alliances and incidents of broadly defined grassroots activism—institutional versus insurgent—had an impact on the council–mayor dynamic. I coded whether a group was a regular SOS participant (1 = yes; 0 = no), which I gleaned from SOS files. I also included the total number of organizations that applied for NOF funds each year (a rough measure of lobbying or normal politics) and the total number of newspaper stories that mentioned housing-related protests or protests against city officials or agencies in the previous twelve months (extra-normal political measures). While the last two count variables are only rudimentary indicators of protest activity,[51] they still help me to broadly understand the utility of protest activism and hint at the protest climate.

Third, another aspect of *context* is captured by the "Context: Collective Identity and Group Networks" battery, including whether an applicant belonged to a block club or neighborhood association, was a Citizen District Council (CDC), or was a housing-related group.[52] Finally, a battery of "Timing: Strategic Advantages" variables are in my models because they answer whether and when it was the right time to have an impact on the mayor–council dynamic. Among these variables are whether it was a local election year (the mayor and City Council were elected at the same time); a year the council overturned all of the mayor's vetoes; a year after the passage of Proposal N; and a year after the introduction of the federal HOME program.[53] While the inclusion of these variables is straightforward, remember that after 1991–92 the federal HOME program gave the mayor and council roughly $9 million more to spend on housing rehabilitation and to distribute to community developers.[54] In addition, to determine whether groups had an advantage by merely being in the funding stream, I included the percentage of times a group received funds, or the number of times a group applied divided by the number of times it was a recipient.

- *Total CDBG Differences*

Results from my analysis confirm that, to varying degrees, SOS's alliance with the City Council and its use of adaptive tactics made a significant difference in increasing overall CDBG allocations, although strategic advantages were significant only in the realm of housing. In Table 5, I present the aforementioned variables' effects on the council's actions minus the mayor's recommendations for all projects (Model 1) and then non-city projects (Model 2). I also estimate the effects of the final total minus the mayor's initial recommendations for all projects (Model 3) and then non-city projects (Model 4). To ensure that each model is either properly specified or theoretically consistent, I occasionally drop variables.

With the "Context: Racial and Economic" battery, one strong and consistent result stands out: The council allocated more funds to tracts with higher total percentages of people in poverty, while the mayor directed more funds to tracts with higher percentages of blacks in poverty. The council appeared, at least initially, to favor non-city projects in these poverty tracts (Model 1 versus Model 2), whereas the mayor was in favor of targeting slightly less funding to non-city projects in these black poverty tracts when compared with total allocations. Also it appears that the council significantly favored requests from areas where white renters outnumbered white homeowners across all models except the third. Consistent with his development philosophy, the mayor significantly favored major redevelopment areas, at least when deciding total CDBG expenditures. Under the "Utility: Disruptive Coalitions and Adaptive Tactics" battery, it is very clear that regular participation in SOS was significantly associated with the council's allocating more funds to a group across all phases of

**Table 5.** Differences between City Council and mayoral CDBG allocations, 1988–1993, clustered by year

| | Model 1 Council's first actions minus Mayor's recommendations (all projects) | Model 2 Council's first actions minus Mayor's recommendations (non-city projects) | Model 3 Final total minus Mayor's recommendations (all projects) | Model 4 Final total minus Mayor's recommendations (non-city projects) |
|---|---|---|---|---|
| *Independent Variables* | | | | |
| *Context: Race, Class, and Regime (1989 census-tracts data)* | | | | |
| Total population | .01 | .00 | .01 | .00[b] |
| | (.00) | (.00) | (.00) | (.00) |
| Black % population | −167.60 | −68.61 | −144.32 | −49.44 |
| | (65.05) | (37.11) | (60.41) | (37.46) |
| White % population | −144.28 | −27.21 | −122.37 | −19.65 |
| | (74.35) | (45.78) | (74.92) | (45.54) |
| % Persons below poverty | 115.80[b] | 127.18[c] | 103.89[b] | 97.91[c] |
| | (17.98) | (20.26) | (25.38) | (18.98) |
| % Blacks below poverty | −97.19[b] | −91.07[c] | −94.94[c] | −69.63[c] |
| | (20.88) | (15.85) | (15.21) | (13.34) |
| % Whites below poverty | −15.19 | −15.77 | −10.07 | 19.34 |
| | (8.75) | (8.37) | (14.18) | (9.52) |
| % Housing vacant | 34.01 | 26.55 | 47.77 | 23.55 |
| | (63.13) | (41.29) | (60.18) | (32.75) |
| % Difference black renters versus owners | −13.37 | −10.50 | −10.46 | −8.14 |
| | (6.20) | (4.07) | (8.19) | (4.22) |
| % Difference white renters versus owners | 20.46[a] | 16.72[a] | 16.35 | 16.90[a] |
| | (5.27) | (5.96) | (7.44) | (5.93) |
| Major development area | −116.60[c] | −45.46 | −124.82[a] | −51.38 |
| | (28.46) | (45.13) | (34.13) | (42.49) |
| *Utility: Disruptive Coalitions and Adaptive Tactics* | | | | |
| SOS participant | 113.95[c] | 104.92[c] | 95.45[b] | 85.29[b] |
| | (20.21) | (18.31) | (21.57) | (19.50) |
| Lobbying: Number of NOF requests | .14[a] | .19[b] | −15.09 | −.08[a] |
| | (.04) | (.05) | (6.15) | (.02) |
| Protest 1: Number of newspaper stories on protests against city agencies (past year) | .70 | 1.80[a] | −165.38 | −93.64 |
| | (.57) | (.69) | (65.19) | (70.31) |

**Table 5.** Continued

| | Model 1 Council's first actions minus Mayor's recommendations (all projects) | Model 2 Council's first actions minus Mayor's recommendations (non-city projects) | Model 3 Final total minus Mayor's recommendations (all projects) | Model 4 Final total minus Mayor's recommendations (non-city projects) |
|---|---|---|---|---|
| Protest 2: Number of newspaper stories on housing-related protests (past year) | — | — | 55.11[a] | 47.54 |
| | — | — | (21.19) | (35.18) |
| *Context: Collective Identity and Group Networks* | | | | |
| Block club / association | 12.87 | 5.80 | 15.28 | 8.78 |
| | (8.05) | (8.36) | (7.30) | (7.42) |
| Citizen district council | −127.28[a] | −9.77[a] | −106.68 | −1.07 |
| | (40.90) | (3.76) | (46.84) | (8.11) |
| Housing-related group | 18.35[c] | 12.54[a] | 14.98[a] | 9.15 |
| | (3.37) | (3.81) | (4.05) | (4.68) |
| *Timing: Strategic Advantages* | | | | |
| Local election year | 6.34 | 13.95[a] | 42.35 | −215.80 |
| | (2.81) | (4.87) | (21.26) | (176.62) |
| Year Council overrides mayor's vetoes | — | — | −564.90 | 365.00 |
| | — | — | (238.61) | (281.79) |
| After Proposal "N" | — | — | −108.13 | −687.20 |
| | — | — | (41.38) | (528.54) |
| HOME allocation year | −14.03[c] | −17.85[c] | 781.87 | — |
| | (1.98) | (2.73) | (321.02) | — |
| % Times group received funds | −.02 | −.02 | −.02 | −.02 |
| | (.01) | (.01) | (.01) | (.01) |
| Constant | −105.63 | −24.24 | 6659.93 | 1315.20 |
| | (50.86) | (20.40) | (2586.75) | (944.37) |
| Number of observations | 2,062 | 1,952 | 2,062 | 1,952 |
| $R^2$ | .14 | .14 | .13 | .13 |
| Root MSE | 127.63 | 87.58 | 127.11 | 83.04 |

*Sources*: City Planning Commission; CDBG Data files.

*Note*: Entries are nonstandardized regression coefficients, clustered by year (6 total), with their corresponding robust standard errors in parentheses. All tests are two-tailed.

[a] Indicates p <.05.

[b] Indicates p <.01.

[c] Indicates p <.005.

the budget process. The council naturally favored allocating slightly fewer dollars to SOS participants to the degree they were not connected to city projects (Model 2 versus Model 4). While SOS leaders lobbied for increased funding for all neighborhood groups partly to deflect the charge that they were parochial and only advocated for their particular neighborhoods, those in the Young camp interpreted council favoritism as evidence that SOS membership had its privileges. To be fair, the lack of a variable in my model that captured each group's resources—budget, staff size, membership size, and so on—makes it difficult to know whether the council favored SOS members because they were SOS members or because they were among the larger groups that potentially had greater service capacity. From my interviews, both SOS leaders and critics concurred that the latter was most likely.[55]

At the beginning of the budget process, the City Council appears to have been somewhat more attentive to the number of NOF requests than was the mayor. At the end of the process, veto politics compelled the mayor to be slightly more attentive to NOF requests of non-city groups (but the coefficient is equivalent to $80). However, the City Council appears to have been more affected by protest demands, for it initially allocated small but higher totals to all projects based on the number of newspaper stories about city agency-related protests (Model 2) and higher final totals to non-city projects based on housing-related protests (Model 4). The council may have used CDBG allocations as one response to frustrated homeless groups, home-repair groups, and public-housing residents, especially in light of the city's well-publicized deficiencies.[56]

The "Context: Collective Identity and Group Networks" estimates reveal what I predicted: The mayor favored citizen district councils. Again, SOS advocates argued that such privileging was congruent with the mayor's focusing dollars in major development areas. Although the signs on the block-club and neighborhood-association estimates are positive, indicating that the council favored these groups, they are not statistically significant. But housing-related groups were significantly favored by the council in all aspects of the budget process except the final total aimed at non-city projects. When this finding is placed in tandem with the understanding that housing protests had a greater impact on the council, it appears that the broader CDBG arena was conducive to varying types of grassroots housing activism. Finally, the "Timing: Strategic Advantages" battery indicates that it mattered more to the council whether it was an election year and requests were from non-city groups. It mattered more to the mayor if it was a year when HOME program funds were available, at least at the beginning of the budget. Surprisingly, there were no significant effects of council overrides in Proposal N years. But overall, a specific focus on CDBG housing allocations divulges a slightly different story.

• *Housing-Related CDBG Differences*

Results from my housing-related analysis confirm that adaptive tactics and strategic advantages mattered more in increasing CDBG allocations, while its alliances with the City Council had no direct impact. Two models in Table 6 tap the differences between the council's final actions and the mayor's initial recommendations for the total sample (Model 1) and the same for non-city projects (Model 2). Table 6 is not a mirror image of the previous table, but there are some consistent relationships. Under the "Context: Race, Class, and Regime" battery, I added a per capita family-income variable to provide another gauge of class differences. Within that battery, it appears that the council directed more dollars to tracts with higher rates of black poverty and with larger overall numbers of blacks than did the mayor. In addition, the council targeted these dollars to neighborhoods with greater housing vacancy. This indirectly corroborates some council members' allegations that the Young administration inordinately funded the demolition of vacant units without equitably funding the rehabilitation of community-based housing.[57]

The "Utility: Disruptive Coalitions and Adaptive Tactics" grouping reveals that the housing sub-domain of CDBG budget politics was an opportune venue for advocates to be heard by the council or the mayor. Although its coefficients remained positive, SOS membership was not a significant indicator of increased council allocations on housing. This corroborates SOS's claim that groups with diverse purposes joined its efforts to put more dollars into the hands of all community-based groups and not specific line items such as U-SNAP-BAC's home-repair program. Mayor Young was sensitive to, and often prickly about, the local news media's portrayal of his leadership and administration, and the activism of public housing and homeless advocates only increased this attention.[58] Subsequently, Models 1 and 2 indicate that the mayor was likely to appropriate more dollars to all housing requests as the number of stories of protests against city agencies increased and a few more dollars to non-city housing requests as the number of housing-related protest stories increased. The results for the "Context: Collective Identity and Networks" battery are the inverse of the results in Table 5. Group characteristics appeared to matter much less in the subdomain of housing than was true with the overall CDBG budget. In fact, all of the estimates were negative and not significant. Possibly multipurpose CDOs proliferated and successfully garnered housing dollars; thus, they blurred the lines between housing and non-housing groups.

**Table 6.** Differences between City Council and mayoral CDBG housing allocations, 1988–1993, clustered by year

| | Model 1 Final total minus Mayor's recommendations (all projects) | Model 2 Final Total minus Mayor's recommendations (non-city projects) |
|---|---|---|
| *Independent Variables* | | |
| *Context: Race, Class, and Regime (1989 census data)* | | |
| Total population | .00 | .00 |
| | (.00) | (.00) |
| Black % population | 47.51[a] | 49.71[a] |
| | (17.05) | (18.04) |
| White % population | 83.59 | 85.47 |
| | (34.16) | (35.22) |
| % Blacks below poverty | 16.66[b] | 20.76[b] |
| | (3.82) | (4.91) |
| % Whites below poverty | −13.70 | −15.04 |
| | (6.54) | (6.31) |
| % Persons below poverty | 13.53 | 7.46 |
| | (24.74) | (25.25) |
| % Housing vacant | 58.19[a] | 57.53[a] |
| | (16.59) | (16.72) |
| % Difference black renters versus owners | −31.39[a] | −32.02[a] |
| | (12.10) | (12.31) |
| % Difference white renters versus owners | 6.64 | 7.36 |
| | (3.56) | (3.53) |
| Per capita family income | −.00 | −.00 |
| | (.00) | (0.00) |
| Major development area | 5.83 | 5.99 |
| | (4.67) | (5.29) |
| *Utility: Disruptive Coalitions and Adaptive Tactics* | | |
| SOS participant | 31.61 | 31.34 |
| | (15.80) | (15.71) |
| Lobbying: Number of NOF requests | −2.97[a] | −.19[c] |
| | (.88) | (.01) |
| Protest 1: Number of newspaper stories on protests against city agencies (past year) | −29.33[a] | 3.39 |
| | (9.04) | (1.55) |

**Table 6.** Continued

| | Model 1 Final total minus Mayor's recommendations (all projects) | Model 2 Final Total minus Mayor's recommendations (non-city projects) |
|---|---|---|
| Protest 2: Number of Newspaper stories on housing-related protests (past year) | 8.39[a] (2.88) | −2.81[a] (.75) |
| *Context: Collective Identity and Group Networks* | | |
| Block club / association | −6.32 (3.77) | −6.59 (3.91) |
| Citizen district council | −13.98 (7.53) | — |
| Housing-related group | −6.54 (2.91) | −6.87 (2.90) |
| *Timing: Strategic Advantages* | | |
| Local election year | 1.53 (3.51) | 1.36 (3.38) |
| HOME allocation year | 144.57[a] (46.54) | — — |
| Year City Council overrides mayoral vetoes | −105.22[a] (35.58) | −11.20 (5.38) |
| After Proposal "N" | 1.02 (3.74) | 42.13[a] (10.60) |
| % Times group received funds | −.00 (.00) | −.00 (.00) |
| Constant | 1193.74[a] (344.80) | −38.47 (56.49) |
| Number of observations | 402 | 391 |
| $R^2$ | .18 | .18 |
| Root MSE | 36.35 | 36.75 |

*Sources*: City Planning Commission; CDBG Data files.

*Note*: Entries are nonstandardized regression coefficients, clustered by year (6 total), with their corresponding robust standard errors in parentheses. All tests are two-tailed.

[a] Indicates p <.05.

[b] Indicates p <.01.

[c] Indicates p <.001.

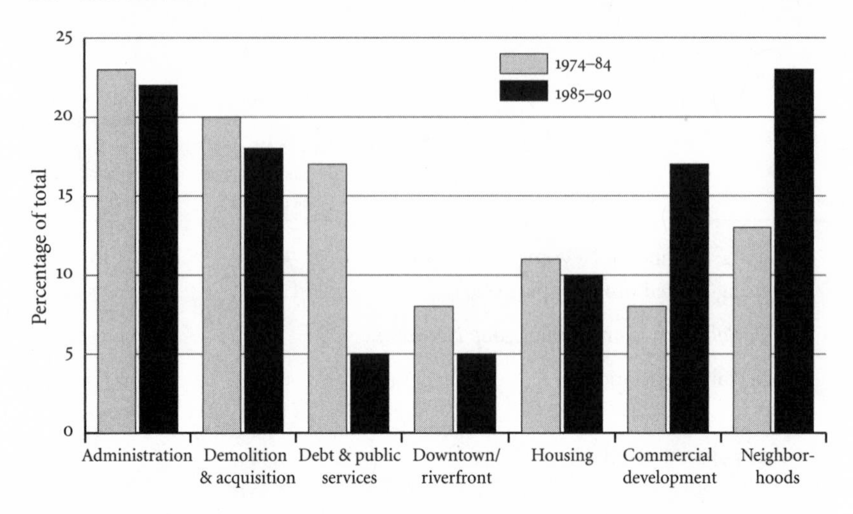


**Figure 10.** CDBG budget allocations by category, 1974–90. *Source*: Beverly Manick (SOS files); Detroit City Planning Department, 1985–91.

Compared with the previous model, however, it appears that the housing subdomain, as tested by the "Timing: Strategic Advantages" battery, provided a different set of opportunities. It is odd that the local-election-year variable is still not significant, while it is positive. Viewed from a different angle, however, this result may be due to the vagaries of 1989. It was both an election year and the first time the council unanimously overrode all of the mayor's vetoes. The mayor attempted to short-circuit the council's opposition to his budget by allocating more overall housing dollars, but the council was emboldened by its post–Proposal N powers and disagreed with the mayor's recommendations. Even the loyal Council Members Collins and Hood implied that they simply had no choice but to vote with the majority, for, as Hood lamented, "My protest vote would not have made any difference."[59] With the mayoral challenger Erma Henderson presiding and Tom Barrow in the audience, Young was compelled to not pick a fight with the council and community activists, and thus he graciously accepted the council's verdict. Two confirmations of these dynamics is the council's willingness to allocate funds more generously after Proposal N (Model 2) and HOME program years (Model 1).

Taken together, this period was a ripe time, and the budget arena was a right context, for effective community development activism. In fact, Figure 10 illustrates the appreciable shifts in the percentages allocated to neighborhood projects prior to the founding of SOS (1974–84) and those after SOS (1985–90). While housing funding remained about the same, neighborhood projects overall greatly increased from 13 percent to 23 percent. Every funding category that was a greater priority for the Young regime witnessed at least a modest decrease.

## CONCLUSION

Although I did not find that effective community development activism in Detroit uniformly required strong allies, advantages, and tactics across the CDBG budget process, I found that combinations of these utility, timing, and contextual variables were necessary for mobilization to prompt greater funding accountability from the mayor or City Council. Both my qualitative and quantitative analyses reveal that SOS groups formed *strong alliances* with members of the City Council, and the council slightly favored community-based groups. In the overall CDBG budget process, SOS was supported by the City Council in the same way that pro-regime CDCs were supported by the mayor. Regarding *strategic advantages*, I found that the mayor recommended higher housing allocations right after the enactment of Proposal N, possibly because it exposed a vulnerability of the regime or decreased the number of council votes needed to override a mayoral veto. Finally, I found that *tactical flexibility* mattered because the protest climate was a complement to the lobbying politics of the budget process. But reported protests had the greater impact on the City Council's total CDBG allocations and on the mayor's housing allocations. In summary, the weight of allies, advantages, and tactics varied according to context: the total CDBG budget domain versus the housing subdomain.

Moreover, SOS carefully traversed the minefield of Detroit race, class, and regime politics. Mayor Young could claim that his CDBG recommendations benefited black and other low-income communities, even while he clearly distrusted activist community developers and favored projects near major development areas. The mayor distrusted SOS partly because it was an outspoken, majority-white coalition with key black spokespeople. Between 1988 and 1993, the council allotted funds to CBOs in census tracts with high black poverty, an average of about $48,000 in CDBG funds, compared with the mayor's recommendation of $16,000. The council even gave CBOs in census tracts with high white poverty an average of about $50,000—a noticeable increase over the mayor's average of $42,000. But the fact that CBOs in census tracts with higher white populations on average received $68,000 from the council, but those in tracts with higher black populations received only $38,000 from the council, was likely not missed by the critics of SOS and its council allies. Like the national community development movement, the SOS leadership confronted the problem of not being descriptively representative of Detroit's black community even though it embraced redistribution and antiracism.[60]

SOS's activism pressured the council and the mayor to target CDBG funds to Detroit's low-income, and often its poor black, communities, especially in the arena of housing. When certain opportunities for advocacy arose, black and white SOS activists had the wherewithal to see them, as is evident from the victory of Proposal N. The same was not true of the electoral arena. In 1989, SOS leaders attempted to broaden their network and expand their political influence by enacting a "PEOPLE's Platform" and running candidates for office. During a special election in 1991, a black SOS leader and community developer, Angela Brown-Wilson, ran for the City Council. Neither the slate of candidates that the PEOPLE's Convention endorsed nor Brown-Wilson's seventh-place finish in the race (with a mere 2,397 votes) proved to be a fruitful a form of activism. Brown-Wilson was outgunned by candidates with more resources, and the PEOPLE's Convention dissolved due to competing visions. Nonetheless, the lesson is that these activists tried various forms of grassroots activism and various tactics to hold those in power responsible.[61]

# 6

## Now Is the Time!

*Public Housing and Anti-Homelessness Activism*

**I know one thing, it's time we put our feet down and demand some action.**
**—Charles Wesley, Detroit/Wayne County Union of the Homeless, 1988**

### NO HOUSING, NO PEACE!

Ill-managed public housing had long compounded the problem of homelessness in Detroit. By the late 1980s, even conservative estimates put Detroit's homeless population at 12,000, while its vacancy rate in public housing was 42 percent.[1] What differentiated the public-housing and homelessness activism of the early 1990s from previous efforts, as I argue in this chapter, was its ability to exploit new strategic advantages, garner stronger group networks, and adapt its protest tactics. Late in October 1989, one hundred supporters of the Detroit/Wayne County Union of the Homeless (DWCUH) disrupted a meeting of the City Council. While chanting "No Housing, No Peace!" and risking police arrest and injury, they pressured the council to call for more vacant public-housing units to be made available to the homeless. Little was gained, because the council was unable to sway the Young administration. Three years later, Preserve Low-Income and Affordable Housing Now! (PLAN) joined the DWCUH, and for two days both occupied the eleventh-floor office of Mayor Young. When this disruption was combined with intense scrutiny from federal officials, modest successes were achieved.[2]

My purpose in this chapter is to demonstrate when a primary tactic or strategy of protest is sufficient and insufficient to compel public accountability to public-housing tenants and homeless citizens. I apply the EBAM to two cycles of public-housing and homelessness activism beginning in the late 1980s: the

Brewster-Douglass anti-demolition campaign and the Parkside-Jeffries campaign. Both groups demanded that the Young administration halt its plans for de-concentrating public-housing poverty by way of demolition and limited construction, but only the latter was successful. Compared with the community development interest groups I examined in chapter 5, the public-housing and homelessness insurgents in this chapter also confronted the hurdles imposed by Detroit black politics, mobilization costs, and Young's development regime but lacked strong City Council support. Nonetheless, the activists of the Parkside-Jeffries campaign learned from the setbacks of the Brewster-Douglass campaign and, at the right time, adapted their protest tactics while exploiting a change in the federal rules for public-housing demolition. I first examine the contextual debates as to how to improve the lives of public-housing residents in Detroit and then use my model to analyze these campaigns.

## THE CONTEXT OF RACE, POVERTY, AND PUBLIC-HOUSING REVITALIZATION

In the 1980s, Congress enacted the Comprehensive Improvement Assistance Program (CIAP) and, later, Comprehensive Improvement Grants (CIGS) to provide local Public Housing Authorities (PHAS) with subsidies to modernize their most distressed properties. Because the Reagan administration believed that government-owned housing unfairly competed with the private market, HUD officials permitted PHAS not only to use these funds to rehabilitate their housing stocks but to demolish a portion of their stocks and reduce vacancy rates. By the early 1990s, the strategic demolition of public housing had gained the ideological support of centrist policymakers, who felt that decades of racial and class segregation had resulted in the alienation of impoverished communities from the economic mainstream. New urbanist architectural layouts of low-rise, mixed-income communities were preferred over the towering brick "warehouses of poverty" of the 1950s that, in the thinking of William J. Wilson, merely concentrated poverty and its social ills.[3] Debates about what constitutes the renewal of public housing led to clashes between the de-concentration-through-demolition and the preservation approach.

Researchers conclude that any neighborhood with a poverty rate in excess of 40 percent suffers from concentrated poverty. Between 1970 and 1990, America's pockets of concentrated poverty more than doubled, from a population of 4.1 million people to 8 million people. Relative to Detroit, the percentage of its population below the poverty line increased from 15 percent in 1970 to 22 percent in 1980, and in 1980 more than half of its population and

75 percent of those living in poverty lived in concentrated poverty tracts. Race clearly mattered, for Detroit was majority black, and black Detroiters were nearly three times as likely as their white counterparts to be living in poverty in 1980.[4]

In this vein, a number of researchers agree that public housing contributes to concentrated poverty. Historically, it has been sited in economically depressed black and Latino neighborhoods, and its income restrictions have had the unintended consequence of warehousing the poor.[5] Between 1970 and 1980, the construction of public housing had a very strong and significant impact on the rates of poverty for Detroit's census tracts, as did the percentage of non-whites. Although the relatively greater poverty in Detroit meant that the concentration of public housing only modestly increased the likelihood of census-tract poverty, it still increased the likelihood of poverty from 57 percent to 65 percent.[6]

Table 7 illustrates this point by indicating how rapidly the Brewster-Douglass neighborhood in downtown Detroit slipped into greater poverty. While the Young administration stressed the economic revitalization of the nearby downtown neighborhoods of Brush Park and the Medical Center, it proposed to demolish half of Brewster-Douglass, or roughly 2,000 units. Partly due to Detroit's declining economy, as well as the neglect of public housing, Brewster-Douglass's census tract lost three-fourths of its population. It remained a majority-female and almost exclusively black neighborhood; it also witnessed a halving of its median family income (in 1990 dollars) and a 30 percent increase in its poverty rate, with 81 percent of all of its families in poverty. Clearly, Brewster-Douglass suffered from concentrated poverty. The housing figures—occupancy rate, percentage of properties occupied by renters, and median home value—reinforce these disparities, although median home values in Brush Park clearly bounced back from a significant drop. Brush Park's median home value of $42,500 in 1990 was nearly twice Detroit's citywide average of $25,600.

Similar patterns are evident in Table 8. Parkside Homes and its annex were located in eastern Detroit, near the Warren-Conner area. Contiguous to Parkside was the neighborhood and park of Chandler Park. Parkside was completed in the late 1930s and was programmed as a whites-only complex, in contrast to Brewster Homes, which was all black. Over the course of the 1970s and 1980s, both Parkside and Chandler Park experienced stark racial segregation and economic decline, although Parkside fared much worse. By the time the Young administration planned to demolish some seven hundred units at the complex in 1990, a whopping 62 percent of the Parkside neighborhood

**Table 7.** Condition of the Brewster-Douglass, Brush Park, and Medical Center neighborhoods, 1970–1990

| | Brewster-Douglass (Census Tract 5176) | | | Brush Park/Woodward East (Census Tract 5174) | | | Medical Center (Census Tract 5180) | | |
|---|---|---|---|---|---|---|---|---|---|
| | 1970 | 1980 | 1990 | 1970 | 1980 | 1990 | 1970 | 1980 | 1990 |
| Total Population | 4,736 | 3,291 | 1,082 | 3,596 | 1,926 | 980 | 4,356 | 2,442 | 1,844 |
| % Female | 60.3 | 61.3 | 62.0 | 45.5 | 40.0 | 34.0 | 50.3 | 50.8 | 45.7 |
| % Black | 99.2 | 99.1 | 99.1 | 71.2 | 71.0 | 82.5 | 83.3 | 76.8 | 73.3 |
| % White | .8[a] | .55 | .55 | 28.8[a] | 27.9 | 15.0 | 16.7[a] | 21.1 | 23.0 |
| Median income (1990 dollars) | 10,755 | 8,702 | 5,629 | 18,570 | 15,532 | 15,000 | 20,679 | 16,542 | 17,273 |
| % Below poverty | 49.2 | 52.3 | 80.7 | 33.3 | 27.6 | 25.0 | 20.8 | 29.5 | 34.8 |
| Occupancy Rate | 96.4 | 88.0 | 36.3 | 84.6 | 77.0 | 70.5 | 77.4 | 83.7 | 82.6 |
| % Renter-occupied | 95.6 | 87.5 | 36.0 | 81.6 | 73.4 | 66.9 | 73.9 | 79.9 | 80.0 |
| Median home value (in 1990 dollars) | — | 51,550 | 15,000 | 44,801 | 27,757 | 42,500 | 40,759 | 27,123 | 25,000 |

*Source*: Census of the Population, Census Tract Details, 1970, 1980, and 1990.

[a] Non-black.

**Table 8.** Conditions of Chandler Park and Parkside neighborhoods, 1970–1990

| | Chandler Park (Census Tract 5121) | | | Parkside (Census Tract 5122) | | |
|---|---|---|---|---|---|---|
| | 1970 | 1980 | 1990 | 1970 | 1980 | 1990 |
| Total Population | 4,947 | 5,107 | 5,818 | 4,266 | 3,386 | 1,734 |
| % Female | 55.2 | 53.6 | 54.8 | 57.8 | 60.5 | 57.4 |
| % Black | .7 | 75.4 | 95.2 | 55.6 | 86.7 | 92.6 |
| % White | 92.3[a] | 24.6 | 4.8 | 44.4[a] | 13.3 | 7.4 |
| Median income (in 1990 dollars) | 35,406 | 21,929 | 14,932 | 4,333 | 5,506 | 6,438 |
| % Below poverty level | 5.5 | 18.9 | 38.7 | 37.8 | 56.5 | 61.6 |
| Occupancy rate | 98.0 | 92.5 | 92.5 | 97.6 | 87.1 | 47.8 |
| Renter-occupied | 56.4 | 49.3 | 50.9 | 81.3 | 75.1 | 38.4 |
| Median housing value (in 1990 dollars) | 55,581 | 32,357 | 23,800 | 48,507 | 29,026 | 20,000 |

*Sources*: Parkside Study Group, "Final Report," July 1994, 129; U.S. Bureau of the Census, "Census of the Population, Census Tract Details," 1970, 1980, 1990.

[a] Non-black.

was in poverty, and 93 percent of its residents were black, as compared with 56 percent in 1970. Chandler Park residents earned more than Parkside's tenants did, but a third of them were below the poverty line. Like Parkside, Chandler Park was 95 percent black. Housing disparities between Chandler Park and Parkside paralleled those between Brewster-Douglass and Brush Park. Basically half of all Chandler Park units were occupied by renters between 1970 and 1990; thus, this community, like the rest of Detroit, maintained a very strong single-family-residential character. But significant decreases in the median home values of both areas motivated Parkside tenant leaders and the Warren / Conner Neighborhood Development Corporation to work together to improve their neighborhoods.[7]

Tenants of Parkside and other public-housing projects in Detroit suffered from concentrated poverty and cited joblessness and crime as persistent problems (for security was terribly lax.) But critics of the de-concentration-through-demolition approach believe that it is problematic because it overlooks tenants' preferences, especially those who want to rehabilitate instead of raze units in their embattled developments.[8] Detroit newspaper accounts and my interviewees with longtime public-housing residents reveal stories about close-knit groups of neighbors who struggled but raised their families, maintained friendships, beautified their properties, participated in project-based organizations, and created communal memories in the face of increasing crime and public neglect. One interviewee who had resided at Brewster-Douglass for more than thirty years explained her attachment to her apartment even when she was given the option to relocate: "We moved out for a little while, and then you got the chance to move back into your same unit if you wanted, which I did because it's just like home to me. My husband became ill and died in the same unit, and it holds a lot of memories for me." Residents of Brewster-Douglass maintained an alumni organization that held a reunion even after units in the complex were demolished. At a reunion in 1991, they recounted stories of Eleanor Roosevelt's christening their development and of its nurturing famous Detroiters such as the boxer Joe Louis and the Motown legends Diana Ross and Stevie Wonder. The public-housing leader Lena Bivens said of Brewster-Douglass: "We're a family. . . . That's why we decided to get together for a good time, instead of waiting to meet at funerals."[9] Into the 1990s, project-based groups like the Brewster Old-Timers or the Friends of Parkside further demonstrated their attachment to their complexes by frequently petitioning the City Council for funds to maintain recreational and other public services.[10]

But my interviewees clearly cited the late 1970s as the turning point in the downfall of public housing, and they laid the blame squarely at the feet of the federal and local authorities. When the Young administration went from a state of increasing neglect to proposing the demolition of public-housing units, a group of black women, who had a communal attachment to and pride in their communities, emerged as the leaders of a new public-housing preservation movement. These women fought not simply for the particularistic interests of keeping their individual apartments but for the broader economic-justice principle of the right to decent and affordable housing.

## PUBLIC-HOUSING DEMOLITION AND YOUNG'S DEVELOPMENT REGIME

Activists believed that the Young administration's failure to properly maintain public housing was not merely incompetence but part of a deliberate plan to find alternative uses for the Brewster-Douglass and Parkside sites—so-called prime pieces of property.[11] Corrine Jones, an activist and longtime resident of Brewster, warned the City Council: "We're being squeezed. They want our homes to make room for all that development and don't care about us."[12] One of my interviewees echoed this outrage in asserting that Coleman Young "just never cared about poor people. Therefore, he put people into [Detroit Housing Department] positions that more or less either owed him favors or he could put them on a string and use them as a puppet to do what we wanted them to do." Whether these assertions are true or not, they reveal a deep distrust and enmity between the administration and these public-housing advocates.

Since the early 1980s, the DHD purposely had relocated tenants and vacated public housing units at Jeffries, Parkside, Brewster-Douglass, Wolverine Towers, and the Charles Terrace complexes. In response to a HUD audit in 1987 that discovered 587 new vacancies in these complexes, the DHD conceded that the 52 percent vacancy rate at Brewster-Douglass was part of a deliberate plan to slate units and buildings for demolition, consolidation, or sale on the private market. This was despite the concession that the department "has either not formally requested HUD approval of its intended actions or not yet received HUD approval on formal requests actually made."[13] But the combined effects of the DHD's failure to address the basic maintenance and upkeep of these buildings (a backlog of more than 8,000 maintenance requests existed in the 1980s), to secure these buildings against vandalism and theft, and to get council and HUD approval for compulsory tenant relocation simply fueled activists' suspicions that the DHD's ulterior motive was "de facto demolition."

As part of a 1986 plan to demolish a total of 2,400 units in Parkside, Charles Terrace, and Brewster-Douglass and thus to reduce Detroit's public-housing vacancies by one-third, the DHD asked to use money from CIAG to demolish about 1,037 two-story units in Brewster-Douglass. It proposed leveling all of the original Brewster buildings, as well as the Brewster annex, and to replace them with 250 newly constructed town houses. In effect, the DHD proposed razing 52 percent of the total number of units in Brewster-Douglass and replacing only 13 percent of the original total. The department submitted its first Brewster-Douglass demolition plan to HUD in June 1986, but final approval was not granted until February 1990.[14] Again, public housing in Detroit was undermined by a politics of disregard coupled with the imperatives of economic development, because (1) the Young administration did not treat public housing as a policy priority; (2) the DHD posts were too often a form of political patronage; and (3) the Bush–Reagan cuts to operating subsidies colluded with their willingness to approve demolition as a vacancy-reduction strategy.[15]

In chapter 4, I described how Tom Lewis, Young's longest serving DHD director, believed that influential members of the mayor's staff were generally uninterested in the efficient management of public housing and were pessimistic about its prospects for revitalization. One defender of public housing corroborated the view that the redevelopment agenda was driving public-housing priorities: "The housing director wasn't calling the shots at this point anymore. . . . It was clear to me that the economic development department was making decisions as to which housing should go." All sides admitted that the location of the complex was very attractive. In the late 1980s, Brewster-Douglass sat at the intersection of the Chrysler Freeway (I-75) and Mack Avenue. It was only minutes away from the Medical Center complex, the theater district, the Renaissance Center, and the Riverfront. While there was clearly a need for economic stabilization in the Brush Park area, the Young administration's actions heightened speculation about the potential gentrification of Brewster-Douglass. Between 1985 and 1993, the mayor asked for $6.3 million of CDBG funds to be spent on infrastructure improvements in Brush Park and Medical Center / Art Center.[16]

Council Member Mel Ravitz confided, "My own suspicions, and that's probably the better word, . . . is that the administration wanted to clear the low-income folks out of the Brewster-Douglass and install instead a more middle-class population that would be perhaps more compatible with the economic interest that were to be developed there."[17] Council Member Maryann Mahaffey agreed: "I think the Mayor really wanted, and he did explore, if he were to tear down Brewster-Douglass, could he use that land for something else. The business people and the Chamber of Commerce and [Mike] Ilitch [developer of the Fox District] all hated public housing. I mean it would interfere with their development."[18] Map 2 lends further credence to the point that Brewster-Douglass was sandwiched between more affluent census tracts, for several areas south and southeast of the site were in the city's top median income quartiles in 1990. To this day, only the Chrysler Freeway separates the remaining complex from Detroit's major baseball and football stadiums, Comerica Park and Ford Field.[19]

Public officials who defended the demolition at Brewster-Douglass differed over whether economic redevelopment was an intended byproduct. During an interview, Council Member Clyde Cleveland bristled at my suggestion that demolition would help the Medical Center's expansion: "Who said that? Don't come in here with that off-the-wall stuff, man! That's off the wall. . . . The expansion of the Medical Center! I don't know where you got it from, and whoever told you that don't know what he's talking about. Bring him or her here, and I'll tell them the same thing!"[20] Cleveland said that the chief problem the demolition addressed was to provide Brewster residents with some "*liebesraum*," or living space, and thus to make the atmosphere safe and comfortable. Council

**Map 2.** Detroit median income in selected neighborhoods, 1990.

Member John Peoples also supported the demolition from what he described as a "sociological perspective" that echoed Wilson's social-isolation argument. He asserted that the tenants' resistance was indeed based on distrust of the administration, but "the distrust idea was kind of a cover-up to hide their [the tenants] own fears."[21]

Next to the concentrated poverty problems of crime, social isolation, and the severe deterioration of these units, Housing Director Lewis argued that demolition was justified because it reduced density. He once told me: "The damn places were too dense." But unlike Council Member Cleveland, Lewis readily conceded that demolition bolstered the administration's objective of redeveloping the Brush Park area: "The bottom line was that if you were attempting to create a community that would complement anything that happens in the proposed Brush Park, and have that public housing fit; if you had risen to the point where [there was a 54 percent vacancy rate] and then you could demolish some and rehabilitate some and bring back to life that neighborhood and still have subsidized housing still have a presence that close to downtown Detroit, what better to do?" On one occasion, Council President Mahaffey remembers, she challenged Lewis's rationale: "Tom Lewis told me himself that 'poor people don't want to live crowded together. It's too high of a density.' I said to him, 'What about Riverfront West [luxury apartments]? Why say that one density is any better than another? . . . 'Oh, you don't know what you're talking about!'"[22]

Another problem was that the depopulation of the city and the proliferation of Section 8 vouchers for rental housing (versus new construction) left the DHD with a "marketing problem." Lewis said, "I wasn't bringing to the low-income marketplace in the city of a Detroit a viable product," for public housing simply was not an attractive prospect for most low-income renters.[23] HUD officials and other critics disagreed with Lewis, and said the staggering depopulation of the city likely increased the demand for public housing, especially given a more impoverished citizenry unable to pay nominal rents. Still, Lewis maintained that Detroit's slack housing supply and other subsidies gave low-income families options that were better than public housing, which already suffered from a stigma in a city of homeowners.[24]

Beyond the question of whether the demolition of these apartments was a good low-income-housing policy, the lack of democratic participation in these modernization plans frustrated several tenants. The administration sanctioned the activities and involvement of a few long-term resident leaders, some of whom served on tenant councils, the Board of Tenant Affairs, and the housing commission.[25] HUD, which was complicit in the lack of transparency, substantiated critics' concerns when its auditors concluded that the DHD had misappropriated large sums of money to the Board of Tenant Affairs, while the Detroit Housing Commission, the department's governing body, often provided weak to nonexistent oversight. At one point, HUD auditors alleged that the board was nothing more than a "pass-through of paper [between the] Mayor and the City Council."[26] To counter this system of patronage and the perceived designs of Young's urban regime, low-income-housing activists mobilized to create several alternative organizations and coalitions.

## THE BREWSTER-DOUGLASS PROTEST CYCLE, 1987–1990

By the end of this campaign or cycle, black grassroots activists did not achieve their goal of preserving all of the Brewster complex's 700 units and the 300 units of the Douglass buildings slated for demolition; nor did they achieve low-income-tenant ownership of HUD properties. Still, this protest cycle laid the groundwork for subsequent learning, alliances, and advantages.[27] The coalition that first framed and demonstrated solidarity between public-housing tenants and homeless citizens included Short End of the Stick and the Detroit / Wayne County Union of the Homeless (DWCUH).

Among public-housing tenants, a core group of African American women—most prominently Corrine Jones, Jackie Nelson, Grace Byers, Bettie Milton, and Janet Hull—formed a group in 1987 that they defiantly named Brewster-Douglass Tenants Get the Short End of the Stick. Black men and people from a variety of backgrounds were involved, but the history of black women's activism and the number of female-headed public-housing households informs us why they were often Short End of the Stick's chief and most vocal spokespeople. To highlight the conclusions about residential displacement and that "the big shots in city hall are trying to take advantage of us," Short End of the Stick had a toothpick as one of its logos. Among homeless citizens, there was the DWCUH. Founded in January 1988 by 400 mostly homeless people with help from the National Union of the Homeless, its aim was to achieve a "victim-led struggle" for decent, permanent housing. Its first president was Sonya Terry, and other executive-committee members and spokespeople included Theresa Smith, Dianne Bernard, Ron Childs, Delphine Shamblin, Wilson O'Neal, Rochelle Porter, Nate Thomas, and Wayne Pippin. Pippin later became the union's long-serving president.[28] The reason this public-housing and anti-homelessness campaign ended in defeat is not lack of vision, energy, or tactical ingenuity. It lacked an effective, disruptive coalition and strategic advantages.[29]

### The Context for Brewster-Douglass Activism

• *Black Politics versus Collective Identity and Framing*

Although Short End of the Stick and the DWCUH contested the irony of the Young administration's proposal to raze public-housing units in the midst of a homelessness crisis, race remained a stronger determinant of black support for Young than was economic redistribution.[30] For example, I received reports of black churches and ministers who were hesitant or unwilling to ally with homelessness activists because they disagreed with the activists' militancy or feared political retribution. A DWCUH leader further lamented that, while many churches engaged in electoral politics, they shied away from homelessness activism: "Most churches on so many other occasions just like with political candidates—the Baptist Council—they make it known who they support. I would like to see them that active in issues such as we're trying to address." True to a racially dominant construction of black politics, tenant activists claimed that they were questioned by black leaders about why they permitted white outsiders to join them in their struggle. In one instance, Marilyn Mullane, a white legal-aid attorney and strong ally of the DWCUH, charged the DHD with illegally evicting Josephine Borrows, a seventy-year-old black woman, from the Jeffries Homes because she failed to "clean the floor in the hall." Director Lewis accused Mullane of "stooping to using this poor black woman, this poor, elderly, ill black woman to further" an agenda.[31]

To counter these politics, Short End of the Stick used both a name and a logo (the toothpick) that implied that citizens living in public housing were unjustly denied the right to high-quality, affordable housing precisely because they were black and poor. One leader shared her belief that HUD's racial indifference colluded with the black-led DHD's economic bias and negligence: "Over the years, nothing has been done, and I have my formula for why it has not been done. Most of public housing is occupied by black people. Low-income black people, and probably no-income black people. A lot of ADC recipients." Thus, the inference advocates drew and the collective identity they attempted to build was that Brewster-Douglass tenants sat on a "gold mine" and they had better band together or be displaced from their homes.[32] It also was no coincidence that homelessness activists called their organization a "union." In the late 1980s, as many as a third of Detroiters belonged to a labor union but also were joining the ranks of the destitute due to losses of manufacturing jobs.[33]

To bridge the divides of race and economics, both the DWCUH and Short End of the Stick framed the issue as a linkage between the problem of public-housing vacancies and Detroit's increasing homelessness. They made this linkage at an opportune moment, when homelessness was receiving increased local and national attention in newspaper headlines and policy hearings. Stories of distressed children and families appealed to that segment of the black and broader Detroit community sympathetic to the plight of the poorly housed, although other issues clearly competed for public attention.[34] Rhonda William's history of black women's organizing in Baltimore public housing directly parallels my investigation, for the female leaders in Detroit also powerfully translated their racial, class, and gender standpoints as black women into a broader empathy for the disadvantaged. "Nobody should be homeless," as one leader reasoned about a subsequent squatting campaign, "so we took the door down." Another leader estimated the racial / ethnic composition of people involved in the campaign's climatic battles as roughly 80 percent black, 20 percent white, and a small percentage Latino.[35]

• *Mobilization Costs versus Group Resources and Networks*

Involvement in these public-housing and homelessness protests carried formidable costs—for example, police arrests, jail time, bodily injury, threats to recipient benefits or housing / shelter rights.[36] For instance, the city threatened to evict Corrine Jones from her apartment for aiding vacant-unit squatters in Brewster-Douglass, and on more than one occasion homeless women and men were arrested, hassled, and injured during demonstrations. One advocate for the homeless summed up the dilemma of facing such costs: "I know from self-experience that it's hard to be talking about standing up and fighting when you don't know where your next meal is coming from."[37] Despite these limitations, an array of group resources and networks created communal incentives for participation.

The most outspoken Short End of the Stick members were from a circle of African American women who were long-term residents with strong ties and enduring memories of their community—Jones, Hull, Milton, Byers, Nelson, and so on. Among their resources were their ties to broader activist networks. The welfare-rights organizers Marian Kramer and Yvette Linebarger heard a rumor through relatives and friends in Brewster-Douglass, as well as counselors at Michigan Legal Services, of an undisclosed demolition plan. Kramer explained, "[Linebarger's] mother kept giving us reports of what was happening over there at Brewster. There was a plan for it to become part of the Medical District. She saw that." These organizers established an advocacy base in the complex from a meeting they held with two hundred or so residents to lobby for the timely payment of recipient checks, and "that gave us the base to have another meeting," Kramer informed me.[38] Soon an interested group of tenants materialized, and in light of the personal and communal costs of losing a thousand units, they committed themselves to challenging the city's plans.

Short End of the Stick was joined and assisted by allies who were key members of the low-income-housing network, including the National Welfare Rights Union and the Michigan Welfare Rights Organization; the United Community Housing Coalition (UCHC); Michigan Legal Services; and Cass United Methodist Church. Maryann Mahaffey was cited as the strongest City

Council ally along with Mel Ravitz and Erma Henderson. The DWCUH was also assisted by a vibrant network. The National Union of the Homeless wanted to make Detroit its fifteenth chapter in the late 1980s and helped found the DWCUH at the invitation of Linebarger and Kramer. Prior to the founding of the DWCUH, these national organizers joined with Detroit welfare-rights and antipoverty activists to initiate the first phase of an ongoing squatters campaign in vacant Brewster-Douglass units. The purpose was to attract media attention to the existence of the homeless union. The DWCUH was preceded by a short-lived homeless advocacy group called the Detroit Homeless Society Union that militated for the Nuisance Abatement Ordinance. Along with Short End of the Stick, the union was a member of the larger umbrella group called the Michigan Up and Out of Poverty Coalition that was to this struggle what SOS was to CDBG budget battles.[39]

## The Utility of Brewster-Douglass Activism

### • *The Black Regime versus Disruptive Coalitions*

Unfortunately, these organizers lacked alliances instrumental enough to derail the Young regime's plans. Because of the City Council's oversight powers and HUD requirements that it approve the final demolition plan, the council became a focal point. In reality, the mayor's political sway and strong executive powers thwarted much of the council's ability to reach independent conclusions about the demolition plan. Nonetheless, the Brewster-Douglass coalition insisted that the council take action on the pending crisis to hold the administration and the DHD accountable. On March 24, 1987, one hundred fifty Brewster-Douglass residents and their supporters mobilized largely under the banner of Short End of the Stick. Earlier they had requested and were granted a public hearing. On behalf of Short End of the Stick, Grace Byers declared, "If the city was serious about solving the problem of homelessness, they wouldn't allow the tearing down of houses."[40] Accompanying the residents at this hearing were its core organizational supporters, including the UCHC, whose board chair, Lee Griffen, wrote in a signed petition, "We question the use of modernization funds to demolish housing units. We believe modernization funds should be used to repair occupied and vacant units at the Brewster-Douglass Development."[41] Each speaker, whose comments were punctuated by loud applause and cheering from the audience, said he or she opposed demolition and distrusted DHD Director Lewis. This at least convinced skeptical council members to directly investigate the administration's claims of the buildings' ramshackle conditions.

In 1987 the council unanimously approved $50,000 in CDBG funds to conduct its own audit of area housing needs and to assess the costs of public-housing preservation. By 1989, council critics resorted to walking tours of the properties to express their reservations about the plan, because Mayor Young summarily declared any budget appropriation for a council audit illegal. He then asserted executive prerogative in refusing to hire the council's selected housing consultant and successfully vetoed its attempts to implement separate line-item appropriations for certain public-housing complexes. Short End of the Stick and its coalition partners were outraged by the council's failure and returned in August to plead their case before they initiated a campaign of occupying units early in 1988. Frustration with the council's incapacity had come to a boiling point by February 1989, and this is when activists occupied the City Council chambers, as described earlier.[42]

• *Electoral Confines versus Adaptive Tactics*

Also as discussed earlier, one of the reason activists took over the mayor's office in 1989 was because it was an election year, and throughout this campaign they devised new tactics—squatting in public-housing units, vacant private units, and HUD-owned properties; using the courts—to expand news coverage. On January 19, 1988, during a casino-gambling ballot measure supported by the mayor, two dozen demonstrators accompanied by their children chanted, "Housing, yes; casinos, no!" and "Open the door for the poor!" They tore open a few units of Brewster-Douglass and briefly squatted in them. Police quickly arrested four persons, including Marian Kramer and her spouse, General Baker. She said that advocates later used "the courtroom as a classroom" to challenge the charges, which eventually were dropped.[43] Meanwhile, the crowd at the original protest grew to at least two hundred persons, including Council Member Mahaffey and members of the press. Shortly thereafter, Lewis agreed to meet with protest leaders and to have the DHD transport prospective homeless applicants from shelters to the housing department. In turn, the department agreed to make two hundred units available for immediate occupancy. Since the takeover had generated "bad press" for the administration, the mayor may have sent a directive to the DHD to cooperate, for as Kramer said, "We knew that Coleman had said that he didn't need that crap there."[44] Sympathetic news coverage from reporters, including Zachare Ball of the *Detroit Free Press*, contributed to the administration's anxiety. To further quell the situation, there was even a point in 1988 when Young invited Corrine Jones from Short End of the Stick to attend a meeting he called at the executive mansion with other tenant leaders. Spokespeople for the homeless publicly voiced optimism about the Lewis agreement; still, they braced themselves when this optimism soured due to a decline in the number of homeless placements.[45]

## Timing and the Brewster-Douglass Protest Cycle

### • *Activists Cycles and Strategic Advantages*

To be sure, it was the right time for the campaign—1988 and 1989 were election years and represented peaks in Detroit's activist cycles—but the campaign still lacked a strategic advantage. The transition in HUD secretaries, from the lackadaisical and scandal-tainted Samuel Pierce under Ronald Reagan to the outspoken, free-market idealist Jack Kemp under George H. W. Bush, resulted in increased scrutiny of the DHD and the Young administration not simply from HUD field offices but from Washington. In addition, because the winter was the most hazardous time for people to remain outdoors, and this attracted several media profiles of the homeless, activists often timed their takeovers during the winter and early spring months. In late February 1989, homeless leaders announced their intentions to mobilize, and three weeks later they squatted in Lewis's office. They believed that the DHD played divide and conquer, for it only completed the housing placements of homeless union leaders. Lewis refused to meet with the protesters but released a statement. A year later, members of the DWCUH again occupied vacant Brewster units during a cold February day. As an antecedent to their most dramatic demonstration, where they literally stood before bulldozers, these activists cited the wasteful practice of maintaining utilities in boarded-up apartments. Even though Short End of the Stick presented Lewis and the DHD with a list of 500 persons who stated their willingness to move into vacant Brewster apartments, nearly everyone on this list was discounted as ineligible and thus not contacted.[46]

However, neither federal officials nor the courts were able or willing to veto the demolition plan, even as they called for greater scrutiny of the DHD. In several instances, campaign leaders appealed directly to members of Congress to counter the city or to reverse federal policies. During a visit to Detroit by HUD Secretary Kemp, residents asked him about the demolition of Brewster units. He attempted to allay their concerns by restating the federal government's commitment to high-quality and affordable housing.[47] Before the demolition of Brewster units was to proceed, activists wired Kemp and asked him to intervene, to no avail. Thus, activists strongly implicated HUD in the neglect of the homeless and public-housing tenants. "You can't just blame Coleman Young and the city of Detroit," Ruth Williams, the leader of PLAN, reasoned. "It first has to come from the federal government."[48] Thus, the poorly housed were left to the vagaries of an already unaccountable and truculent housing department. A DHD official coarsely responded to my inquiry about whether activists' concerns were legitimate: "All those fuckers wanted to do was to tear the boards off and grandstand and get political. You ask anyone of those son-of-a-bitches, 'How many of you have ever applied to live in public housing?' Not one of those fuckers raised their hand. They had never applied to live there! They were playing the political game."[49]

## Race, Class, and Accountability from Brewster-Douglass Activism

In the end, the city administration won the fight for demolition at Brewster-Douglass in June 1990 on procedural grounds, because activists lacked one necessary strategic advantage: the one-for-one replacement rule. It was part of the 1990 Housing Act and went into effect weeks after HUD approved Detroit's application for demolition. It would have required the administration to rebuild as many units as it demolished. Attorneys with Michigan Legal Services argued that the act of demolition, not the approval of the application, was the starting point, and thus the rule applied. The First Circuit Court disagreed. Furthermore, the City Council provided no redress because Council Members Mahaffey, Ravitz, and Butler were out voted by a majority persuaded by the administration's argument that 1,037 apartments were obsolete and required only 250 modern replacements. When I asked Council Member Nicholas Hood Sr. about the opposition of "community groups" to demolition, he denied that any such opposition existed and instead framed the problem in terms of race and poverty: "It wasn't any community groups. It was just some of the white liberals on the City Council. They figured they knew best what these folks needed, and those of us who live out here in the community knew that they needed something better than that old worn-out housing built in 1938. Even though it was brick and steel it was worn out. It had the wrong image. It was infested with drugs, crime, and other things that go along with vacancy and a lack of security."[50] At the time, Hood was the pastor of Plymouth Congregational Church and had an adult development center; both of them were in the neighborhood of Brewster-Douglass.

In September 1990, a dramatic scene ensued when about seventy-five activists chained themselves to construction fences or hid inside units so that the police had to do an exhaustive search prior to demolition. Having lost this campaign, however, advocates won a limited victory. Lewis's political isolation in the administration was increased by his criticism of Secretary Kemp's tenant homeownership plan. This infuriated Kemp, and he accused Lewis of "disrespecting" tenants' abilities. In October 1990, Young accepted Lewis's resignation as DHD director.[51]

## THE PARKSIDE AND JEFFRIES PROTEST CYCLES, 1990–1993

Activists regrouped after the Brewster-Douglass demolition aware that it was only the first of a multiphase plan to thin out Detroit's public-housing stock, and thus units in the city's other major projects, especially Parkside and Jeffries, were next in line. In October 1989, a Detroit coalition of more than 1,000 persons consisting of homeless advocates (120 persons sponsored by the DWCUH), public-housing tenant groups, and community development organizations traveled to Washington, D.C., to participate in the "Housing Now!" march. Mobilized by an umbrella group that included the National Low-Income Housing Coalition, the National Housing Coalition, the National Union of the Homeless, and the Community for Creative Non-Violence, these Detroit activists were joined by 200,000 participants from across the nation. Local events were held in dozens of communities in support of the march and its Capitol Hill lobbying.[52]

After the march, the Detroit steering committee decided to form a group called Preserve Low-Income and Affordable Housing Now! (PLAN) in March 1990. This umbrella formation's unique contribution to the movement was its assistance in establishing separate affiliates at Detroit's large public-housing developments, and these affiliates served as local bases for residents' and activists' mobilization in opposition to DHD policies. Like Short End of the Stick, PLAN was led predominantly but not exclusively by black women who were long-term residents and passionately wanted to save their homes. Among the leaders were Ruth Williams from Herman Gardens Homes, Delores Eaton and Elizabeth Mack from Jeffries Homes, and Betty Cole and Bobbie Hurd from Parkside Homes. PLAN claimed several hundred individual members, and its chief organizational supporters and executive-board representatives were all connected to the same low-income-housing network that supported Short End of the Stick.[53] Overall, the protest opportunity structure that confronted PLAN was somewhat different from Short End of the Stick's experience, and PLAN had an important strategic advantage that made a difference in forestalling demolition.

The Context of Parkside-Jeffries Activism

• *Black Politics versus Collective Identity and Framing*

Akin to Short End of the Stick, PLAN framed the DHD's negligence as a problem that should concern all black Detroiters but met resistance from black leaders in three chief ways. First, the main reason PLAN gave for its existence was its belief that the formal representatives of Detroit public-housing tenants, the Board of Tenant Affairs and the elected resident councils, were too closely aligned with the Young administration in a patron–client relationship. This was partially corroborated by HUD's assessment that the BTA was over-funded at the expense of many resident councils. PLAN's executive-board chair, Lenora Lewis, maintained: "For so long we've been forced to accept the leadership the Housing Department has put on us. We need to recognize our own leadership, leaders who are about building something, not tearing it down!" One organizer, Doug Smith, directly decried these politics and compared them to those of Chicago's infamous political machine.[54]

Second, race and black politics not only complicated HUD's scrutiny of the DHD but tempered the support of black community leaders, including ministers. Another PLAN organizer recounted one meeting with a ministerial alliance:

> See, the churches here were against PLAN—the African American churches. When we attempted to do the first paint up in Jeffries Homes in early May 1991 (I don't remember), we went to the Detroit Ecumenical Council to get support for that. A Detroit city official, one of the mayor's aides, came in, and the discussion got so vicious and he brought up the fact that there were "legitimate public housing groups and illegitimate ones." The question became, "Is this [PLAN] a legitimate public housing group?" And he [the official] said, "No." They voted not to help us. We were going to paint one hundred senior citizens' apartments in Jeffries we could identify that had not been painted in twelve to fifteen years.

Later, she clarified that the vote had gone "down racial lines. The black ministers [voted] 'no,' and the white ministers [voted] 'yes.'"

Not all black leaders shunned alliances with PLAN, but there was a third problem of how PLAN challenged black politics. At times, PLAN and its allies disagreed with how mainline black leaders framed the interests of the poor as they led anti-homelessness and antipoverty movements. For example, in the fall of 1990, the Michigan Up and Out of Poverty Coalition, which included PLAN and the homeless unions, vehemently opposed Republican Governor John Engler's decision to cut 90,000 persons off of General Assistance. The coalition set up several "Englerville" tent cities on city properties, including the Jeffries Homes, and tried to embarrass the Young administration for insisting that the tents were a fire hazard. They had several supporters, including student activists at the University of Michigan, who set up their own tent city in Ann Arbor.[55] Civil-rights leaders and a handful of black ministers joined the campaign, but activists admonished Reverend Jesse Jackson Sr. when he led his own protest, without their participation, and later failed to recognize the multiracial character of their coalition. As Marian Kramer complained, "Don't pull us into no all-black meeting, because poverty has no color!"[56] While also a strong critic of Engler, Reverend Charles Adams of Hartford Memorial Baptist Church staunchly supported the Young administration and deflected any suggestion that mismanaged public housing bolstered the crisis: "How can we honestly blame Coleman Young and the City's Housing Department for the failure in public housing when the funds from the federal government have been drastically, deliberately and relentlessly reduced?"[57]

To help bridge this construction of black politics, PLAN projected a collective identity that was somewhat broader than the Brewster-Douglass campaign because it claimed members throughout the Detroit public-housing system and not just one specific complex. With a mantra of "UNITY + ACTION = POWER!" its name, "Preserve Low-Income Income and Affordable Housing Now!" and its acronym, PLAN, stated its intent to rally those in housing poverty around themes of self-empowerment and participation in determining the future of Detroit's public and subsidized housing. In fact, these themes echoed the ideal of community control, which was a key principle of the community-organizing and Black Power movements of the 1960s and 1970s. At least two key PLAN organizers, Ruth Williams and Annie Sanders (Kaleema Sumareh), had affiliations with these earlier movements.[58]

With a brochure that displayed the smiling faces and locked arms of mainly black women and men, PLAN said, "We are folks just like you! Folks who deserve a safe, decent place to live and bring up our families." The brochure emphasized their commitment "to fighting the demolition of subsidized units, as well as forced relocation."[59] PLAN informed the homeless that "under federal law you should have first priority to available vacant public housing units," and it expanded the list of previous demands for preservation and rehabilitation to include "tenant empowerment—Resident Management!"[60] While my interviews with activists revealed their belief that such frame bridging did not insulate PLAN's female leaders from the sexist attitudes of a few male comrades or its low-income black leadership from the racially patronizing attitudes of some white supporters, this group had an expansive identity as a multiracial and class-elastic movement of women and men.[61]

• *Mobilization Costs versus Group Resources and Networks*

To reiterate, police arrest and further mistreatment by the public-housing bureaucracy were heavy burdens for the poor to bear. However, black women's circles of personal contact and involvement not only emboldened PLAN leaders such as Elizabeth Mack and Ruth Williams but planted seeds of dissent among ordinary participants willing to bear the costs of otherwise extraordinary actions.[62] For example, in the wake of Engler's welfare cuts, PLAN and Michigan Up and Out of Poverty led two hundred and fifty demonstrators in protests outside Jeffries Building D as seventy persons squatted on a vacant sixth floor. For seven hours, protesters tussled with a phalanx of Detroit police and made the latter so apprehensive that Chief Stanley Knox and his deputy arrived by helicopter to lead a charge. A total of eight people were arrested. Richard Williams, a coalition spokesperson, declared their fearlessness: "We are saying we don't have a damn thing to loose. They've taken everything else they can take." Echoing sentiments said during the Brewster-Douglass takeovers, one protester scoffed, "They want to put us in jail? Fine. It would be a step up." Picketers chanted, "No Housing, No Peace. . . . They say cut back, we say fight back." Council President Mahaffey arrived to lend support and admonish the mayor and the DHD for not opening up vacant units. Mayor Young implied his hands were tied: "To illegally occupy housing is not the answer, and I certainly understand the crisis. . . . But anything that we do at this level of government is minimal."[63]

In general, organizational resources and networks subsidized PLAN's activities. Along with Taylor and Kramer, PLAN was supported by the public-housing organizers Annie Sanders and Doug Smith of UCHC, anti-homelessness activists including Wayne Pippin and Nate Thomas, and the community development groups of Karen McCleod of Cass Corridor, Maggie DeSantis of Warren/Conner, and Rosa Sims and Roz Edwards of U-SNAP-BAC. PLAN and UCHC organizers helped to establish the Jeffries Homes Resident Empowerment Committee, which was a pivotal contributor to several takeover actions in the Jeffries buildings; they also organized the first democratic tenant-council election that Parkside Homes had witnessed in several years.[64]

## The Utility of the Parkside-Jeffries Protest Cycle

• *The Black Regime versus Disruptive Coalitions*

It was reasonable for PLAN to fear that Parkside Homes—as surrounded by working-class to middle-income tracts, as well as a golf course, commercial areas, and a hospital—was susceptible to the same regime agenda that targeted Brewster-Douglass units. Again, the DHD planned to demolish 737 units and replace them with 257 at an estimated cost of $23 million. Residents who could not be newly accommodated would be given housing vouchers. Poverty deconcentration was the DHD's stated goal. Had there been an atmosphere of trust, the city and the residents might have pondered cooperatively how to turn around a complex that was more than 80 percent vacant. But there was not. What disrupted the administration's plans for Parkside and Jeffries, however, was an imperfect but still powerful storm of external and internal pressure that included skeptical HUD field agents, a Republican administration in Washington that encouraged demolition as a scheme to reduce vacancy but considered the Young administration incompetent, and a militant low-income housing alliance in Detroit that was vehemently against demolition. All three created a disruptive coalition of sorts.[65]

In November 1991 HUD Secretary Kemp repackaged $222 million in emergency housing aid to respond to the aftershocks of Governor Engler's cuts but demanded that the Young administration make responsible use of these funds. To ensure this, Kemp appointed Elmer Binford of Kansas City to head a response team whose mission was "Operation Occupancy," or the relocation of a thousand homeless persons into vacant public housing. Binford was an interesting choice because in the 1970s he investigated the massive HUD housing scandal. Throughout his investigations in Detroit, especially his unannounced site visits, Binford was praised by PLAN members and council allies for the full disclosure of his findings. He once told a *Detroit Free Press* reporter, "We find it indefensible that almost half of [the DHD's] 8,000 units . . . are vacant. Many of them in our judgment could be rehabbed . . . and put back on the market . . . within a couple of months."[66] Along with the media attention his investigations received, Binford gave PLAN activists additional, concrete evidence to challenge the DHD. When combined with PLAN-related protests, this pressure gained new homes in the Jeffries buildings for 172 families—a small dent in the citywide waiting list of 800—and bolstered PLAN's case for greater housing occupancy.[67]

• *Electoral Confines versus Adaptive Tactics*

Federal allies notwithstanding, the strong-arm politics of the Young administration and its supporters still thwarted PLAN as it demanded local accountability to the homeless. One of the council members who eventually voted for Parkside demolition was Kay Everett. Although she began as a critic of the Parkside plan—for she accompanied Council Members Mahaffey and Jack Kelley on a walking tour—advocates believed she was later pressured by the administration during her reelection bid in 1993. Shortly thereafter, she became adamantly in favor of demolition. At a subsequent public hearing, according to one account, Everett prefaced remarks to PLAN spokespeople by expressing sympathy with their situation but proceeded to accuse the spokesperson of being "duped by plantation politics." The inference was that disingenuous white organizers were merely using this older black woman and her fellow Parkside residents as a cover for their own self-interested policy agendas. The woman broke into tears after the comment.[68]

Activists devised new tactics to attract media attention or to directly serve the needs of the homeless, and often they did both. Between 1991 and 1993, PLAN and its allies orchestrated a series of actions to move a number of homeless families and individuals into vacant Jeffries units. PLAN and Up and Out of Poverty formed a third group called Help Everybody Live Properly (HELP) headed by Tommy Rudolph, a homeless mechanic. Although some residents complained about the squatters and suspected them of crime, Rudolph reasoned, "No one should live in a cardboard box."[69] Due to the lax state of public-housing management, Rudolph easily commandeered first-floor office space in Jeffries (complete with a working telephone and cherry-wood desk) and supervised the preparation of apartments and the move-in of more than a dozen families before the DHD got wind. Evictions were served against these formerly homeless families, but Steve Lockhart, an attorney with the UCHC, aided in their defense. Forty families eventually were given formal leases by the Archer administration after a 36th District judge gave them a reprieve.[70]

## Timing and the Parkside-Jeffries Protest Cycle

### • *Activist Cycles and Strategic Advantages*

Political-opportunity theorists remind us that regimes are particularly open to dissent when they have powerful external critics or suffer from periods of transition and instability. In this case, the Parkside-Jeffries cycle emerged at a moment when the Young administration was more vulnerable to criticism than had been true with the Brewster-Douglass cycle. While the administration retained considerable power, it critics possessed a significant veto. After successive audits discovered that public housing in Detroit was in a state of severe neglect and Lewis was forced to resign, top HUD officials were increasingly critical of the DHD and no longer overlooked infractions. In addition, Kemp's tenant ownership and management thrust provided empowerment advocates with a platform. Overall, HUD pressured the DHD to allocate more of its vacant units to the homeless just when, unknown to most, Young's long tenure in office was ending.[71]

What most differed about the Parkside episode was the strategic advantage activists enjoyed from the federal one-for-one replacement requirement (effective as of February 1990). It ensured that the Parkside plan came under wider scrutiny than had the Brewster-Douglass plan. One interesting council ally for the activists was Reverend Keith Butler, who, due to his Republican ties with Kemp and HUD, kept HUD from taking back $50 million in unspent CDBG funds.[72] When the City Council approved the Parkside demolition plan in a 6–3 vote, with Mahaffey, Ravitz, and Butler dissenting, HUD officials deemed cost estimates exorbitant and eventually halted the plan because it was in violation of the rule. Furthermore, HUD mandated that the administration soften its posture toward tenant advocates and include them as participants in a $27 million revitalization planning grant. Modest reconciliation even occurred between the DHD, HUD, and tenant leaders (including representatives from Parkside) under the auspices of Young's last DHD director, John Codwell. Still, Kemp remained so frustrated with the DHD that he moved to place it under federal receivership on the eve (as in the noon before) of the Clinton presidential inauguration. Only lobbying from the new Clinton administration aborted this move.[73]

## Race, Class, and Public Accountability from PLAN's Activism

Along with the temporary halting of the demolition plan, activists claimed another victory with the "Operation Occupancy" plan of the Binford–Hagood team, but it was fleeting. By October 1992, about 389 new occupants out of a goal of 1,000 were placed, but afterward the number of placements slowed to a trickle. HUD and the DHD sent very conflicting signals. Whereas the DHD administrators ignored the policies issued by the department's Board of Commissioners, which mandated that priority be given to homeless people, HUD agreed with this policy in one instance and backtracked shortly thereafter. Furthermore, a majority of the placements were single men, who, due to a lack of programming funds, were given no intervening social services in buildings composed predominantly of elderly black women. PLAN activists took a self-help approach and did all they could by organizing committees to clean up the designated apartments and the surrounding areas before new residents moved in. They also located furniture and household appliances and connected these new residents with social services and job-training referrals. Yet when I asked Ruth Williams what difference these efforts made in improving public housing and the lives of the homeless, she responded, "A drop in the bucket."[74]

PLAN was able to effectively use the lessons of Brewster-Douglass to gain at least a modicum of leverage against an administration that, from the view of activists, up until that point had not been accountable. When the new administration of Mayor Dennis Archer came into office a year later and had the generous support of the Clinton administration under HUD Secretary Henry Cisneros, PLAN and its allies were cautiously optimistic. Still, they used takeovers in the Jeffries Homes to aggressively push Archer's administration. PLAN assumed that the change in administrations was only a cosmetic improvement until there was concrete and sustained evidence of responsiveness.[75]

## CONCLUSION

As in previous chapters, this chapter's purpose has been to describe how low-income-housing advocates overcame the obstructions to effective black grassroots activism. At odds with the Young administration's de-concentration-through-demolition approach to public-housing renewal, a group of public-housing tenants and homeless citizens, led by black women, demanded that the city preserve and rehabilitate Detroit's scare public-housing stock. The two interrelated campaigns I have examined in this chapter fit the pattern of what social-movement scholars call "protest cycles." But overall, the second campaign—the Parkside-Jeffries campaign—was more successful than the Brewster-Douglass campaign.

Table 9 summarizes why the Parkside-Jeffries campaign had greater success. Within the cells of the table, the plus and minus signs are relative indicators of whether the Brewster-Douglass or Parkside-Jeffries campaign confronted greater or smaller barriers to activism and enjoyed greater or smaller advantages and contingent solutions to these barriers. The more plus signs, the stronger a factor's influence; the more minus signs, the weaker its influence.

Both groups were passionate, earnest, and ingenious in how they contested demolition, but the Parkside-Jeffries campaigned had more allies, advantages, and (to a degree) tactical innovations. Along the dimensions of context, timing, and utility, both groups confronted formidable "barriers." But the Parkside-Jeffries cycle gained momentum precisely when the Young administration, already in its twilight, faced greater federal scrutiny. So the second cycle's mobilization costs modestly decreased as the regime weakened and usual electoral confines loosened. From the "solutions" side, the Parkside-Jeffries campaign enjoyed the "context" benefit of greater group resources and networks because it was the beneficiary of pre-existing affiliations. "Timing" was on the side of both movements, but it benefited the Parkside-Jeffries campaign more, for it

**Table 9.** Opportunities for effective black grassroots activism: Brewster-Douglass versus Parkside / Jeffries campaigns

| | Context | | Timing | | Utility | | |
|---|---|---|---|---|---|---|---|
| Barriers → | Construction of black politics | Costs of mobilization | Rules of the game | Regime transition | Constraints of black urban regime | Confines of electoral arena | Accountability |
| Brewster-Douglass 1987–90 | ( – – ) | ( – – ) | ( – – ) | ( – ) | ( – – ) | ( – ) | |
| Parkside Jeffries 1989–93 | ( – – ) | ( – ) | ( – – ) | ( + ) | ( – ) | ( + ) | |
| Solutions → | Collective identity and framing | Group resources and networks | Strategic advantages | Activist cycles | Disruptive coalitions | Adaptive tactics | |
| Brewster-Douglass 1987–90 | ( + ) | ( ++ ) | ( – – ) | (+) | ( – – ) | ( + ) | Placed more than 30 persons; lost fight to stop demolition |
| Parkside Jeffries 1989–93 | ( + ) | ( + ) | ( + ) | ( ++ ) | ( + ) | ( ++ ) | Placed more than 389 homeless persons; temporarily stopped demolition due to one-for-one replacement rule |

began on the heels of a national low-income-housing movement and belonged to a more intense activist cycle. Moreover, Parkside-Jeffries had the strategic advantage of a federal one-for-one replacement rule, which temporarily halted demolition at the Parkside Homes and ordered the Young administration to assume a more cooperative posture in re-planning Parkside. Finally, under "utility," the Parkside-Jeffries cycle made a few tactical innovations, though neither campaign was able to form an effective disruptive coalition with the City Council. However, these activists did form an uneasy alliance with Secretary Kemp and federal auditors to the degree the federal government became increasingly critical of the Young administration. In this regard, one can say that the protests of Parkside-Jeffries, which were relatively larger in magnitude, helped to compel the administration to account for its actions, even if the administration was not self-motivated in its responsive to public-housing residents and thus was not very accountable.

Compared with the community development activists I discussed in chapter 5, the political-opportunity structure and activist efficacy of public housing and anti-homelessness advocates clearly differed in at least three ways. First, the anti-homelessness activists were predominantly though not solely African American and had fewer allies on the City Council, in contrast to the often black-led but majority-white SOS. Second, community development activism benefited from a shift in the balance of power between the city's legislative and executive branches, where public housing and anti-homelessness activism had to rely on an external rule change and the federal government. Third, the insurgent protest strategy of these public housing and anti-homelessness activists clearly differed from SOS's primarily interest-group strategy of lobbying for public funds through an institutionalized process, with secondary uses of protests. Across chapters 5 and 6, I have shown that, when we hold context and timing relatively constant (same city and same decade of activism), we gain theoretical purchase in understanding utility variances or, rather, differing forms of grassroots activism. In the last section of this book, I hold utility and timing constant as I vary context by examining housing policy and activism after Young and beyond Detroit. This permits me to more fully comment on the democratic implications of this work.

# PART III

*Black Grassroots Activism after Young and beyond Detroit, 1993–2005*

# 7

## A Change Is Gonna Come?

*The Archer Regime and Housing Politics beyond Detroit*

**While [we] want the city to boom and you build a building here a building there, don't forget to build the human beings to be able to appreciate the buildings you have built.**
**—Elizabeth Mack, Jeffries Homes Resident Empowerment Committee, 1995**

### FROM PROTEST TO PARTICIPATION

Coleman Young's Detroit has been my focus for much of this book. This chapter expands that focus and examines the years after Young and cities other than Detroit where grassroots leaders used new tactics to ensure policy accountability to the black poor. In the mid-1990s, public-housing activists shifted tactics from protest activities to routine participation in the Homeownership for People Everywhere (HOPE VI) program. Residents served on revitalization task forces and thus contemplated the physical redesign of and new social services for their beleaguered developments. Effectively they turned to the same kind of activities community developers had employed since the late 1970s. HOPE VI garnered praise for the way its "mixed-income" innovations reduced public housing's concentrated poverty. However, I examine how it posed a set of missed and mixed opportunities with regard to policy accountability to the poorly housed in black-led cities.[1]

Several public-housing leaders shared the initial optimism of other Detroiters when newly elected Mayor Dennis Archer's close alliance with the Clinton administration resulted in $126 million in HOPE VI funds to revitalize Detroit's public housing. The Westside complex of Herman Gardens was designated as one of Detroit's three HOPE VI sites and received $24 million. In 1995, Herman Gardens' tenant president, Ruth Williams, said of Archer's housing director, Carl Greene: "We know Carl and what he stands for. He worked for the tenants and has a strong backbone; he respects us and is compassionate."[2] At the time, she and several other Herman Garden residents were hard at work devising the first of several revitalization plans for their long neglected development. In 2006 nearly ten years after Herman Gardens was completely razed, a DHC brochure implied that on this same site, admittedly "prime real estate" close to downtown, a sparkling new "Gardenview Estates" was built, with "an innovative educational expansion, a state-of-the-art recreational center, a tree-lined central park, and trendy retail shopping."[3] When I visited the site, all that existed, except for the foundation for a new Boys and Girls Club, was a huge, prairie-grass-strewn lot with a fallen sign that read, "Detroit Housing Commission Herman Gardens Revitalization—Together We're Rebuilding Neighborhoods." Clearly, the city administration missed this opportunity for HOPE VI to make a real difference. Revitalization at Parkside Homes or the Villages at Parkside reveals an entirely different story, due in part to this community's stronger ally network (see Figures 11–12).

In this chapter, Mayor Archer's new liberal regime for development and housing is the backdrop against which I contrast the successful tenant activism and HOPE VI rebuilding of Parkside Homes with the less successful tenant activism and the then unrealized HOPE VI rebuilding of Herman Gardens. To extend beyond Detroit, I compare these two cases to a case in the black-led city of Atlanta (Techwood / Clark Howell Homes) and, to a lesser extent, cases in Newark (Archbishop Walsh Homes) and Washington, D.C. (Ellen Wilson Dwellings). When combined, all five of these cases demonstrate my contention that higher levels of tenant involvement led, in relative terms, to smaller degrees of tenant dislocation and neighborhood gentrification.

My purpose is to advance two larger points. First, the context for effective black grassroots activism in the 1990s and early 2000s was shaped by whether a regime and its public housing authority *missed opportunities* to properly use new federal subsidies and the period's growing economy to create genuinely mixed-income public-housing communities, not simply gentrified inner-city havens. Second, effective activism was determined by the *mixed opportunities* grassroots leaders had and acted on to recruit allies, exploit advantages, and adapt their tactics to HOPE VI, which professed that the participation of lower-income citizens was vital to the renewal of public-housing communities. What mattered is whether regime politics did not corrode the collective identity of tenants and prevent them from framing a project's goals and implementation. Overall, this chapter demonstrates how my Effective Black Activism Model and its broader considerations of activist utility, timing, and context can be generalized beyond Detroit.

**Figure 11.** Gardenview Estates site. Photograph by the author.

**Figure 12.** Villages at Parkside complex, July 2006. Photograph by the author.

## MISSED OPPORTUNITIES: ECONOMIC CHANGE AND THE ARCHER REGIME

Dennis Archer's election as mayor in 1993 was significant for several reasons, but especially for his regime's implicit break with a Young regime that had endorsed his opponent, Sharon McPhail. Four years later, a final indicator of regime change appeared as thousands of Detroiters mourned the passing of Mayor Young, "the old lion."[4] Archer's election was also significant because he pledged to change the tone or reshape the construction of black politics by building new bridges between Detroit and its previously hostile white suburbs and between disenchanted Detroiters and City Hall. Similar to Mayor Bill Campbell of Atlanta, Mayor Cory Booker of Newark, and Mayor Anthony Williams and Mayor Adrian Fenty of Washington, D.C., it is fair to argue that Archer's first mayoral campaign was "de-racialized," for he promised to transcend old racial divides, work with a Republican governor, and spur new business investments. Still, he clothed many of his appeals in a populist, self-help rhetoric when once he told Detroiters not to wait for City Hall but to "go with your neighbor to cut the weeds in the lot down the way on your street."[5]

In an early campaign document whose stated purpose was to solicit public comment, housing was one of the nine priorities that candidate Archer foresaw as critical to Detroit's renaissance over the next decade. He envisioned a comprehensive housing strategy led by "a strong leader, a civic entrepreneur" who could facilitate public–private partnerships: "Our public housing needs to become a priority and units need to be repaired and rehabilitated. We also have sufficient vacant land that virtually new communities and entire new neighborhoods can be built."[6] Such statements signaled Archer's intention to establish a new liberal regime of free-market initiatives.

Archer assembled on his transition team, as well as hired in his administration, several people who were active in the city's low-income-housing advocacy network and frequent dissenters of Young's policies. Most notably, he hired Angela Brown-Wilson, former deputy director of the Warren / Conner Development Coalition, as one of his chief executive aides. Many of these community leaders endorsed and worked on his campaign and were members of the SOS or other grassroots advocacy coalitions. When coupled with the city's improving economic fortunes and the announcement of Detroit as an Empowerment Zone (EZ), such changes had, in the minds of many citizens, set the stage for "a New Day in Detroit."[7]

## An Improved Economic Context

The decade of the 1990s was a period of unprecedented national economic growth that partially benefited black Americans, including black Detroiters. Table 10 presents a mixed picture with regard to housing, but an optimistic one overall. A quarter of Detroit's black households were still below the poverty line in 2000, but this was nearly four points lower than the median for the comparison cities. In fact, the table reveals that whereas Atlanta, Newark, and Washington, D.C., each witnessed percentage increases in black poverty, Detroit's black poverty fell by 8 percent. Detroit's unemployment rate also dropped from 20 percent to 14 percent while Atlanta's increased from 9 percent to 14 percent. To be sure, Detroit far outpaced these cities with regard to population loss and housing-unit demolition, but black Detroiters witnessed the greatest increases in their median incomes and clearly had higher rates of homeownership. Detroit historically has been a residential city, and its depressed housing market ensured that moderate-income renters, on average, paid less than a third of their income in rent. Black poverty and housing poverty were still formidable in Detroit, but a buoyant automobile industry, coupled with public–private investments such as the EZ, likely provided opportunities to combat poverty.[8] All the same, Detroit spent only two-thirds of the comparison group's median per capita expenditure on housing and community development.

## Archer's New Liberal Regime and Downtown Redevelopment

A new liberal philosophy motivated the Archer administration's strategy to spark economic development and revive low-income housing. President Bill Clinton and Mayor Archer developed a political affinity because Clinton led and Archer was an active member of the centrist Democratic Leadership Council. Like other "New Democrats," both were promoters of middle-of-the-road policy solutions that appealed to their liberal bases, in some respects, but also relied on alliances with, if not ideas advocated by, conservatives.[9] In racial terms, new liberals like Clinton and Archer galvanized their left-leaning bases by symbolically endorsing racial justice and social diversity while eschewing explicit appeals for black empowerment. So while Archer incorporated grassroots advocates into his administration and at times used black populist oratory, his "de-racialized" governing strategy infuriated the Black Nationalist Black Slate, especially when he rejected the casino bid of the only black-led developer or agreed with Republican Governor John Engler's plan to partially

**Table 10.** Detroit racial, economic, and housing comparisons with selected cities, 1990–2000

| | Detroit | Atlanta | Newark, N.J. | Washington, D.C. | Median |
|---|---|---|---|---|---|
| Total population, 2000 (in thousands) | 951.0 | 416.4 | 275.2 | 606.9 | 511.7 |
| Population growth, 1970–2000 | −37.0 | −16.2 | −19.6 | −5.2 | −17.9 |
| % Total population black, 2000 | 81.2 | 61.0 | 58.5 | 65.9 | 63.4 |
| % Blacks[a] in poverty, 2000 (1990–2000 difference) | 25.7 (−8.1) | 33.5 (+3.2) | 31.7 (+2.2) | 23.7 (+4.5) | 28.7 |
| Black[a] median income, 2000 (1990–2000 difference) | $30,664 (+$5,441) | $27,637 (+$3,703) | $27,552 (+$1,751) | $34,248 (−$906) | $29,151 ($2,727) |
| % Black[a] homeowners, 2000 (1990–2000 difference) | 54.9 (+3.4) | 40.9 (0.0) | 23.8 (+2.0) | 39.8 (+2.3) | 40.35 (+2.15) |
| % Moderate renters paying more than 30% in rent, 2000 | 23.4 | 43.3 | 41.4 | 36.6 | 39.0 |
| Building permits, 2000: single-family and (multi-family) units | 72 (294) | 803 (5,016) | 110 (751) | 187 (619) | 148.5 (685) |
| Number of single-family units demolished, 1990 | 1,945 | 202 | 9 | 89 | 146 |
| Housing and community development expenditure, per capita, 1997 | $98 | $36 | $89 | $214 | $156 |

*Source*: U.S. Department of Housing and Urban Development, State of the Cities data set.

[a] Household measure.

take over Detroit's schools. In terms of redistribution, William J. Wison's "hidden agenda" thesis inspired new liberal attacks on black poverty by promoting policies with universal economic benefits. Archer's early policy statement also advocated attacking "aberrant" underclass behavior through a de-concentrated housing strategy akin to what would become HOPE VI.[10]

By definition, new liberalism quietly privileges the interests of capital and requires an urban regime or a development coalition to bolster corporate preferences with public authority. To be sure, a formidable set of challenges confronted the new Archer administration as it tried to put a fresh face on Detroit's beleaguered image and extend olive branches to a hostile white suburbia. After years of the racially proud but irascible Coleman Young, Archer pleasantly surprised the pundits and the white business community when he made important accountability reforms and was committed to aggressively pursuing economic development. Still, one critic drew parallels between Young and Archer: "Now [Archer] is on the Tiger stadium, big-ticket stuff, Fox Town, the Casino stuff. He's trying to land [an auto] plant. Sounds like somebody else we know, doesn't it [laughter]?"[11] During his two mayoral terms, Archer succeeded in ways Young could not and built a new liberal urban regime, which affected his priorities toward low-income constituencies.[12]

Early in his first term, Archer hired Gloria Robinson, former director of development for Wayne County, to lead a newly created Planning and Development Department, a merger of the Community & Economic Development Department and the City Planning Department. For a time, she helped coordinate Detroit Empowerment Zone planning. Detroit Renaissance, an organization whose members included forty-three of the region's most powerful CEOs, was one of the initial corporate stakeholders the Archer administration consulted to plan the EZ. Later, this organization launched a new initiative, the Empowerment Zone Financial Institutions Consortium, which made a commitment to lend $1.1 billion to prospective businesses and homeowners within the EZ. Detroit Renaissance also established a $53 million Detroit Investment Fund whose purpose was to help fill the "gaps" between what new EZ businesses could borrow and the start-up or improvement capital they needed. Another spin-off of Detroit Renaissance members was the Greater Downtown Partnership, many of whose members Archer not only appointed to the Detroit Economic Growth Corporation (DEGC) and Downtown Development Agency but helped to gain title to the old Hudson's Building property to redevelop the site.[13]

For eight years, Archer's urban regime navigated around various City Council objections to and community protests of the "privatization" of city planning, although Archer respected planning as process more than Young had. Archer's regime enjoyed a long list of development victories, including the construction of a new baseball stadium (Comerica Park), a new football stadium (Ford Field), and three casinos (the MGM Grand, Greektown, and Motor City); the construction of a new Compuware corporate headquarters; the construction of the Campus Martius downtown park and forum; the General Motor's takeover and the $500 million redevelopment of Detroit's Renaissance Center office complex; the construction of several new downtown condominium developments (especially Woodward Commons); and the scheduling of Super Bowl XL for 2006.[14] It was in tandem with this new form of urban renewal and its guiding philosophy that the Detroit EZ and HOPE VI emerged. As was later true of HOPE VI, some of the outcomes of the EZ coincided with the regime's goals, even though this was not the intention of grassroots advocates.

## The Empowerment Zone's Political Opportunities and Problems

Reminiscent of the Community Action Program and Model Cities programs of President Lyndon Johnson, the Empowerment Zones and Empowerment Communities (EZ/EC) program created new political opportunities for Detroit community developers and other advocates to influence the targeting of federal dollars at economically distressed neighborhoods. However, these community leaders enjoyed mixed success, for despite the alliances they formed and the strategic advantages they took, the EZ/EC program paralleled HOPE IV in its unintended displacement of the very poor.

The EZ/EC program began as part of the 1993 Omnibus Budget Reconciliation Act's Title XIII. To newly attack poverty and spur inner-city revitalization, this program had four key policy components, including the use of tax incentives, targeted spending, strategic planning, and public–private partnerships. True to Bill Clinton's policy-triangulation approach, this "hybrid" approach combined conservative, free-market ideas such as tax breaks for businesses to locate in the inner-city with traditional liberal ideas such as direct grants for education, job training, and child care.[15]

In December 1994 the Clinton administration announced Detroit as one of only six EZ cities. The others were Atlanta, Baltimore, Chicago, New York, and Philadelphia / Camden. Newark was among a third tier of sixty designees named Enterprise Communities. As of 2000, these communities had received $1.5 billion in performance grants, not including the millions of dollars leveraged from private investments.[16] Once completed, the Detroit EZ included just over 100,000 persons (roughly a tenth of the city's population) and encompassed neighborhoods within the Southwest, Woodward Corridor, East Central, and Eastside—18.4 square miles. While Detroit in 1990 was 73 percent African American, 21 percent white, and 3 percent Hispanic, the zone, as a concession to Detroit's ethnic diversity, was 60 percent African American, 21 percent white, and 11 percent Hispanic. Forty-seven percent of all EZ residents lived below the poverty line, compared with 32 percent across the city. Eighteen percent of the houses in the EZ were vacant, and only 31 percent were occupied by their owners, while the respective rates for the whole city were 9 percent vacant and 53 percent owner-occupied.[17]

Because the EZ planning process emerged in the long shadow of the Young era, the Archer administration first had to contend with the lingering distrust community activists harbored against City Hall's development motives. Such fears were never completely allayed, but the outcomes of the process validate my broader thesis. The community participation victories that community-based organizations (CBOs) and community development organizations (CDOs) enjoyed were partly due to their ability to form disruptive coalitions (or create alliances) and to use strategic advantages.

First, these groups were able to form disruptive coalitions that reminded Archer they were among the major backers of his candidacy and thus could legitimately assess whether he was keeping his pledge to be accountable to community groups ignored by the Young regime. For example, one of my interviewees claimed that the first Archer campaign heavily relied on the PEOPLE's Platform of 1989 to devise its community-revitalization proposals. Key leaders of the SOS coalition who had backed Archer later formed a CDO trade association called the Community Development Advocates of Detroit (CDAD). Charlene Allen observes that at an initial public meeting, CDAD representatives directed their lengthy testimony at the administration to demand the significant inclusion of CDOs and CBOs in the initial Working Group, due to their disenchantment with other non-inclusive planning efforts such as Archer's "Master Plan Task Force." In one heated meeting where CDO leaders confronted the mayor, they walked away with the agreement that community representatives would hold 60 percent of the seats on the EZ's governing board.[18]

Second, they exploited strategic advantages as they underlined the broad federal requirement of a "bottom-up" planning process and capitalized on their connections with insiders in the Archer administration who relied on CDOs' expertise. Janice Bockmeyer observes that mutual work on past advocacy campaigns helped cement a niche network among Detroit CDOs. Again, this network enabled the CDAD to stress in Detroit's application the evidence that Clinton officials expected of significant community collaboration. A number of SOS or former SOS leaders took key roles or memberships in various EZ planning groups, including Angela Brown-Wilson, Maggie DeSantis, Donald Softley, and Karen McCleod. In an interview during the first several months of Archer's administration, DeSantis, of the Warren / Conner Community Development Coalition, expressed a genuine confidence that Archer greatly differed from Young in his leadership, but she also cautioned that his administration was "in a mess of trouble. So they are just going to have to make some hard decisions, and he's not going to be popular."[19]

According to an interim assessment of the Detroit EZ in 2001, the zone appears to have witnessed dramatic improvements in its employment rate, number of businesses, poverty rate, and vacancy rate. However, there are strong indications that these improvements were due to the dislocation of poor families out of the zone, especially given the demolition of public housing through the HOPE VI program. Taken at its worst, the EZ and HOPE VI, as I explain, unwittingly were new forms of urban renewal in Detroit as well as Atlanta. Despite the best efforts of community advocates, most low-income families were not the chief beneficiaries of these new economic opportunities.[20]

## MIXED OPPORTUNITIES: HOPE VI AND SHIFTS IN BLACK GRASSROOTS ACTIVISM

My purpose in this section is to understand the mixed opportunities for public-housing activism to be effective as it tactically shifted from protest to programming in Detroit, Atlanta, Newark, and Washington, D.C. During this particular period (i.e., timing), protest was viewed as less necessary (i.e., utility), because the political environment (i.e., context) had changed. In fact, between 1993 and 2000, housing issues may have constituted as little as 1 percent of all the protest issues newspapers covered.[21] When viewed through the lens of my theory, shifts in regimes and resources prompted new forms of participation, which meant that this period likely constituted a valley in Detroit's housing-protest cycles. There was a tactical shift from protest to program participation not simply because Archer was a new mayor who described himself as a responsive reformer. New resources—tens of millions of HOPE VI programming and revitalization dollars—encouraged tenants to start up businesses, participate in social-service activities, and devise revitalization plans.

### Public Housing and HOPE VI's De-concentration Approach

The Clinton administration inherited parts of the Reagan-Bush de-concentration-through-demolition strategy to improve public housing. The Department of Housing and Urban Development Reform Act of 1989 created a National Commission on Severely Distressed Public Housing with the hope of tackling the fundamental disrepair of many public-housing complexes. In 1992 the commission forwarded a set of recommendations, and Congress enacted the Urban Revitalization Demonstration, or HOPE VI, program. The program had several objectives, but principally it tackled concentrated poverty through a host of public and market-rate incentives that encouraged newly remodeled and class-integrated communities. As of 2004, HUD had awarded some 446 HOPE VI grants in 166 cities. These funds were targeted at 63,000 severely distressed units, and 20,000 units were slated for demolition. Only 15 out of 165 programs funded by HOPE VI had been completed by 2002.

A bevy of other de-concentration initiatives supported HOPE VI's objectives, such as the post-1994 repeal of the "one-for-one replacement" rule for public-housing demolition; the one-strike rule that punished criminal infractions in public housing; tenant-based assistance or community-support services (job training, child care) as opposed to project-based assistance; and the recruitment of higher-income families to reside in "mixed-income" public-housing neighborhoods while low-income families were urged to take more scattered-site Section 8 vouchers. The latter initiatives stemmed from the Quality Housing and Work Responsibility Act of 1998, the public-housing analog to the Republican Congress's welfare-reform bill of 1996. The combined programs of the de-concentration-through-demolition approach—Comprehensive Grant Program, the Major Reconstruction of Obsolete Projects (MROP), and HOPE VI—had razed some 137,000 units by the end of the 1990s and fundamentally reduced the scale of public housing in the United States. Public housing officials assumed that a smaller program was preferable to the threat of concentrated poverty.[22]

HOPE VI provided the Archer administration with a unique opportunity to dramatically improve the livelihoods of low-income citizens and turn around public housing in a way that was consistent with economic-development goals. From the very beginning of Archer's tenure, HUD Secretary Henry Cisneros strongly supported his efforts to rejuvenate Detroit public housing. Table 11 compares Detroit's public-housing department and its 1993–95 federal funding streams to those in Atlanta, Newark, and Washington, D.C. By 1995, Detroit had the smallest number of units of the three Public Housing Authorities (PHAS),

**Table 11.** Comparisons of public-housing management and funding, fiscal years 1993–95

| | Detroit | Atlanta | Newark, N.J. | Washington, D.C. | Median |
|---|---|---|---|---|---|
| Total public housing units, 1995 | 8,159 | 14,461 | 11,553 | 11,666 | 11,610 |
| % Buildings large and old (non-elderly units)[a] | 72.7 | 56.4 | 66.3 | 39.4 | 61.35 |
| PHMAP[b] PHA scores | 37.35 | 55.45 | 70.88 | 22.38 | 46.4 |
| PHA-wide vacancy rate | 39.6 | 15.0 | — | 19.0 | 17.0 |
| Average Comprehensive Grant amount, 1993–95 (in millions) | $28.261 | $30.418 | — | $27.814 | $28.037 |
| Total HOPE VI Implementation Grant, 1993–95 (in millions) | $87.927 | $42.412 | $49.996 | $15.671 | $46.204 |
| Ratio of HOPE VI to CGP, 1993–95 | 2.89 | 1.50 | — | — | 1.03 |
| Total HOPE VI Implementation Grant, since 2000 (in thousands) | $111,651 | $164,669 | $84,996 | $161,152 | $136,000 |

*Source*: U.S. Department of Housing and Urban Development, *A Historical Baseline Assessment of* HOPE VI, Volume 1: *Cross-Site Report*, July 1996; HOPE VI Revitalization Grants, revised June 2007.

[a] "Large" means developments with more than 300 units; "old" means developments constructed before 1960.

[b] PHMAP is a quality score used by HUD to rate a local PHA. The scores range from 0 to 100. PHAs with scores lower than 60 are considered "management-troubled"; those with scores higher than 90 are considered "high-performing."

the highest number of large and old buildings, and the highest authority-wide vacancy rate (nearly 40 percent) and was second only to Washington, D.C., in its PHA quality rating (70 is a passing grade). By 1995, Detroit had by far the largest HOPE VI award, $88 million, which was $41 million above the median amount. The ratio of its HOPE VI to Comprehensive Grants was nearly 3–1, whereas for its counterparts there was roughly a 1–1 match. Again, by 2001 Detroit had been awarded a total of $126 million, but by 2007 it only retained $111 million. By 2007, Atlanta had been awarded $164 million, or $30 million more than the median amount.[23]

Table 12 compares the HOPE VI project characteristics of the four cities. Detroit's three HOPE VI projects were Jeffries Homes, Herman Gardens / Gardenview, and Parkside Homes. Of the four PHAs, the Archer administration planned to demolish the largest number of units, even though Detroit had the smallest public-housing stock of a city of its size. As evidence that the lack of replacement tenants was well under way by the mid-1990s, all four cities had vacancy rates ranging between 50 percent and 100 percent. In the three Detroit projects, plans were to demolish as little as half and as much as the entire development and, as was true with the Brewster-Douglass development years earlier, to replace only a fraction. Compared with those in its counterparts, residents in Detroit's HOPE VI sites were equally segregated by race and income, although greater numbers of Atlanta's Clark Howell residents relied on public assistance. It is difficult from the very limited survey information to discern whether residents across these developments were equally satisfied, but probably a majority of them did not want to relocate.

## Detroit: Eastside and Westside Development versus the Parkside and Herman Gardens Plans

As discussed in the previous chapters, the activists of PLAN and their allies occupied vacant public-housing units during Archer's transition period to pressure Lisa Webb, acting director of the Detroit Housing Commission (DHC), and other administration officials to address unit vacancy.[24] As these advocates claimed victory and made the transition from protest to programming, the administration proved incapable of meeting its commitment to improve public housing. Part of the blame for the DHC's deficiencies can be attributed to HUD's continued lack of oversight, which meant there was no real assurance that the DHC had the capacity to implement HOPE VI projects. Beyond managerial acumen, however, resident leaders had to contend with the ideological stigma some HOPE VI personnel and DHC staff members harbored against

**Table 12.** Comparison of characteristics of HOPE VI modernization projects, 1993–1996

| | Detroit | | Atlanta | | | Newark, N.J. | Washington, D.C. |
|---|---|---|---|---|---|---|---|
| | Jeffries[a] | Herman Gardens/ Gardenview[b] | Parkside[c] | Techwood | Clark Howell | Walsh | Ellen Wilson |
| 1996 residents | 998 | 554 | 375 | 411 | 587 | 359 | 134 |
| Year opened | 1950 | 1943 | 1938 | 1936 | 1940 | 1953 | 1941 |
| Total units | 2,170 | 1,444 | 737 | 624 | 457 | 630 | 134 |
| % Estimated units vacant, 1994–96 | 54 | 56 | 100 | 94 | 1 | 56 | 0 |
| Estimated units planned for demolition, 1996 | 1,344 | 906 | 737 | 624 | 457 | 630 | 134 |
| Estimated units replaced on-site/ off-site, 1996 | 626/264 | 538/342 | 345/180 | 360/284 | — | 502/0 | 134/0 |
| % Black | 99 | 99 | 99 | 95 | 98 | — | — |
| Estimated resident household income, 1993 | $5,508 | — | $5,508 | $3,950 | $3,960 | $5,856 | — |
| % Residents on public assistance | 43 | — | 46 | 51 | 62 | 46 | — |
| % Tenants satisfied with apartments | 76 | — | — | 76 | — | — | — |
| (total surveys) | (41) | — | — | (50) | — | — | — |

*Sources*: U.S. Department of Housing and Urban Development, *A Historical Baseline Assessment of HOPE VI*, Volume I: *Cross-Site Report*, July 1996.

[a] Missing estimates from Tom Nut-Powell (Capital Needs Unlimited) Memo to Detroit Housing Department, May 12, 1995.

[b] Missing estimates from Herman Gardens Resident Design Team and CMTS, Inc., *Herman Gardens Revitalization Plan: Executive Summary, Vision on the Move*, revised 1 March 1996.

[c] Missing estimates from Parkside Resident Design Team and Capital Needs Unlimited. *Parkside Revitalization Plan*, circa 1996.

their demands for decent and affordable housing. One staff member tersely concluded that such demands rested on "this whole concept of entitlement that they [tenants] allowed to be stacked into their brains as opposed to, shit, go out and go to work!"

### • *Public-Housing Management under Archer*

During the mid-1990s, there was modest progress in public housing, but its results proved to be mixed and transitory. Archer appointed experienced and well-received professionals as his first housing directors, such as Betty Turner from Sacramento, California, and, later, Carl Greene. Turner initially established good rapport with tenants but resigned after only seventeen months. To this day, it is not known whether she resigned because she felt that Detroit's problems were intractable.[25] Greene succeeded Turner as director and by 1997 had instituted reforms, including Section 3 tenant-run programs, that managed to raise Detroit's public-housing-quality score enough for the authority to be temporarily removed from HUD's troubled list. There was even an appreciable decrease in crime rates in Detroit's public housing. On the strength of these reforms, Mayor Archer recommended in September 1998 that the DHC become a fully autonomous PHA, a move that the City Council and city labor unions resisted for several years.[26]

By 1999 these modest reforms had evaporated. A backlog of 14,000 citizens were waiting for rental subsidies; possibly as much as $18 million in HOPE VI funds had been misappropriated; projects had been delayed for several years; and the administration conceded that it needed HUD's assistance to administer $430 million in housing funds.[27] After Greene, Irene Hannah served as interim director of the DHC for a year and was replaced by John Nelson, a housing professional from Indianapolis. Moreover, it took the Archer administration seven years after the demolition of several Jeffries buildings to begin constructing the replacement family dwellings, Woodbridge Estates. HUD alleged enormous cost overruns with the Villages of Parkside complex, to the tune of at least $7 million. And the city lagged in its efforts to find $100 million in private investment to break ground on the new Herman Gardens units after relocating four hundred families and razing every unit.[28]

### • *Resident Involvement and HOPE VI Politics: Parkside versus Herman Gardens*

One of the clear strategic advantages advocates had is HOPE VI's requirement that residents participate in the redesign and approval of plans to deconcentrate public housing. Yet Susan Popkin and colleagues note, "Because

HOPE VI guidelines never clearly stated what constitutes 'participation,' individual sites have had considerable latitude in defining it."[29] The difference between misplaced and realized hopes in each context depended on whether tenants could unite among themselves (collective identity) and recruit allies (coalitions) able to align tenants' aspirations with specific redevelopment priorities (framing) while retaining a modest strategic advantage.

**PARKSIDE** • Of all of my cases, the Parkside community demonstrated the strongest community capacity because of its strong collective identity, framing ability, network of allies, strategic advantages, and programmatic innovations. After all, its community leaders benefited from extensive advocacy experience, for during its most recent protest cycle (1990–93) it had successfully resisted Mayor Young's Parkside demolition plan. With various allies, especially the Warren / Connor Neighborhood Development Coalition, Parkside leaders used their anti-demolition victory as leverage when they drafted the first HOPE VI / Urban Revitalization Demonstration grant. Roughly five years after formal planning began, the first complexes of the "Villages at Parkside" opened, in August 1999. The 737 units of the old complex and its annex of 329 units were mainly composed of two-story, two-bedroom town houses sitting on a forty-acre parcel. Overall, Parkside's attractive environs included a golf course, a community college, and a bustling commercial area.[30] The neighborhood to the east of it in the late 1980s was solidly middle class and stable. As of May 2001 HUD had awarded the Villages at Parkside project one of Detroit's largest HOPE VI grants—almost $48 million—and more than $500,000 for a planning grant. Parkside's resident leaders and their developer allies leveraged this award into a total of $82 million, and by June 2000 they had constructed or revitalized 462 units and 43 buildings within the Villages of Parkside II and IV complexes.

Even while its original mixed-income criteria were greatly relaxed, the Parkside design group's imaginative plans called for the development of four villages—a total of 987 rehabilitated or newly built units, including 427 on-site and 350 off-site homeownership units—financed with HOPE VI funds and "silent second" mortgages or collateral from conventional bank loans. Residents planned several community-support services, such as day care, youth and senior services, a parenting-skills program, and a job-referral network. Among the most imaginative ideas was the creation of a limited liability corporation called the Parkside Services Endowment, Inc., in which $4 million (netted from Low Income Housing Tax Credit investments) was to be deposited in an interest-bearing account and yield $400,000 annually to fund community services. Unfortunately, the DHC never followed through with the groundwork needed to pursue the idea.[31]

The Parkside Services Endowment was the brainchild of Thomas Nutt-Powell of Capital Needs Unlimited (CNU), an expert in housing, planning, and development. Although he was white and Parkside's leaders were African American, Nutt-Powell eventually earned these leaders' trust because of his persistent desire to empower them by designing the highest-quality housing possible. My interviews with people who helped coordinate the Parkside planning process revealed that there were initial tensions among residents and between residents and project developers, especially as one set of leaders was succeeded by another. Nonetheless, Parkside greatly benefited from a strong network of leaders and allies. Virgil Hammond, Catherine Rowe, Carol Mayes, and Helen Nesbitt were among these key leaders. The Parkside Resident Council was a vital participant in the process, as was a longstanding support organization called the Friends of Parkside.

As a way to strengthen the bonds between the residents and project managers, Nutt-Powell hired a native Detroiter and African American, Curtis Smith, to serve as the on-site coordinator. He also earned the residents' respect. In turn, Nutt-Powell subcontracted a number of African American firms for the construction and rehabilitation work on the Villages. Parkside likewise had a number of community partners, such as the Northeast Guidance Center, Project Safe Havens, and Operation Get-Down, as well as allies on the City Council, especially Council President Mahaffey. The entire design process was highly participatory and involved the use of a unique, full-scale design laboratory where resident designers could visually contemplate the dimensions of units by positioning walls and unit features. Unfortunately, the collaboration between Parkside and CNU came to an end in 1999 when Greene departed as director. Nelson was appointed in his place, and according to one source, the "race card" was used to justify a shift from a white contractor (Nutt-Powell) to a black contractor.[32] Nonetheless, the relative successes of this process stood in sharp contrast to the frustrations of Herman Gardens residents.

**HERMAN GARDENS** • Herman Gardens represents a case in which outspoken leaders' best efforts to create a strong collective identity, a network of allies, strategic advantage, and programmatic vision were undermined by regime politics and bureaucratic malaise. To reiterate, its site remained a huge, barren parcel as late as the fall of 2006. Herman Gardens was originally built in 1943 and contained 1,444 units on 160 acres of land, which it shared with Gardenview apartments. First designated as a HOPE VI project through an MROP grant in 1995, Herman Gardens received $24 million in HOPE VI funds, not including a portion of $400,000 for an earlier planning grant. In 1998, all of its remaining residents were relocated, and in April 2000, all of its remaining units were razed. This dislocation fundamentally undermined Herman Gardens' community capacity. Two years later, while its latest revitalization plan lay dormant, HUD notified the DHC that it was in default of its agreement. A 2007 construction plan slated $4 million for community-support services and called for $232 million in mixed-income development, or "804 units—470 rental units (including 258 public housing units) and 334 homeownership units." Other elements of the plan included construction of a regional athletic facility on the site and "250,000 square feet of institutional space for a new community college."[33]

It is no wonder that resident leaders expressed disappointment about DHC's failure to act on no fewer than six separate revitalization plans. Marlita Jenkins, Carol Brantley, Jacqueline Wright, James Fuller, and Ruth Williams, who also was vice-chair of the Resident Council, were among the members of the Resident Design Team, led by then president Evelyn Bradshaw. They unanimously approved the first plan in February 1996. Mildred Ray, Mary Square, and Carla King also became involved. Working over a twenty-eight-week period and assisted by J. Scot Rogers of CMTS, Inc., they devised an innovative plan for their new community that made use of the Parkside real-time design laboratory and called for 400 to 600 renovated units, with limited to no demolition, especially with MROP funds. The low-income advocates Ted Phillips and Annie Sanders (Kaleema Sumareh) of the United Community Housing Coalition, as well as Marilyn Mullane of Michigan Legal Services, also worked with these residents.[34]

Unlike at Parkside, the regime's displacement and dispersal of the Herman Gardens community thwarted its best efforts to press for the implementation of its rebuilding plan in several ways. First, this displacement eroded its strong collective identity and active network of residents and allies. Williams believed that Greene isolated critics like her and actively courted or rewarded resident supporters. She stated that she discovered plans to completely demolish Herman Gardens only when, at a HOPE VI conference, Greene casually informed those present, "Oh, we're tearing it down." Another resident leader sitting behind Williams registered her reaction: "Every strand of hair on my neck stood up."[35] Williams further alleged that, prior to this announcement, Greene had briefed other resident leaders on the demolition, who likely knew that an earlier pledge of $1 million in renovation funds was untrue. Second, the razed complex was subjected to passing speculation about whether a more productive use of its land would be commercial or industrial redevelopment as opposed to housing. Housing officials readily conceded that the property was so well-placed and "massive" that it "provides a potential locational advantage for a variety of non-residential uses."[36] Allegedly, when one DHC developer and consultant asked Williams about her reaction to the construction of a Toyota plant on the site, she claimed that her vociferous response was, "Hell, nah, not in this lifetime!"[37]

Third, Herman Gardens was literally out of "site" and out of mind and thus suffered from the DHC's extreme administrative delays. Ironically, HUD demanded that the authority give greater priority to the Jeffries and Parkside projects. In what became a war of attrition, the Herman Gardens Resident Council suffered from neglect (it was eventually disbanded), garnered much less support from prospective community-service providers, and had fewer strong allies than Parkside. Similar to Parkside, some supporters of Herman Gardens believed the "race card" figured into why its plans stalled. Subtle staff and client tensions existed, and (according to one account) both black and white allies declined to sue the black-led Archer administration partly due to the fear of being perceived as disloyal or racist.[38]

### Atlanta: Olympic Development versus the Techwood / Clark Howell Plans

Atlanta provides an excellent point of comparison and contrast for Detroit, for as a headquarters of the Civil Rights Movement and an epicenter of the post-movement progress of the black middle class, it, too, experienced at least thirty years of black political empowerment, black mayoral leadership, and noteworthy grassroots activism. In contrast to Detroit, the work of Clarence Stone firmly establishes Atlanta as a classic black urban regime. Its first three black mayors—Maynard Jackson (1974–82, 1990–94), Andrew Young (1982–90), and Bill Campbell (1994–2002)—in conjunction with the downtown white business elite, clearly formed public–private partnerships to push through a number of central business district and area redevelopment projects such as the construction of Hartsfield International Airport, Peachtree Plaza, the Underground, and the 1996 Olympics complex.[39] While Atlanta's black homeownership rate is smaller than Detroit's, its black housing culture carries no less of a stigma against public housing. And as in Detroit, the redevelopment priorities of Atlanta's regime, especially the 1996 Olympics, rather than the critical needs of Atlanta's poorly housed citizens drove the HOPE VI revitalization process. Akin to the situation of Herman Gardens, the Atlanta regime was able to displace Techwood and Clark Howell residents and thus lessen their collective identity, ally networks, and strategic advantages, thus making planning a less effective form of activism. Unlike at Herman Gardens, the resulting Centennial Place complex is hailed as a HOPE VI exemplar.[40]

• *Atlanta's Housing Poverty and Techwood / Clark Howell*

Similar to other major cities, Atlanta witnessed a mushrooming homeless population in the 1980s and early 1990s. By the end of the 1990s, counts of the homeless varied widely from 11,000 to 47,200. Needless to say, the 2,500 available shelter beds fell woefully short of estimated needs. The Atlanta City Council further complicated the situation when it bowed to the image-conscious demands of Olympics organizers and passed a stringent anti-loitering ordinance that enacted "Vagrant Free Zones" in central Atlanta and around Olympics venues. Later, the city razed three nearby homeless shelters. Low-income renters who were unable to find housing confronted a tight rental market. Roughly 50 percent of all Atlantans paid more than a third of the fair market rate determined by HUD for a two-bedroom apartment by 2000. Thus, there was a pressing need for well-maintained public housing.[41]

Similar to the experience of Detroit, public housing in Atlanta was created by the federal government's coupling slum clearance and urban renewal with affordable housing. The Techwood and Clark Howell Homes were originally programmed as white projects when they were built in 1936 and 1940, respectively. Located in north-central Atlanta between North Avenue and Simpson Street, Techwood consisted of 604 units arranged in thirteen three-story apartment buildings, while Clark Howell consisted of 630 town homes in fifty-eight two-story buildings. The Atlanta Municipal Housing Authority designated both whites-only projects and removed as well as re-segregated the remaining black neighborhood from this predominantly white northside community. Even with the desegregation of Techwood / Clark Howell in 1968, white working-class flight served to isolate the remaining inhabitants racially and economically. Blacks made up 60 percent of the residents by 1975 and about 96 percent by 1990.[42]

The Atlanta Housing Authority (AHA), formerly the Atlanta Municipal Housing Authority, which earlier had doubled as one of the city's urban-renewal agencies, had an extremely checkered history of management and maintenance. In 1974, Mayor Jackson was appalled by the conditions he encountered when he spent a weekend at Bankhead Courts, and he immediately ordered improvements. Likewise, in the early 1980s some 10,000 violations at Techwood and Clark Howell compelled Jackson to use $17 million in HUD modernization funds, nearly the state's entire allocation, to bring these complexes into compliance with building codes. Despite these moves, Jackson initially agreed to, and then backed away from, a proposal to demolish and rebuild the project that was pushed by Paul Austin and Robert W. Woodruff of Coca-Cola and by John Portman of Central Atlanta Progress (CAP). (Coca-Cola's headquarters bordered Techwood and Clark Howell.) By the end of Jackson's third term, the AHA had so neglected the complex that residents pleaded with the governor to mobilize the National Guard to protect them from crime and drug-related violence. The AHA spent only a fraction of $19 million in HUD anti-crime funds as Clark Howell and Techwood became the city's most dangerous developments. After an inspection in 1994, HUD concluded that the authority had been so derelict in its obligations that receivership was necessary. HUD examiners gave the AHA a PHA quality score of 39 out of 100 and declared it one of the nation's most troubled public-housing authorities.[43]

• *The Olympics Plan and Pre–HOPE VI Politics*

It is against this backdrop of neglect that, in 1990, the real-estate lawyer Billy Payne and the Atlanta Olympic Committee (AOC) helped win the bid for Atlanta to host the 1996 Olympic Games. The AOC's successor, the Atlanta Committee for the Olympic Games (ACOG), which included many of the urban regime's downtown corporate stakeholders, revived interest in the plan to demolish and partly renovate Techwood / Clark Howell. The project was in the ACOG's sights because of its proximity to Coca-Cola's world headquarters, the campus of Georgia Tech, a planned Olympic Village, and a Centennial Olympic Park. A flurry of competing interests attempted to shape a Techwood / Clark Howell revitalization proposal. When Patrick Cecine, president of Georgia Tech and a member of the ACOG, independently met with a committee of Techwood residents to make a buyout and scattered-site relocation offer, he was criticized by Raymond Sales, Mayor Jackson's housing adviser, and Jane Forsten, chair of the AHA Board of Commissioners. Forsten favored a plan to rent out vacant units to Olympic athletes. City Council President Marvin Arrington opposed any demolition. Resident Association President Margie Scott said of the mayor's Olympic plans: "People need to understand that they're dealing with our lives. To them it's just politics, but it's our damn lives."[44]

These regime politics became corrosive to tenants' collective identity and any strategic advantages they might have commanded. Jackson stepped in and formed a Techwood Advisory Committee that included representatives from the Techwood Residents' Association, the AHA, CAP, and the ACOG. In July 1991, the committee hired a professional planning team, PATH, which devised an extremely vague proposal approved by 428 of 791 tenants (56 percent). The proposal called for the renovation of Techwood and the demolition and partial replacement of Clark Howell as mixed-income communities. Completely absent from the proposal and survey was any consideration of whether tenants wanted to preserve these complexes or agreed with a "mixed-income" formula.

A group of tenants, as represented by the Atlanta Legal Aid society, contested the vote and sued to overturn it, for they believed that PATH had purposely deceived them. Scott's fears that the process had irreparably divided the resident association and created intense factions were realized when Andrell Crowder-Jordan and Sammie Bolton led the opposition group and gained control of the association. HUD eventually rejected the PATH proposal on several grounds, including the failure to comply with the one-for-one replacement rule. But all of this took place prior to HOPE VI and the Republican Congress's rescinding of the one-for-one rule.[45]

• *Resident Involvement and HOPE VI Politics*

The resulting "Centennial Place" design process was mostly driven by the objectives of the Olympics and Atlanta's urban regime as the latter gentrified a low-income area it considered an eyesore in the midst of its central commercial zone. Tenant participation was difficult to muster precisely because of a vicious cycle of "de facto demolition" in which vacancy was produced when the AHA required some tenants relocate, which in turn made remaining tenants fearful of living among vacant buildings. The ranks of tenants participating in the HOPE VI process were depleted by a whopping 90 percent—from a high of 791 in 1991 to 165 in 1995.[46]

Despite the lingering misgivings of many tenants, Earl Phillips, director of the AHA under Mayor Jackson, built at least a limited partnership with Techwood / Clark Howell tenants to secure and implement the HOPE VI grant. This might have evolved into a disruptive coalition. In 1992, Phillips employed an architect with a strong background in public housing, Richard Bradfield, to follow tenants' preferences and preserve Techwood / Clark Howell while not repeating the PATH plan's mixed-income approach. Bradfield used some of PATH's design concepts but called for the rehabilitation and not the demolition of 492 units. The Phillips–Bradfield plan was approved by tenants and submitted to HUD in August 1993. Atlanta received a $42.4 million HOPE VI grant later that year, which was leveraged into $82 million for the Centennial Place project. By November, however, Mayor Bill Campbell had been elected. He articulated a new liberal vision of demolition and privatization and compelled Phillips to resign. Campbell appointed Renee Glover, one of his campaign aides, as director. While Glover has been widely credited for reforming the AHA and working with the remaining Techwood / Clark Howell tenants to design the path-breaking "Centennial Place," she also clearly embraced the regime's vision when she assured CAP that Techwood / Clark Howell "[has] to be part of the downtown agenda."[47]

With little collective identity and few genuine allies, I reiterate that Techwood / Clark Howell residents faced a dilemma like the one before Herman Garden residents. While some tenants greatly distrusted the Jackson and Campbell administrations and other regime stakeholders, others cooperated with those in power, which fueled internecine conflict. For example, Margie Scott,[48] a longtime housekeeping employee of Georgia Tech, challenged Techwood / Clark Howell leaders and became president of the Techwood / Clark Howell Resident Association and later the Redevelopment Task Force chair. Frank Johnson's field work confirmed that Scott faithfully attended all meetings and tried to have a good rapport with Glover, AHA officials, project designers, and various residents. However, veteran activists, such as Louise Whatley—a Fannie Lou Hamer protégé and leader of the militant Georgia Tenants Organization—was cynical of Scott and even led a small protest during the Techwood / Clark Howell's demolition ceremony. For all of the above reasons, it is difficult to argue that the tenants, for all of their agency and vision, had democratic control over the design process.[49]

• *HOPE VI and Centennial Place*

As mentioned, Centennial Place has been hailed as one of HOPE VI's brightest success stories. The AHA planned for and created a "mixed-income, mixed-use project with residential, commercial, community, and educational uses."[50] Along with on-site job-training programs and other social services, a $12 million state-of-the-art magnet school (Centennial Place Elementary School), a $4 million YMCA fitness center, and a new commercial area with a bank, grocery store, hotel, and police mini-station were constructed. Negotiations between tenants and other stakeholders resulted in the retention of only 540 of the original 1,081 units of public housing, which meant a 50 percent reduction. Of the 900 total units built, 40 percent, or 360 units, were rented at the full market rate. The remaining 60 percent were rented for no less than 40 percent of the market rate. Market-rate single-family condominiums were planned after 2000. Glover and the lead developers of Integral Group, Inc., insisted on these rent levels to consciously deflect the stigma of public housing, but these requirements also coincided with the regime's tacit gentrification of the area. The AHA did not issue Section 8 vouchers to all displaced tenants. In 1990, only 545, or 49 percent, of the 1,115 Techwood / Clark Howell residents received Section 8 vouchers or relocated to other public-housing units. The rest moved or were evicted, and absolutely no tracking was done until the late 1990s.[51]

## Other HOPE VI Snapshots: Newark and Washington, D.C.

• *Newark: Archbishop Walsh Homes and Delayed Opposition*

Newark is a Northeastern sister city to Detroit that in many ways is just as impoverished. Unlike Detroit, it gained very little from the buoyant economy of the 1990s and continued to suffer extreme housing poverty. New Jersey's largest city, Newark had the state's largest homeless population by 2000 and the highest proportion of public housing per capita of any city in the United States. Precisely because public housing remains central to Newark's scarce affordable housing stock, and because Newark is a city with a long history of community development advocacy and black grassroots housing activism—from its Black Power era forward—it is interesting that initial quiescence among tenants accompanied the HOPE VI redevelopment of its Archbishop Walsh Homes.[52]

Much like Coleman Young, Mayor Sharpe James built a formidable political machine to remain in office for twenty years (1986–2006). He beat Newark's first black mayor, Kenneth Gibson, and in 2002 used the "race card" to fend off the young reformer Corey Booker. Also like Young, the charismatic and hard-knuckled James built a machine-based regime, which some have identified as new liberal in its aspirations. A strong testament to his machine regime's legacy is the recent federal conviction of James and a girlfriend for their fraudulent sale of city-owned properties. When in power, his regime's list of successes included a $180 million New Jersey Performing Arts Center, a downtown condominium and commercial boom, and a minor-league ballpark. Still, Newark is a city pockmarked with vacant lots where an affordable-housing crisis looms large.[53] During James's tenure, the Newark Housing Authority (NHA) took on enormous responsibilities but had a checkered history of performance. With modernization and, later, HOPE VI funds, the NHA demolished all of its non-senior-citizen high-rise buildings, including Stella Wright, comprising some 7,500 units, and replaced only about 1,250, or 16 percent, of them with single-family town houses. In 1989, the Newark Coalition for Low Income Housing won a historic consent decree that ordered the NHA to replace or repair about 3,000 units. But all of these rehabbed units were later demolished.[54]

It is was within this context that in 1993–94 the NHA was awarded a $50 million HOPE VI grant for the revitalization of the Archbishop Walsh Homes in the city's diverse North Ward. Built in 1953, the Walsh Homes consisted of 603 apartments in nine eight-story and three-story high-rise complexes. About 62 percent of the North Ward was Latino in 1990, but about 93 percent of Walsh Homes tenants were black. A constant concern with this public-housing neighborhood was its isolation, next to busy Route 21 and along the Passaic River and thus susceptible to crime and drug trafficking. Its tenant revitalization team devised a plan to build 230 town homes and 143 off-site public-housing units—all of which were to be subsidized housing—and thus no mixed-income housing. In fact, this spurred strong tenant support for the plan. In a show of both racial and redistributive politics during a reelection bid, Mayor James claimed that he had fended off offers by high-priced developers to gentrify the complex. Furthermore, when a white tenant leader and newspaper editorialist recommended the gentrification of the Walsh Homes, James fired back that such views were "an attack on the African-Americans of the city, an attack on the public housing, and attack on the city."[55] Ironically, mixed-income was the precise formula the mayor endorsed with the other HOPE VI projects. But these racial politics might partly explain why tenants had limited initial opposition to the Walsh Homes plans. This contrasts with the controversy and protracted tenant protest over the demolition of the Central Ward's Brick Towers building (a non-HOPE VI project), which became a cause célèbre for Councilman Corey Booker, its most famous tenant and Newark's current mayor. Having said this, there was subsequent strong tenant opposition and litigation against the NHA once tenants discovered new plans for demolition and extreme delays in rebuilding parts of Walsh Homes with some money being diverted elsewhere.[56]

• *Washington, D.C.: Ellen Wilson Dwellings and* NIMBY

It is difficult for Table 10 to capture the stark differences in housing wealth and housing poverty found in the nation's capital. A recent housing survey found that the median income for home-loan applicants was $92,000, but Washington, D.C., also contained nearly half of the metropolitan area's federally subsidized units. In 2000, more than a third of those in its moderate income range paid more than a third of their incomes in rent. Given that Washington, D.C., is the capital of American politics and advocacy, it has a fertile history of public-housing activism, neighborhood advocacy, and black grassroots activism, not the least of which includes its racialized and "de-racialized" black politics. Its HOPE VI politics reflected the class and racial tensions left unresolved by new liberal approaches to poverty.[57]

As a veteran of the Civil Rights Movement and charismatic mayor, Marion Barry—with his rise (1979–91), fall (due to infamous drug charges in 1989), and resurrection (1995–99)—testifies to the power of race in black politics. Like Young and James, Barry was not beyond using the "race card" to mobilize African Americans and white liberals to electorally defeat formidable black and white opponents. While he initially linked the economic growth of downtown with the needs of neighborhood revitalization, he later was hotly criticized, especially by black community developers, for not targeting more dollars toward black and low-income communities such as Anacostia.[58] The post-1994 Republican Congress excoriated his administration for its fiscal disarray, and HUD as well as tenant groups concluded that the District of Columbia Housing Authority (DCHA) was the worst PHA in the nation. In May 1995, it was placed in receivership. Plaintiffs charged that the DCHA had demolished viable public-housing units with little regard for reuse and rehabilitation and that some of its properties were unsafe and unsanitary. In 1999, legislation was enacted to make the DCHA an authority completely independent of the mayor. Federal receivership lasted until September 2000, when the authority's public-housing-quality score sufficiently increased.[59]

With a cloud over the DCHA's operations, a group of Capitol Hill residents met and formed the Ellen Wilson Neighborhood Redevelopment Corporation. They were concerned that, since 1988, the Ellen Wilson Dwellings had lain abandoned. Located at Six and G Streets Southeast, it was composed of 13 three-story brick buildings and included 132 apartments. Subject to partial demolition from urban renewal in the 1970s and a nearby highway extension, Ellen Wilson required revitalization to keep it from further deterioration and from affecting its surrounding communities, some of which were low-income. In 1993, the redevelopment corporation persuaded the DCHA to apply for a HOPE VI grant and thus received $25 million. With a team of developers, it created the Ellen Wilson Redevelopment Limited Liability Corporation. Like Parkside planners, they used innovative urbanist designs to create a 134 unit "mixed-income cooperative" that included an additional 13 market-rate homes and a community center. The four income categories they created to ensure that the development and its "shareholders" had mixed incomes were much higher than some of the low-income members hoped. And despite the ingenuity of this shareholder approach, it encountered vociferous opposition from the Sousa Neighborhood Association, a middle-class and partly black-led group concerned that the developers did not promote outright homeownership. As James Didden, a bank vice-president and former board member, declared: "I firmly believe we're going to end up with another ghetto here in 10 years."[60] Although the new development was built, occupied by tenants (62 percent of whom were black), and fairly well received by its neighbors, these class conflicts added to its six-year delay.

## CONCLUSION

In this chapter, my purpose was to examine the varying effects of housing-related activism in Detroit as it shifted tactics in the 1990s from protest to program participation. We can only assess the effectiveness of this new participation, however, if we fully understand its outcomes. In appendix 2, Tables 17 and 18, I report census-tract figures for the three Detroit HOPE VI projects for 1990 versus 2000, as well as those in Atlanta, Newark, and Washington, D.C. Admittedly, the population, economic, and housing figures capture these projects in very different stages of completion, but is still clear that all six tracts were undergoing enormous changes, especially a 13 percent decrease in the poverty rate.[61] Thomas Kingsley and colleagues provide limited evidence that recipients of HOPE VI Section 8 vouchers who moved to non-HOPE VI sites in several cities, including the four discussed here, were relocated from census tracts of higher poverty to those of lower poverty. But most HOPE VI relocatees did not receive Section 8 vouchers, and thus this conclusion does not hold for the entire population of movers.[62] So what outcomes are clear?

First, activists were justifiably suspicious that poverty de-concentration under some HOPE VI projects had gentrification as an ulterior motive.[63] During the 1990s, Detroit's Jeffries and Herman Gardens sites and Atlanta's Techwood / Clark Howell site experienced dramatic depopulation of between 85 percent and 41 percent. But Jeffries and Techwood / Clark Howell witnessed at least a $14,000 increase in median family income, while Herman Gardens and Techwood / Clark Howell witnessed at least a 20 percent drop in their poverty rates. It is no coincidence that these projects confronted the most intense debates over their compatibility with the regime's downtown-redevelopment objectives. Second, the HOPE VI sites of Parkside and Archbishop Walsh achieved decreases in poverty on the order of 9 percent, with a minimal or, at least, a smaller decline in their populations. Parkside was the more successful case of the two, however, because it opened its first Villages at Parkside complex in 1999. The Newark project faced long delays.[64] Third, one site made greatest use of the mixed-income formula: Ellen Wilson was already an affluent tract with a median family income of $68,000 in 1990. It experienced an $18,000 decrease in median family income and a roughly 7 percent increase in poverty, with virtually no decrease in its population. Such trends very likely were the proof middle-class critics of Ellen Wilson used to argue that the new development was deleterious to the neighborhood.

Figure 13 indicates that communities that suffered less physical displacement and fewer communal divisions—Parkside and Ellen Wilson—had stronger hands to play. They recruited allies, devised innovative design and ownership concepts, and used HOPE VI's advantage of tenant participation to avert displacement and strike a better balance between mixed-income development and gentrification. Of the case studies I examined,[65] resident leaders of Techwood / Clark Howell and Herman Gardens suffered the greatest losses to the

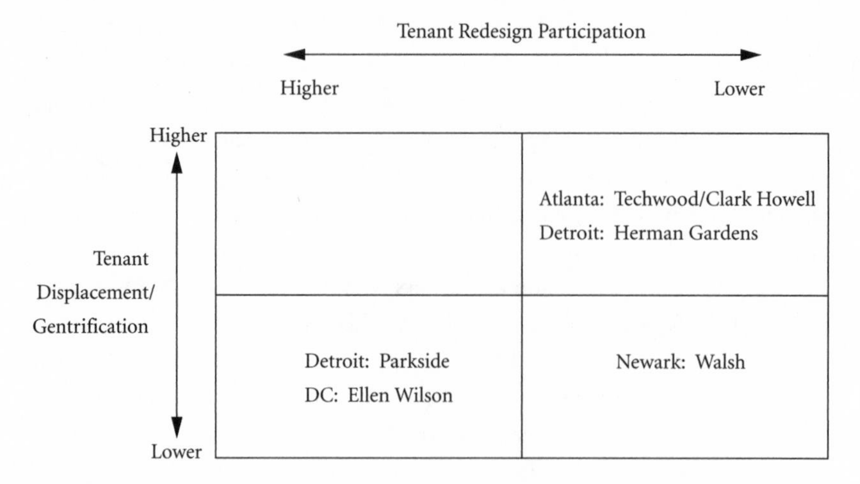


**Figure 13.** HOPE VI tenant participation versus displacement / gentrification.

forces of displacement and gentrification, partly because their tenants' unity was sapped. The Archbishop Walsh case, like Parkside, is on the lower end of the economic gentrification scale per se, but due to Sharpe James's machine-regime politics, Walsh tenants initially were less mobilized than Parkside tenants under the Archer regime. Notwithstanding the success one can attribute to Atlanta's Centennial Place, cases closer to the table's upper-right-hand corner represent public-housing authorities' *missed opportunities* to have HOPE VI principally benefit and empower current residents in the redesign of their communities. Cases in the lower-left-hand corner are the *mixed opportunities* tenants and their allies took to achieve improved public-housing communities, absent tenant displacement. More resident participation generally meant less displacement.

In the end, none of the regimes I analyzed in this chapter were fully accountable to tenants' preferences. What ultimately determined the outcome in each case is that public-housing leaders were able to recognize policy openings for what they were and creatively seize the moment. So I conclude this book as I began it: Political opportunities for black grassroots activism exist when attentive activists see them and, with imagination and courage, select the best weapon for the right battlefield.

## EPILOGUE

# More than a Drop

*The Visions of Black Grassroots Activism*

**The service that I do today is the payment that I pay my Lord for him allowing me to occupy his space right here on earth.**
**—Ruth Williams, former Herman Gardens tenant leader, 2006**

### THIS STUDY

One central premise has guided this book and my Effective Black Activism Model: Contemporary black grassroots activism and protest in majority-black cities such as Detroit can at least modestly induce black and other public officials to be accountable to black and other low-income communities when activists imaginatively use the right tactic (utility), at the right time (timing), in the right place (context.) My work has shown that strong allies, strategic advantages, and adaptive tactics (my triple As) are essential ingredients of successful grassroots activism, often as supplemented by expansive group identities, attractive goal framing, and necessary organizational resources.

Although groups that participate in interest-group systems, such as the community-developer-led SOS coalition, require the use of protest less than do insurgent groups such as the public-housing and anti-homelessness advocates of PLAN, dissident political action still plays a vital role in grassroots and post-Civil Rights Movement black politics. Different political-opportunity configurations of race, class, gender, and regime politics indicate why SOS, a predominantly white but often black-led advocacy coalition that sought to represent black and other lower-income communities, enjoyed a greater level of policy success than did predominantly black-led public-housing and anti-homelessness groups, especially Brewster-Douglass Gets the Short End of the Stick. On the utility and timing dimensions, holding context constant, strategic advantages are critically important to the success of such black-led insurgent groups, especially when they lack strong allies at the targeted level of government. On the contextual dimension (holding utility and timing constant), alliances are pivotal. Both internal to Detroit and in comparison with Atlanta, Newark, and Washington, D.C., the ability of regimes to displace HOPE VI tenant communities (and thus erode their solidarity and support) helped determine the strength of grassroots involvement and public-housing outcomes. An array of mixed and missed opportunities confronted such activists even when regimes changed—from the Coleman Young to Dennis Archer administrations in Detroit—or when programs were touted as successes, such as Atlanta's Centennial Place community.

In the final analysis, my work seamlessly melds and greatly contributes to the social-movements, African American politics, and urban-policy literature. It shows the cross-field, theoretical applicability of collective identity and framing, group resources and networks, disruptive coalitions, adaptive tactics, and strategic advantages. Moreover, my work is a realistic assessment of what is required if activists want to overcome black urban regimes, expand black politics, act beyond the electoral arena, and reduce grassroots-mobilization costs. Having summarized my key findings, the rest of this epilogue addresses a few grassroots visions that loom outside the scope of this study but motivate the activist genius I placed at the center of my model.

## BEYOND THIS STUDY: DEMOCRATIC FAITH AND DEEP DEMOCRACY

As mentioned in the introduction to this book, two theoretical bookends for my model are *democratic faith* on the front end and *deep democracy* on the back end. John Dewey also used the term "democratic faith" in his educational philosophy, and his conception partly inspires mine. Religion has played a central, though not exclusive, role in motivating the willingness of black grassroots activists to remain vigilant until social change arrives. I invoke the term, however, for a more secular—or, at least, a more ecumenical—purpose. By democratic faith, I mean the conviction that *deep democracy*—the mobilization and representation of the most marginalized citizens—will eventually compel meaningful political reform and thus induce accountability to black low-income citizens. Political scientists call such beliefs "political efficacy," internal and external, because a citizen is convinced she can make a difference through her political participation.[1] More plainly, democratic faith is the belief that, if citizens do their part, social change is not only possible but inevitable. As the great South Carolina civil-rights activist Septima P. Clark reasoned, "The only thing that is really worthwhile is change . . . and it's coming." As Martin Luther

King Jr. once poignantly declared as he paraphrased a quote by Theodore Parker: "Let us realize the arc of the moral universe is long but it bends toward justice." Closer to home, the Detroit-based leaders of the Michigan Welfare Rights Organization recruited members by using this appeal: "If you *believe* that the U.S. needs to be refocused, if you *agree* that poverty is surmountable, and *if you agree that we are capable of being better than what we see today*, then join us and let's make this thing happen!"[2]

From my work in Detroit, a wonderful exemplar of this democratic faith is the quote by Ruth Williams that begins this chapter. It was a common refrain echoed among the black and other women in Detroit I interviewed as they gave reasons for continuing in the movement despite significant setbacks. In an interview in 1994, Williams lamented that all of her group's activism had produced only "a drop in the bucket." But her comments during a follow-up interview in 2006 reinforced my conclusion that black grassroots activists—from New Orleans to Oakland, California—believe an equitable and democratic America would grant the poor and working class much "more than a drop" in the bucket. The opening quote indicates just how deeply Williams's service was fueled by a reservoir of spirituality intrinsic to black women's "activist mothering." Her second reason was linked to her first: "I would not be living where I stay at today in a decent, low-income, affordable housing unit if it wasn't for people before me that kept on pushing out there. And you have to remember, I'm the mother of eight children who raised twelve, who has twenty-four grandchildren, and five greats. I have to fight for them and all the rest of them. That's why I keep on doing the things that I'm doing until the day after."[3] Several black feminist scholars have cited black women's sentiments of spirituality, historical indebtedness, family obligations, and communal well-being as core ethics of black feminist or womanist activism. Such a faith likely believes that even if social change such as a government guarantee of high-quality, affordable housing is slow and inconsistent, and even if their grassroots activism is merely a drop of water on a rock, eventually the persistence of this activism can create small breakthroughs or, at least, smooth some of the more jagged edges of social policy.[4]

While a belief in democratic faith is a motivating vision of black grassroots activism, the realization of deep democracy is a motivating goal. J. Phillip Thompson's work nicely extended on Benjamin Barber and critiqued democratic theories that view deep democracy as a deliberative or dialogic process in which a fundamental community consensus arrives from free exchange and public forums of debate. Like Thompson, I believe that deep democracy, or what he relabeled "deep pluralism," is more fundamentally an ethic and a collective action that demands not only that those in government be accountable to their most marginalized constituencies, but that those grassroots groups that purport to represent the marginalized also hold themselves accountable to and do "not avoid the dynamics of" race, class, gender, and regime conflicts.[5]

Activists in New Orleans and Detroit continue to rely on their democratic faith to call for deep grassroots democracy. In the wake of Hurricane Katrina's devastation of New Orleans in 2005, further exposing the unnerving inequalities of race and poverty in America, the People's Organizing Committee of the New Orleans Survivor Council, a black radical coalition, demanded a "bottom-up" rebuilding process reminiscent of Ella Baker and early SNCC activism. In fact, this coalition attacked white organizers as paternalistic when the organizers attempted to predominantly speak on behalf of displaced public-housing residents in the struggle to prevent the government's demolition of salvageable public-housing developments. The resulting organization, Residents of Public Housing (RPH), led a number of demonstrations in late 2006 and throughout 2007 to protest the demolition plans of HUD and the Housing Authority of New Orleans. Along with ACORN, the RPH was one of several grassroots advocacy groups insisting that public–private partnerships such as the United New Orleans Plan or Mayor Ray Nagin's regime-oriented Bring News Orleans Back Commission reflect the voices, as well as the preferences, of the majority-black and frequently poor New Orleans citizenry and post-Katrina diaspora.[6]

Detroit's worsening economy, losses in tax revenue, and mounting budget crisis prompted new cycles of activism due to the city's cuts in vital services. Beginning in 2002, the Michigan Welfare Rights Organization (MWRO) protested the plans of the Detroit Water Department to shut off the utilities of about 5,000 Detroit residents unable to pay their water bills, and by 2006 it had pressured members of the City Council to pass ordinances that would provide partial payment options to the poor. This movement was related to similar "water wars" occurring in nearby Highland Park, Michigan. True to its long history, the MWRO's recent campaign also sought to organize what it saw as the victims of poverty.[7] So whether in the wake of Katrina's torrential rains or the Detroit River's potable waters, these New Orleans and Detroit episodes indicate how the early-twenty-first century has manifested new waves of late-twentieth-century movements for economic and racial justice.

## THE NEXT DETROIT

With these grassroots visions in mind, what possibilities do Detroit's future and the future of other black-led cities hold? The picture is very mixed. In his "State of the City Address" in 2006, Mayor Kwame Kilpatrick called for the emergence of the "Next Detroit." For all of his optimism, given that the city hosted the 2006 Super Bowl, he soberly reported that Detroit faced an enormous budget deficit of some $144 million, while negative job growth greatly depressed the city and regional economies. Four months earlier, in 2005, opponents were stunned and supporters were elated when Kilpatrick was reelected to a second term over his rival, Freeman Hendrix, a deputy mayor under Archer. In 2001, Kilpatrick was thirty-one years old and thus the youngest person ever elected mayor of Detroit, as well as the third African American. In a fashion reminiscent of Young, he overcame voters' apprehension with troubles that dogged his administration—for example, a suspected police coverup of misconduct at the mayoral mansion, improprieties in executive spending, an enormous city deficit—and mobilized his ground troops to take 53 percent of the general-election vote. To gear up for a tough race, he shed his "Hip Hop Mayor" image and gave the impression of a new political maturity by making tough decisions.[8]

Among these tough decisions was his concession in July 2005 to place the Detroit Housing Commission under a limited federal receivership; a move that his predecessors had avoided since 1979 and that Ruth Williams's housing group, PLAN, had been calling for at least since the early 1990s. HUD Secretary Alphonso Jackson announced the resignation of the DHC commission, which three years earlier had elected the tenants Betty Scott and Carol Mayes its president and vice-president, and reduced the commission to an advisory body under Lindsey Reames, the recovery administrator. Later, the DHC's executive director, Cassandra Smith-Gray, stepped down. Since the receivership, there has been limited progress. Early in 2007, the DHC still had a $4 million deficit, and, as I have discussed, ten years passed before it broke ground on the third HOPE VI site, Gardenview Estates, formerly Herman Gardens. While there were other signs of progress, including the redevelopment of Jeffries East, housing-development problems such as crime, drug trafficking, and greatly delayed maintenance persisted. HUD spokespeople simply asked residents "to hold on" for changes.[9]

On the housing-rehabilitation front, the administration of George W. Bush echoed the Reagan administration and proposed devastating cuts of as much as 50 percent to the CDBG budget. Advocates lobbied the Kilpatrick administration, as they had the Young and Archer administrations before it, to direct more money to neighbors, but a recent report found that depopulation in Detroit meant losses in the total number of CDBG dollars the city received amid its sagging economy. Overall, the housing advocates I recently interviewed were not optimistic about the prospects for real reform, especially since the same weekend that I visited in July 2006, Maryann Mahaffey, the City Council member and president who for decades had been the leading voice for the city's poor, died at eighty-one.[10]

We are in a period of transition and crisis for black politics in several black-led cities, such as Detroit and New Orleans, Newark, and Washington, D.C. In 2006 Newark and Washington, D.C., respectively elected their "Generation Next" mayors Cory Booker and Adrian Fenty. For all of the promise this new generation of black elected officials brings, some black grassroots advocates are uncertain whether they can fulfill the democratic faith placed in them to achieve deep democracy. In the spring of 2008 Kilpatrick and Christine Beatty, his aide as well as his presumed mistress, were indicted and later convicted for a perjury coverup among other charges. Just as Detroit and many other cities need local leaders able to weather the latest housing crisis and economic downturn, this scandal sparked grassroots debates about whether Kilpatrick should have resigned or continued to fight a supposedly overzealous prosecution. At the time this manuscript entered production, Senator Barack Obama (D-Ill.), a former community organizer, among other callings, was the first African American to be nominated as a presidential candidate by a major American political party, and he has since been elected president of the United States. Despite Obama's great popularity, there is vigorous grassroots debate both inside and outside the black community as to what and who the Obama administration will represent.[11] Whatever constitutes the "Next Detroit"—the next major battlefield for black political and economic justice—my work argues that the prospects for real change depend on a new and visionary grassroots leadership able and willing to demand accountability to the disadvantaged, no matter who walks the corridors of power.

# Appendix 1

*List of Personal Interviews, April 1994–April 1998, and July 2006*

| ORGANIZATION / OFFICE | NAME AND TITLE AT TIME OF INTERVIEW |
|---|---|
| ***Public Officials*** | |
| Mayor of Detroit | Coleman Young (former) |
| Detroit City Council | Erma Henderson, president (former)<br>Maryann Mahaffey, president (former)<br>Gil Hill, president pro tem<br>Rev. Nicholas Hood Sr., member (former)<br>Mel Ravitz, member<br>Rev. John Peoples, member (former)<br>Clyde Cleveland, member<br>Jack Kelly, member (former) |
| Office of the Mayor (Young) | Pamela Johnson, executive aide (former) |
| Office of the Mayor (Archer) | Lisa Webb Sharpe, executive aide<br>Angela Brown-Wilson, executive aide |
| Detroit Community and Economic Development Department (Young) | Henry Hagood, director (former) |
| Detroit Housing Department (Young) | Thomas Lewis, executive director (former)<br>Leonard Karle, superintendent of operations (former) |
| Detroit Housing Department (Archer) | Betty Turner, executive director (former) |
| Detroit Housing Department (Kilpatrick) | Dan Jones, HOPE VI construction coordinator |
| Michigan State Housing Development Authority | Darryl Sills, housing specialist |
| U.S. Department of Housing and Urban Development, Regional Office | Robert Prescott, director (telephone interview) |

| ORGANIZATION / OFFICE | NAME AND TITLE AT TIME OF INTERVIEW |
|---|---|
| ***Housing and Community Development*** | |
| Michigan Avenue Community Organization | Maryann Johnson, executive director<br>Sue Karczewski, commercial coordinator |
| Islandview Village Development Corporation | Donald Softley, director |
| U-SNAP-BAC | Rosa Sims, executive director (former)<br>Roz Edwards, associate director (former) |
| Church of the Messiah Housing Corporation | Richard Cannon Jr., executive director (former) |
| Holy Trinity Non-Profit Housing Corporation (and Michigan Housing Coalition) | Shirley Beaupre, president (former) |
| Cass Corridor Neighborhood Development Corporation | Karen McCleod, executive director |
| REACH, Inc. | Pamela Martin Turner, executive director<br>Linda Smith, director of housing and administration |
| Michigan Neighborhood Partnership | Charlene Johnson, president (also former president and CEO of REACH, Inc.) |
| CORE City Neighborhoods, Inc. | Travis Harmon, interim executive director (former)<br>Pat Alexander, associate director of housing<br>Sister Theresa Blaquiere, executive director (former) |
| Warren / Conner Development Coalition | Maggie DeSantis, executive director |
| People in Faith United Housing Corporation, Inc. | Margaret Williamson, executive director |
| YouthBuild, Inc. (and MACO) | Beverly Manick, program director (former housing director, MACO) |
| ***Low-Income Activists / Advocates*** | |
| Franklin-Wright Settlement Association of Communities for Reform Now (ACORN) | Derrick Brown, community organizer<br>Elizabeth Davis, director (former)<br>Retha Wilkins, Elizabeth Spencer, and other members |

| ORGANIZATION / OFFICE | NAME AND TITLE AT TIME OF INTERVIEW |
|---|---|
| Cass Community United Methodist Church | Rev. Ed Rowe, senior minister (former) |
| Michigan, Up and Out of Poverty | Maureen Taylor, president |
| *Detroit Free Press* | Zachare Ball, reporter, housing beat (former) |
| National Welfare Rights Union | Marian Kramer, president |
| Michigan Legal Services | Marilyn Mullane, staff attorney |
| Operation Get-Down | Bernard Parker, executive director (former); also Wayne County Commission |
| Hunger Action Coalition | Bernard Trice, training and technical assistance coordinator |
| Detroit Organization of Tenants (defunct) | Vicki Kovari, organizer |
| Detroiters Uniting (and many others) | Grace Boggs, activist |
| Westside Mothers | Selma Goode, organizer |
| ***Anti-Homelessness Activists / Advocates*** | |
| Detroit / Wayne County Union of the Homeless | Wayne Pippin, president |
| Cass Church Homeless Drop-In Center | Yvette Linebarger, program director |
| Coalition on Temporary Shelters | Peggy Posa, director |
| ***Public-Housing Activists / Advocates*** | |
| Brewster-Douglass Gets the Short End of the Stick | Bettie Milton, member |
| Jeffries Resident Empowerment Committee | Elizabeth Mack, president (co-chair, PLAN) |
| Preserve Low-Income and Affordable Housing Now! (PLAN) | Ruth Williams, co-chair |
| Friends of Parkside | Catherine Rowe, executive director |
| Parkside Tenants Council | Betty Cole, president |
| Parkside Homes | James Cartwright, resident |

| ORGANIZATION / OFFICE | NAME AND TITLE AT TIME OF INTERVIEW |
|---|---|
| United Community Housing Services | Ted Phillips, executive director<br>Annie Sanders (Kaleema Sumareh), organizer |
| Parkside Homes, HOPE VI Program | Thomas Nutt-Powell, president, Capital Needs Unlimited, Inc.,<br>Curtis Smith, site coordinator |
| Herman Gardens, HOPE VI Program | J. Scott Rogers, planner, CMTS, Inc. |

# Appendix 2

*Miscellaneous Tables*

**Table 13.** Black attitudes toward redistribution and race relations, 1976 Detroit Area Study

| | Model 1 Government guarantee of job and standard of living[a] | Model 2 Government guarantee of housing[a] | Model 3 Have nothing to do with whites[a] | Model 4 Whites want to keep blacks down[b] |
|---|---|---|---|---|
| % Agree | 84[c] | 77[c] | 5 | 33 |
| *Independent Variables* | | | | |
| Family income | −.046[e] | −.022[d] | −.094[e] | −.000 |
| | (.017) | (.010) | (.035) | (.001) |
| Education | −1.015 | 2.000[d] | 1.161 | .038 |
| | (1.543) | (1.006) | (2.529) | (.113) |
| Age | .065 | .005 | −.085[d] | −.000 |
| | (.035) | (.018) | (.042) | (.001) |
| Female | .253 | .393 | −4.449[f] | −.047 |
| | (.652) | (.463) | (1.505) | (.051) |
| Black identification | −.229 | 1.099 | 6.805[f] | .209[e] |
| | (1.127) | (.710) | (1.998) | (.078) |
| All black neighborhood | −.216 | 1.032 | 11.068[f] | .138 |
| | (1.524) | (1.103) | (3.692) | (.118) |
| Church attendance | −1.236 | −.594 | −2.628[d] | −.102 |
| | (.756) | (.524) | (1.239) | (.054) |
| Length of residence | −.038 | −.030 | .015 | −.001 |
| | (.027) | (.019) | (.036) | (.001) |
| Homeowner | 1.678[d] | .722 | 2.789[d] | .135[d] |
| | (.760) | (.538) | (1.259) | (.053) |
| Constant | 3.048 | −.035 | −9.405[e] | .423[f] |
| | 1.831 | 1.346 | (3.333) | (.142) |
| Log likelihood | −40.68 | −76.038 | −23.124 | — |
| Pseudo-$R^2$ | .218 | .087 | .501 | — |
| Adjusted $R^2$ | — | — | — | .060 |
| Standard error | — | — | — | .359 |
| Total cases | 142 | 134 | 279 | 278 |

[a] Logit coefficients.

[b] Ordinary Least Squares coefficients.

[c] Averages from combined split-sample questions with a total $N = 396$. Standard errors are in parentheses.

[d] Indicates $p < .05$.

[e] Indicates $p < .01$.

[f] Indicates $p < .005$.

**Table 14.** Black attitudes toward neighborhood mixtures, 1976 Detroit Area Study

| | Model 1 Important for neighbors to have same race | Model 2 Important for neighbors to have same income |
|---|---|---|
| % Agree | 18.3 | 52.5 |
| *Independent Variables* | | |
| Family income | −.000 | .001[a] |
| | (.001) | (.000) |
| Education | −.184[a] | −.292[c] |
| | (.081) | (.092) |
| Age | −.002 | .006[c] |
| | (.001) | (.001) |
| Female | −.009 | −.020 |
| | (.036) | (.041) |
| Length of residence | −.003[c] | −.004[b] |
| | (.001) | (.001) |
| Church attendance | −.013 | −.020 |
| | (.039) | (.044) |
| Black identification | .155[b] | .182[b] |
| | (.056) | (.064) |
| All-black neighborhood | .159 | .013 |
| | (.083) | (.095) |
| Homeowner | .007 | .009 |
| | (.038) | (.043) |
| Constant | .226[a] | .310[b] |
| | (.102) | (.116) |
| Adjusted $R^2$ | .076 | .151 |
| Standard error of the estimate | .259 | .295 |
| Number of cases | 284 | 284 |

*Note:* All are Ordinary Least Squares estimates. Standard errors are in parentheses.

[a] Indicates $p < .05$.

[b] Indicates $p < .01$.

[c] Indicates $p < .005$.

**Table 15.** Black attitudes toward voting, protest, and Coleman Young, 1989 Detroit Area Study

| | Model 1 Voting is my only say (1976)[a] | Model 2 Voted in 1988 election (1989)[b] | Model 3 Protested before 1988 (1989)[b] | Model 4 Coleman Young (1989)[b] |
|---|---|---|---|---|
| % Agreed / average | 70.6 | 68.2 | 33.7 | 71.4 |
| Family income | .016 | .293 | .067 | 5.416 |
| | (.012) | (.166) | (.190) | (11.138) |
| Education | −2.624[c] | .024[c] | .027[c] | −1.831[c] |
| | (1.211) | (.011) | (.013) | (.800) |
| Age | .091[e] | .008[e] | .005[c] | .144 |
| | (.024) | (.001) | (.001) | (.112) |
| Female | 1.105[c] | .076 | −.118[c] | 4.374 |
| | (.560) | (.051) | (.087) | (3.458) |
| Church attendance | .058 | — | — | — |
| | (.536) | — | — | — |
| Belongs to activist church | — | .186[d] | −.0176 | 6.372 |
| | — | (.063) | (.072) | (4.228) |
| Whites keep blacks down | .534 | .142 | .038 | 11.582[c] |
| | (.601) | (.085) | (.096) | (5.635) |
| All-black neighborhood | −2.499 | −.232 | −.301[c] | −.022 |
| | (1.365) | (.129) | (.143) | (.088) |
| Length of residence | −.010 | .123 | −.111 | .359 |
| | (.020) | (.077) | (.453) | (5.143) |
| Homeowner | −1.650[d] | .121[c] | .074 | −2.278 |
| | (.630) | (.057) | (.065) | (3.832) |
| Working class | .268 | — | — | — |
| | (.479) | — | — | — |
| Union member | — | .012 | .089 | .238 |
| | — | (.056) | (.064) | (3.770) |
| Protest is effective | — | .066 | .205 | 15.693[e] |
| | (.080) | (.092) | (5.411) | |
| −2 log likelihood | −65.6556 | — | — | — |
| Pseudo-$R^2$ | .211 | — | — | — |

**Table 15.** Continued

| | Model 1 Voting is my only say (1976)[a] | Model 2 Voted in 1988 election (1989)[b] | Model 3 Protested before 1988 (1989)[b] | Model 4 Coleman Young (1989)[b] |
|---|---|---|---|---|
| Adjusted $R^2$ | — | .236 | .088 | .065 |
| Standard error | — | .399 | .457 | 26.745 |
| Number of cases | 136 | 295 | 297 | 296 |

[a] Logit estimates.

[b] Ordinary Least Squares estimates. Standard errors are in parentheses.

[c] Indicates $p < .05$.

[d] Indicates $p < .01$.

[e] Indicates $p < .005$.

**Table 16.** Detroit City Council members, 1985–1993, CDBG veto overrides

| Name | Term of office/ select Council president terms | % Times voted to override Mayor's veto | Number of votes cast |
|---|---|---|---|
| Henderson, Erma | 1972–89<br>Council president, 1978–89 | 99 | 154 |
| Mahaffey, Maryann | 1974–2002<br>Council president, 1990–88, 2002–5 | 100 | 470 |
| Ravitz, Mel | 1960–73, 1982–97 | 100 | 429 |
| Hill, Gill | 1990–2001<br>Council president, 1999–2001 | 83 | 319 |
| Hood, Rev. Nicholas, Sr. | 1964–93 | 24 | 471 |
| Cleveland, Clyde | 1974–2000 | 88 | 471 |
| Collins, Barbara-Rose | 1980–90 | 9 | 209 |
| Eberhard, David | 1970–93 | 60 | 471 |
| Kelley, Jack | 1974–93 | 100 | 471 |
| Peoples, Rev. John | 1980–89 | 100 | 154 |
| Butler, Rev. Keith | 1990–93 | 100 | 315 |
| Everett, Kay | 1991–2004 | 100 | 120 |
| Median | | 99.6 | 374 |

*Sources*: Detroit City Clerk's Office; *Journal of the City Council*, 1988–93; Community Development Block Grant, 1988–93.

**Table 17.** Population, Economic, and Housing Figures, Detroit HOPE VI Sites (Jeffries, Parkside, and Herman Gardens), 1990–2000

| | Jeffries (Census Tract 5218) | | Parkside (Census Tract 5122) | | Herman Gardens (Census Tract 5454) | |
|---|---|---|---|---|---|---|
| | 1990 | 2000 | 1990 | 2000 | 1990 | 2000 |
| Total population | 1,326 | 205 | 1,734 | 1,698 | 2,962 | 749 |
| % Female | 65.1 | 61.0 | 57.4 | 55.7 | 54.9 | 52.0 |
| % Black | 97.6 | 98.0 | 92.6 | 95.8 | 91.3 | 85.7 |
| % White | 1.3 | 1.5 | 7.4 | 2.5 | 8.1 | 11.5 |
| Median family income (in 2000 dollars) | 10,202 | 26,250 | 11,396 | 16,402 | 10,992 | 17,188 |
| % People below poverty | 66.1 | 56.2 | 61.6 | 52.2 | 67.4 | 46.5 |
| % Units occupied | 50.1 | 42.4 | 47.8 | 92.3 | 57.7 | 89.8 |
| % Owner-occupied | .7 | .6 | 19.8 | 22.7 | 8.4 | 26.0 |

*Sources*: Parkside Study Group, "Final Report," July 1994, 129; U.S. Bureau of the Census, "Census Tract Details," 1990, 2000.

**Table 18.** Population, Economic, and Housing Figures, Non-Detroit HOPE VI Sites—Techwood / Howell (Atlanta), Archbishop Walsh (Newark, N.J.), and Ellen Wilson Dwellings (Washington, D.C.), 1990–2000

| | Techwood / Clark Howell (Census Tract 21) | | Archbishop Walsh (Census Tract) | | Ellen Wilson (Census Tract) | |
|---|---|---|---|---|---|---|
| | 1990 | 2000 | 1990 | 2000 | 1990 | 2000 |
| Total population | 2,706 | 1,573 | 3,859 | 3,071 | 2,150 | 2,132 |
| % Female | 53.1 | 42.0 | 51.5 | 49.2 | 40.5 | 50.9 |
| % Black | 84.4 | 67.5 | 56.2 | 32.9 | 22.0 | 23.3 |
| % White | 11.9 | 21.0 | 24.8 | 30.6 | 74.3 | 70.2 |
| Median family income (in 2000 dollars) | 6,586 | 20,972 | 27,282 | 31,563 | 68,200 | 50,046 |
| % People below poverty | 68.8 | 43.6 | 37.8 | 27.7 | 7.0 | 13.5 |
| % Units occupied | 93.2 | 94.1 | 84.8 | 81.8 | 84.6 | 91.0 |
| % Owner-occupied | 7.0 | 7.2 | 25.9 | 32.0 | 48.2 | 66.2 |

*Source*: U.S. Bureau of the Census, "Census Tract Details," 1990, 2000.

# Notes

### INTRODUCTION

1. For an interesting examination of Parker's improvisational genius, see Martin, *Charlie Parker and Thematic Improvisation*. For specific discussions about the history and performance of the song "Now's the Time," see Priestly, *Chasin' the Bird*, 57–58, 109–10, 113–14, 209–10.
2. The "Motown sound" not only revolutionized rhythm and blues but served as protest music on the picket line: see Smith, *Dancing in the Street*, 4–5, 221–22.
3. Lipsky, "Protest as a Political Resource," 55; Pitkin, *The Concept of Representation*.
4. See Gotham, "Political Opportunity, Community Identity, and the Emergence of Local Anti-Expressway Movement"; Haines, "Issue Structure, 'Frameability,' and Political Opportunity"; Meyer and Staggenborg, "Movements, Countermovements, and the Structure of Political Opportunity."
5. Again, see Goodwin and Jasper, "Caught in the Winding, Snarling Vine." But in all fairness, some of the most prominent theorists of political opportunity structure are among its most adept critics: see Gamson and Meyer, "Framing Political Opportunity."
6. "Millions Join Global Anti-War Protests," BBC News Online, 2003, available at http://news.bbc.co.uk/1/hi/world/europe/2765215.stm (accessed September 29, 2007); Whoriskey, "Thousands Protest Blacks' Treatment."
7. Halpern, *Rebuilding the Inner City*; Smith, *We Have No Leaders*; Jackson, "The State, the Movement, and the Urban Poor"; Reed, "Sources of Demobilization in the New Black Political Regime." For a broader discussion, see Shaw, "The Expanding Boundaries of Black Politics."
8. Halpern, *Rebuilding the Inner City*; Jackson, "The State, the Movement, and the Urban Poor"; Reed, "Sources of Demobilization in the New Black Political Regime," 120; Rustin, "From Protest to Politics"; Smith, *We Have No Leaders*, 3–26.
9. Jennings, *The Politics of Black Empowerment*, 32; Thompson, *Double Trouble*, 23.
10. Among the data I present are those of Olzak and West, *Ethnic Collective Action in Contemporary Urban U.S.*
11. Spence, "Strings of Life." For a discussion of welfare-rights unions in New York City, see Tait, "Workers Just like Anyone Else."

12. Good distillations of urban-regime theory are in Mossberger and Stoker, "The Evolution of Urban Regime Theory"; Stone, *Regime Politics*, 4, 6–11. Several fascinating revisions of urban regime theory are provided in Bennett, "Harold Washington and the Black Urban Regime"; DeLeon, *Left Coast City*; Jessop, "A Neo-Gramscian Approach to the Regulation of Urban Regimes"; McGovern, *The Politics of Downtown Development*.
13. Among the myriad discussions of the "urban crisis" and Detroit are Edwards, "The Resolution of an 'Urban Crisis'"; Hill, "Crisis in the Motor City"; Sugrue, *The Origins of the Urban Crisis*. For a comparison of poverty rates among cities with high percentages of minorities in the 1990s, see Downs, *New Visions for Metropolitan America*, 74; Mast, *Detroit Lives*, 118–23; Rich, *Coleman Young and Detroit Politics*, 116–17.
14. Among the vocal grassroots critics of the administration who emerged to challenge this hegemony was a group called Detroiters for a Rationale Economy (DARE), led by the astute and articulate Marxist attorney and City Council Member Kenneth Cockrel: see Bush, "Detroit"; Hill, "Crisis in the Motor City," 112–13. An excellent discussion of the narrow construction of blackness and black group interests is in Cohen, *The Boundaries of Blackness*, 16–20.
15. Black Radical Congress, "Freedom Agenda of the Black Radical Congress," April 17, 1999, available online at http://www.blackradicalcongress.org/aboutus/freedom angenda.html (accessed May 20, 2008); Cooper Hamilton and Hamilton, *The Dual Agenda*; Dawson, *Behind the Mule*; Goldfield, *The Color of Politics*; Iton, *Solidarity Blues*; Tate, *From Protest to Politics*.
16. Various works have discovered intraracial class differences among African Americans with regard to spending on social-welfare programs, including Dawson, *Behind the Mule*, 192–94; Giddings, *When and Where I Enter*; Locke, "Deconstruct to Reconstruct"; Tate, *From Protest to Politics*, 20–49.
17. In his dissertation, Lester Spence examined the motives underpinning black women's political participation in Detroit: see Spence, "Strings of Life." The concept of "multiple consciousness" is examined and articulated in King, "Multiple Jeopardy, Multiple Consciousness"; Robinson, "The Effect of Group Identity among Black Women on Race Consciousness." However, Patricia Hill Collins wrote one of the first and most seminal works expounding on "standpoint theory": see Hill Collins, *Black Feminist Thought*, 24–45.
18. Garcelon, *Revolutionary Passage*, 114–55; Schneider, "On the Fault-Line"; Seaoane, "From Seattle to Porto Alegre."
19. A number of works have documented the persistent deficit between demand and supply in the market for lower-income housing, including Bartelt, "Housing the 'Underclass'"; Bove et al., "Dilemmas of Community-Based Housing Development." See also Hirsch, *Making the Second Ghetto*, and the more recent analysis in Venkatesh, *American Project*.
20. Goetz, "Retrenchment, Devolution and Local Housing Policy in the Postfederal Era"; Nathan et al., *Reagan and the States*; Popkin et al., "A Decade of HOPE VI"; Steuerle, "An Ownership Society or a Society for Those Who Already Own?"

21. Just a few of these works are Darden et al., *Detroit*; Farley et al., *Detroit Divided*; Fine, *Violence in the Model City*; Rich, *Coleman Young and Detroit Politics*; Sugrue, *The Origins of the Urban Crisis*; Thomas, *Redevelopment and Race*.
22. Giugni, "How Social Movements Matter," xxiv–xi.
23. In my reporting, I generally maintained the anonymity of respondents as per the dictates of human-subject protocols: see Lofland and Lofland, *Analyzing Social Settings*, 29–30. Given the special nature of my project, in which some episodes were very public and involved public officials, however, I used two special procedural rules to determine whether I should attribute a statement to a person. First, I asked all respondents whether they were willing to observe a "limited confidentiality" in that they had no problem with my mentioning their names and organizational affiliations or public offices but would let me know when a matter was "on and off the record." All of the people I interviewed agreed to this rule. When interview subjects directly criticized other individuals or groups, I generally refrained from direct attribution even if the subjects did not stipulate that the statements were off the record. In a few instances, I have switched the gender pronouns of respondents to help protect their identities. Second, I was more liberal in the use of the names of public officials, because they are public personalities and are often quoted by the media and in public sources.
24. As a general rule, I relied on the memories and perceptions of these actors for substantive knowledge and normative interpretation. I also did participant-observation research of the SOS in the springs of 1994 and 1995 and thus gained firsthand insights into how these community-developer-led activists mobilized participants and lobbied City Council members.
25. Castells, *The City and the Grassroots*, xvi (my emphasis).

## 1. MAKING BLACK ACTIVISM MATTER

1. Browning et al., *Protest Is Not Enough*, 240–41.
2. Reed, "Sources of Demobilization in the New Black Political Regime"; Smith, *We Have No Leaders*. Contemporary community organizing is examined in Orr, "Community Organizing and the Changing Ecology of Civic Engagement."
3. See Smiley, *Moral Responsibility and the Boundaries of Community*. The quote is from PEOPLE Convention, "The PEOPLE's Platform," 4.
4. Kelling et al., *Police Accountability and Community Policing*; Pitkin, *The Concept of Representation*, 55–57; Stone, *Changing Urban Education*.
5. Goode, *In Goode Faith*, 208–209.
6. See Eulau and Karps, "The Puzzle of Representation." A discussion of Washington's community-development priorities is in Clavel and Wiewel, *Harold Washington and the Neighborhoods*.
7. Grassroots activism is synonymous with the term "community organizing": see Delgado, "Building Multiracial Alliances"; Fisher, *Let the People Decide*; idem, "Neighborhood Organizing." More recently, there is Orr, "Community Organizing and the Changing Ecology of Civic Engagement."

8. Franklin, "Community Organizing and Strategy in Post-Black Power Grass-Roots Activism"; Owens, *God and Government in the Ghetto*, 8–12.
9. Calpotura and Fellner, "Square Pegs Find Their Groove"; Delgado, *Beyond the Politics of Place*; Fisher and Shragge, "Contextualizing Community Organizing"; Miller, "Beyond the Politics of Place"; Shaw and Spence, "Race and Representation in Detroit's Community Development Coalitions"; Stoecker, "Understanding the Development-Organizing Dialectic." One study that illuminates the varying protest potential of ad hoc urban interest groups is Woliver, *From Outrage to Action*.
10. Eisinger, "The Conditions of Protest Behavior in American Cities," 13.
11. Supporting evidence for the previous claim by Peter Eisinger is in the classic Gamson, *The Strategy of Social Protest*, 14–17. The Rucht reference is in Rucht et al., *Acts of Dissent*.
12. Among the scholars who have systematically examined the effectiveness of protest are Andrews, "The Impact of Social Movements on the Political Process," and Fording, "The Political Response to Black Insurgency." Wagner and Cohen, "The Power of the People," explores this problem from the vantage point of the homeless. The other references are to Lipsky, "Protest as a Political Resource"; Moore, *Carol B. Stokes and the Rise of Black Political Power*; Schattschneider, *The Semisovereign People*, 143–44.
13. Piven and Cloward, *Poor People's Movement*, 24.
14. Ibid., 25.
15. Kelley, "The Black Poor and the Politics of Opposition in a New South City," 295; Scott, *Domination and the Arts Resistance*, 36–44, 183–84. For a searing critique of infrapolitics, see Reed, "Sources of Demobilization in the New Black Political Regime," 151.
16. A strong empirical test of Frances Fox Piven's and Richard A. Cloward's claim that permanent organizations are incapable of sustaining protest is in Meyer and Minkoff, "Conceptualizing Political Opportunity," 1482, while a strong theoretical critique is in Gamson and Schmeidler, "Organizing the Poor."
17. Euchner, *Extraordinary Politics*, 238; Teles, *Whose Welfare?* 7.
18. The thinking of John Lewis is captured in Zieger, *John L. Lewis*. The pivotal role Dianne Nash and other black women played in theorizing and acting up nonviolent direct-action tactics is captured in Giddings, *When and Where I Enter*, 278–80. For various other accounts of civil-rights conflict theory, see Branch, *Parting the Waters*; King, *Where Do We Go From Here?*; Payne, *I've Got the Light of Freedom*. The Frederick Douglass quote is from Foner and Taylor, *Frederick Douglass*, 367.
19. Eisinger, "The Conditions of Protest Behavior in American Cities," 25–28.
20. McAdam, "Conceptual Origins, Current Problems, and Future Directions," 27.
21. Goodwin and Jasper, "Caught in the Winding, Snarling Vine," 29.
22. Gamson and Meyer, "Framing Political Opportunity." More broadly, the volume in which Gamson's and Meyer's essay appears is an exemplar of self-critique.
23. Meyer and Minkoff, "Conceptualizing Political Opportunity," 1476.

24. "Millions Join Global Anti-War Protests."
25. Dreier et al., "What Cities Can Do to Address Poverty," 157–71; Schattschneider, *The Semisovereign People*; Shaw and Spence, "Race and Representation in Detroit's Community Development Coalitions," 132–40.
26. For a discussion of windows of policy opportunity as discussed in the American policy process, see Kingdon, *Congressmen's Voting Decisions*, 166–95. Evidence that Piven's and Cloward's contention is applicable to Detroit is in Brewster-Douglass Strike Committee, "Re: Rent Strike Demands," 1969, in Welfare Papers of the Commission on Community Relations, Archive of Labor and Urban Affairs, Walter P. Reuther Library, Wayne State University, Detroit (hereafter, ALUA), Welfare Rights box 78; Fine, *Violence in the Model City*, 382–83; Piven and Cloward, *Poor People's Movement*; Snow and Benford, "Master Frames and Cycles of Protests."
27. For a few of any number of examples of how context shapes ideology, see Gelb and Hurt, "Feminist Politics in a Hostile Environment"; Gotham, "Political Opportunity, Community Identity, and the Emergence of Local Anti-Expressway Movement." Social structure matters, as is evident in Alex-Assensoh and Stanford, "Gender, Participation, and the Black Urban Underclass"; Berry et al., "The Political Behavior of Poor People"; Kelley, "The Black Poor and the Politics of Opposition in a New South City." In addition, scholars of African American politics have also noted how context—i.e., community or neighborhood—as well as social class can fundamentally shape racial attitudes and ideology: see Cohen and Dawson, "Neighborhood Poverty and African American Politics"; Gamson and Meyer, "Framing Political Opportunity"; Gay, "Putting Race in Context"; Walton, *African American Power and Politics.*
28. See Banks, "A Changing Electorate in a Black Majority City"; Bennett, "Harold Washington and the Black Urban Regime"; Reed, "Sources of Demobilization in the New Black Political Regime."
29. See Tilly, *From Mobilization to Revolution*, chap. 6, but also Tarrow, *Power in Movement*, 20–21. For other references to collective and contentious actions, see Ayres, "Transnational Activism in the Americas"; Bearman and Everett, "The Structure of Social Protest"; Krinsky, "Organizing the Organizing of the Unorganized"; Verba and Nie, *Participation in America*; Verba et al., "Citizen Activity."
30. Again, I rely on Tilly, *From Mobilization to Revolution*, chap. 6, for theoretical support.
31. Burnstein, "Social Movements and Public Policy"; Guth et al., "Thunder on the Right?"; McCann, *Rights at Work*.
32. Sidney Tarrow earlier articulated this concept in *Struggling to Reform*. The quote is from Snow and Benford, "Master Frames and Cycles of Protests," 41.
33. This point is empirically substantiated by Minkoff, "The Sequencing of Social Movements."
34. See Bello and Montemurri, "Maryann Mahaffey"; Georgakas and Surkin, *Detroit I Do Mind Dying*, 55–58, 175–87; Teles, *Whose Welfare?* 109–16.
35. Friedman and McAdam, "Collective Identity and Activism," 156.

36. Melucci, *Nomads of the Present*. The quote is from Snow and Benford, "Master Frames and Cycles of Protests," 139.
37. Among the earliest and best explications of frame theory is provided in Snow et al., "Frame Alignment Processes, Micromobilization, and Movement Participation."
38. King, "Multiple Jeopardy, Multiple Consciousness"; Robinson, "The Effect of Group Identity among Black Women on Race Consciousness."
39. Cress and Snow, "Mobilization at the Margins," 1107; McCarthy and Zald, *The Trend in Social Movements in America*; Robnett, *How Long?* 13–15; Walker, *Mobilizing Interest Groups in America*.
40. Melucci, *Nomads of the Present*, 72; Morris, *The Origins of the Civil Rights Movement*, 40–76; Muller and Opp, "Rational Choice and Rebellious Collective Action"; Oberschall, *Social Movements*, 25–31.
41. Despite the broader psychic costs imposed on the poor (see, e.g., Lusane, "If I Were a Rich Man"; Reed, "The Underclass as Myth and Symbol"), it is quite possible to subsidize the costs of participation: Rosenstone and Hansen, *Mobilization, Participation, and Democracy in America*.
42. Downs, *New Visions for Metropolitan America*, 45–94; Mollenkopf and Swanstrom, *Place Matters*, 133–72.
43. Rustin, "From Protest to Politics," 26. A fascinating discussion of Rustin and the history behind the essay is in Anderson, *Bayard Rustin*, 284–86; D'Emillio, *Lost Prophet*; Levine, *Bayard Rustin and the Civil Rights Movement*, 172–74.
44. Rustin, "From Protest to Politics," 26.
45. Garrow, *Bearing the Cross*; McKnight, *The Last Crusade*; Smith, *We Have No Leaders*, 189–91; Rustin, "From Protest to Politics," 25.
46. Cohen, *The Boundaries of Blackness*, 13–16, explains the concept of "cross-cutting cleavages" as relevant to black politics and questions of sexual orientation or health status. Along with sexual orientation and health status, gender and class are among many other potential cleavages: see Dawson, *Behind the Mule*; Gay, "Putting Race in Context"; Gay and Tate, "Doubly Bound"; Gilliam, "Black America"; Hochschild, *Facing Up to the American Dream*; Tate, *From Protest to Politics*; Landry, *The New Black Middle Class*; Wilson, *The Declining Significance of Race*. For the Harris research, see Harris et al., *Countervailing Forces in African-American Civic Activism*.
47. Burbank et al., "Antigrowth Politics or Piecemeal Resistance?" 345–48; Eisinger, *The Politics of Displacement*; Marable, *Speaking Truth to Power*.
48. The quote is from Smith, *We Have No Leaders*, 23. For larger argument, see ibid., 3–28, 127–63, 277–81.
49. Reed, "Sources of Demobilization in the New Black Political Regime," 18.
50. Ibid., 19, 119–20.
51. Jennings, *The Politics of Black Empowerment*, 32.
52. Ibid., 15–16 (my emphasis); Thompson, *Double Trouble*, 12–13, 37–74.
53. Other black politics scholars who posit black demobilization include Harris et al., *Countervailing Forces in African-American Civic Activism*; Hill, "Crisis in the Motor City"; Dawson, *Black Visions*, 35–42.
54. Harris et al., *Countervailing Forces in African-American Civic Activism*, 65–79.

55. For details about the racial and political transitions that occurred in Detroit and sister cities as they shifted to black-majority control, see Colburn, "Running for Office"; Germany, *New Orleans after the Promises*; Johnson, *Revolutionaries to Race Leaders*. Support for my specific claims about Detroit's plight is in Anton, *Federal Aid to Detroit*; Darden et al., *Detroit*, 67–108; Farley et al., *Detroit Divided*, 53–106; Wilson, "Restructuring and the Growth of Concentrated Poverty in Detroit"; Young and Wheeler, *Hard Stuff*, 255–326.
56. Minkoff, "The Sequencing of Social Movements"; Tarrow, *Struggling to Reform*.
57. Checkoway and Zimmerman, *Correlates of Participation in Neighborhood Organizations*; Detroit Area Study, "Separate and Unequal." For further validation that protest is still a non-conventional form of political participation, see Conway, *Political Participation in the United States*, 63–64, 68–69, 83–84; Verba et al., *Voice and Equality*, 50–51.
58. Carbado, "The Million Man March." Examinations of the anti-Confederate flag movement in South Carolina are in Hill, "Understanding the Drive to Make the Confederate Flag Official in South Carolina"; Woliver et al., "The South Carolina Confederate Flag."
59. Cooper Hamilton and Hamilton, *The Dual Agenda*; Dewan, "Gentrification Changing Face of Atlanta"; Smith, *We Have No Leaders*; Landry, *The New Black Middle Class*.
60. Gregory, *Black Corona*; Moore, "What's Class Got to Do with It?"; Pattillo-McCoy, *Black Picket Fences*. Moreover, Manuel Castells revised his neo-Marxist thinking to concede that one of the surprising traits shared by urban protest movements is their invariable propensity to foment a class-elastic insurgency: see Castells, *The City and the Grassroots*, 318–31.
61. Boston, *Race, Class, and Conservatism*, 9–19, 29–31; Obama, *Dreams from My Father*, 133–63.
62. Hill Collins, *Black Feminist Thought*, 21–43; King, "Multiple Jeopardy, Multiple Consciousness"; Williams, *The Alchemy of Race and Rights*, 181–201.
63. White, "Talking Black, Talking Feminist." The Tillmon quote is from Hancock, *The Politics of Disgust*, 210.
64. Among the works that provide good overviews of black women's activism and urban activism are Hill Collins, *Black Feminist Thought*, 201–25; Naples, *Grassroots Warriors*. Toward the end of understanding the long-term economic realities and class conflicts of black women's lives and activism, see DeSena, "What's a Mother to Do?"; Malveaux, "The Political Economy of Black Women"; Myers, "Racial Unity in the Grassroots?" Two fascinating discussions of women's and black women's "work" in the movement field of environmental justice are Krauss, "Women and Toxic Waste Protests"; Simpson, "Public Hazard, Personal Peril."
65. Dawson, *Behind the Mule*, 181–203; Thompson, *Double Trouble*, 254, 265–74.
66. The quote is from Mossberger and Stoker, "The Evolution of Urban Regime Theory," 89, as quoted in Stone, *Regime Politics*, 4. Other works began or expanded on urban regime theory: Sanders and Stone, "Developmental Politics Reconsidered"; Stone, "Systemic Power in Community Decision Making," 4. Two works that creatively

consider local ideology and culture in their accounts of urban regimes are DeLeon, *Left Coast City*; Ferman, *Challenging the Growth Machine in Chicago and Pittsburgh Neighborhood Politics*.

67. Reed, "The Black Urban Regime," 161.
68. Brown, "Race and Politics Matter."
69. Reed, "The Black Urban Regime," 162.
70. The difficulties and possibilities of such dynamics are discussed in Bennett, "Harold Washington and the Black Urban Regime"; Edwards, "The Resolution of an 'Urban Crisis'"; Hill, "Crisis in the Motor City." Later I discuss Marion Orr's and Gerry Stoker's conclusion that Young had a non-regime in Detroit: Orr and Stoker, "Urban Regimes and Leadership in Detroit."
71. Cohen, *The Boundaries of Blackness*, 10–27; Dawson, *Behind the Mule*; Gurin et al., *Hope and Independence*; Tate, *From Protest to Politics*; White, "Talking Black, Talking Feminist." For a more recent, empirical examination of the uses of common fate, see McClerking, *We Are in This Together*.
72. Dyson, "Introduction," xviii; West, "The Crisis of Black Leadership." One incendiary account of Marion Barry's rise and fall is in Barras, *The Last of the Black Emperors*.
73. Robnett, *How Long?*, 13. Of course, the racial thinking of the black middle and upper classes was studied long ago: see Frazier, *Black Self-Determination*. For a recent and fascinating study of significant differences within the black middle class, see Lacy, *Blue-Chip Blacks*.
74. Robnett, *How Long?*, 13–14; Snow et al., "Frame Alignment Processes, Micromobilization, and Movement Participation." The quote is from King, "Letter from Birmingham City Jail," 290.
75. Transformative versus transactional politics are examined in Burns, *Leadership*; Cohen, *The Boundaries of Blackness*, 251–55. As mentioned earlier, frame amplification is nicely explained in Robnett, *How Long?*, 13–14; while Babson, *Working Detroit*, gives a pictorial history of Detroit's and black Detroit's deep labor roots. I further describe the issues confronting anti-homelessness activists in chapter 6.
76. Ferman, *Challenging the Growth Machine in Chicago and Pittsburgh Neighborhood Politics*, 4–6.
77. Dahl, *A Preface to Democratic Theory*; Gilbert, "Race, Location, and Education"; Krebs, "The Determinants of Candidate's Vote Share and the Advantages of Incumbency in City Council Elections"; Mayhew, *Congress*. The Wood quote is from Wood, "Higher Power," 170. The election observations come from my field research in Detroit.
78. Tilly, *From Mobilization to Revolution*; *Malcolm X Speaks*, 3–17, 23–44.
79. Ganz, "Resources and Resourcefulness"; Wood, "Higher Power," 173–75.
80. Chwe, "Structure and Strategy in Collective Action"; Wood, "Higher Power," 173–75.
81. Shaw, "Responsible for Their Deeds," 407–84.

**2. WHERE ARE THE PEOPLE?**

1. For a discussion of Detroit's housing and economic woes, see Boyer, *Cities Destroyed for Cash*; Rasmussen and Struyk, *A Housing Strategy for the City of Detroit*; U.S. Department of Housing and Urban Development, *Maintenance Review*. More recently, see Farley et al., *Detroit Divided*, 1; McWhirter and Nichols, "Detroit Tops U.S. in Lost Housing."
2. Chafets, *Devil's Night*. Some observers have gone as far as to number Detroit among a group of so-called pariah cities: Neill et al., *Reimaging the Pariah City*.
3. Sugrue, *The Origins of the Urban Crisis*, 3–31. Much to Thomas Sugrue's credit, his structural analysis extended the origins of Detroit's urban crisis even further back than Fine's voluminous *Violence in the Model City*.
4. Bates et al., "Where Are the People?" 14–15.
5. Thompson, *Whose Detroit?*
6. Deskins, "Residential Mobility of Negroes in Detroit." How race shaped patterns of black housing and neighborhood formation, especially in Paradise Valley, is discussed in Moon, *Untold Tales*, 89–91, 118–19, 184–85, 188; Sugrue, *The Origins of the Urban Crisis*, 35–37, 185; Thomas, *Life for Us Is What We Make It*, 89–91.
7. Velie, "Housing," 15.
8. Detroit Housing Commission, *Eleventh Annual Report of the Detroit Housing Commission*, 11; idem, *Public Housing in Detroit*, 11; idem, *Tenth Annual Report*, 10; National Association for the Advancement of Colored People, Detroit Branch, paper presented at the Housing Conference, August 29–30, 1945, in Papers of the Citizens Housing Council, Detroit Public Library, box 60, file 5; Velie, "Housing," 75.
9. Black, "Restrictive Covenants in Relation to Segregated Housing in Detroit," 24; Sugrue, *The Origins of the Urban Crisis*, 194–97; Velie, "Housing," 15. For a discussion of the larger problem of housing and historical residential segregation, see Berry, *The Open Housing Question*; Hirsch, *Making the Second Ghetto*; Jackson, *Crabgrass Frontier*; Massey and Denton, *American Apartheid*; Molotch, *Managed Integration*.
10. Sugrue, *The Origins of the Urban Crisis*, 231–58; Widick, *Detroit*, 5–22. The fascinating political and cultural contexts surrounding the Ossian Sweet case are recounted in Boyle, *Arc of Justice*.
11. Black, "Restrictive Covenants in Relation to Segregated Housing in Detroit"; Darden et al., *Detroit*; Gelfand, *A Nation of Cities*; Jackson, *Crabgrass Frontier*; Teaford, *The Rough Road to Renaissance*. In "The Structures of Urban Poverty," 63–72, Sugrue tells of an infamous wall that was built to separate the homes of middle-class blacks on Eight Mile and Wyoming from their white counterparts so that the latter could qualify for federally subsidized home loans.
12. Conot, *American Odyssey*, 363; Darden et al., *Detroit*, 86–98, 102–104; Moon, *Untold Tales*, 152.
13. Capeci, *Race Relations in Wartime Detroit*; Sugrue, *The Origins of the Urban Crisis*, 40–41. The quote is from Moon, *Untold Tales*, 199.

14. Sugrue, *The Origins of the Urban Crisis*, 203–207.
15. Krainz Woods Community Council, "All Conant Gardens Home Owners Should Attend."
16. Such antipathies among the black middle class against public housing and the poor are not new or unique to Detroit, as is evident in Moore, *Carol B. Stokes and the Rise of Black Political Power*, 101–106; Pattillo-McCoy, *Black Picket Fences*.
17. The quote from Sanders interview. See also Moon, *Untold Tales*, 121.
18. Detroit Housing Commission, *Second Annual Report of the Detroit Housing Commission*; Friedman, *Government and Slum Housing*; Gelfand, *A Nation of Cities*; Hays, *The Federal Government and Urban Housing*; Thomas, *Redevelopment and Race*, 19–28, 55–66.
19. The DHC's policy is stated in Detroit Housing Commission, *First Annual Report of the Detroit Housing Commission*, 10. For discussions of racial attitudes and clashes, see Jenkins, *The Racial Policies of the Detroit Housing Commission and Their Administration*; Kornhauser, *Attitudes of Detroit People toward Detroit*; Sugrue, "Crabgrass-Roots Politics."
20. Capeci, *Race Relations in Wartime Detroit*; Sugrue, *The Origins of the Urban Crisis*, 80.
21. Some jewels in the Cobo redevelopment crown included the $54 million Cobo Exhibition Hall, the namesake of the mayor and, at that time, the largest convention center in the world; the $12.6 million Detroit / Wayne County City-County Building; and the $16 million Detroit Metropolitan Airport, not to mention the Gratiot / Lafayette Park Project: see Darden et al., *Detroit*, 163–65; Mowitz and Wright, *Profile of a Metropolis*, 159–66, 335; Sugrue, *The Origins of the Urban Crisis*, 84–87, 222–25; Thomas, *Redevelopment and Race*, 58–60.
22. Detroit Housing Commission, *Slum Clearance and Public Housing in Detroit*, 1952, 6; Thomas, "Racial Crisis and the Fall of the Detroit Plan Commission." As an aside, the DHC also succumbed to McCarthyism, for in a report from the early 1950s it stated, "The Detroit Housing Commission held a special meeting to find means of evicting known Communists from public housing projects": Detroit Housing Commission, *Slum Clearance and Public Housing in Detroit*, 1952, 6.
23. Mowitz and Wright, *Profile of a Metropolis*, 27–33.
24. Sugrue, *The Origins of the Urban Crisis*, 51.
25. Detroit Housing Commission, *A Tour of Detroit's Urban Renewal Projects*, 4; Wolf and Leabeaux, *Change and Renewal in an Urban Community*.
26. Conot, *American Odyssey*, 436–37.
27. Darden et al., *Detroit*, 167–70; Fine, *Violence in the Model City*, 62–64; Gans, "The Failure of Urban Renewal."
28. For an extensive discussion of Detroit's early black politics, see Kilson, "Political Change in the Negro Ghetto"; Meier and Rudwick, *Black Detroit and the Rise of the UAW*; Orr, "Black Political Incorporation—Phase Two"; Stovall, *The Growth of Black Elected Officials in the City of Detroit*.
29. Rich, *Coleman Young and Detroit Politics*, 45.

30. Stovall, "Before Coleman Young," 65–81.
31. Babson, *Working Detroit*, 57–58; Detroit Housing Commission, *Second Annual Report of the Detroit Housing Commission*; idem, *Fifth Annual Report of the Detroit Housing Commission.*
32. Thomas, *Life for Us Is What We Make It*, 94–97.
33. Shaw, "We Refused to Lay Down Our Spears"; Wolcott, *Remaking Respectability.*
34. Darden et al., *Detroit*, 109–50. The Hubbard quote is from ibid., 122.
35. Dillard, *Faith in the City*, chap. 6, conclusion. The quote is from Fine, *Violence in the Model City*, 429.
36. X, *Malcolm X Speaks*, 3, 11.
37. Fine, *Violence in the Model City*, 27; Mast, *Detroit Lives*, 306; Thompson, *Whose Detroit?* 103–27.
38. Fine, *Violence in the Model City*, 69–70; Goode interview; Meier and Rudwick, CORE; Naison, "Rent Strikes in New York." The Farmer quote is from Sauter, "Rights Unit Calls Slums Top Issue," 1A.
39. Meier and Rudwick, CORE, 316, 377–78; Goode interview; Sauter, "Pickets at New Hotel Tell Landlord."
40. Hoyt, "Tenants Strike," 3.
41. Sauter, "Pickets at New Hotel Tell Landlord," 1A.
42. "Death-Trap House Falls Wednesday," 1A; "Evicted Chain-In Sponsors Take Landlord to Court," 4B; Fine, *Violence in the Model City*, 73.
43. Sauter and Blonston, "Court Seeks Landlord for Cutting off Utilities," 2A.
44. Sauter, "Judge Orders Arrest of Vanishing Slumlord," 3A.
45. "United Tenants for Collective Action, 1967–1968," in Papers of the Detroit Commission on Community Relations, ALUA, box 30, file 18. For discussions of FBI and Detroit police attacks on black militants and revolutionaries, see Churchill and Vander Wall, *Agents of Repression*; Georgakas and Surkin, *Detroit I Do Mind Dying*, 18–19.
46. Daniel Bogus, "State of Welfare Legislation under Consideration in Washington," 1972, in Papers of the Welfare Employees' Union, ALUA, box 18, folder 4; "Rent Strike Set for Inner City"; Mast, *Detroit Lives*, 297–98; Stanton, "Housing Experiment"; Urban Law Program, "Tenant Rights and Code Enforcement: New Legislation in Michigan, ca. 1968, in Papers of the Commission on Community Relations, ALUA, box 121, file 7.
47. Blanchard, "City's Poor Get Dynamic Organizer." See the following for a discussion of Alinsky's background and philosophy: Horwitt, *Let Them Call Me Rebel*; Lancourt, *Confront or Concede*. The Venus quote is from Fine, *Violence in the Model City*, 30.
48. Alinsky, *Rules for Radicals*; Fisher, *Let the People Decide*; Daya et al., *Self Determination*; "United Tenants for Collective Action, 1967–1968"; West Central Organization, *By-Laws / West Central Organization*; idem, "West Central Organization: A People's Union," 1965, in Papers of the Office of Religious Affairs, ALUA, box 26.
49. As a general reference, see idem, "Voiceless People Organize for Power," 1965, in

Papers of the Office of Religious Affairs, ALUA, box 26. The specific exchange between Del Rio and Ravitz is recorded in Cohen, "Neighborhood Urges Council."

50. The specific image and story was recorded, in part, by DeWolfe, "Model Policeman Punches Superior at Picketing Scene." The beginning of the demolition process is recorded in "We Are Making Progress Now."
51. Stanton, "Urban Renewal Protesters Break Up Council Session"; Thomas, "Neighborhood Response to Redevelopment in Detroit"; idem, "Racial Crisis and the Fall of the Detroit Plan Commission"; idem, *Redevelopment and Race*, 108–11.
52. Black, "Urban Renewal." The quote is from West Central Organization, "For Immediate Release," in Papers of the Office of Religious Affairs, ALUA, box 26.
53. Fine, *Violence in the Model City*, 63–64. The quote is from *South End Press*, January 18, 1966.
54. Fine, *Violence in the Model City*, 63–64. The Hood quote is from Stanton, "Housing Director Finds a Defender," 1A. See also Hood interview.
55. Among the WCO's competitors when it helped form urban-renewal councils were Grass Roots Organized Workers (GROW) and the Jeffries Tenant Council Division: Commission on Community Relations, Field Division, "Letter to R. V. Marks," 1966, Papers of the Commission on Community Relations, ALUA, box 35. Among the young leaders the WCO influenced was John Watson of the League: see Georgakas and Surkin, *Detroit I Do Mind Dying*, 254; Geschwender, *Class, Race, Working Insurgency*. Also, Shelia Murphy-Cockrel, spouse of the popular and militant Kenneth Cockrel, was a future member of the City Council: see Mast, *Detroit Lives*, 181–82. There were ideological and personal disagreements among these young leaders and others that later contribute to the decline of the League: Georgakas and Surkin, *Detroit I Do Mind Dying*, 133–35, 147–50; Thompson, *Whose Detroit?* 168–73.
56. For a discussion of the opportunities and contradictions of the War on Poverty, see Conot, *American Odyssey*, 654; Fine, *Violence in the Model City*, 71–93; Jackson, "The State, the Movement, and the Urban Poor"; Katz, *The Undeserving Poor*, 79–123; Barbara Knox, "Federation for Aid to Dependent Children," 1966, in Papers of the Welfare Employees Union, ALUA, Welfare Rights (1960s) box 78; Mayor's Committee for Community Renewal, "Total Action against Poverty."
57. Shaw, "We Refused to Lay Down Our Spears," 177–79. The Tillmon quote is cited in Hancock, *The Politics of Disgust*, 210.
58. The quotes are from Linebarger interview.
59. Kramer and Linebarger interviews; Metropolitan Detroit Welfare Reform Coalition, "The Welfare Reform Coalition?," 1973, in Papers of the Welfare Employees Union, ALUA, Welfare Rights (1960s) box 78, file 28.
60. West, *The National Welfare Rights Movement*. The quote is from Kramer interview. See also Kramer, "Speaking for Ourselves"; Shaw, "We Refused to Lay Down Our Spears," 177.
61. Conot, *American Odyssey*, 560; Falbaum, "Housing Outlook Here Remains Gloomy"; Robert Holland, "Public Housing Rent Strike Report," 1969, in Papers of the Commission on Community Relations, ALUA, Welfare Rights box 78; Neuman, "City Seeks to Avoid Rent Strike," 560.

62. Mast, *Detroit Lives*, 104.
63. See Askins, "Tenant Board Makes New Demands"; Commission on Community Relations, Field Division, "Letter to R. V. Marks, Inter-Office Correspondence re: January 27 Meeting at the University of Detroit—Subject: 'Can Rent Strikes Be Successful?'" 1968, Papers of the Commission on Community Relations, ALUA, Welfare Rights box 78.
64. Neuman, "City Seeks to Avoid Rent Strike"; Holland, "Public Housing Rent Strike Report."
65. Brewster-Douglass Strike Committee, "Re: Rent Strike Demands," 1.
66. Ibid.
67. Holland, "Public Housing Rent Strike Report," 2; Morris, "Poor to Fight Rent in Court."
68. Askins, "Real Housing Issue."
69. Idem, "Tenants Hold Upper Hand in Public Housing."
70. The first quote by Scott is from idem, "City Tenant Board Leaders Demand Salaries and Staff"; the second is from idem, "Tenant Board Makes New Demands," 5-A.
71. From idem, "Tenant Affairs Board Is Struggling to Define Its Power."
72. Seigel, "Harassment Charged by Tenant Affairs Chairman," A10.
73. A brief description of the Brooke Amendment is in Salins, "America's Permanent Housing Problem," 24. See the following for an explanation of strike resolution: Holland, "Housing Talks Set in Hotel"; Morris, "Tenants in Herman Gardens End Year-Long Rent Strike." The quote is from Hallas, "City Hosts $3,000 Parley for 16 Public Tenants."
74. Fine, *Violence in the Model City*, 57–58, 291–301.
75. Babson, *Working Detroit*, 168–71; Darden et al., *Detroit*; Fine, *Violence in the Model City*, 291–301, 445; Graves, "New Detroit Committee / New Detroit, Inc."
76. Michigan Coalition on Housing, "For Immediate Release" and "Meeting Minutes," 1972, in Papers of the Commission on Community Relations, ALUA, box 35; LaMore, "Community Economic Development in Michigan."

**3. TRADING ACTIVISM**

1. Along with the City-County Building, or Detroit's City Hall, being renamed the Coleman A. Young Municipal Center in 1998, a number of community organizations still bear his name, and thus his legacy, including the Coleman A. Young Foundation and Coleman A. Young Community Center. For a discussion of his career and legacy, see Rich, *Coleman Young and Detroit Politics*.
2. A detailed discussion of the convention and Young's storming out is in Smith, *We Have No Leaders*, 29–52. The quotes are from Van DeBurg, "Modern Black Nationalism," 140, 144.
3. Jennings, *The Politics of Black Empowerment*; Reed, "Sources of Demobilization in the New Black Political Regime." For a detailed overview of the National Black Political Conventions of the 1970s and 1980s, see Walters, *Black Presidential Politics*, 85–109; Johnson, *Revolutionaries to Race Leaders*, 85–130.

4. For a review of black class dynamics and their implications, see Lacy, *Blue-Chip Blacks*; Landry, *The New Black Middle Class*; Pattillo-McCoy, *Black Picket Fences*; Wilson, *The Declining Significance of Race*.
5. Moon, *Untold Tales*, 72–73; Sugrue, *The Origins of the Urban Crisis*, 39–41.
6. Lawrence Graham provides a fascinating account of Detroit's "black elite" in Graham, *Our Kind of People*, 294–320, esp. 308–309. See also Boston, *Race, Class, and Conservatism*; Eisinger, *Black Employment in City Government*; Farley et al., *Detroit Divided*, 308–309.
7. Jargowsky, *Poverty and Place*, 157; Wilson, "Restructuring and the Growth of Concentrated Poverty in Detroit."
8. Those families labeled "poor" have incomes that are below the poverty level. Families labeled "near poor" have incomes that are a 100 percent to 199 percent of the poverty line. The "middle class" enjoys incomes that are from two to three times the poverty line, and the highest echelon, or the "upper class," have incomes that are four times or greater than the poverty line: see Farley et al., *Detroit Divided*, 49–50. They derived their data from Steven Ruggles, Matthew Sobek, Trent Alexander, Catherine A. Fitch, Ronald Goeken, Patricia Kelly Hall, Miriam King, and Chad Ronnander, *Integrated Public Use Microdata Series*, version 3.0 (machine-readable database), Minnesota Population Center, 2004.
9. Conley, *Being Black, Living in the Red*; Hochschild, *Facing Up to the American Dream*, 47–51; Oliver and Shapiro, *Black Wealth / White Wealth*. See also U.S. Bureau of the Census and U.S. Bureau of Labor Statistics, "Annual Demographic Survey, March Supplement."
10. Mirel, "After the Fall"; Farley et al., *Detroit Divided*, 97–103.
11. Boston, *Race, Class, and Conservatism*; Spence, "Parlor Tricks and Politics."
12. The 1976 Detroit Area Study was a split sample, partial telephone interview conducted by Reynolds Farley and Howard Schuman at the University of Michigan, Ann Arbor. The total number of respondents was 1,134. The total number of black respondents was 397, and the total number of white respondents was 729: Farley and Schuman, *Detroit Area Study Code Book with Final Marginals*, 7. I derived my income categories by simply dividing the self-reported family-income distribution of the black respondents into roughly even quartiles.
13. An analysis of the National Election Study (NES) cumulative data files for the years 1970 to 1996 corroborated my finding that income has a negative relationship with blacks' support for guaranteed jobs and a living standard during this period: see Brown et al., "Is It Cause I'm Broke or Cause I'm Black?" For an understanding of the odd ratios technique I use to report some results, see Pampel, *Logistic Regression*.
14. For a discussion of Detroit's housing crisis in the 1970s, see Ball, "HUD Speculators Are Accused of Arson for Profit"; Boyer, *Cities Destroyed for Cash*; Rasmussen and Struyk, *A Housing Strategy for the City of Detroit*.
15. Welch et al., *Race and Place*, 83–93, 107–109. In an earlier work, Timothy Bledsoe, Michael Combs, and Lee Sigelman discovered by examining Detroit Area Studies

from the late 1960s to the early 1990s that black attitudinal suspicion of whites not only failed to lessen in the post-Civil Rights Movement era but actually heightened: see Bledsoe et al., "Trends in Racial Attitudes in Detroit."

16. Wilbur Rich briefly discusses the Black Slate's importance to Young's electoral coalition and in the black community in Rich, *Coleman Young and Detroit Politics*, 82, 274, 276. See also Widick, *Detroit*. Contact in mixed-race communities actually make both blacks and whites more aware of racial discrimination, according to Welch et al., *Race and Place*, 83–91.
17. For a discussion of the confines of the electoral arena, see Pinderhughes, *Race and Ethnicity in Chicago Politics*, 109–40. For a discussion of Young's political dominance and the political agenda of black mayors, see Edwards, "The Resolution of an 'Urban Crisis'"; Hill, "Crisis in the Motor City"; Williams, "Detroit Politics and Urban Theory."
18. Rich, *Coleman Young and Detroit Politics*, 172–200; Stovall, "Before Coleman Young." Evidence of the urgency on the part of African American voters to elect black officeholders is in Morris, *The Politics of Black America*; Nelson and Meranto, *Electing Black Mayors*; Walton, *Black Politics*.
19. Cheyfitz, "The Survivor," 48; Young and Wheeler, *Hard Stuff*, 42.
20. Darden et al., *Detroit*, 213–14; Young and Wheeler, *Hard Stuff*, 79–142.
21. Jackson interview; Josar, "FBI Papers Offer Insight on Young."
22. Cheyfitz, "The Survivor," 50–53, 97; Thompson, "Rethinking the Collapse of Postwar Liberalism," 223, 233–34.
23. Darden et al., *Detroit*, 75–76; Rich, *Coleman Young and Detroit Politics*, 103–109; Thompson, "Rethinking the Collapse of Postwar Liberalism," 231–33. David Colburn provides a good review of the electoral conditions and platforms of the first generation of black mayors: Colburn, "Running for Office."
24. The quote is from Mast, *Detroit Lives*, 187–88. For further details, see Rich, *Coleman Young and Detroit Politics*, 91–125.
25. Rich, *Coleman Young and Detroit Politics*, 109–24.
26. Ibid., 122; Bobo and Gilliam, "Race, Sociopolitical Participation, and Black Empowerment"; Gilliam and Kaufman, "Is There An Empowerment Life Cycle?"
27. Cohen, *The Boundaries of Blackness*. I am quite sympathetic to Heather Ann Thompson's assertion that, compared with previous, overtly racist and conservative white regimes, Young assembled a progressive black-led regime: see Thompson, "Rethinking the Collapse of Postwar Liberalism," 225. Yet she overstates her thesis. At the end of his tenure, Young consciously described his own approach to governing as a form of bare-knuckled pragmatism that in many outward respects was overtly non-ideological, hostile toward white (and black) liberal critics of his regime, and often saw the economic ends justifying the means: see Young and Wheeler, *Hard Stuff*, 220–21.
28. McGraw et al., "It's a Rematch." The quote about "Aunt Jemimas" is from Wilson, "Young Blasts Media Coverage," A1.
29. John Conyers went as so far as to disclose, "The mayor's flunkies keep telling me,

'Wait, John, one more term.' No more terms, Coleman. It's all over, big daddy. I'm running": see Huskisson, "Conyers to Young." Erma Henderson inaugurated her campaign on a subtler note. In the City Council Budget Message in 1989, she simply stated, as a veiled overture to running, "Unfortunately . . . the dream . . . the vision that I have always followed for these many years has not always been fulfilled": Henderson, "Detroit City Council Budget Message," 1989, 2.

30. Adams, "Political Suicide Not the Way." However, it is clear from Angela Denise Dillard's work that at times black clergy and the radical preaching tradition have been progressive contributors to black politics in Detroit: Dillard, *Faith in the City*.
31. Mast, *Detroit Lives*, 199; Sheffield, "Reactionary Bid to Dump Young Calls on Blacks to Close Ranks."
32. A feeling thermometer is a psychometric measure of a respondent's psychological affect toward a public figure or group. In this case, a respondent is asked to score her feelings toward Young along a range of 0–100 in which "100" is extremely warm, "0" is extremely cold, and "50" is in the middle. The principal investigator of the 1989 Detroit Area Study was Steven J. Rosenstone. This study had a total sample of 916 respondents and was composed of a "core sample" of 466 persons taken from the three metropolitan Detroit counties—Wayne, Oakland, and Macomb—and a supplemental sample of 450 persons who resided in Detroit. Of the Detroit residents, 415 were black. "Women, blacks, the poor, voters, and the young are slightly over represented in the sample." The purpose of the study was to address issues of racial and economic inequality, community problems, and political participation in community problems: see Rosenstone, *Detroit Area Code Book*, 7.
33. The first five variables of Table 3 are control variables that should generally explain black sentiments toward Young in light of core constituencies, such as black churches. Also, a discussion of the use of the black self-help measure as a Black Nationalist measure is in Brown and Shaw, "Separate Nations." For a discussion of the clash between the Young administration and antipoverty protesters, see Ball, "City Police Fold Tent as Being Hazardous"; Mast, *Detroit Lives*, 55, 174–75.
34. Graham, *Our Kind of People*, 306.
35. Boggs, *Living for Change*; Bush, "Detroit"; Mast, *Detroit Lives*; Sims interview.
36. Mast, *Detroit Lives*, 175.
37. Young and Wheeler, *Hard Stuff*, 316.
38. Rich, *Coleman Young and Detroit Politics*, 104–108, 208–209, 219–25, 232–34, 249–63.
39. Ibid., 18–31; Anton, *Federal Aid to Detroit*; Stewart, "Blacks Are Hard Hit By City Layoffs."
40. Fuchs, *Mayors and Money*; Nathan et al., *Reagan and the States*; Rich, *Coleman Young and Detroit Politics*, 172–200, 212–13; Young, "Mayor's Message," 1986.
41. "Annual Personnel Figures"; Anton, *Federal Aid to Detroit*; Hill, "Crisis in the Motor City." See also Eisinger, *Black Employment in City Government*.
42. Ravitz interview.
43. The quotes are from Mast, *Detroit Lives*, 145; Trice interview.

44. To review Stone's criteria for an urban regime, see Mossberger and Stoker, "The Evolution of Urban Regime Theory." Otherwise, see Neill, "Lipstick on the Gorilla"; Orr and Stoker, "Urban Regimes and Leadership in Detroit."
45. The quotes are from Young and Wheeler, *Hard Stuff*, 20, 29. Furthermore, see Bachelor and Jones, "Managed Participation"; Ewen, *Corporate Power and Urban Crisis in Detroit.*
46. Darden et al., *Detroit*, 44–62. The quote is from Young interview.
47. The quote is from Hill, "Crisis in the Motor City," 103.
48. June Thomas wrote an excellent analysis of the perils and problem confronting urban planning and development in Detroit's racialized context: see Thomas, *Redevelopment and Race*, 188–89.
49. Rich, "Coleman Young and Detroit Politics, 1972–1986," 146.
50. Fainstein and Fainstein, "Regime Strategies, Communal Resistance, and Economic Forces."
51. Fasenfast, "Community Politics and Urban Redevelopment."
52. Thomas, "Neighborhood Response to Redevelopment in Detroit"; Wylie, *Poletown.*
53. Hill, "Crisis in the Motor City"; Wylie, *Poletown*. Bryan D. Jones and Lynn W. Bachelor provide a more extensive discussion of the financing of this plan: Jones and Bachelor, *The Sustaining Hand*, 95–103.
54. Buckowczyk, "The Poletown Case and the Future of Detroit's Neighborhoods"; Darden et al., *Detroit*, 175–81; Thomas, "Neighborhood Response to Redevelopment in Detroit"; Wylie, *Poletown.*
55. Darden et al., *Detroit*, 175–81; Wylie, *Poletown*. To more fully understand the racial fissures and politics of the Poletown case, see Jones and Bachelor, *The Sustaining Hand*, 161–62.

### 4. PICKING UP SPEARS

1. Flanigan, "Local Project Tenants' Temperatures Rise in Wake of Heating Drop."
2. U.S. Department of Housing and Urban Development, *Low-Income Housing Program*, 21.
3. The Young quote is in Young and Wheeler, *Hard Stuff*, 200. For a more extensive discussion of this "Hollow Prize" phenomenon, see Friesema, "Black Control of Central Cities"; Keller, "The Impact of Black Mayors on Urban Policy"; Kraus and Swanstrom, "Minority Mayors and the Hollow-Prize Problem"; Nelson, "Black Mayoral Leadership"; and, esp., Brown, "Race and Politics Matter."
4. A discussion of housing disparities in the 1970s is in Rasmussen and Struyk, *A Housing Strategy for the City of Detroit*, as well as Anton, *Federal Aid to Detroit*. For an examination of federal housing scandals, see Boyer, *Cities Destroyed for Cash*; Chandler, *Urban Homesteading.*
5. City of Detroit Commission on Community Relations, "Housing Task Force," 1973, in Papers of the Commission on Community Relations, ALUA, box 121, file 7.
6. Boyer, *Cities Destroyed for Cash*, 24–36; Ball, "HUD Speculators Are Accused of Ar-

son for Profit"; idem, "HUD Plans Homes Sales Speed Up"; idem, "HUD Speculators Ordered Two Killings"; Chandler, *Urban Homesteading.*

7. These housing figures come from the 1970 and 1990 Census of Population for Michigan. Discussions of the number of jobs at the Poletown plant are in Thomas, "Neighborhood Response to Redevelopment in Detroit"; Wylie, *Poletown*, 96. The neglect of low-rental housing was national in scope. Testifying before the U.S. Senate Committee on Banking, Housing, and Urban Affairs in 1990, Peggy Posa, director of the Detroit Coalition on Temporary Shelter (COTS), noted, "In the 10 years before the mid-1970s and the mid-1980s the number of rental units available for $300 or less in this country decreased by 1 million units. The number of rental units available for over $400 in that same period increased by 4.5 million units. That sounds to me like a decision about who we are going to house." Her comments received loud applause: see U.S. Senate, "Hearing on Homeless Situation in Michigan," 34.
8. U.S. Bureau of the Census, "Current Housing Reports"; U.S. Department of Housing and Urban Development, "American Housing Survey for the Detroit Metropolitan Area."
9. Farley and Frey, "Changes in the Segregation of Whites from Blacks during the 1980s."
10. Welch et al., *Race and Place.*
11. In my interviews with Mayor Young and former City Council President Erma Henderson, they derided the decision to place Section 8 tenants in the historically middle-class apartment complex of Lafayette Park. Young fumed, "They have created a potential slum right there in the heart of Lafayette Park, which was years ago . . . an ideal middle-class settlement in the city of Detroit." In a separate interview, Henderson, a longtime advocate of fair housing, concurred: "You don't bring the slums into the finer apartments and still charge the great amount of rent." As a contrast to these sentiments, a black community developer confided to me, "When you talk about low-income rental housing [long-established homeowners] began to think Section 8, and start to think raggedy buildings, and 'folks doing all kinds of God knows what up in there.'" The community developer was resigned to the subtle class tensions in black neighborhoods that clearly constrained advocacy for low-income housing.
12. Robert Conot recounts the plight of Detroit's homeless during the Great Depression in *American Odyssey*, 332–33. President Reagan's infamous comment about the voluntary nature of homelessness is recounted in Roberts, "Reagan on Homelessness." For extensive discussions of homelessness prior to and during the 1980s and 1990s, see Hopper and Hamberg, "The Making of America's Homeless," 12–40; Jencks, *The Homeless*; Marcuse, "Homelessness and Housing Policy"; Tucker, *The Excluded Americans*; Wagner, *Checkerboard Square.*
13. Brand-Williams, "U.S. Counts the Homeless in Detroit"; Burt and Cohen, "America's Homeless"; "More Homeless in Detroit."
14. For a discussion of African Americans and the politics of homelessness, see Hopper

and Millburn, "Homelessness among African Americans." The homeless-service providers I consulted include Linebarger, Pippin, and Posa.

15. Caton, *Homeless in America*; Hoch and Slayton, *New Homeless and Old*; Rossi, *Down and Out in America*; Joint Center for Housing Studies, "The State of the Nation's Housing"; Wolch and Dear, *Malign Neglect*.
16. Babson, *Working Detroit*, 212–15; Jeter, "Young Wants Grants for Shelters"; Lynch and Leonard, "A Place to Call Home."
17. Pippin interview.
18. Wright, *Out of Place*.
19. Thomas, "Racial Crisis and the Fall of the Detroit Plan Commission," and *Redevelopment and Race*, 140–45.
20. U.S. Department of Housing and Urban Development, *Low-Income Housing Program*, 6.
21. Among independent public-housing authorities were Philadelphia and St. Louis: Bauman, *Public Housing, Race, and Renewal*, 6–8; Monti, *Race, Redevelopment, and the New Company Town*. Several advocates and some HUD officials complained about the DHD not being an independent authority: U.S. Department of Housing and Urban Development, *Coordinated Management Review*; Parkside Study Group, "Final Report"; Prescott telephone interview. But some in the administration believed it made no appreciable difference: Hagood interview.
22. U.S. Department of Housing and Urban Development, *Coordinated Management Review*, 6, 11, 13, 21–22, 24–25.
23. Rich, *Coleman Young and Detroit Politics*, 143–49; Thomas, *Redevelopment and Race*, 145–46, 185. As an urban and neighborhood planner and sociology instructor at Wayne State University, Council Member Mel Ravitz once wrote a searing critique of the mayor's failing to plan: Ravitz, "Community Development: Salvation or Suicide?"
24. Mullane interview; Planning Department, "Request for Proposals (RFP) for the 1985–1986 Neighborhood Opportunity Fund (NOF)/Community Development Block Grant (CDBG) Program," 1984, Community and Economic Development Department, City of Detroit.
25. Hagood interview.
26. Anton, *Federal Aid to Detroit*; Cheyfitz, "The Survivor," 97–98; Heldman, "Herman Gardens Gets $10 Million for Fix-Up."
27. Goetz, *Shelter Burden*, 29–37; Low Income Housing Information Service, "Special Memorandum"; Nathan et al., *Reagan and the States*; Rich, *Coleman Young and Detroit Politics*, 144; Stone, *Shelter Poverty*, 152–62. "U.S. Housing Programs Overhauled."
28. Goetz, "Retrenchment, Devolution and Local Housing Policy in the Postfederal Era."
29. U.S. President's Commission on Housing, *Report of the President's Commission on Housing*; see also Hartman, "Housing Policies under the Reagan Administration," 363.

30. Hartman, "Housing Policies under the Reagan Administration," 363–64. Shelia Ards discusses the impact the Reagan administration's greater reliance upon vouchers had upon African American communities in Ards, "The Theory of Vouchers and Housing Availability in the Black Community."
31. Hartman, "Housing Policies under the Reagan Administration," 366–67.
32. See Hays, *The Federal Government and Urban Housing*; Rich, *Federal Policymaking and the Poor*, 43–49.
33. U.S. Department of Housing and Urban Development, *Low-Income Housing Program*, 6–9.
34. Ibid., 17.
35. Young interview.
36. Lewis telephone interview.
37. Jackson interview.
38. Hagood interview; Lewis telephone interview; Prescott telephone interview; U.S. Department of Housing and Urban Development, *Low-Income Housing Program*, 6. A reference to mayoral nepotism is in Cannon and Vance, "Detroit Has 'Worst' Public Housing," 5A. Arguably, the mayor had a similar disregard for hiring professional urban planners, as reported in Thomas, *Redevelopment and Race*, 183–84.
39. Lewis telephone interview.
40. Ibid.
41. U.S. Department of Housing and Urban Development, *Low-Income Housing Program*, 12.
42. Ibid., 12, 14, 16.
43. Mack interview. Mack's type of account is corroborated by earlier findings by HUD: U.S. Department of Housing and Urban Development, *Low-Income Housing Program*, 6–7.
44. Impropriety by the staff is corroborated by several interviews with public officials and housing advocates: Mack, Jackson, Prescott, Sanders, and Williams. HUD auditors alleged that employees improperly used public-housing resources such as the personal use of department vehicles: U.S. Department of Housing and Urban Development, *Low-Income Housing Program*, 16, 44–46. The copying-machine example is recorded in idem, *Coordinated Management Review*, 70.
45. Idem, *Low-Income Housing Program*, 8–9; Stone, *Shelter Poverty*, 54–55. See also Katz, *In the Shadow of the Poorhouse*, 295–99.
46. Lewis telephone interview.
47. Prescott telephone interview.
48. Mahaffey interview.
49. Sanders interview.
50. The quote is from Kramer interview.
51. See Bobo and Gilliam, "Race, Sociopolitical Participation, and Black Empowerment"; Gay, "The Effect of Black Congressional Representation on Political Participation"; Gilliam and Kaufman, "Is There an Empowerment Life Cycle?"; Reed, "Sources of Demobilization in the New Black Political Regime"; Smith, *We Have No Leaders*; Tate, *Black Faces in the Mirror*.

52. Among the good overviews of Detroit and various examples of "activist mothering" are Naples, *Grassroots Warriors*; Spence, "Strings of Life"; Springer, *Still Lifting, Still Climbing*. Jan E. Leighley and her colleagues discovered that, while homeownership is positively associated with the likelihood of people contacting pubic officials, this effect was positive but not significant for African Americans: Leighley and Vedlitz, "Race, Ethnicity, and Political Participation," 1103, 1106.
53. Shaw and Spence, "Race and Representation in Detroit's Community Development Coalitions"; Tate, "Black Political Participation in the 1984 and 1988 Presidential Elections."
54. See Eisinger, "The Conditions of Protest Behavior in American Cities"; Lipsky, "Protest as a Political Resource"; McAdam, *Political Process and the Development of Black Insurgency*, 117–228; Rucht et al., *Acts of Dissent*; Smith et al., "From Protest to Agenda Building."
55. To review these protest opportunities and protest cycle concepts, see Euchner, *Extraordinary Politics*; Minkoff, "The Sequencing of Social Movements"; Snow and Benford, "Master Frames and Cycles of Protests"; Tarrow, *Struggling to Reform*; Tilly, *From Mobilization to Revolution*.
56. Thompson, *Double Trouble*, 90–93.
57. This sentiment was echoed by several advocates I interviewed: Brown-Wilson, DeSantis, Kramer, Manick, Martin-Turner and Smith, Sanders, Sims, and Trice.
58. Berry et al., "The Political Behavior of Poor People"; Boyte, *The Backyard Revolution*; Delgado, *Organizing the Movement*; Halpern, *Rebuilding the Inner City*.
59. Bush, "Detroit," 193–94.
60. Ibid.; Dosmet, "Council Approves Low-Cost Housing"; English, "Cockrel Calls West Side Housing Foes 'Elitist'"; "Groups Back Cockrel in Canfield Dispute"; Hill, "Crisis in the Motor City"; "Our Opinions."
61. Michigan Avenue Community Organization, "Revitalization Plan," 3.
62. Darden et al., *Detroit*, 197–98; Dolezal, "The Squeaky Wheel Gets the Grease"; Manick interview.
63. Kovari interview; Lee, "HUD Tenants Protest"; Mast, *Detroit Lives*, 154; Michigan Tenants Rights Coalition, "Federal Cutbacks Hurt the Poor," *MRTC Newsletter*, in Papers of the Commission on Community Relations, ALUA, box 121, folder 7.
64. Citizens for Welfare Reform, "Meeting Minutes," 1977, in Papers of the Welfare Employees Union, ALUA, Welfare Rights (1960s) box 78, file 28.
65. Borgos, "Low-Income Homeownership and the ACORN Squatters Campaign"; Boyte, *The Backyard Revolution*; West, *The National Welfare Rights Movement*.
66. Ball, "HUD's Inventory Soars"; Borgos, "Low-Income Homeownership and the ACORN Squatters Campaign"; Chandler, *Urban Homesteading*, 53–54; Henderson interview; Mleczko and Hindes, "'Bargain' House Isn't."
67. Association of Communities for Reform Now, "Standard Agenda for NAO"; Bailey, "Castles"; Cleveland interview; Freedberg, "Break-In to Protest HUD a Bust"; Freedman and Alpert, "Squatter Law Upheld"; Sawyers, "'Door Was Open'"; idem, "Squatters Can Take Vacant Homes"; idem, "Young Does Nothing." Andrew Dick further explains the shortcomings of nuisance abatement and repair-to-own, as

well as the Wayne County government's additional powers, which have made a larger dent in the problem: Dick, "Blight Flight."

**5. HOLDING THEM RESPONSIBLE**

1. Save Our Spirit, "SOS Builds 'Spirit House' and Garden on Vacant Lot." Discussions of activism and the politics of veto overrides are in Alpert, "City Council Overrides Young's Budget Vetoes"; Save Our Spirit, "Action Alert!" 1987, SOS files, Cass Corridor Neighborhood Development Corporation, Detroit; Vance, "Young Wins Budget War with Council."
2. Libby V. Morris and Gina L. Gilbreath derived an interesting model of black community-development organizing, some of whose assumptions parallel SOS's approach: Morris and Gilbreath, "African-American Community Development in Theory and Practice."
3. Hays, *The Federal Government and Urban Housing*, 208–11; Judd and Swanstrom, *City Politics*, 183–87; Rich, *Federal Policymaking and the Poor*, 36–49.
4. The Williams quote is from "Neighborhood Leaders," 1A. See the following regarding the other community-development politics: Darden et al., *Detroit*; Goetz, *Shelter Burden*, 114–38; idem, "The Community-Based Housing Movement and Progressive Local Politics"; Henderson, "Detroit City Council Budget Message," 1989; Rubin, *Renewing Hope within Neighborhoods of Despair*; Save Our Spirit, "The Community Development Block Grant Program"; Vidal, "Rebuilding Communities."
5. Mel Ravitz, "Letter to My Colleagues," 1985, files of the Detroit City Planning Commission, Cass Corridor Neighborhood Development Corporation, Detroit.
6. Coleman Young, "Letter to the Honorable City Council," 1985, Files of the City Planning Commission, Files of City Planning Commission, Detroit.
7. City of Detroit, "Community and Economic Development Department"; Karen McCleod, "Re: Proposed City Council Block Grant Task Force, To: Council President Mahaffey," 1990, Files of City Planning Commission, Detroit; O'Regan and Quigley, "Federal Policy and the Rise of Nonprofit Housing Providers"; Walker, "Community Development Corporations and Their Changing Support Systems," 31. SOS asks for council to consider problems in grant administration and Mahaffey responds: Save Our Spirit, "Open Letter Asks Council to Vote for Neighborhoods"; Toy, "Mahaffey Wants to Shorten Wait for Federal Block Funds." For a discussion of the 1993 Grantee Performance Report data, see Shaw and Spence, "Race and Representation in Detroit's Community Development Coalitions," 200–201.
8. Young, "Letter to the Honorable City Council," 314–15.
9. Hagood interview.
10. Walker, "Community Development Corporations and Their Changing Support Systems," 8, 29, 41. The figures come from my calculations using CDBG data between 1985 and 1993.
11. Young interview.

12. See series "Mayor's Message, City of Detroit Budget," circa April 1985–92, Files of City Planning Commission, City of Detroit. The figures for CDBG housing allocations are from Shaw, "Responsible for Their Deeds," 425. For a discussion of nonprofits as client-actors of political machines, see Marwell, "Privatizing the Welfare State."
13. Bachelor and Jones, "Managed Participation," 524–26; Beaupre interview; Thomas, *Redevelopment and Race*, 182. This coalition was also very concerned about the practice of suburban Detroit communities opting not to apply for CDBG to discourage programs and housing of benefit to low-income citizens and minorities: see Coalition for Block Grant Compliance, "Housing for All People: A Citizen-Based Program to Facilitate Affirmative Suburban Housing Initiatives in the Community Development Block Grant Program in Three Southeastern Michigan Counties," 1978, in Papers of the Commission on Community Relations, ALUA, box 121, folder 13.
14. My figures for the HUD Grantee Performance reports come from the files of Save Our Spirit, Cass Corridor Neighborhood Development Corporation, Detroit, and especially the tabulations by Beverly Manick. This is partly the basis for the numbers reported in Figure 8. For the other facts about CDBG, see Bachelor and Jones, "Managed Participation," 532–33; Rich, *Federal Policymaking and the Poor*, 295–321.
15. City of Detroit, "Preliminary Statement of Community Development Objectives and Projected Use of Funds"; Planning Department, "Request for Proposals," 1–8; Shaw, "Responsible for Their Deeds," 404–405.
16. Atlas and Dreier, "The Tenants' Movement and American Politics"; City of Detroit, "Preliminary Statement of Community Development Objectives and Projected Use of Funds," 2–3; Hartman, "Housing Policies under the Reagan Administration"; Marcuse, "Homelessness and Housing Policy." See also Manick, McCleod, and Sims interviews.
17. Tschirhart, "Mrs. Henderson to Battle Mayor."
18. Young and Wheeler, *Hard Stuff*, 316.
19. Nicholas Hood, "Council Colleagues / City Planning Commission. Re: Amendments to CDBG Recommendations," 1985, Files of the City Planning Commission, Detroit; Vance, "Young Wins Budget War with Council."
20. Hood interview.
21. The quotes about Mahaffey are from Kramer and McCleod interviews. Young's comments are from Young and Wheeler, *Hard Stuff*, 227–28.
22. City Clerk's Office, "Council Members since 1919 (City of Detroit) in Order—per Votes Received," Files of City Planning Commission, Detroit; Mahaffey interview.
23. See "Congressman George W. Crockett, Jr., Endorses Maryann Mahaffey."
24. Mast, *Detroit Lives*, 133; Save Our Spirit, "Brief History of SOS," 1989, SOS files, Cass Corridor Neighborhood Development Corporation, Detroit.
25. Save Our Spirit, "Principles of SOS Members."
26. Manick interview; Save Our Spirit, "Brief History of SOS." Also, these conclusions

are based on my participant observation field notes from SOS meetings, as well as from the Detroit City Council's NOF and CDBG public hearings in the spring of 1994.

27. Young and Wheeler, *Hard Stuff*, 229.
28. Save Our Spirit, "City Council, an Open Letter," 1987, SOS files, Cass Corridor Neighborhood Development Corporation, Detroit, 1.
29. Idem, "Save Our Spirit: Neighborhoods Are the Spirit of Detroit; Restore the Balance!" 1990; idem, "SOS Testimony [before the City Council]" (1990); idem, "SOS Testimony [before the City Council]," 1991, all in SOS files, Cass Corridor Neighborhood Development Corporation, Detroit. Again, these observations come from my field notes of the City Council's public hearings of NOF and CDBG appeals in the spring of 1994.
30. Ravitz, "Letter to My Colleagues."
31. City of Detroit, "Statement by Mel Ravitz."
32. Olson, *The Logic of Collective Action*.
33. Chong, *Collective Action and the Civil Rights Movement*; Hardin, *Collective Action*; McAdam, *Political Process and the Development of Black Insurgency*; Morris, *The Origins of the Civil Rights Movement*.
34. Mossberger and Stoker, "The Evolution of Urban Regime Theory"; Orr and Stoker, "Urban Regimes and Leadership in Detroit"; Reed, "The Black Urban Regime."
35. Shaw and Spence, "Race and Representation in Detroit's Community Development Coalitions," 137–39.
36. Clingmayer and Feoick, "Council Views toward Targeting Economic Development Policy Benefits."
37. Save Our Spirit, "S.O.S. Coalition Urges Equity in Block Grant Spending."
38. Brown-Wilson interview; Kovari interview; McCleod interview; Save Our Spirit, "Council President Maryann Mahaffey," 1990, SOS files, Cass Corridor Neighborhood Development Corporation, Detroit; Dolores Weber, City Planning Commission, Citizen Review Committee, 1991, City of Detroit, Files of the City Planning Commission, Detroit.
39. Save Our Spirit, "City Council, an Open Letter" (my emphasis). See also Sims interview.
40. Kovari interview; Mahaffey, "Making the Tough Decisions"; Ravitz, "Community Development Block Grant Ordinance"; Save Our Spirit, "SOS Alert," 1991, SOS files, Cass Corridor Neighborhood Development Corporation, Detroit; Sims interview.
41. Save Our Spirit, "Principles of SOS Members."
42. Ravitz interview.
43. Alpert, "City Groups Ask Council for Share of Federal Aid"; Save Our Spirit, "The Community Development Block Grant Program"; idem, "Save Our Spirit Campaign Persuades Council"
44. Darden et al., *Detroit*, 197–98; Vance and Zeiger, "Detroit Council Members Oppose Many Young Cuts."
45. Save Our Spirit, "Save Our Spirit Campaign Persuades Council."

46. Bailey, "Henderson Moves to Cut Mayor's Veto Clout"; Eberhard, "Councilman Eberhard Comments on 1988/89 Budget Veto"; Mahaffey, "Statement for the Record," 1393; Vance, "Young Fights Override Proposal." For a discussion of the Detroit politics of casino gaming around this period, see Eisinger, "The Politics of Bread and Circuses Building"; Warren Connor Development Coalition, "Casino Gambling."
47. Amend the Charter to Improve Our Neighborhoods, "The Following Organizations and Individuals Have Endorsed Proposal N," 1988, SOS Files, Cass Corridor Neighborhood Development Corporation, Detroit; Bailey, "Coalition Plans Campaign to Give Council More Budget Control"; Jones, "Push Grows to Cut Young Budget Power."
48. The results of the Proposal N and Proposal J can be retrieved from Detroit Election Commission, *General Election*. The Young quote is recorded in Vance, "Mayor."
49. Shaw, "Race, Regime and Redevelopment," 197–98.
50. I control for temporal dependence in my models by using robust standard errors with cluster analysis in which I cluster by year. The robust standard errors and clustered regression analysis method of estimation is a well-accepted method for handling the problem of conditional dependence among a model's error terms. I thank Christopher Zorn for his invaluable assistance and patience in explaining various methodological options: see Zorn, "Comparing GEE and Robust Standard Errors for Conditionally Dependent Data." I cannot assume that a group's request in any one year or the mayor's recommendations and City Council actions at any point in time are uninfluenced by, and thus independent of, previous years or previous steps in the budget process. Thus, "robust standard errors" permit me to control this conditional dependence between cases. The clustering of analysis by year (six of them) and the use of difference measures controls the conditional dependence between years. My thanks also to Nancy Glenn for her broader insights about nonparametric statistics but particularly difference-in-difference estimators: see Neumark et al., "The Effects of Minimum Wages on the Distribution of Family Incomes." Having said this, I was unable to control for spatial correlation or dependence between proximate census tracks as geographic units. I thank David Darmofal for his insights: see Darmofal, "Spatial Econometrics in Political Science." First, the specific design of my panel data set did not permit the STATA statistics program to properly read the year variable and thus perform procedures that could correct for spatial correlation. Second, it is difficult to perfectly control for both spatial and temporal correlation. Nonetheless, I have confidence in my estimations because they are partially corroborated by what subsequent examiners of the Detroit CDBG allocations have discovered. Lyke Thompson conducted extensive CDBG research in the late 1990s and early 2000s: see also Michigan Neighborhood Partnership, "Detroit State of the Neighborhoods Report"; Planning and Development Department, "Analysis of Funding for Programs as specified by the City Council."
51. Earl et al., "The Use of Newspaper Data in the Study of Collective Action"; Wisler and Barranco, "Validity and Systematicity of Newspaper Data in Event Analysis."

52. Among the groups included were homeless-service providers and homeless shelters; home repair and rehabilitation groups; tenant advocacy organizations; and public-housing resident organizations. All of these variables were coded 1 if "yes" and 0 if "no."
53. All of these variables were coded 1 if "yes" and 0 if "no."
54. City of Detroit, "Community and Economic Development Department."
55. Hood interview; Phillips interview.
56. Ball, "Housing Protesters Try to See Young."
57. Henderson, "Detroit City Council Budget Message," 1989.
58. Cheyfitz, "The Survivor"; Kramer interview; Rich, "Coleman Young and Detroit Politics, 1972–1986"; idem, *Coleman Young and Detroit Politics*; Sharrott, *"Operation Occupancy" and Activities to House Homeless Families*; Thompson, "Rethinking the Collapse of Postwar Liberalism."
59. Jones and Cannon, "Council Kills Veto," 14A.
60. The figures come from the author's unreported analysis of the average CDBG funds the mayor versus the city council allocated by census tract demographics. For a discussion of the racial representation problem in the community-development movement, see Shaw and Spence, "Race and Representation in Detroit's Community Development Coalitions."
61. Brown-Wilson interview; PEOPLE Convention, "The PEOPLE's Platform"; "Vote Totals."

**6. NOW IS THE TIME!**

1. Cannon and Vance, "Young to Review Housing Department"; Chargot and Hundley, "The New Homeless"; Gunther, "A Strong Dose of Reality"; McTyre, "A Place to Stay"; Rossi, *Down and Out in America*; "Shelters Inundated by Nation's Homeless."
2. Ball, "Housing Protesters Try to See Young"; Dozier, "Homeless Protest Includes a Brawl"; Sharrott, "To John Codwell, Director, DHD."
3. Bennett and Reed, "The New Face of Urban Renewal"; Goetz, "The Politics of Poverty Deconcentration and Housing Demolition"; Wilson, *The Truly Disadvantaged*, 56, 58, 60–62.
4. Alex-Assensoh, "Race, Concentrated Poverty, Social Isolation, and Political Behavior"; Jargowsky, *Poverty and Place*, 77–78; Wilson, "Restructuring and the Growth of Concentrated Poverty in Detroit."
5. Goetz, "The Politics of Poverty Deconcentration and Housing Demolition."
6. Carter et al., "Polarisation, Public Housing, and Racial Minorities in U.S. Cities"; Hirsch, *Making the Second Ghetto*; Holloway et al., "Exploring the Effect of Public Housing on the Concentration of Poverty in Columbus, OH"; Massey and Kanaiaupuni, "Public Housing and the Concentration of Poverty."
7. DeSantis interview; Parkside Study Group, "Final Report," 128–29.
8. Bennett and Reed, "The New Face of Urban Renewal"; Goetz, "The Politics of

Poverty Deconcentration and Housing Demolition"; Venkatesh, *American Project*, 263–77. Edward Goetz has also written a more recent work to detail the politics of de-concentration: Goetz, *Clearing the Way*. One study concluded that renovation was more feasible than demolition and new construction: see On-Site Insight, "Final Report." Although it is not a major focus of my work, my interview subjects frequently shared the belief that DHD had a wholly inadequate system of public safety to secure their complexes. One firm, JOWA, was accused of impropriety, including drug dealing among its officers, and was drastically overpaid: see Parkside Study Group, "Final Report," 24–25, 37–40, 64–69; U.S. Department of Housing and Urban Development, *Coordinated Management Review*, 45.

9. The quotes are from Sweeney, "Brewster 'Family' Returns to Projects"; "When Life in the Projects Was Good." Additional testimony of fond Brewster Homes memories is in Hunter and Manlove, "Discussion on the Life in the Brewster Housing Projects."
10. This conclusion is based on my observations of several years of CDBG applications.
11. A series of HUD audit reports, to which I frequently referred in chapter 4, assert that Detroit public housing was grossly mismanaged: U.S. Department of Housing and Urban Development, *Coordinated Management Review*; idem, *Low-Income Housing Program*; idem, *Maintenance Review*; idem, *Review*. But my interviews with public-housing activists first introduced the claim that demolition and de-concentration had an ulterior motive: interviews with Kramer, Linebarger, Mack, Milton, Phillips, Pippin, Sanders, Taylor, Williams.
12. Tschirhart, "Project Residents Raise Protest."
13. U.S. Department of Housing and Urban Development, *Low-Income Housing Program*, 9.
14. Bailey, "Life Is Hard for Detroiters in the Projects"; U.S. Department of Housing and Urban Development, *Low-Income Housing Program*; Vance, "Brewster Razing Bid Faulted"; idem, "Project Residents Protest Demolition."
15. Clements, "HUD Urges Shake-Up in City Housing"; Trent, "HUD to City"; U.S. Department of Housing and Urban Development, *Coordinated Management Review*; idem, *Low-Income Housing Program*.
16. Mel Ravitz, "Re: Community Development Block Grant Budget," 1986, to Members of the Detroit City Council, Files of the City Planning Commission, Detroit; Young, "Mayor's Message," 1986, City of Detroit Budget, 1986–87, presented to the Detroit City Council, Files of the City Planning Commission, Detroit. The figures for the Brush Park/Medical Center improvements come from my analysis of the CDBG data compiled between 1983 and 1993.
17. Ravitz interview.
18. Mahaffey interview.
19. These conclusions are from my field research.
20. Cleveland interview.
21. Peoples interview.

22. Bailey, "Life Is Hard for Detroiters in the Projects"; Lewis telephone Interview; Mahaffey interview; U.S. Department of Housing and Urban Development, *Low-Income Housing Program.*
23. Bratt, "Public Housing," 367; Hays, *The Federal Government and Urban Housing*, 239. The quote is from Lewis telephone interview. This quote is reiterated in U.S. Department of Housing and Urban Development, *Low-Income Housing Program*, 20.
24. Among the accounts and reports that differ with Lewis's claim are Lynch and Leonard, "A Place to Call Home"; Mahaffey interview; Prescott telephone interview; U.S. Bureau of the Census, "Current Housing Reports"; U.S. Department of Housing and Urban Development, *Low-Income Housing Program.*
25. Smith, "Tenant Council?"
26. U.S. Department of Housing and Urban Development, *Coordinated Management Review*, 8–9. The quote is from idem, *Briefing on Detroit Public Housing*, 4.
27. Minkoff, "The Sequencing of Social Movements." There is evidence that low-income clients' experiences with public bureaucracies shape political learning and political participation more broadly: Soss, "Lessons of Welfare."
28. Tschirhart, "Project Residents Raise Protest"; Zablit, "Group Vows to be Advocate for Homeless."
29. Brian P. Conway's and David S. Hachen Jr.'s attitudinal findings regarding the key determinants of participation in public-housing tenant associations parallel my assumptions—efficacy (collective identity), grievances (framing), resources and constraints (group resources), and neighborhood attachments (networks): see Conway and Hachen, "Attachments, Grievances, Resources, and Efficacy."
30. There is evidence that by 1993 some prominent civil-rights leaders began to question the practices of the administration relative to the issues of homelessness. By 1993, the Detroit Urban League had invited the UCHC, among others, to sit on the Detroit / Wayne County Homeless Strategy Coalition. It issued a final report that generally was quite critical of the administration of DHD: see United Community Housing Coalition, "Detroit Urban League Detroit Wayne County Homeless Strategy Coalition."
31. Among those advocates who expressed concern they were willingly to share about the involvement of churches were Kramer, Linebarger, Milton, and Sanders. The quote is from Vance and Farrell, "City Acts to Evict Woman."
32. Hood interview; Katz, *The Undeserving Poor.*
33. Union membership is derived from "State of the Cities Dataset," Lewis Mumford Center for Comparative Urban and Regional Research, 2004, available online at http://mumford.albany.edu/census/data.html#state (accessed September 30, 2004). Babson, *Working Detroit*, 211–15, documents the dire economic context these union members and autoworkers confronted in the 1980s.
34. Caton, *Homeless in America*; Detroit Area Study, "Separate and Unequal"; Hopper, "Advocacy for the Homeless in the 1980s"; Hopper and Hamberg, "The Making of America's Homeless"; "More Homeless in Detroit"; Wolch and Dear, *Malign Neglect.*

35. See Williams, *The Politics of Public Housing*. To reiterate from chapter 1, standpoint theory is found in the work of Hill Collins, *Black Feminist Thought*. The quotes are from Taylor interview.
36. Pope, *Biting the Hand That Feeds Them*; Rosenthal, *Homeless in Paradise*; Wagner, *Checkerboard Square*; Wagner and Cohen, "The Power of the People"; West, *The National Welfare Rights Movement*.
37. Milton interview testifies to the efforts to evict Jones. Dozier, "Homeless Protest Includes a Brawl," provides evidence of the arrest of a public-housing and anti-homelessness protester. The quote is from Pippin interview.
38. Kramer interview.
39. Delgado, *Organizing the Movement*; "Homeless Unite"; Kotz and Kotz, *A Passion for Equality*; Zablit, "Group Vows to be Advocate for Homeless." Firsthand knowledge of the homeless union's founding is from Kramer, Linebarger, and Taylor interviews.
40. The quote is from Vance, "Project Residents Protest Demolition." See also Parkside Study Group, "Final Report"; U.S. Department of Housing and Urban Development, *Review*.
41. Griffen, "Letter to the Detroit City Council."
42. Dozier, "Homeless Protest Includes a Brawl"; Henderson, "Detroit City Council Budget Message," 1989; Tschirhart, "Project Residents Raise Protest"; Young, "From the Mayor," 1222–23.
43. The information and quotes, respectively, are from Kamuda, "Activists for Homeless Protest," and Kramer interview.
44. Chargot, "Homeless in Shelters Get Offer of Public Housing"; Kramer and Linebarger interviews; Shaw, "Race, Regime and Redevelopment."
45. Ball and Kramer interviews.
46. Blossom and Kaplan, "Council Considers Housing Homeless"; Kaplan, "Union Says City's Too Slow in Providing Public Housing"; "Protesters: Promises Broken."
47. Chargot, "Kemp Rips City Official on Public Housing Stand"; U.S. Senate, "Hearing on Homeless Situation in Michigan."
48. Williams interview.
49. Given the highly incendiary nature of this remark, I have decided to make this an anonymous quote. But still it demonstrates the animus some housing officials harbored toward activists.
50. Kleinknecht, "Brewster Demolition Plan Gets City Council Backing"; idem, "Crew Begins Demolition at Brewster-Douglass"; Mullane interview; Stone, *Shelter Poverty*; "U.S. Housing Programs Overhauled." The quote is from Hood interview. The council vote for the Brewster-Douglass renovation plan is recorded in Detroit City Council, "Resolution: Brewster Douglass Housing Renovation."
51. Cannon, "HUD Likes City's Plan to Overhaul Its Troubled Housing Program"; Chargot, "Kemp Rips City Official on Public Housing Stand"; Fears, "Brewster-Douglas Demolition Protested."
52. Ball, "Activist Criticizes Detroit's Homeless Program"; idem, "Homeless Wash Cars

to Get Money for Rally"; Goetz, *Shelter Burden*, 75; May, "Advocates for the Homeless to March for Federal Money."

53. Preserve Low Income and Affordable Housing Now! *Preserve Low Income and Affordable Housing Now! for Detroit.*
54. Ball, "Public Housing Official Says Some Rules Lacking"; Preserve Low Income and Affordable Housing Now! *Preserve Low Income and Affordable Housing Now! for Detroit*, 13–16; Smith, "Tenant Council?"; idem, "Public Housing Residents Organize to Fight for Improved Conditions."
55. Ball, "City Police Fold Tent as Being Hazardous"; Kramer interview.
56. Huskisson, "In Detroit, Jackson to Protest State Cuts"; Kramer interview; Wimberley, "Leaders Blast Engler on Homelessness."
57. Adams, "Problem Identified, Now Fix It."
58. Boyte, "The Growth of Citizen Politics"; Fisher, "Neighborhood Organizing"; Franklin, "Community Organizing and Strategy in Post-Black Power Grass-Roots Activism"; Jackson, "The State, the Movement, and the Urban Poor"; Preserve Low Income and Affordable Housing Now! *Preserve Low Income and Affordable Housing Now! for Detroit*; Williams and Sanders interviews.
59. Preserve Low Income and Affordable Housing Now! *Preserve Low Income and Affordable Housing Now! for Detroit*; idem, "Receivership Now!!!"
60. Idem, *Preserve Low Income and Affordable Housing Now! for Detroit.*
61. Mack, Sanders, and Williams interviews.
62. Mack and Williams interviews.
63. Dozier and Ball, "Police Charge Floor Held by 250 Protesters"; idem, "Poor Seize on Empty Housing."
64. Parkside Resident Council, "Parkside Community in Action"; Preserve Low Income and Affordable Housing Now!, "Operation Occupancy"; idem, "Tenants' Voice"; Williams interviews.
65. Prescott telephone interview; Sharrott, "Memo to John Codwell, Director, DHD," 2; Trent, "Low-Income Units Should Be Repaired."
66. Sharrott, *"Operation Occupancy" and Activities to House Homeless Families*. The Binford quote is from Trent, "HUD to City." See also Ball, "HUD Boss Says City Didn't Meet Goals as Claimed"; idem, "No Stranger to Trouble"; Parkside Study Group, "Final Report," 22; Preserve Low Income and Affordable Housing Now! "Tenants' Voice."
67. Parkside Study Group, "Final Report"; Preserve Low Income and Affordable Housing Now! "Tenants' Voice."
68. Parkside Study Group, "Final Report"; Toy, "City Council Approves Plan to Raze Parkside Homes"; Trent, "Low-Income Units Should Be Repaired."
69. Ball, "Man Takes Risk to Help Squatters Fill Vacant Units."
70. Ball, "Squatters Face Eviction"; Williams interview.
71. Clements, "HUD Urges Shake-Up in City Housing"; Gamson and Meyer, "Framing Political Opportunity"; Huskisson, "U.S. to Help Detroit with Housing Team"; U.S. Department of Housing and Urban Development, *Coordinated Management Review*, 17.

72. Parkside Study Group, "Final Report"; Trent, "HUD Official Scolds City for Not Meeting Public Housing Goals."
73. Ball, "Razing of Public Housing Rejected"; Parkside Study Group, "Final Report"; Prescott, "DHD Partnership Planning Retreat"; Toy, "City Council Approves Plan to Raze Parkside Homes." For records of the two council attempts to approve the Parkside replacement plan, see Detroit City Council, "Resolution: Replacement Housing Plan for Parkside Homes."
74. HUD's contradictory stances are recorded in Sharrott, *"Operation Occupancy" and Activities to House Homeless Families*, versus U.S. Department of Housing and Urban Development, *Maintenance Review*, 7. The quote is from Williams interview.
75. Ball, "City Leases End Fight with Homeless Families"; Williams interview.

### 7. A CHANGE IS GONNA COME?

1. Owens, *God and Government in the Ghetto*; Popkin et al., "A Decade of HOPE VI."
2. Migoya, "HUD Won't OK Detroit Plan until New Housing Chief Picked."
3. Detroit Housing Commission, *Gardenview Estates*, 1.
4. McGraw and Montemurri, "Detroit Throng Bids Farewell to Young."
5. Banks, "A Changing Electorate in a Black Majority City"; Coleman, "Swearing-in Ceremony of Dennis W. Archer," 4A; McCormick and Jones, "The Conceptualization of Deracialization"; Salim Muwakkil, "Black Politics' Paradigm Paradox," available online at http://www.inthesetimes.com/site/main/article/2714 (accessed June 26, 2006).
6. Archer, "Thoughts for a Great Detroit," 49–50.
7. Coleman, "Swearing-in Ceremony of Dennis W. Archer"; "Detroit Election Totals"; McGraw, "Archer Has a Lot to Learn and Fast Transition Team's Job Crucial at Start."
8. Naughton and Higgins, "Chrysler's Sales Surge May Create 6,000 Jobs"; Thomas, "Applying for Empowerment Zone Designation."
9. At the end of his first year in office, President Clinton gave a speech to the Democratic Leadership Council in which he celebrated the new election as well as the DLC membership of Mayor Archer: see William J. Clinton, "Remarks to the Democratic Leadership Council University of California," 1993, available online at http://www.presidency.ucsb.edu/ws/print.php?pid=46193 (accessed February 3, 2007). See also Hackworth, *The Neoliberal City*. I use the term "new liberal" as opposed to "neoliberal" partly to emulate Klinkner's and Reed's terminology and their inference that regimes like those of Clinton and Archer occupy the center-left of the neoliberal ideological spectrum: Klinkner, "Bill Clinton and the Politics of New Liberalism"; Reed, "The Black Urban Regime."
10. Archer, "Inaugural Address," 6; idem, "Thoughts for a Great Detroit"; Boyle, "APSA Economic Empowerment Zone Panel," 8; Klinkner, "Bill Clinton and the Politics of New Liberalism"; McCormick and Jones, "The Conceptualization of Deracialization"; Williams, *The Constraint of Race*, 312–28.

11. Hagood interview.
12. Burns and Thomas, "The Failure of the Nonregime," 518; Orr and Stoker, "Urban Regimes and Leadership in Detroit"; Stone, *Regime Politics*.
13. Boyle, "APSA Economic Empowerment Zone Panel," 3; Committee to Elect Freeman Hendrix Mayor, "Freeman Hendrix for Mayor: Leadership That Works," 2006, available online at http://www.fremanhendrix.com/economic.htm (accessed February 14, 2007); Downtown Detroit Partnership, "The Year in Review." See also Thomas, *Redevelopment and Race*, 182.
14. Bockmeyer, "Community Coup"; Hagood interview; McGraw, "The Mayoral Legacy"; Siegel, "Protesters Urge Conversion of Hudson's"; Thomas, *Redevelopment and Race*, 189–93.
15. Judd and Swanstrom, *City Politics*, 196–97; Liebschutz, "Empowerment Zones and Enterprise Communities."
16. Allen, "Community Based Organizations as Policy Entrepreneurs," 20; Herbert et al., "Interim Assessment of the Empowerment Zones and Enterprise Communities (EZ/EC) Program," 1–4, 1–8; McGraw and Johnson, "Clinton Sees Hope in Detroit."
17. Boyle, "APSA Economic Empowerment Zone Panel," ii.
18. Allen, "Community Based Organizations as Policy Entrepreneurs," 28–29, 52; Bockmeyer, "A Culture of Distrust," 2430–34; Brown-Wilson interview.
19. Bockmeyer, "A Culture of Distrust"; Detroit Empowerment Zone Coordinating Council, "Detroit Empowerment Zone." At one public meeting, the CDAD even displayed letters of support from various foundations—Annie E. Casey; the Local Initiatives Support Corporation (LISC), Brown's former employer; Kresge—to stress that it knew how to create partnerships in the EZ process: see Allen, "Community Based Organizations as Policy Entrepreneurs," 27. For interview, see DeSantis interview.
20. Herbert et al., "Interim Assessment of the Empowerment Zones and Enterprise Communities (EZ/EC) Program," 2–9, 2–11, 13–14, 13–15; U.S. Government Accountability Office, "Empowerment Zones and Enterprise Community Program," 89, 104.
21. Follow-up interviews with public-housing activists and allies corroborated the view that there was a shift from protest to programming to take advantage of new opportunities: Sumareh interview (second Sanders interview); Williams interview. The newspaper analysis is not shown but was conducted by the author with thanks to the graduate research assistant A. J. Bargothi, who coded newspaper stories from the *Detroit Free Press* between 1993 and 2000.
22. Popkin et al., "The Gautreaux Legacy"; Popkin et al. "A Decade of HOPE VI"; Vardy et al., "Attracting Middle-Income Families in the HOPE VI Public Housing Revitalization Program."
23. Office of the Inspector General, "Audit Report," 1; Trent, "HUD Chief Offers New Hope."
24. Ball, "City Leases End Fight with Homeless Families"; McGraw, "New Mayor Making Changes at a Fast Clip"; Williams interview.

25. I conducted a brief interview with Betty Turner in the spring of 2007.
26. Archer and Greene, "Detroit Housing Commission Accomplishment Report"; Bivins, "Feds Say Detroit Public Housing Improving"; Fine, *Violence in the Model City*; Hackney, "Detroit Removed from List of Troubled Housing"; McConell, "Archer Wants Public Housing Agency to Be Separate."
27. Dixon, "Housing Has Cracks"; idem, "Housing Rehab Plans Crumbling Soberly Needed."
28. Idem, "Archer Requests HUD's Help"; U.S. General Accounting Office, "Public Housing: HUD's Oversight of HOPE VI Sites Needs to be More Consistent."
29. Popkin et al., "A Decade of HOPE VI," 40.
30. Nutt-Powell, *Capital Needs Unlimited.*
31. Office of the Inspector General, "Audit Report."
32. Nutt-Powell, *Capital Needs Unlimited*; Smith telephone interview.
33. Nutt-Powell, *Capital Needs Unlimited*; Planning Commission, "Minutes of Regular Meeting"; U.S. General Accounting Office, "Public Housing: HUD's Oversight of HOPE VI Sites Needs to be More Consistent."
34. Rogers telephone interview; Williams interview.
35. Williams interview.
36. Nutt-Powell, *Capital Needs Unlimited*, 10.
37. U.S. General Accounting Office, "Public Housing: HUD's Oversight of HOPE VI Sites Needs to be More Consistent," 91; Williams interview.
38. U.S. General Accounting Office, "Public Housing: HUD's Oversight of HOPE VI Sites Needs to be More Consistent," 91.
39. Keating, *Atlanta*; Orr and Stoker, "Urban Regimes and Leadership in Detroit"; Rutheiser, *Imagineering Atlanta*, 4; Stone, *Regime Politics.*
40. Naperstek et al., "HOPE VI."
41. Atlanta Task Force for the Homeless, "Homelessness in Metropolitan Atlanta," as cited in Wilkes, "A Case Study of Homelessness in the City of Atlanta," 11–14; Fernandez, "Judge Rejects Plea to Block Arrests of Homeless"; Jargowsky, *Poverty and Place*, 223, 225, 227; Kasarda, "Inner-City Concentrated Poverty and Neighborhood Distress"; National Coalition for the Homeless and National Law Center on Homelessness and Poverty, "A Dream Denied," 15; "Plan for Olympic Park Spurs Atlanta Protest"; Stone, *Regime Politics*, 141–42; Towns, "Homeless Numbers Vary."
42. Ferguson, *Black Politics in New Deal Atlanta*, 165–85; Keating, *Atlanta*, 175–76; Newman, "The Atlanta Housing Authority's Olympic Legacy Program," 6–7.
43. Keating and Flores, "Sixty and Out," 284–87; Newman, "The Atlanta Housing Authority's Olympic Legacy Program," 7–8.
44. Burbank et al., "Antigrowth Politics or Piecemeal Resistance?" 344; Keating, *Atlanta*, 288–89; Keating and Flores, "Sixty and Out," 175–77.
45. Keating and Flores, "Sixty and Out," 289–94.
46. Ibid., 295.
47. Ibid. The Glover quote comes from ibid., 295.
48. For the sake of consistency, I refer to her by the same name Larry Keating uses in

his work: ibid., 289–94. But in his doctoral dissertation, Frank Johnson refers to her as "Ella Johnson": see Johnson, "Let the Games Begin," 205–18.

49. Johnson, "Let the Games Begin," 183–218.
50. Horwich et al., *Rebuilding Homes and Lives*, 10; Naperstek et al., "HOPE VI." Quote from Salama, "The Redevelopment of Distressed Public Housing," 106.
51. Ambrose et al., "Mixed Income Housing Initiatives in Public Housing," 7–10; Buron et al., *The HOPE VI Resident Tracking Study*; Naperstek et al., "HOPE VI"; Salama, "The Redevelopment of Distressed Public Housing," 106.
52. Sidney, "The Urban Slums Report"; U.S. Bureau of the Census, "Emergency and Transitional Shelter Population," 16; Woody, *Managing Crisis Cities*, 59–87.
53. Sidney, "The Urban Slums Report," 5–6; Robert Anthony Watts, "Not the Old Newark: Has Newark Emerged from the Ashes of the 1967 Riots," Brookings Institution, 2004, available online at http://www.livingcites.org/pdf/Not_The_Old_Newark.pdf (accessed February 1, 2007). For an explanation of the recent conviction of James, see Miller and Jones, "Ex-Newark Mayor Convicted of Fraud."
54. Sidney, "The Urban Slums Report," 12. A *New York Times* article revealed that the NHA's executive director, Harold Lucas, claimed that the authority during his term (1992–98) went from "worst to first" are not accurate and that some of the NHA's quality scores were inflated: see Cave, "Report Suggests That Newark Housing Agency Had a History of Troubles."
55. Buron et al., *The HOPE VI Resident Tracking Study*, 17–21; Roberts, "Another Newark Housing Project Has Date with Wrecking Ball." The James quote is from idem, "Newark Mayor Lambastes Columnist."
56. Carter, "City Continues to Upgrade Housing Skyline"; idem, "Newarkers Protest Threat to Their Home"; Newman, "Newark, Decline and Avoidance, Renaissance and Desire," 41–47; Newark Housing Authority, "FY2007–2009 Annual Plan," 8.
57. Neighborhood Info D.C., "District of Columbia Housing Monitor," 1; Gillette, "Protest and Power in Washington, D.C."; McGovern, *The Politics of Downtown Development*.
58. Gillette, "Protest and Power in Washington, D.C.," 202–207; McGovern, *The Politics of Downtown Development*, 260–61.
59. U.S. General Accounting Office, "Public Housing: Information on Receiverships at Public Housing Authorities," 31–32.
60. Holin and Amendolia, "Interim Assessment of the HOPE VI Program," 1–8. The Didden quote and additional details are in Loeb, "At Wilson Dwellings, a Dream Gets Hope."
61. These census tract figures are only rough estimates because the geographic boundaries of each HOPE VI project and the census tracts do not perfectly match.
62. Kingsley et al., "Patterns of Section 8 Relocation in the HOPE VI Program."
63. Dixon, "Housing Has Cracks."
64. Newark Housing Authority, "City View Landing Construction in Progress, Newark Housing Authority," 2007, available online at http://www.newarkha.org/nha/city%20view.html (accessed November 13, 2007).

65. Jeffries is not included in this table because I was unable to reach key participants in the case. However, I include its census-tract figures because it was one of Detroit's HOPE VI revitalization projects.

## EPILOGUE

1. A good reference for Dewey's democratic philosophy is Westbrook, *John Dewey and American Democracy*. For a classic political-science investigation into black political efficacy, see Shingles, "Black Consciousness and Political Participation."
2. The quote from Clark is in Hansen and Foner, *Women of Hope*, 10. King used this quote in 1967 in his presidential address to the SCLC: King, *Where Do We Go from Here*, 252. For the MWRO quote, see Michigan Welfare Rights Organization, "Donate to MWRO," 2006, available online at http:www.mwro.org/toc.htm (accessed March 18, 2006).
3. Williams interview.
4. Hill Collins, *Black Feminist Thought*; Naples, *Grassroots Warriors*; Williams, *The Politics of Public Housing*. In previous work, I have referred to this faith as a belief in "diversionary politics" or the politics of diverting the welfare policy agenda from more draconian alternatives: see Shaw, "We Refused to Lay Down Our Spears," 172–76.
5. Barber, *Strong Democracy*; Green, *Deep Democracy*; Thompson, *Double Trouble*, 23–28, 30.
6. Association of Communities for Reform Now, "The People's Plan for Overcoming the Hurricane Katrina Blues"; Burns and Thomas, "The Failure of the Nonregime"; People's Organizing Committee of the New Orleans Survivor Council, "Public Housing Residents Take Back Their Homes," February 11, 2007, available online at http://www.peoplesorganizing.org/breaking_news.html#ph (accessed February 13, 2007); United New Orleans Plan, "Preliminary Report Updated."
7. Lefebvre, "Water Woes"; Pope, "MWRO Protests against Winter Utility Shutoffs"; Williams interview. For a documentary that explains the passionate equity campaign for water in Highland Park, see Miller, *The Water Front*. I thank Curtis Smith for bringing this work to my attention.
8. Bello and Montemurri, "Kilpatrick Has Ten Days 'til Layoffs"; idem, "Report Shows Detroit Finances in Worse Shape"; Elrick, "Mayor Comes Back"; Kilpatrick, "State of the City Address."
9. Pratt, "Housing Project Gets under Way." The HUD quote is from Bello and Montemurri, "City-Owned Slum Awaits Wreckers," 3; Detroit Housing Commission, "DHC Makes History"; Preserve Low Income and Affordable Housing Now! "Receivership Now!!!"; U.S. Department of Housing and Urban Development, "HUD Assumes Control of Detroit Housing Commission to Restore Public Confidence in Agency."
10. Bello and Montemurri, "Maryann Mahaffey"; Mahaffey, "Detroit City Council's 2005–2006 Budget"; Richardson, "Redistribution Effect of Introducing Census

2000 Data in CDBG Formula," 50; Sumareh (Sanders) interview; Weisman, "Bush Plans Sharp Cuts in HUD Community Efforts"; Williams interviews.

11. Montgomery, "In Sweep, Fenty Draws on Uniting to Conquer"; Slater, "Obama Reels in Austin Crowd"; Wang and Mays, "After Two Decades under James, Residents Heed Call for Change." For an article that deftly critiques the unorthodox politics of Cory Booker and implicitly the newest generation of African American politicians, see Muwakkil, "Black Politics' Paradigm Paradox." Peter Burns and Matthew O. Thomas offer an interesting discussion of how, for all of his efforts, Nagin lacked an urban regime in New Orleans: Burns and Thomas, "The Failure of the Nonregime." Discussions of the Kilpatrick–Beatty indictment and Detroit's latest housing woes are in Aguillar, "Wayne Co[unty] Foreclosure Rate Leads the Nation"; Krolicki, "Detroit Faces Racial Issues with Mayoral Crisis."

# Bibliography


Adams, Charles G. "Political Suicide Not the Way." *Michigan Chronicle*, July 18, 1989, 4.

———. "Problem Identified, Now Fix It." *Michigan Chronicle*, January 8, 1992, A7.

Aguillar, Louis. "Wayne Co[unty] Foreclosure Rate Leads the Nation." *Detroit News*, February 13, 2007.

Alex-Assensoh, Yvette. "Race, Concentrated Poverty, Social Isolation, and Political Behavior." *Urban Affairs Review* 33 (1998): 209–27.

Alex-Assensoh, Yvette, and Karin Stanford. "Gender, Participation, and the Black Urban Underclass." In *Women Transforming Politics: An Alternative Reader*, ed. by Cathy J. Cohen, Kathleen Jones and Joan C. Tronto. New York: New York University Press, 1997.

Alinsky, Saul. *Rules for Radicals: A Practical Primer for Realistic Radicals*. New York: Vintage Books, 1972.

Allen, Charlene J. "Community Based Organizations as Policy Entrepreneurs: Getting Neighborhood's on the Policy Agenda." Paper presented at the National Conference of Black Political Scientists, Atlanta, March 6–9, 2002.

Alpert, Bruce. "City Council Overrides Young's Budget Vetoes." *Detroit News*, June 4, 1986, A3.

———. "City Groups Ask Council for Share of Federal Aid." *Detroit News*, April 29, 1987, 4B.

Ambrose, Brent, William Grigsby, Samuel Zell, and Robert Laurie. "Mixed Income Housing Initiatives in Public Housing." Unpublished ms., 1999, Zell / Lurie Center Working Papers. Wharton School Samuel Zell and Robert Lurie Real Estate Center. University of Pennsylvania, Philadelphia.

Anderson, Jervis. *Bayard Rustin: Troubles I've Seen, a Biography*. New York: HarperCollins, 1997.

Andrews, Kenneth T. "The Impact of Social Movements on the Political Process: The Civil Rights Movement and the Black Electoral Politics in Mississippi." *American Sociological Review* 62 (1997): 800–19.

"Annual Personnel Figures, 2000." Department of Human Resources, City of Detroit, 2000.

Anton, Thomas J. *Federal Aid to Detroit*. Washington, D.C.: Brookings Institution, 1983.

Archer, Dennis W. "Inaugural Address: Mayor Dennis W. Archer." *Journal of the City Council* (1998): 4–8.

———. "Thoughts for a Great Detroit . . . Draft for Community Input." Report, Detroit, 1991.

Archer, Dennis W., and Carl R. Greene. "Detroit Housing Commission Accomplishment Report." Detroit, 1996.

Ards, Shelia. "The Theory of Vouchers and Housing Availability in the Black Community." In *Race, Politics, and Economic Development*, ed. by James Jennings. London: Verso, 1992.

Askins, John. "City Tenant Board Leaders Demand Salaries and Staff." *Detroit Free Press*, August 15, 1969, 3A-2.

———. "Real Housing Issue: Power." *Detroit Free Press*, July 1, 1969, 6D.

———. "Tenant Board Makes New Demands." *Detroit Free Press*, August 21, 1969, 3A-4.

———. "Tenants Hold Upper Hand in Public Housing." *Detroit Free Press*, August 14, 1969, 3A.

Association of Communities for Reform Now (ACORN). "The People's Plan for Overcoming the Hurricane Katrina Blues: A Comprehensive Strategy for Building a More Vibrant, Sustainable, and Equitable 9th Ward." Report, New Orleans, 2007.

———. "Standard Agenda for NAO." Detroit, 1990.

Atlanta Task Force for the Homeless. "Homelessness in Metropolitan Atlanta: June 1994." Atlanta Task Force for the Homeless, Atlanta, 1994.

Atlas, John, and Peter Dreier. "The Tenants' Movement and American Politics." In *Critical Perspectives on Housing*, ed. by Rachel G. Bratt, Chester Hartman and Ann Meyerson. Philadelphia: Temple University Press, 1986.

Ayres, Jeffrey M. "Transnational Activism in the Americas: The Internet and Innovations in the Repertoire of Collective Action." *Research in Social Movements, Conflicts, and Change* 26 (2005): 35–61.

Babson, Steve. *Working Detroit: The Making of a Union Town*. Detroit: Wayne State University Press, 1986.

Bachelor, Lynn W., and Bryan D. Jones. "Managed Participation: Detroit's Neighborhood Opportunity Fund." *Journal of Applied Behavioral Science* 17, no. 4 (1981): 518–36.

Bailey, Chauncey. "'Castles,' but Transforming Empty Homes Won in Lottery is a Slow Process." *Detroit News*, October 14, 1982, 2B, 3B.

———. "Coalition Plans Campaign to Give Council More Budget Control." *Detroit News*, September 30, 1988, B3.

———. "Henderson Moves to Cut Mayor's Veto Clout." *Detroit News*, June 1, 1988, 1.

———. "Life Is Hard for Detroiters in the Projects." *Detroit News*, March 9, 1986, 2, 8.

Ball, Don. "HUD Speculators Are Accused of Arson for Profit." *Detroit News*, January 18, 1976, 1A, 10A.

———. "HUD Plans Homes Sales Speed Up." *Detroit News*, February 14, 1976, 3A.

———. "HUD Speculators Ordered Two Killings." *Detroit News*, January 19, 1976, 1A, 4A.

———. "HUD's Inventory Soars, but Turnabout Is Slated." *Detroit News*, May 2, 1978, 2B.

Ball, Zachare. "Activist Criticizes Detroit's Homeless Program." *Detroit Free Press*, October 6, 1989, 4A.

———. "City Leases End Fight with Homeless Families." *Detroit Free Press*, January 12, 1994, 2B.

———. "City Police Fold Tent as Being Hazardous." *Detroit Free Press*, November 18, 1991, 1B.

———. "Homeless Wash Cars to Get Money for Rally." *Detroit Free Press*, October 1, 1989, 3A.

———. "Housing Protesters Try to See Young: Homeless Say Detroit Fails on Promise." *Detroit Free Press*, October 27, 1992, 3A.

———. "HUD Boss Says City Didn't Meet Goals as Claimed." *Detroit Free Press*, December 6, 1991, 2B.

———. "Man Takes Risk to Help Squatters Fill Vacant Units: But Some at Jeffries Homes Complain." *Detroit Free Press*, November 20, 1993, 3A.

———. "No Stranger to Trouble: Crisis Chief Tackled HUD Scandal in '70s." *Detroit Free Press*, November 21, 1991, 8A.

———. "Public Housing Official Says Some Rules Lacking." *Detroit Free Press*, February 13, 1991, 3A.

———. "Razing of Public Housing Rejected: United Renovation Costs Inflated, HUD Says." *Detroit Free Press*, March 10, 1992, 3A, 4A.

———. "Squatters Face Eviction, Vow to Fill Courtroom." *Detroit Free Press*, December 18, 1993, 16.

Banks, Manley Elliott. "A Changing Electorate in a Black Majority City: The Emergence of a Neo-Conservative Black Urban Regime in Contemporary Atlanta." *Journal of Urban Affairs* 22, no. 3 (2000): 265–78.

Barber, Benjamin R. *Strong Democracy: Participatory Politics for a New Age*. Berkeley: University of California Press, 1984.

Barras, Jonetta Rose. *The Last of the Black Emperors: The Hollow Comeback of Marion Barry in the New Age of Black Leaders*. Baltimore: Bancroft Press, 1998.

Bartelt, David W. "Housing the 'Underclass.'" In *The Underclass Debate: Views from History*, ed. by Michael B. Katz. Princeton: Princeton University Press, 1993.

Bates, Beth, Timothy Bates, and Grace Lee Boggs. "Where Are the People? Review Essay on Thomas Sugrue's *The Origins of the Urban Crisis*." *Review of Black Political Economy* 27, no. 4 (2000): 13–26.

Bauman, John F. *Public Housing, Race, and Renewal: Urban Planning in Philadelphia, 1920–1974*. Philadelphia: Temple University Press, 1987.

Bearman, Peter S, and Kevin D. Everett. "The Structure of Social Protest, 1961–1983." *Social Networks* 15, no. 2 (1993): 171–200.

Bello, Marisol, and Patricia Montemurri. "City-Owned Slum Awaits Wreckers: Some Residents Welcome Plans to Rebuild Jeffries Project." *Detroit Free Press*, January 12, 2007, 1–6.

———. "Kilpatrick Has Ten Days 'til Layoffs." *Detroit Free Press*, August 5, 2005.

———. "Maryann Mahaffey, 1925–2006: She Spoke for Those Who Needed a Voice." *Detroit Free Press*, July 26, 2006, 1A, 9A.

———. "Report Shows Detroit Finances in Worse Shape." *Detroit Free Press*, April 4, 2006, 1–2.

Bennett, Larry. "Harold Washington and the Black Urban Regime." *Urban Affairs Quarterly* 28 (1993): 423–40.

Bennett, Larry, and Adolph J. Reed. "The New Face of Urban Renewal: The Near North Redevelopment Initiative and the Cabrini-Green Neighborhood." In *Without Justice for All: The New Liberalism and Our Retreat from Racial Equality*, ed. by Adolph Reed Jr. Boulder, Colo.: Westview Press, 1999.

Berry, Brian J. L. *The Open Housing Question: Race and Housing in Chicago, 1966–1976*. Cambridge, Mass.: Ballinger, 1979.

Berry, Jeffrey, Kent Portney, and Ken Thomson. "The Political Behavior of Poor People." In *The Urban Underclass*, ed. by Christopher Jencks and Paul E. Peterson. Washington, D.C.: Brookings Institution, 1991.

Bivins, Larry. "Feds Say Detroit Public Housing Improving: Focus on Services, Management Helps Raise System's Troubled Status." *Detroit News*, January 26, 1997.

Black, Harold. "Restrictive Covenants in Relation to Segregated Housing in Detroit." Master's thesis, Wayne State University, Detroit, 1947.

———. "Urban Renewal: A Program Involving a Multiplicity of Participants." Ph.D. diss., University of Michigan, Ann Arbor, 1973.

Blanchard, Allan. "City's Poor Get Dynamic Organizer." *Detroit News*, August 15, 1965, 1A, 9A.

Bledsoe, Timothy, Michael Combs, Lee Sigelman, and Susan Welch. "Trends in Racial Attitudes in Detroit, 1968–1992." *Urban Affairs Review* 31, no. 4 (1996): 508–28.

Blossom, Theresa, and Deborah Kaplan. "Council Considers Housing Homeless." *Detroit Free Press*, February 24, 1989, 3A.

Bobo, Lawrence, and Franklin Gilliam. "Race, Sociopolitical Participation, and Black Empowerment." *American Political Science Review* 84 (1990): 377–93.

Bockmeyer, Janice. "Community Coup: CDC Activism in the Detroit Empowerment Zone." Paper presented at the Annual Meeting of the American Political Science Association, San Francisco, 1996.

———. "A Culture of Distrust: The Impact of Local Political Culture on Participation in the Detroit EZ." *Urban Studies* 37, no. 13 (2000): 2417–40.

Boggs, Grace Lee. *Living for Change: An Autobiography*. Minneapolis: University of Minnesota Press, 1998.

Borgos, Seth. "Low-Income Homeownership and the ACORN Squatters Campaign." In *Critical Perspectives on Housing*, ed. by Rachel G. Bratt, Chester Hartman, and Ann Meyerson. Philadelphia: Temple University Press, 1986.

Boston, Thomas D. *Race, Class, and Conservatism*. Boston: Unwyn Hyman, 1988.

Bove, Eric, Phillip Brown, Peter Hollands, Sarah Snow, and John Thoma. "Dilemmas of Community-Based Housing Development: Case Studies." In *Rebuilding a Low-Income Housing Policy*, ed. by Rachel G. Bratt. Philadelphia: Temple University Press, 1989.

Boyer, Brian. *Cities Destroyed for Cash: The FHA Scandal at HUD*. Chicago: Follet Publishing, 1973.

Boyle, Kevin. *Arc of Justice: The Saga of Race, Civil Rights, and Murder in the Jazz Age*. New York: Henry Holt, 2004.

Boyle, Robin. "APSA Economic Empowerment Zone Panel: Notes on Detroit." Paper presented at the Annual Meeting of the American Political Science Association, Chicago, 1995.

Boyte, Harry C. *The Backyard Revolution: Understanding the New Citizen Movement*. Philadelphia: Temple University Press, 1980.

———. "The Growth of Citizen Politics: Stages in Local Community Organizing." *Dissent* (1990): 513–18.

Branch, Taylor. *Parting the Waters: America in the King Years, 1954–63*. New York: Simon and Schuster, 1988.

Brand-Williams, Oralandar. "U.S. Counts the Homeless in Detroit: Workers Visit Shelters, Abandoned Buildings to Ensure Accuracy." *Detroit News*, March 28, 2000.

Bratt, Rachel G. "Public Housing: The Controversy and Contribution." In *Critical Perspectives on Housing*, ed. by Rachel G. Bratt, Chester Hartman and Ann Meyerson. Philadelphia: Temple University Press, 1986.

Brown, Robert A. "Race and Politics Matter: Black Urban Representation and Social Spending during the Urban Crisis." *National Black Political Science Review* 11 (2007): 17–41.

Brown, Robert A., Heather Dash, and Tharius Sumter. "Is It 'Cause I'm Broke or 'Cause I'm Black? An Empirical Analysis of the Race versus Class Debate in African Americans' Political Attitudes." Paper presented at the Midwest Political Science Association, Chicago, 2000.

Brown, Robert A., and Todd C. Shaw. "Separate Nations: Two Attitudinal Dimensions of Black Nationalism." *Journal of Politics* 64, no. 1 (2002): 22–44.

Browning, Rufus P., Dale Rogers Marshall, and David H. Tabb. *Protest Is Not Enough: The Struggle of Black and Hispanics for Equality in Urban Politics*. Berkeley: University of California Press, 1984.

Buckowczyk, John. "The Poletown Case and the Future of Detroit's Neighborhoods." *Michigan Quarterly Review* (1988): 449–57.

Burbank, M. J., C. H. Heying, and G. Andronovich. "Antigrowth Politics or Piecemeal Resistance? Citizen Opposition to Olympic-Related Economic Growth." *Urban Affairs Review* 35, no. 3 (2000): 334–57.

Burns, James McGregor. *Leadership*. New York: Harper and Row, 1978.

Burns, Peter, and Matthew O. Thomas. "The Failure of the Nonregime: How Katrina Exposed New Orleans as a Regimeless City." *Urban Affairs Review* 41, no. 4 (2006): 517–27.

Burnstein, Paul. "Social Movements and Public Policy." In *How Social Movements Mat-*

*ters*, ed. by Marco Giugni, Doug McAdam, and Charles Tilly. Minneapolis: University of Minnesota Press, 1999.

Buron, Larry F., Susan J Popkin, Dianne Levy, Laura Harris, and Jill Khadduri. *The HOPE VI Resident Tracking Study: A Snapshot of the Current Living Situation of Original Residents from Eight Sites*. Washington, D.C.: Abt Associates and Urban Institute, 2002.

Burt, Martha R, and Barbara E. Cohen. *America's Homeless: Numbers, Characteristics, and Programs That Serve Them*. Washington, D.C.: Urban Institute, 1989.

Bush, Rod. "Detroit: Victory of a Black Radical. Interview with Ken Cockrel." In *The New Black Vote: Politics and Power in Four American Cities*, ed. by Rod Bush. San Francisco: Synthesis Publications, 1984.

Calpotura, Francis, and Kim Fellner. "Square Pegs Find Their Groove: Reshaping the Organizing Circle." Manuscript. Center for Third World Organizing, Oakland, Calif., n.d.

Cannon, Angie. "Detroit Has 'Worst' Public Housing." *Detroit News*, March 6, 1991, 1A, 5A.

———. "HUD Likes City's Plan to Overhaul Its Troubled Housing Program." *Detroit News*, January 6, 1991, 1C, 2C.

Cannon, Angie, and N. Scott Vance. "Young to Review Housing Department." *Detroit News*, September 6, 1990, 1A, 2B.

Capeci, Dominic, Jr. *Race Relations in Wartime Detroit: The Sojourner Truth Housing Controversy of 1942*. Philadelphia: Temple University Press, 1984.

Carbado, Devon W. "The Million Man March: Racial Solidarity or Division?" In *Black Men on Race, Gender, and Sexuality*, ed. by Devon W. Carbado. New York: New York University Press, 1999.

Carter, Barry. "City Continues to Upgrade Housing Skyline: $50 Million Federal Grant to Put Townhouse on Site of Walsh Homes." *Star-Ledger*, July 20, 2000, 1.

———. "Newarkers Protest Threat to Their Home: Rally Decries HUD Proposal to Close Building." *Star-Ledger*, March 14, 2000, 40.

Carter, William H, Michael H Schill, and Susan M. Wachter. "Polarisation, Public Housing, and Racial Minorities in U.S. Cities." *Urban Studies* 35, no. 1 (1998): 1889–1911.

Castells, Manuel. *The City and the Grassroots: A Cross-Cultural Theory of Urban Social Movements*. Berkeley: University of California Press, 1983.

Caton, Carol. *Homeless in America*. New York: Oxford University Press, 1990.

Cave, Damien. "Report Suggests That Newark Housing Agency Had a History of Troubles." *New York Times*, September 29, 2004, 1–3.

Chafets, Ze'ev. *Devil's Nights: And Other True Stories of Detroit*. New York: Random House, 1990.

Chandler, Mittie Olion. *Urban Homesteading: Programs and Policies*. Westport, Conn.: Greenwood Press, 1988.

Chargot, Patricia. "Homeless in Shelters Get Offer of Public Housing." *Detroit Free Press*, January 27, 1988, 5A.

———. "Kemp Rips City Official on Public Housing Stand. *Detroit Free Press*, April 21, 1990, 1A, 6A.

Chargot, Patricia, and Tom Hundley. "The New Homeless: Special Report." *Detroit Free Press*, February 18, 1988, 1B, 4B.

Checkoway, Barry, and Marc A Zimmerman. *Correlates of Participation in Neighborhood Organizations*. Philadelphia: Haworth Press, 1992.

Cheyfitz, Kirk. "The Survivor." *Monthly Detroit*, February 1981, 41–53, 97–100.

Chong, Dennis. *Collective Action and the Civil Rights Movement*. Chicago: University of Chicago Press, 1991.

Churchill, Ward, and Jim Vander Wall. *Agents of Repression: The FBI's Secret War against the Black Panther Party and the American Indian Movement*. Boston: South End Press, 1990.

Chwe, Michael. "Structure and Strategy in Collective Action." *American Journal of Sociology* 105 (1999): 128–56.

City of Detroit. "Community and Economic Development Department—May 18, 1992—HOME Rehab—from Henry Hagood, Director." *Journal of the Detroit City Council* (1992): 1039–40.

———. "Preliminary Statement of Community Development Objectives and Projected Use of Funds." Detroit, 1985.

———. "Statement by Mel Ravitz re: Budget Veto Override." *Journal of the Detroit City Council* (1987): 1237.

Clavel, Pierre, and Wim Wiewel. *Harold Washington and the Neighborhoods: Progressive City Government in Chicago, 1983–1987*. New Brunswick, N.J.: Rutgers University Press, 1991.

Clements, Michael. "HUD Urges Shake-Up in City Housing." *Detroit News*, January 30, 1992, 1A, 11A.

Clingmayer, James C., and Richard C. Feoick. "Council Views toward Targeting Economic Development Policy Benefits." *Journal of Politics* 57 (1995): 508–20.

Cohen, Cathy. *The Boundaries of Blackness: AIDS in the Black Community*. Chicago: University of Chicago Press, 1999.

Cohen, Cathy, and Michael Dawson. "Neighborhood Poverty and African American Politics." *American Political Science Review* 87, no. 2 (1993): 286–301.

Cohen, Hal. "Neighborhood Urges Council: 'Raze Those Houses!'" *Detroit Free Press*, July 2, 1965, 1A.

Colburn, David R. "Running for Office: African-American Mayors from 1967 to 1996." In *African-American Mayors: Race, Politics, and the American City*, ed. by David R. Colburn and Jeffrey S. Adler. Urbana: University of Illinois Press, 2001.

Coleman Jr., Kenneth. "Swearing-In Ceremony of Dennis W. Archer: Thousands Attend Emotion-Filled Ceremony." *Michigan Chronicle*, January 11, 1994, 1A, 4A.

"Congressman George W. Crockett, Jr., Endorses Maryann Mahaffey." *Michigan Chronicle*, October 28, 1989, 2A.

Conley, Dalton. *Being Black, Living in the Red: Race, Wealth, and Social Policy in America*. Berkeley: University of California Press, 1999.

Conot, Robert. *American Odyssey*. Detroit: Wayne State University Press, 1986.

Conway, Brian P., and David S. Hachen Jr. "Attachments, Grievances, Resources, and Efficacy: The Determinants of Tenant Association Participation among Public Housing Tenants." *Journal of Urban Affairs* 27, no. 1 (2005): 25–52.

Conway, Margaret. *Political Participation in the United States*, 3d ed. Washington, D.C.: CQ Press, 2000.

Cooper Hamilton, Donna, and Charles V. Hamilton. *The Dual Agenda: Race and Social Welfare Policies of the Civil Rights Organizations*. New York: Columbia University Press, 1997.

Cress, Daniel M., and David Snow. "Mobilization at the Margins: Resources, Benefactors, and the Viability of Homeless Social Movement Organizations." *American Sociological Review* 61 (1996): 1089–1109.

Dahl, Robert. *A Preface to Democratic Theory*. Chicago: University of Chicago Press, 1956.

Darden, Joe T., Richard C. Hill, June Thomas, and Richard Thomas. *Detroit: Race and Uneven Development*. Philadelphia: Temple University Press, 1987.

Darmofal, David. "Spatial Econometrics and Political Science." Unpublished ms., Society for Political Methodology Working Archive, 2006.

Dawson, Michael. *Behind the Mule: Race and Class in African American Politics*. Princeton: Princeton University Press, 1994.

———. *Black Visions: The Roots of Contemporary African-American Political Ideologies*. Chicago: University of Chicago Press, 2001.

Daya, Dalpha Kasan, Willie Fuller, Richard Leon Lindsey, Marilyn E. M. Ross. *Self Determination: An Exploratory Study of the Characteristics of Participants and Non-Participants in the West Central Organization*. Detroit: Wayne State University, 1966.

"Death-Trap House Falls Wednesday." *Detroit Free Press*, July 28, 1965, 1A.

DeLeon, Richard E. *Left Coast City: Progressive Politics in San Francisco, 1975–1991*. Lawrence: University Press of Kansas, 1992.

Delgado, Gary. *Beyond the Politics of Place: New Directions in Community Organizing in the 1990s*, 2d ed. Oakland, Calif.: Applied Research Center, 1994.

———. "Building Multiracial Alliances: The Case of People United for a Better Oakland." In *Mobilizing the Community: Local Politics in the Era of the Global City*, ed. by Robert Fisher and Joe Kling. Newbury Park, Calif.: Sage Publications, 1993.

———. *Organizing the Movement: The Roots and Growth of ACORN*. Philadelphia: Temple University Press, 1986.

D'Emillio, John. *Lost Prophet: The Life and Times of Bayard Rustin*. New York: Free Press, 2003.

DeSena, Judith N. "'What's a Mother to Do?' Gentrification, School Selection, and the Consequences for Community Cohesion." *American Behavioral Scientist* 50, no. 2 (2006): 241–57.

Deskins, Donald, Jr. "Residential Mobility of Negroes in Detroit, 1836–1965." Report, Department of Geography, University of Michigan, Ann Arbor, 1972.

Detroit Area Study. "Separate and Unequal: The Racial Divide. Strategies for Reducing Political and Economic Inequalities in the Detroit Area." Report to the Detroit Tri-County Area. University of Michigan, Ann Arbor, 1989.

Detroit City Council. "Resolution: Brewster Douglass Housing Renovation." *Journal of the Detroit City Council* (1990): 829.

———. "Resolution: Replacement Housing Plan for Parkside Homes Mich. 1–14." *Journal of the Detroit City Council* (1992): 82, 1970–71.

Detroit Election Commission. *General Election.* Detroit, 1988.

"Detroit Election Totals." *Detroit Free Press,* November 4, 1993, 6B.

Detroit Empowerment Zone Coordinating Council. "Detroit Empowerment Zone: Progress Report to the Community." Detroit, 1994.

Detroit Housing Commission. "DHC Makes History: Public Housing Residents Elected to Both Top Board Positions." *Resident DHC News,* 2002, 1, 3.

———. *Eleventh Annual Report of the Detroit Housing Commission.* Detroit, 1946.

———. *Fifth Annual Report of the Detroit Housing Commission.* Detroit, 1938.

———. *First Annual Report of the Detroit Housing Commission.* Detroit, 1934.

———. *Gardenview Estates.* Detroit, n.d.

———. *Public Housing in Detroit, 1946–1948.* Detroit, 1948.

———. *Second Annual Report of the Detroit Housing Commission.* Detroit, 1935.

———. *Slum Clearance and Public Housing in Detroit.* Detroit, 1952.

———. *Slum Clearance and Public Housing in Detroit.* Detroit, 1953.

———. *Tenth Annual Report.* Detroit, 1944.

———. *A Tour of Detroit's Urban Renewal Projects.* Detroit, 1965.

Dewan, Shaila. "Gentrification Changing Face of New Atlanta." *New York Times,* March 11, 2006.

DeWolfe, Robert. "Model Policeman Punches Superior at Picketing Scene." *Detroit Free Press,* July 27, 1965.

Dick, Andrew. "Blight Flight: Detroit's Aggressive Approach to Nuisance Abatement Is Sparking Some Redevelopment." *Planning* 73, no. 6 (2007): 44–47.

Dillard, Angela Denise. *Faith in the City: Preaching Radical Social Change in Detroit.* Ann Arbor: University of Michigan Press, 2007.

Dixon, Jennifer. "Archer Requests HUD's Help, City Looks for Advice on Best Use of Funds." *Detroit Free Press,* March 26, 1999, 1B.

———. "Housing Has Cracks, City HUD Vowed Changes, but Residents Are Frustrated." *Detroit Free Press,* March 25, 1999, 1B.

———. "Housing Rehab Plans Crumbling Soberly Needed, Public Projects Are Way Over Budget." *Detroit Free Press,* February 16, 2000, 1B.

Dolezal, Suzanne. "The Squeaky Wheel Gets the Grease." *Detroit Free Press Magazine,* August 2, 1981, 7.

Dosmet, Kate. "Council Approves Low-Cost Housing." *Detroit News,* October 3, 1978, BD02.

Downs, Anthony. *New Visions for Metropolitan America.* Washington, D.C.: Brookings Institution, 1994.

Downtown Detroit Partnership. *The Year in Review, the Year Ahead—Partnering for Progress*. Detroit: Downtown Detroit Partnership, 2006.

Dozier, Marian. "Homeless Protest Includes a Brawl: Union Presses Council for Audience, Action." *Detroit Free Press*, October 28, 1989, 1A.

Dozier, Marian, and Zachare Ball. "Police Charge Floor Held by 250 Protesters." *Detroit Free Press*, October 30, 1991, 1A–2A.

———. "Poor Seize on Empty Housing." *Detroit Free Press*, October 30, 1991, 1.

Dreier, Peter, John H. Mollenkopf, and Todd Swanstrom. "What Cities Can Do to Address Poverty." In *Place Matters: Metropolitics for the Twenty-first Century*. Lawrence: University Press of Kansas, 2001.

Dyson, Michael. "Introduction, Beyond Essentialism: Expanding African-American Cultural Criticism." In *Reflecting Black: African-American Cultural Criticism*. Minneapolis: University of Minnesota Press, 1993.

Earl, Jennifer, Andrew Martin, John D. McCarthy, and Sarah A. Soule. "The Use of Newspaper Data in the Study of Collective Action." *Annual Review of Sociology* 30 (2004.): 65–80.

Eberhard, David. "Councilman Eberhard Comments on 1988 / 89 Budget Veto." *Journal of the Detroit City Council* (1988): 1392.

Edwards, Jeffrey. "The Resolution of an 'Urban Crisis': Racial Formation in Detroit, 1961–1981." Ph.D. diss., University of Minnesota, Minneapolis, 1992.

Eisinger, Peter K. *Black Employment in City Government, 1973–1980*. Washington, D.C.: Joint Center for Political Studies, 1983.

———. "The Conditions of Protest Behavior in American Cities." *American Political Science Review* 67 (1973): 11–28.

———. "The Politics of Bread and Circuses Building: The City for the Visitor Class." *Urban Affairs Review* 35, no. 3 (2000): 316–33.

———. *The Politics of Displacement: Racial and Ethnic Transition in Three American Cities*. New York: Academic Press, 1980.

Elrick, M. L. "Mayor Comes Back: Kilpatrick Grabs Victor in Early-Morning Finish." *Detroit Free Press*, November 9, 2005, 1A.

English, Carey. "Cockrel Calls West Side Housing Foes 'Elitist.'" *Detroit Free Press*, October 3, 1978, 4C.

Euchner, Charles C. *Extraordinary Politics: How Protest and Dissent Are Changing American Democracy*. Boulder: Westview Press, 1996.

Eulau, Heinz, and Paul D. Karps. "The Puzzle of Representation: Specifying Components of Responsiveness." *Legislative Studies Quarterly* 2, no. 3 (1977): 233–354.

"Evicted Chain-In Sponsors Take Landlord to Court." *Detroit Free Press*, June 3, 1965, 4B.

Ewen, Lynda. *Corporate Power and Urban Crisis in Detroit*. Princeton: Princeton University Press, 1978.

Fainstein, Susan S., and Norman I. Fainstein. "Regime Strategies, Communal Resistance, and Economic Forces." In *Restructuring the City: The Political Economy of Urban Development*, ed. by Susan S. Fainstein and Norman I. Fainstein, Richard Child Hill, Dennis Judd, and Michael P. Smith. New York: Longman, 1983.

Falbaum, Berl. "Housing Outlook Here Remains Gloomy." *Detroit Free Press*, August 28, 1968, 12B.

Farley, Reynolds, and William H. Frey. "Changes in the Segregation of Whites from Blacks during the 1980s: Small Steps toward a More Integrated Society." *American Sociological Review* 59, no. 1 (1994): 23–45.

Farley, Reynolds, and Howard Schuman. *Detroit Area Study Code Book with Final Marginals*. Ann Arbor: University of Michigan, Detroit Area Study, 1976.

Farley, Reynolds, Sheldon Danziger, and Harry J. Holzer. *Detroit Divided*. New York: Russell Sage Foundation, 2000.

Fasenfast, David. "Community Politics and Urban Redevelopment: Poletown, Detroit, and General Motors." *Urban Affairs Quarterly* 22, no. 1 (1986): 101–23.

Fears, Darryl. "Brewster-Douglas Demolition Protested." *Detroit Free Press*, September 22, 1990, 3A.

Ferguson, Karen. *Black Politics in New Deal Atlanta*. Chapel Hill: University of North Carolina Press, 2002.

Ferman, Barbara. *Challenging the Growth Machine in Chicago and Pittsburgh Neighborhood Politics*. Lawrence: University Press of Kansas, 1996.

Fernandez, Maria Elena. "Judge Rejects Plea to Block Arrests of Homeless, but Sets Some Limits." *Atlanta Journal-Constitution*, July 18, 1996, C5.

Fine, Sidney. *Violence in the Model City: The Cavanagh Administration, Race Relations, and the Detroit Riot of 1967*. Ann Arbor: University of Michigan Press, 1989.

Fisher, Robert. *Let the People Decide: Neighborhood Organizing in America*. Boston: Twayne Publishers, 1984.

———. "Neighborhood Organizing: The Importance of Historical Context." In *Revitalizing Urban Neighborhoods*, ed. by W. Dennis Keating, Norman Krumholz, and Philip Star. Lawrence: University Press of Kansas, 1996.

Fisher, Robert, and Eric Shragge. "Contextualizing Community Organizing: Lessons from the Past, Tensions in the Present, Opportunities for the Future." In *Transforming the City: Community Organizing and the Challenge of Political Change*, ed. by Marion Orr. Lawrence: University Press of Kansas, 2007.

Flanigan, Brian. "Local Project Tenants' Temperatures Rise in Wake of Heating Drop." *Michigan Chronicle*, January 22, 1977, 1, 4.

Foner, Philip, and Yuval Taylor, eds. *Frederick Douglass: Selected Speeches and Writings*. Chicago: Lawrence Hill Books, 1999.

Fording, Richard C. "The Political Response to Black Insurgency: A Critical Test of Competing Theories of the State." *American Political Science Review* 95. no. 1 (2001): 115–30.

Franklin, Sekou. "Community Organizing and Strategy in Post-Black Power Grass-Roots Activism." Unpublished paper, Middle Tennessee State University, Murfreesboro, TN, 2002.

Frazier, E. Franklin. *Black Bourgeoisie*. New York: Free Press, 1957.

Freedberg, Sydney. "Break-In to Protest HUD a Bust." *Detroit News*, November 2, 1980, B2.

Freedman, Eric, and Bruce Alpert. "Squatter Law Upheld: Detroit Told to Allow Use of Vacant Homes." *Detroit News*, April 11, 1987, 1A, 14A.

Friedman, Debra, and Doug McAdam. "Collective Identity and Activism: Networks, Choices, and the Life of a Social Movement." In *Frontiers in Social Movement Theory*, ed. by Aldon D. Morris and Carol M. Mueller. New Haven, Conn.: Yale University Press, 1992.

Friedman, Lawrence M. *Government and Slum Housing: A Century of Frustration*. Chicago: Rand McNally, 1968.

Friesema, H. Paul. "Black Control of Central Cities." *American Institute of Planners Journal* 35 (1969): 75–79.

Fuchs, Ester. *Mayors and Money: Fiscal Policy in New York and Chicago*. Chicago: University of Chicago, 1990.

Gamson, William A. *The Strategy of Social Protest*, 2d ed. Belmont, Calif.: Wadsworth Publishing, 1990.

Gamson, William A., and David S. Meyer. "Framing Political Opportunity." In *Comparative Perspectives on Social Movements: Political Opportunities, Mobilizing Structures, and Cultural Framings*, ed. by Doug McAdam, John D. McCarthy and Mayer N. Zald. Cambridge: Cambridge University Press, 1996.

Gamson, William A., and Emile Schmeidler. "Organizing the Poor." *Theory and Society* 13 (1984): 567–85.

Gans, Herbert. "The Failure of Urban Renewal." In *Urban Renewal: The Record and the Controversy*, ed. by James Q. Wilson. Cambridge, Mass.: MIT Press, 1966.

Ganz, Marshall. "Resources and Resourcefulness: Strategic Capacity in the Unionization of California Agriculture, 1959–1966." *American Journal of Sociology* 105 (2000): 1003–63.

Garcelon, Marc. *Revolutionary Passage: From Soviet Union to Post-Soviet Russia, 1985–2000*. Philadelphia: Temple University Press, 2005.

Garrow, David. *Bearing the Cross: Martin Luther King, Jr., and the Southern Christian Leadership Conference*. New York: William Morrow, 1986.

Gay, Claudine. "The Effect of Black Congressional Representation on Political Participation." *American Political Science Review* 95, no. 3 (2001): 589–602.

———. "Putting Race in Context: Identifying the Environmental Determinants of Black Racial Attitudes." *American Political Science Review* 98, no. 4 (2005): 547–62.

Gay, Claudine, and Katherine Tate. "Doubly Bound: The Impact of Gender and Race on the Politics of Black Women." *Political Psychology* 1 (1998): 169–84.

Gelb, Joyce, and Vivien Hurt. "Feminist Politics in a Hostile Environment: Obstacles and Opportunities." In *How Social Movements Matter*, ed. by Marco Giugni, Doug McAdam, and Charles Tilly. Minneapolis: University of Minnesota Press, 1999.

Gelfand, Mark I. *A Nation of Cities: The Federal Government and Urban America, 1933–1965*. New York: Oxford University Press, 1975.

Georgakas, Dan, and Marvin Surkin. *Detroit I Do Mind Dying*, updated ed. Cambridge, Mass.: South End Press, 1998.

Germany, Kent B. *New Orleans after the Promises: Poverty, Citizenship, and the Search for the Great Society*. Athens: University of Georgia Press, 2007.

Geschwender, James. *Class, Race, Working Insurgency: The League of Revolutionary Black Workers*. Cambridge: Cambridge University Press, 1979.

Giddings, Paula. *When and Where I Enter: The Impact of Black Women on Race and Sex in America*. New York: Bantam Books, 1984.

Gilbert, Michele A. "Race, Location, and Education: The Election of Black Mayors in the 1990s." *Journal of Politics* 36, no. 3 (2006): 318–33.

Gillette, Howard, Jr. "Protest and Power in Washington, D.C.: The Troubled Legacy of Marion Barry." In *African-American Mayors: Race, Politics, and the American City*, ed. by David R. Colburn and Jeffrey S. Adler. Urbana: University of Illinois Press, 2001.

Gilliam, Frank. "Black America: Divided by Class?" *Public Opinion* 9 (1986.): 53–57.

Gilliam, Franklin D., Jr., and Karen Kaufman. "Is There an Empowerment Life Cycle? Long-Term Black Empowerment and Its Influence on Voter Participation." *Urban Affairs Review* 33, no. 6 (1998): 741–66.

Giugni, Marco. "How Social Movements Matter: Past Research, Present Problems, Future Developments." In *How Social Movements Matters*, ed. by Marco Giugni, Doug McAdam, and Charles Tilly. Minneapolis: University of Minnesota Press, 1999.

Goetz, Edward G. *Clearing the Way: Deconcentrating the Poor in Urban America*. Washington, D.C.: Urban Institute Press, 2003.

———. "The Community-Based Housing Movement and Progressive Local Politics." In *Revitalizing Urban Neighborhoods*, ed. by W. Dennis Keating, Norman Krumholz, and Philip Star. Lawrence: University Press of Kansas, 1996.

———. "The Politics of Poverty Deconcentration and Housing Demolition." *Journal of Urban Affairs* 22, no. 2 (2000): 157–73.

———. "Retrenchment, Devolution and Local Housing Policy in the Postfederal Era." Paper presented at the Annual Meeting of the American Political Science Association, New York, 1994.

———. *Shelter Burden: Local Politics and Progressive Housing Policy*. Philadelphia: Temple University Press, 1993.

Goldfield, Michael. *The Color of Politics: Race and the Mainsprings of American Politics*. New York: New York University Press, 1997.

Goode, Wilson. *In Goode Faith: Philadelphia's First Black Mayor Tells His Story*. Valley Forge, Penn.: Judson Press, 1992.

Goodwin, Jeff, and James M. Jasper. "Caught in the Winding, Snarling Vine: The Structural Bias of Political Process Theory." *Sociological Forum* 14, no. 1 (1999): 27–54.

Gotham, Kevin Fox. "Political Opportunity, Community Identity, and the Emergence of Local Anti-Expressway Movement.: *Social Problems* 46, no. 3 (1999): 332–54.

Graham, Lawrence. *Our Kind of People: Inside America's Black Upper Class*. New York: HarperCollins, 1999.

Graves, Helen Mataya. "New Detroit Committee / New Detroit, Inc.: A Study of an Urban Coalition, 1967–1972." Ph.D. diss., Wayne State University, Detroit, 1975.

Green, Judith. *Deep Democracy: Community, Diversity, and Transformation*. Lanham, Md.: Rowman and Littlefield, 1999.

Gregory, Steven. *Black Corona: Race and the Politics of Place in an Urban Community.* Princeton: Princeton University Press, 1998.

Griffen, Lee. "Letter to the Detroit City Council." United Community Housing Coalition, Detroit, 1987.

"Groups Back Cockrel in Canfield Dispute." *Michigan Chronicle,* November 4, 1978, 1, 4.

Gunther, Marc. "A Strong Dose of Reality." *Detroit Free Press,* March 20, 1988, 7G.

Gurin, Patrica, Shirley Hatchett, and James Jackson. *Hope and Independence: Blacks' Response to Electoral and Party Politics.* New York: Sage Foundation, 1989.

Guth, James L., Lyman A. Kellstedt, Corwin E. Smidt, and John C. Green. "Thunder on the Right? Religious Interest Group Mobilization in the 1996 Election." In *Interest Group Politics,* ed. by Allan J. Cigler and Burdett A. Loomis. Washington, D.C.: CQ Press, 1998.

Hackney, Suzette. "Detroit Removed from List of Troubled Housing." *Detroit News,* April 16, 1997.

Hackworth, Jason. The *Neoliberal City: Governance, Ideology, and Ideology in American Urbanism.* Ithaca, N.Y.: Cornell University Press, 2007.

Haines, Herbert. "Issue Structure, 'Frameability,' and Political Opportunity." Unpublished ms., presented at the Annual Meeting of the Society for the Study of Social Problems, Washington, D.C., 2000.

Hallas, Clark. "City Hosts $3,000 Parley for 16 Public Tenants." *Detroit News,* January 9, 1970, 3A.

Halpern, Robert. *Rebuilding the Inner City: A History of Neighborhood Initiatives to Address Poverty in the United States.* New York: Columbia University Press, 1995.

Hancock, Ange-Marie. *The Politics of Disgust: The Public Identity of the Welfare Queen.* New York: New York University Press, 2004.

Hansen, Joyce, and Moe Foner. *Women of Hope: African Americans Who Made a Difference.* New York: Scholastic Press, 1998.

Hardin, Russell. *Collective Action.* Baltimore: John Hopkins University Press, 1982.

Harris, Fredrick C., Valeria Sinclair-Chapman, and Brian McKenzie. *Countervailing Forces in African-American Civic Activism, 1973–1994.* Cambridge: Cambridge University Press, 2006.

Hartman, Chester. "Housing Policies under the Reagan Administration." In *Critical Perspectives on Housing,* edited by Rachel G. Bratt, Chester Hartman, and Ann Meyerson. Philadelphia: Temple University Press.

Hays, R. Allen. *The Federal Government and Urban Housing: Ideology and Change in Public Policy.* Albany: State University of New York Press, 1985.

Heldman, Louis M. "Herman Gardens Gets $10 Million for Fix-Up." *Detroit Free Press,* October 4, 1978, 3A, 17A.

Henderson, Erma. "Detroit City Council Budget Message." Presented to the Detroit City Council, 1987.

———. "Detroit City Council Budget Message." Presented to the Detroit City Council, 1989.

Herbert, Scott, Avis Vidal, Greg Mills, Franklin James, and Debbie Gruenstein. "Interim Assessment of the Empowerment Zones and Enterprise Communities (EZ/EC) Program: A Progress Report." U.S. Department of Housing and Urban Development, Washington, D.C., 2001.

Hill Collins, Patricia. *Black Feminist Thought: Knowledge, Consciousness, and the Politics of Empowerment*, 2d ed. New York: Routledge, 2000.

Hill, Richard C. "Crisis in the Motor City: The Politics of Economic Development in Detroit." In *Restructuring the City: The Political Economy of Urban Redevelopment*, ed. by Susan S. Fainstein and Norman I. Fainstein. New York: Longman, 1983.

Hill, Rickey. "Understanding the Drive to Make the Confederate Flag Official in South Carolina." In *Beyond the Color Line? Race, Representation, and Community in the New Century*, ed. by Alex Willingham. New York: Brennan Center for Justice, New York University School of Law, 2002.

Hirsch, Arnold. *Making the Second Ghetto: Race and Housing in Chicago, 1940–1960*. Cambridge: Cambridge University Press, 1983.

Hoch, Charles, and Robert A. Slayton. *New Homeless and Old: Community and the Skid Row Hotel*. Philadelphia: Temple University Press, 1989.

Hochschild, Jennifer. *Facing Up to the American Dream: Race, Class, and the Soul of the Nation*. Princeton: Princeton University Press, 1995.

Holin, Mary Joel, and Jean Amendolia. "Interim Assessment of the HOPE VI Program: Case Study of the Ellen Wilson Dwellings in Washington, D.C." Abt Associates, Cambridge, Mass., 2001.

Holland, John. "Housing Talks Set in Motel." *Detroit Free Press*, January 9, 1970, 3A.

Holloway, Steven R., Deborah Bryan, Robert Chabot, Donna M. Rogers, and James Rulli. "Exploring the Effect of Public Housing on the Concentration of Poverty in Columbus, OH." *Urban Affairs Review* 33, no. 6 (1998): 767–89.

"Homeless Unite: National Activists Visit Detroit to Help Those without Shelter." *Detroit Free Press*, January 29, 1988, 12D.

Hopper, Kim. "Advocacy for the Homeless in the 1980s." In *Homeless in America*, ed. by Carol Caton. New York: Oxford University Press, 1990.

Hopper, Kim, and Jill Hamberg. "The Making of America's Homeless: From Skid Row to New Poor, 1945–1984." In *Critical Perspectives on Housing*, ed. by Rachel G. Bratt, Chester Hartman, and Ann Meyerson. Philadelphia: Temple University Press, 1986.

Hopper, Kim, and Norweeta Millburn. "Homelessness among African Americans: A Historical and Contemporary Perspective." In *Homelessness in America*, ed. by Jim Baumohl. Phoenix: Orxy Press, 1996.

Horwich, Joel, Jason Lakin, Lydia Bean, Jal Metha, and Derek R. B. Douglas. *Rebuilding Homes and Lives: Progressive Options for Housing Policy Post-Katrina*. Washington, D.C.: Center for American Progress and New Vision, 2006.

Horwitt, Sanford. *Let Them Call Me Rebel: Saul Alinsky, His Life, and Legacy*. New York: Knopf / Random House, 1989.

Hoyt, Clark. "Tenants Strike: 'Rats Wall to Wall.'" *Detroit Free Press*, October 3, 1968, 3.

Hunter, Gloria Manlove, and Eleanor Manlove. "Discussion on the Life in the Brewster Housing Projects: Gloria Manlove Hunter and Eleanor Manlove." In *Untold Tales, Unsung Heroes: An Oral History of Detroit's African American Community, 1918–1967*, ed. by Elaine L. Moon. Detroit: Wayne State University Press, 1994.

Huskisson, Gregory. "Conyers to Young: 'It's All Over.'" *Detroit Free Press*, August 2, 1989, 2A–1.

———. "In Detroit, Jackson to Protest State Cuts; Engler's Spokesman Suggests Talking Instead." *Detroit Free Press*, December 27, 1991, 6B.

———. "U.S. to Help Detroit with Housing Team: $220 Million Available, Kemp Says." *Detroit Free Press*, November 20, 1991, 1A.

Iton, Richard. *Solidarity Blues: Race, Culture, and the American Left*. Chapel Hill: University of North Carolina Press, 2000.

Jackson, Kenneth. *Crabgrass Frontier: The Suburbanization of the United States*. New York: Oxford University Press, 1985.

Jackson, Thomas. "The State, the Movement, and the Urban Poor: The War on Poverty and Political Mobilization in the 1960's." In *The Underclass Debate: Views from History*, ed. by Michael B. Katz. Princeton: Princeton University Press, 1993.

Jargowsky, Paul A. *Poverty and Place: Ghettos, Barrios, and the American City*. New York: Russell Sage Foundation, 1997.

Jencks, Christopher. *The Homeless*. Cambridge, Mass.: Harvard University Press, 1994.

Jenkins, Bette Smith. "The Racial Policies of the Detroit Housing Commission and Their Administration." Master's thesis, Wayne State University, Detroit, 1951.

Jennings, James. *The Politics of Black Empowerment: The Transformation of Black Activism in Urban America*. Detroit: Wayne State University Press, 1992.

Jessop, Bob. "A Neo-Gramscian Approach to the Regulation of Urban Regimes: Accumulation Strategies, Hegemonic Projects, and Governance." In *Reconstructing Urban Regime Theory: Regulating Urban Politics in a Global Economy*, ed. by Mickey Lauria. Thousand Oaks, Calif.: Sage Publications, 1997.

Jeter, Jon. "Young Wants Grants for Shelters." *Detroit Free Press*, October 14, 1992, 2A.

Johnson, Cedric. *Revolutionaries to Race Leaders: Black Power and the Making of African American Politics*. Minneapolis: University of Minnesota Press, 2007.

Johnson, Frank W. "Let the Games Begin: Relocation and Redevelopment of Public Housing in Atlanta, GA." Ph.D. diss., Temple University, Philadelphia, 2002.

Joint Center for Housing Studies. *The State of Nation's Housing*. Report, Harvard University, Cambridge, Mass., 1993.

Jones, Bryan D., and Lynn W. Bachelor. *The Sustaining Hand: Community Leadership and Corporate Power*. Lawrence: University Press of Kansas, 1993.

Jones, Linda. "Push Grows to Cut Young Budget Power." *Detroit News*, October 6, 1988, 3B.

Jones, Linda, and Angie Cannon. "Council Kills Veto: Casts Historic Veto Override." *Detroit News*, June 3, 1989, 1A, 14A.

Josar, David. "FBI Papers Offer Insight on Young." *Detroit News*, January 9, 2000, 1–6.

Judd, Dennis R., and Todd Swanstrom. *City Politics: The Political Economy of Urban America*. New York: Longman, 2006.

Kamuda, Al. "Activists for Homeless Protest, Break into Brewster-Douglass Town Houses." *Detroit Free Press*, January 18, 1988, 8D.

Kaplan, Deborah. "Union Says City's Too Slow in Providing Public Housing." *Detroit Free Press*, February 22, 1988, 3A.

Kasarda, John. "Inner-City Concentrated Poverty and Neighborhood Distress: 1970 to 1990." *Housing Policy Debate* 4, no. 3 (1993.): 253–302.

Katz, Michael B. 1996. *In the Shadow of the Poorhouse: A Social History of Welfare in America*, 10th ed. New York: HarperCollins, 1989.

———. *The Undeserving Poor: From the War on Poverty to the War on Welfare*. New York: Pantheon Books, 1989.

Keating, Larry. *Atlanta: Race, Class, and Urban Expansion*. Philadelphia: Temple University Press, 2001.

Keating, Larry, and Carol A. Flores. "Sixty and Out: Techwood Homes Transformed by Enemies and Friends." *Journal of Urban History* 26, no. 3 (2000): 275–311.

Keller, Edmond. "The Impact of Black Mayors on Urban Policy." *Annals of the American Academy of Political and Social Science* 439 (1978): 40–52.

Kelley, Robin. "The Black Poor and the Politics of Opposition in a New South City, 1929–1970." In *The "Underclass" Debate: Views from History*, ed. by Michael B. Katz. Princeton: Princeton University Press, 1993.

Kelling, George L., Robert Wasserman, and Hubert Williams. *Police Accountability and Community Policing*. Washington, D.C.: Office of Justice Programs, U.S. Department of Justice, 1989.

Kilpatrick, Kwame M. "State of the City Address." Office of the Mayor, Detroit, 2006.

Kilson, Martin. "Political Change in the Negro Ghetto, 1990–1940." In *Key Issues in the Afro-American Experience*, ed. by Nathan I. Huggins, Martin Kilson, and Daniel Fox. New York: Harcourt Brace, 1971.

King, Deborah. "Multiple Jeopardy, Multiple Consciousnesses: The Context of Black Feminist Ideology." In *Black Women in America: Social Science Perspectives*, ed. by Micheline R. Malson. Chicago: University of Chicago Press, 1990.

King, Martin Luther, Jr. "Letter from Birmingham City Jail." In *A Testament of Hope: The Essential Writings of Martin Luther King, Jr.*, ed. by James M. Washington. San Francisco: Harper and Row, 1963.

———. *Where Do We Go From Here: Chaos or Community?* New York: Harper and Row, 1967.

Kingdon, John. *Congressmen's Voting Decisions*. New York: Harper and Row, 1989.

Kingsley, G. Thomas, Jennifer Johnson, and Kathryn L. S. Pettit. "Patterns of Section 8 Relocation in the HOPE VI Program." *Journal of Urban Affairs* 25, no. 4 (2003): 427.

Kleinknecht, William. "Brewster Demolition Plan Gets City Council Backing." *Detroit Free Press*, January 21, 1990, 2B.

———. "Crew Begins Demolition at Brewster-Douglass." *Detroit Free Press*, September 19 19, 1990, 2B.

Klinkner, Philip A. "Bill Clinton and the Politics of New Liberalism." In *Without Justice for All: The New Liberalism and Our Retreat from Racial Equality*, ed. by Adolph Reed Jr. Boulder: Westview Press, 1999.

Kornhauser, Arthur W. *Attitudes of Detroit People toward Detroit: Summary of a Detailed Report*. Detroit: Wayne State University Press, 1952.

Kotz, Nick, and Marilyn Kotz. *A Passion for Equality: George A. Wiley and the Movement*. New York: W. W. Norton, 1977.

Krainz Woods Community Council. "All Conant Gardens Home Owners Should Attend." *Michigan Chronicle*, December 6, 1966.

Kramer, Marian. "Speaking for Ourselves: A Lifetime of Welfare Rights Organizing." In *For Crying Out Loud: Women's Poverty in the United States*, ed. by Diane Dujon and Ann Withorn. Boston: South End Press, 1996.

Kraus, Neil, and Todd Swanstrom. "Minority Mayors and the Hollow-Prize Problem." *Political Science and Politics* 35, no. 1 (2001): 99–105.

Krauss, Celene. "Women and Toxic Waste Protests: Race, Class, and Gender as Resources of Resistance." *Qualitative Sociology* 16, no. 3 (1993): 247–62.

Krebs, Timothy B. "The Determinants of Candidate's Vote Share and the Advantages of Incumbency in City Council Elections." *American Journal of Political Science* 42, no. 3 (1998): 921–35.

Krinsky, John. "Organizing the Organizing of the Unorganized: Opposition to Workfare in New York and the Recombination of Contentious Repertoires." Paper presented at the Annual Meeting of the American Sociological Association, Washington, D.C., 1998.

Krolicki, Kevin. "Detroit Faces Racial Issues with Mayoral Crisis." *Washington Post*, March 27, 2008.

Lacy, Kayrn. *Blue-Chip Blacks: Race, Class, and Status in the New Black Middle Class*. Los Angeles: University of California Press, 2007.

LaMore, Rex L. "Community Economic Development in Michigan." *Exchange* 9, no. 9 (1986.): 5–6.

Lancourt, Joan. *Confront or Concede: The Alinsky Citizen Action Organization*. Lexington, Mass.: Lexington Books, 1979.

Landry, Bart. *The New Black Middle Class*. Berkeley: University of California Press, 1987.

Lee, Cynthia. "HUD Tenants Protest." *Detroit News*, July 3, 1981, 1B–2B.

Lefebvre, Ben. "Water Woes: Increased Detroit Rates Put Pressure on Poor." *Metro Times*, June 14, 2006.

Leighley, Jan E., and Arnold Vedlitz. "Race, Ethnicity, and Political Participation: Competing Models and Contrasting Explanations." *Journal of Politics* 61, no. 4 (1999): 1092–1114.

Levine, Daniel. *Bayard Rustin and the Civil Rights Movement*. New Brunswick, N.J.: Rutgers University Press, 2000.

Liebschutz, Sarah F. "Empowerment Zones and Enterprise Communities: Reinventing Federalism for Distressed Communities." *Journal of Federalism* 25, no. 3 (1995.): 117–32.

Lipsky, Michael. "Protest as a Political Resource." *American Political Science Review* 62 (1968): 1144–58.

Locke, Mamie. "Deconstruct to Reconstruct: African American Women in the Post-Civil Rights Movement Era." In *Black and Multiracial Politics in America*, ed. by Yvette M. Alex-Assensoh and Lawrence J. Hanks. New York: New York University Press, 2000.

Loeb, Vernon. "At Wilson Dwellings, a Dream Gets Hope." *Washington Post*, January 23, 1997, J1.

Lofland, John, and Lyn H. Lofland. *Analyzing Social Settings: A Guide to Qualitative Observation and Analysis*. Belmont, Calif.: Wadsworth Publishing, 1984.

Low Income Housing Information Service (LIHIS). "Special Memorandum: The Reagan Budget and Low Income Housing." Washington, D.C., 1982.

Lusane, Clarence. "If I Were a Rich Man: Race, Gender, and Poverty." In *Race in the Global Era: African Americans at the Millennium*. Boston: South End Press, 1997.

Lynch, Timothy, and Paul Leonard. *A Place to Call Home: The Crisis in Housing for the Poor: Detroit, Michigan*. Washington, D.C.: Center for Budget and Policy Analysis, 1991.

Mahaffey, Maryann. "Detroit City Council's 2005–2006 Budget." Council President's Address, City Council, Detroit, 2006.

———. "Making the Tough Decisions: Budget Process Continues: Council President Mahaffey's Budget Message, 1991." *Exchange* (July 1991): 1, 8–9.

———. "Statement for the Record: Override of Mayor's Vetoes [by] Council Member Maryann Mahaffey." *Journal of the Detroit City Council* (1988): 1392–93.

Malcolm X. *Malcolm X Speaks*, ed. by by G. Brietman. New York: Pathfinder Press, 1989.

Malveaux, Julianne. "The Political Economy of Black Women." In *Race, Politics, and Economic Development: Community Perspectives*, ed. by James Jennings. London: Verso, 1992.

Marable, Manning, ed. "Toward a Renaissance of Progressive Black Politics." In *Speaking Truth to Power: Essays on Race, Resistance, and Radicalism*. Boulder: Westview Press, 1996.

Marcuse, Peter. "Homelessness and Housing Policy." In *Homeless in America*, ed. by Carol Caton. New York: Oxford University Press, 1990.

Martin, Henry. *Charlie Parker and Thematic Improvisation*. Lanham, Md.: Scarecrow Press, 1996.

Marwell, Nicole P. "Privatizing the Welfare State: Nonprofit Community-Based Organizations as Political Actors." *American Sociological Review* 69 (2004): 265–91.

Massey, Douglass, and Nancy Denton. *American Apartheid: Segregation and the Making of the Underclass*. Cambridge, Mass.: Harvard University Press, 1993.

Massey, Douglass, and Shawn M. Kanaiaupuni. "Public Housing and the Concentration of Poverty." *Social Science Quarterly* 74, no. 1 (1993): 109–22.

Mast, David H, ed. *Detroit Lives*. Philadelphia: Temple University Press, 1994.

May, Jeanne. "Advocates for the Homeless to March for Federal Money." *Detroit Free Press*, July 26, 1989, 7B.

Mayhew, David. *Congress: The Electoral Connection*. New Haven, Conn.: Yale University Press, 1974.

Mayor's Committee for Community Renewal. "Total Action against Poverty: Mayor's Committee for Community Renewal." Detroit, 1964.

McAdam, Doug. "Conceptual Origins, Current Problems, and Future Directions." In *Comparative Perspectives on Social Movements: Political Opportunities, Mobilizing Structures, and Cultural Framings*, ed. by Doug Adam, John D. McCarthy, and Mayer N. Zald. Cambridge: Cambridge University Press, 1996.

———. *Political Process and the Development of Black Insurgency, 1930–1970*. Chicago: University of Chicago Press, 1982.

McCann, Michael. *Rights at Work: Pay Equity Reform and the Politics of Legal Mobilization*. Chicago: University of Chicago Press, 1987.

McCarthy, John D., and Mayer N. Zald. *The Trend in Social Movements in America: Professionalization and Resource Mobilization*. Morristown, N.J.: General Learning Press, 1973.

McClerking, Harwood. "We Are in This Together: The Origins and Maintenance of Black Common Fate Perceptions." Ph.D. diss., University of Michigan, Ann Arbor, 2001.

McConell, Darci. "Archer Wants Public Housing Agency to Be Separate, Plan Would Make It Independent." *Detroit Free Press*, March 21, 1998, 6B.

McCormick II, Joseph, and Charles E. Jones. "The Conceptualization of Deracialization: Thinking through the Dilemma." In *Dilemmas of Black Politics: Issues of Leadership and Strategy*, ed. by Georgia A. Persons. New York: HarperCollins, 1993.

McGovern, Stephen J. *The Politics of Downtown Development: Dynamic Political Cultures in San Francisco and Washington, D.C.* Lexington: University Press of Kentucky, 1998.

McGraw, Bill. "Archer Has a Lot to Learn and Fast: Transition Team's Job Crucial at Start." *Detroit Free Press*, November 13, 1993, 1A.

———. "The Mayoral Legacy: A Better Downtown, Archer Aimed High, with Mixed Results." *Detroit Free Press*, April 18, 2001, 1A.

———. "New Mayor Making Changes at a Fast Clip." *Detroit Free Press*, January 29, 1994, 3A.

McGraw, Bill, and L. A. Johnson. "Clinton Sees Hope in Detroit." *Detroit Free Press*, March 4, 1994, 1A, 6A.

McGraw, Bill, and Patricia Montemurri. "Detroit Throng Bids Farewell to Young." *Pittsburgh Post-Gazette*, December 7, 1997, B5.

McGraw, Bill, David Ashenfelter, and Dori J. Maynard. "It's a Rematch: Young versus Barrow, Conyers Loses a Close Race." *Detroit Free Press*, September 13, 1989, 1A.

McKnight, Gerald. *The Last Crusade: Martin Luther King, Jr., the FBI, and the Poor People's Campaign*. Boulder, Colo.: Westview Press, 1998.

McTyre, Robert E. "A Place to Stay." *Michigan Chronicle*, November 5, 1988, 1A, 4A.

McWhirter, Cameron, and Darren A. Nichols. "Detroit Tops U.S. in Lost Housing." *Detroit News*, May 23, 2001, 1A.

Meier, August, and Elliot Rudwick. *Black Detroit and the Rise of the UAW*. Oxford: Oxford University Press, 1979.

———. *CORE: A Study in the Civil Rights Movement, 1942–1968*. Urbana: University of Illinois Press, 1975.

Melucci, Alberto. *Nomads of the Present: Social Movements and Individual Needs in Contemporary Society*, ed. by John Keane and Paul Mier. Philadelphia: Temple University Press, 1989.

Meyer, David, and Debra Minkoff. "Conceptualizing Political Opportunity." *Social Forces* 82, no. 4 (2004): 1457–92.

Meyer, David, and Suzanne Staggenborg. "Movements, Countermovements, and the Structure of Political Opportunity." *American Journal of Sociology* 101, no. 6 (1996): 1628–60.

Michigan Avenue Community Organization. *Revitalization Plan*. Detroit, 1982.

Michigan Neighborhood Partnership. "Detroit State of the Neighborhoods Report." Report, College of Urban, Labor, and Metropolitan Affairs, Wayne State University, Detroit, 2002.

Migoya, David. "HUD Won't OK Detroit Plan until New Housing Chief Picked." *Detroit Free Press*, August 17, 1995, 3B.

Miller, Jonathan, and Richard G. Jones. "Ex-Newark Mayor Convicted of Fraud." *New York Times*, April 17, 2008.

Miller, Liz, dir. *The Water Front*. Documentary, Bullfrog Films, Oley, Penn., 2008.

Miller, Mike. "Beyond the Politics of Place: A Critical Review, Notes toward a Conversation on Community Organizing." Report, Organize Training Center, San Francisco, 1996.

Minkoff, Debra. "The Sequencing of Social Movements." *American Sociological Review* 62 (1997): 779–99.

Mirel, Jeffrey. "After the Fall: Continuity and Change in Detroit, 1981–1995." *History of Education Quarterly* 38, no. 3 (1998): 237–76.

Mleczko, Louis, and Martha Hindes. "'Bargain' House Isn't, Mother Finds." *Detroit News*, December 18, 1980, 1B, 13B.

Mollenkopf, John H., and Todd Swanstrom. *Place Matters: Metropolitics for the Twenty-First Century*. Lawrence: University Press of Kansas, 2001.

Molotch, Harvey L. *Managed Integration: Dilemmas of Doing Good in the City*. Berkeley: University of California Press, 1972.

Montgomery, Lori. "In Sweep, Fenty Draws on Uniting to Conquer." *Washington Post*, September 14, 2006, A1.

Monti, Daniel J. *Race, Redevelopment, and the New Company Town*. Albany: State University of New York Press, 1990.

Moon, Elaine Latzman. *Untold Tales, Unsung Heroes: An Oral History of Detroit's African American Community, 1919–1967*. Detroit: Wayne State University Press, 1994.

Moore, Kesha S. "What's Class Got to Do with It? Community Development and Racial Identity." *Journal of Urban Affairs* 27, no. 4 (2005): 437–51.

Moore, Leonard N. *Carol B. Stokes and the Rise of Black Political Power*. Urbana: University of Illinois Press, 2002.

"More Homeless in Detroit." *Detroit Free Press*, November 15, 1988, 4A.

Morris, Aldon. 1984. *The Origins of the Civil Rights Movement: Black Communities Organizing for Change*. New York: The Free Press.

Morris, Julie. "Poor to Fight Rent in Court." *Detroit Free Press*, June 6, 1969, 10A.

———. "Tenants in Herman Gardens End Year-Long Rent Strike." *Detroit Free Press*, February 26, 1970, 14A.

Morris, Libby V, and Gina L Gilbreath. "African-American Community Development in Theory and Practice: A Georgia Case Study." *Journal of Community Development Society* 27, no. 2 (1996): 161–75.

Morris, Milton D. *The Politics of Black America*. New York: Harper and Row, 1975.

Mossberger, Karen, and Gerry Stoker. "The Evolution of Urban Regime Theory: The Challenge of Conceptualization." *Urban Affairs Review* 36, no. 6 (2001): 810–35.

Mowitz, Robert J., and Deil S. Wright. *Profile of a Metropolis: A Case Book Study*. Detroit: Wayne State University Press, 1962.

Muller, Edward N., and Karl-Dieter Opp. "Rational Choice and Rebellious Collective Action." *American Political Science Review* 80, no. 2 (1986): 471–87.

Myers, Kristin. "Racial Unity in the Grassroots? A Case Study of a Women's Social Service Organization." In *Still Lifting, Still Climbing: African American Women's Contemporary Activism*, ed. by Kimberly Springer. New York: New York University Press, 1999.

Naison, Mark D. "Rent Strikes in New York." In *Tenants and the Urban Housing Crisis*, ed. by Stephen Burghardt. Dexter, Mich.: New Press, 1972.

Naperstek, Arthur J., Susan R. Freis, G. Thomas Kingsley, Dennis Dooley, and Howard E. Lewis. "HOPE VI: Community Building Makes a Difference." Office of Public and Indian Housing, U.S. Department of Housing and Urban Development, Washington, D.C., 2000.

Naples, Nancy. *Grassroots Warriors: Activist Mothering, Community Work, and the War on Poverty*. New York: Routledge, 1998.

Nathan, Richard, Frederick Doolittle, and Associates. *Reagan and the States*. Princeton: Princeton University Press, 1987.

National Coalition for the Homeless and National Law Center on Homelessness and Poverty. *A Dream Denied: The Criminalization of Homelessness in U.S. Cities*. Washington, D.C.: National Coalition for the Homeless, 2006.

Naughton, Keith, and James V. Higgins. "Chrysler's Sales Surge May Create 6,000 Jobs." *Detroit News*, March 4, 1994, 1A, 8A.

Neighborhood Info D.C. "District of Columbia Housing Monitor." Urban Institute, Washington, D.C., 2006.

"Neighborhood Leaders: Land Deal Wasted Our Money." *Detroit News*, 1988, 1A, 4A.

Neill, William J. V. "Lipstick on the Gorilla: The Failure of Image-led Planning in Coleman Young's Detroit." *International Journal of Urban and Regional Research* 19, no. 4 (1995): 639–53.

Neill, William J. V., Diana Fitzsimons, and Brendan Murtagh. *Reimaging the Pariah City: Urban Development in Belfast and Detroit*. Aldershot: Avebury, 1995.

Nelson, William E. "Black Mayoral Leadership: A Twenty-Year Perspective." *National Political Science Review* 2 (1990): 188–95.

Nelson, William, and Phillip Meranto. *Electing Black Mayors: Political Action in the Black Community*. Columbus: Ohio State University Press, 1977.

Neuman, Ladd. "City Seeks to Avoid Rent Strike." *Detroit Free Press*, January 28, 1969, 5A.

Neumark, David, Mark Schweitzer, and William Wascher. "The Effects of Minimum Wages on the Distribution of Family Incomes: A Nonparametric Analyses." *Journal of Human Resources* 25, no. 4 (2005): 868–94.

Newark Housing Authority. "FY2007–2009 *Annual Plan*." Newark Housing Authority, Newark, N.J, 2007.

Newman, Harvey. "The Atlanta Housing Authority's Olympic Legacy Program: Public Housing Projects to Mixed Income Communities." Atlanta: Research Atlanta, 2002.

Newman, Kathe. "Newark, Decline and Avoidance, Renaissance and Desire: From Disinvestment to Reinvestment." *Annals of the American Academy of Political and Social Science* 594 (2004): 34–48.

Nutt-Powell, Thomas. *Capital Needs Unlimited*, ed. by B. Turner and C. R. Greene. Report, Detroit, 1995.

Obama, Barack. *Dreams from My Father: A Story of Race and Inheritance*. New York: Three Rivers Press, 2004.

Oberschall, Anthony. *Social Movements: Ideologies, Interests, and Identities*. New Brunswick, N.J.: Transaction, 1993.

Office of the Inspector General. "Audit Report: Detroit Housing Commission HOPE VI Program." Office of Audit, Midwest, U.S. Department of Housing and Urban Development, Chicago, 2001.

Oliver, Melvin L., and Thomas Shapiro. *Black Wealth / White Wealth: A New Perspective on Racial Inequality*. New York: Routledge, 1995.

Olson, Mancur, Jr. *The Logic of Collective Action*. Cambridge, Mass.: Harvard University Press, 1965.

Olzak, Susan, and Elizabeth West. *Ethnic Collective Action in Urban Contemporary U.S.: Project Description and Coding Manual*. Palo Alto, Calif.: Stanford University, 1995.

On-Site Insight. "Final Report: Physical Needs Assessment—Parkside Homes." Detroit, 1992.

O'Regan, Katherine M., and John M. Quigley. "Federal Policy and the Rise of Nonprofit Housing Providers." *Journal of Housing Research* 11, no. 2 (2000): 297–317.

Orr, Marion. "Black Political Incorporation—Phase Two: The Cases of Baltimore and Detroit." Ph.D. diss., University of Maryland, College Park, 1992.

———. "Community Organizing and the Changing Ecology of Civic Engagement." In *Transforming the City: Community Organizing the Challenge of Political Change*, ed. by Marion Orr. Lawrence: University Press of Kansas, 2007.

Orr, Marion, and Gerry Stoker. "Urban Regimes and Leadership in Detroit." *Urban Affairs Quarterly* 30 (1994): 48–73.

"Our Opinions: The Battle of West Canfield." *Detroit News*, October 19, 1978, A26.

Owens, Michael Leo. *God and Government in the Ghetto: The Politics of Church-State Collaboration in American Cities*. Chicago: University of Chicago Press, 2007.

Pampel, Fred C. *Logistic Regression: A Primer, Quantitative Applications in the Social Sciences*. New York: Sage Publications, 2000.

Parkside Resident Council. "Parkside Community in Action." *Tenants' Voice*! 2, nos. 3–4 (1993): 1, 4.

Parkside Study Group. "Final Report." Detroit, 1994.

Pattillo-McCoy, Mary. *Black Picket Fences: Privilege and Peril among the Black Middle Class*. Chicago: University of Chicago Press, 1999.

Payne, Charles. *I've Got the Light of Freedom: The Organizing Tradition and the Mississippi Freedom Struggle*. Berkeley: University of California Press, 1995.

PEOPLE Convention. "The PEOPLE's Platform." Detroit, 1989.

Pinderhughes, Dianne. *Race and Ethnicity in Chicago Politics: A Reexamination of Pluralist Theory*. Urbana: University of Illinois Press, 1987.

Pitkin, Hannah. *The Concept of Representation*. Berkeley: University of California Press, 1967.

Piven, Frances Fox, and Richard A. Cloward. *Poor People's Movement: Why They Succeed, How They Fail*. New York: Vintage Books, 1979.

"Plan for Olympic Park Spurs Atlanta Protest." *New York Times*, November 21, 1993, 17.

Preserve Low Income and Affordable Housing Now! *Preserve Low Income and Affordable Housing Now! for Detroit: An Organization with a Plan to Preserve and Improve Detroit's Public Housing*. Detroit: PLAN, 1990.

———. "Operation Occupancy." *Tenants' Voice!* 2, nos. 3–4 (1992): 1.

———. "Tenants' Voice." *Tenants' Voice!* 2, nos. 3–4 (1992.): 1–12.

———. "Receivership Now!!!" *Tenants' Voice!* 3, no. 2 (1993): 1.

Planning and Development Department. "Analysis of Funding for Programs as Specified by the City Council." Office of the Auditor General, Detroit, 1996.

Planning Commission. "Minutes of Regular Meeting." City Planning Commission, Detroit, 2007.

Pope, Eric. "MWRO Protests against Winter Utility Shutoffs." *Pipeline* 14, no. 1 (2003): 6.

Pope, Jacqueline. Biting *the Hand That Feeds Them: Organizing Women on Welfare at the Grass Roots Level*. New York: Praeger, 1989.

Popkin, Susan J., Larry F. Buron, Diane K. Levy, and Mary K. Cunningham. "The Gautreaux Legacy: What Might Mixed-Income and Dispersal Strategies Mean for the Poorest Public Housing Tenants?" *Housing Policy Debate* 11, no. 4 (2000): 911–31.

Popkin, Susan J., Bruce Katz, Mary K. Cunningham, Karen D. Brown, Jeremy Gustafson, and Margery A. Turner. "A Decade of HOPE VI: Research Findings and Policy Challenges." Washington, D.C.: Urban Institute and Brookings Institution, 2004.

Pratt, Chastity. "Housing Project Gets Under Way." *Detroit Free Press*, February 7, 2007. 2B.

Prescott, Robert. "Re: DHD Partnership Planning Retreat, To: H. Sharrott." U.S. Department of Housing and Urban Development, Detroit, 1993.

Priestly, Brian. *Chasin' the Bird: The Life and Legacy of Charlie Parker*. Oxford: Oxford University Press, 2005.

"Protesters: Promises Broken." *Detroit Free Press*, March 9, 1988, 19A.

Rasmussen, David, and Raymond Struyk. *A Housing Strategy for the City of Detroit: Policy Perspective Based on Economic Analysis*. Washington, D.C.: Urban Institute Press, 1981.

Ravitz, Mel. "Community Development Block Grant Ordinance: Sponsored by City Council Member Mel Ravitz." *Exchange* 8, no. 5 (1985.): 1–2.

———. "Community Development: Salvation or Suicide?" *Social Policy* (1988): 17–21.

Reed, Adolph, Jr. "The Black Urban Regime: Structural Origins and Constraints." In *Power, Community, and the City: Comparative Urban and Community Research*, ed. by Michael P. Smith. New Brunswick, N.J.: Transaction, 1988.

———. "Sources of Demobilization in the New Black Political Regime: Incorporation, Ideological Capitulation, and Radical Failure in the Post-Segregation Era." In *Stirrings in the Jug: Black Politics in the Post-Segregation Era*, ed. by Adolph Reed Jr. Minneapolis: University of Minnesota Press, 1999.

———. "The Underclass as Myth and Symbol: The Poverty of Discourse about Poverty." *Radical America* 24, no. 1 (1991): 21–40.

"Rent Strike Set for Inner City." *Detroit Free Press*, September 27, 1968, 3B.

Rich, Michael J. *Federal Policymaking and the Poor: National Goals, Local Choices, and Distributional Outcomes*. Princeton: Princeton University Press, 1993.

Rich, Wilbur. *Coleman Young and Detroit Politics: From Social Activist to Power Broker*. Detroit: Wayne State University Press, 1989.

———. "Coleman Young and Detroit Politics, 1972–1986." In *The New Black Politics: The Search for Political Power*, ed. by Michael B. Preston, Paul L. Puryear, and Lenneal J. Henderson. New York: Longman, 1987.

Richardson, Todd. "Redistribution Effect of Introducing Census 2000 Data in CDBG Formula." Office of Policy Development and Research, U.S. Department of Housing and Urban Development, Washington, D.C., 2003.

Roberts, Reginald. "Another Newark Housing Project Has Date with Wrecking Ball." *Star-Ledger*, April 24, 1997, 33.

———. "Newark Mayor Lambastes Columnist." *Star-Ledger*, August 12, 1997, 40.

Roberts, Steven V. "Reagan on Homelessness: Many Choose to Live in the Streets." *New York Times*, December 23, 1988, A26.

Robinson, Deborah. "The Effect of Group Identity among Black Women on Race Consciousness." Ph.D. diss., University of Michigan, Ann Arbor, 1987.

Robnett, Belinda. *How Long? How Long? African-American Women in the Struggle for Civil Rights*. New York: Oxford University Press, 1997.

Rosenstone, Steven J. *Detroit Area Code Book, 1989*. Ann Arbor: University of Michigan, Detroit Area Study, 1989.

Rosenstone, Steven J., and John Mark Hansen. *Mobilization, Participation, and Democracy in America*. New York: Macmillan, 1993.

Rosenthal, Rob. *Homeless in Paradise: A Map of the Terrain*. Philadelphia: Temple University Press, 1994.

Rossi, Peter H. *Down and Out in America: The Origins of Homelessness*. Chicago: University of Chicago Press, 1989.

Rubin, Herbert J. *Renewing Hope within Neighborhoods of Despair: The Community-Based Development Model*. Albany: State University of New York Press, 2000.

Rucht, Dieter, Ruud Koopmans, and Friedhelm Niedhardt. *Acts of Dissent: New Developments in the Study of Protest*. Lanham, Md.: Rowman and Littlefield, 1999.

Rustin, Bayard. "From Protest to Politics." *Commentary* 39, no. 2 (1965): 25–31.

Rutheiser, Charles. *Imagineering Atlanta: The Politics of Place in the City of Dreams*. London: Verso, 1996.

Salama, Jerry J. "The Redevelopment of Distressed Public Housing: Early Results from HOPE VI Projects in Atlanta, Chicago, and San Antonio." *Housing Policy Debate* 10, no. 1 (1999.): 95–142.

Salins, Peter D. "America's Permanent Housing Problem." In *Housing America's Poor*. Chapel Hill: University of North Carolina Press, 1987.

Sanders, Heywood T., and Clarence N. Stone. "Developmental Politics Reconsidered." *Urban Affairs Review* 30 (1995): 407–31.

Sauter, Van G. "Judge Orders Arrest of Vanishing Slumlord: Rep Diggs Plays Hero to Evictees." *Detroit Free Press*, September 27, 1966, 3A–b.

———. "Pickets at New Hotel Tell Landlord: 'Fix Up Our Place.'" *Detroit Free Press*, May 1, 1965, 1A–2A.

———. "Rights Unit Calls Slums Top Issue." *Detroit Free Press*, May 17, 1965, 1A.

Sauter, Van G., and Gary Blonston. "Court Seeks Landlord for Cutting Off Utilities: Tenants in Dark for the Weekend." *Detroit Free Press*, September 26, 1966, 4A-1.

Save Our Spirit. "The Community Development Block Grant Program, 1987–88: SOS Proposes More CDBG Funds to Be Invested in Neighborhoods." *Exchange* 10, no. 2 (1987): 1–2.

———. "Open Letter Asks Council to Vote for Neighborhoods." *Exchange* (May 1991): 1.

———. "Principles of SOS Members." N.d., SOS Files, Cass Corridor Neighborhood Development Corporation, Detroit.

———. "Save Our Spirit Campaign Persuades Council: $10 Million Moved to Neighborhoods." *Exchange* 8, no. 5 (1985): 3, 6.

———. "SOS Builds 'Spirit House' and Garden on Vacant Lot." *Exchange* 9, no. 5 (1986): 3.

———. "SOS Coalition Urges Equity in Block Grant Spending." *Exchange* 9, no. 4 (1986): 1.

Sawyers, Arlena. "'Door Was Open,' so ADC Mom Made Home Her Own." *Detroit News*, August 4, 1982, 3A, 6A.

———. "Squatters Can Take Vacant Houses, City Says." *Detroit News*, July 28, 1983, 3A.

———. "Young Does Nothing—Squatters' Law in Effect." *Detroit News*, August 4, 1983, 1G.

Schattschneider, E. E. *The Semisovereign People*. Hindsdale, Ill.: Dryden Press, 1975.

Schneider, Helen. "On the Fault-Line: The Politics of AIDS in contemporary South Africa." *African Studies* 61, no. 1 (2002): 145–67.

Scott, James C. *Domination and the Arts Resistance: Hidden Transcripts*. New Haven, Conn.: Yale University Press, 1990.

Seaoane, Jose. "From Seattle to Porto Alegre: The Anti-Neoliberal Globalization Movement." *Current Sociology* 50, no. 1 (2002): 99–122.

Seigel, Ron. "Harassment Charged by Tenant Affairs Chairman." *Michigan Chronicle*, October 4, 1969, 10A.

Sharrott, Henry I. "Memorandum to John Codwell, Director, DHD, re: Maintenance Review." Detroit Office Region V, U.S. Department of Housing and Urban Development, Chicago, 1992.

———. *"Operation Occupancy" and Activities to House Homeless Families*, ed. by J. E. Codwell. Detroit: U.S. Department of Housing and Urban Development, 1992.

———. "To John Codwell, Director, DHD, re: FFY 1992 Comprehensive Grant Program (CGP)." Detroit Office Region V, U.S. Department of Housing and Urban Development, Detroit, 1992.

Shaw, Todd C. "The Expanding Boundaries of Black Politics." *National Black Political Science Review* 11 (2007): 3–11.

———. "Race, Regime and Redevelopment: Opportunities for Community Coalitions in Detroit, 1985–1993." *National Political Science Review* 9 (2003): 186–205.

———. "Responsible for Their Deeds: Political Accountability and Black, Low-Income, Housing Advocacy in Detroit, 1933–1993." Ph.D. diss., University of Michigan, Ann Arbor, 1996.

———. "'We Refused to Lay Down Our Spears': The Persistence of Welfare Rights Activism in the Post-Welfare Era, 1966–1996." In *Black Political Organizations in the Post-Civil Rights Era*, ed. by Karlin L. Stanford and Ollie A. Johnson. New Brunswick, N.J.: Rutgers University Press, 2002.

Shaw, Todd C., and Lester K. Spence. "Race and Representation in Detroit's Community Development Coalitions." *Annals of the American Academy of Political and Social Science* 594 (2004): 125–42.

Sheffield, Horace, Jr. "Reactionary Bid to Dump Young Calls on Blacks to Close Ranks." *Michigan Chronicle*, July 29, 1989, A7.

"Shelters Inundated by Nation's Homeless: Search Continues for More Beds." *Detroit Free Press*, December 23, 1988, 12C.

Shingles, Richard. "Black Consciousness and Political Participation: The Missing Link." *American Political Science Review* 75 (1981): 76–91.

Sidney, Mara S. "The Urban Slums Report: The Case of Newark, USA." Report, Department of Political Science, Rutgers University, Newark, N.J., 2003.

Siegel, Suzanne. "Protesters Urge Conversion of Hudson's." *Detroit Free Press*, October 25, 1997, 9A.

Simpson, Andrea Y. "Public Hazard, Personal Peril: The Impact of Non-Governmental Organizations in Environmental Justice Claims." Paper presented at the Annual Meeting of the American Political Science Association, Boston, 2002.

Slater, Wayne. "Obama Reels in Austin Crowd: Sea of People Brushes Off Rain to Hear Democrat's Promise of Change." *Dallas Morning News*, February 24, 2007.

Smiley, Marion. *Moral Responsibility and the Boundaries of Community: Power and Accountability from a Pragmatic Point of View*. Chicago: University of Chicago Press, 1992.

Smith, Doug. "Public Housing Residents Organize to Fight for Improved Conditions." *Exchange* (1991): 1, 8.

———. "Tenant Council? What Tenant Council?" *Tenants' Voice* (PLAN newsletter), vol. 1, no. 2, 1991, 7.

Smith, Jackie, John D. McCarthy, Clark McPhail, and Boguslaw Augustyn. "From Protest to Agenda Building: Description Bias in Media Coverage of Protest Events in Washington, D.C." *Social Forces* 79, no. 4 (2001): 1397–1423.

Smith, Robert C. *We Have No Leaders: African Americans in the Post-Civil Rights Era*. Albany: State University of New York Press, 1996.

Smith, Suzanne E. *Dancing in the Street: Motown and the Cultural Politics of Detroit*. Cambridge, Mass.: Harvard University Press, 1999.

Snow, David A., and Robert D. Benford. "Master Frames and Cycles of Protests." In *Frontiers in Social Movement Theory*, ed. by Aldon D. Morris and Carol M. Mueller. New Haven, Conn.: Yale University Press, 1992.

Snow, David A., E. Burke Rochford, Steven K. Worden, and Robert Benford. "Frame Alignment Processes, Micromobilization, and Movement Participation." *American Sociological Review* 51, no. 4 (1986): 464–81.

Soss, Joe. 1999. Lessons of Welfare: Policy Design, Political Learning, and Political Action. *American Political Science Review* 93 (2): 363–380.

Spence, Lester K. "Parlor Tricks and Politics: Nationalism, Gender, and Political Participation in Detroit." Paper presented at the Annual Meeting of the Midwest Political Science Association, Chicago, April 19–22, 2001.

———. "Strings of Life: Gender and Political Participation in Detroit." Ph.D. diss., University of Michigan, Ann Arbor, 2001.

Springer, Kimberly, ed. *Still Lifting, Still Climbing: African American Women's Contemporary Activism*. New York: New York University Press, 1999.

Stanton, Barbara. "Housing Director Finds a Defender." *Detroit Free Press*, September 27, 1966, 1A, 4A.

———. "Housing Experiment: Arson Sets Back Tenant Project." *Detroit Free Press*, July 11, 1969., 3A–4A.

———. "Urban Renewal Protesters Break Up Council Session." *Detroit Free Press*, November 17, 1965, 4A.

Steuerle, C. Eugene. "An Ownership Society or a Society for Those Who Already Own?" *Tax Analysts*, January 31, 2005, 597.

Stewart, Agnes. "Blacks Are Hard Hit By City Layoffs." *Michigan Chronicle*, January 4, 1975, 1A.

Stoecker, Randy. "Understanding the Development–Organizing Dialectic." *Journal of Urban Affairs* 25, no. 4 (2003): 493–512.

Stone, Clarence N. *Regime Politics: Governing Atlanta, 1946–1988*. Lawrence: University Press of Kansas, 1989.

———. "Systemic Power in Community Decision Making: A Restatement of Stratification Theory." In *Readings in Urban Politics*, ed. by Harlan Hahn and Charles H. Levine. New York: Longman, 1980.

Stone, Clarence N., ed. *Changing Urban Education*. Lawrence: University Press of Kansas, 1998.

Stone, Michael E. *Shelter Poverty: News Ideas on Housing Affordability*. Philadelphia: Temple University Press, 1993.

Stovall, A. J. "Before Coleman Young: The Growth of the Detroit Black Elected Officialdom, 1870–1973." Ph.D. diss., Union for Experimenting Colleges and Universities, Cincinnati, 1983.

———. *The Growth of Black Elected Officials in the City of Detroit, 1870–1973*. Lewiston, N.Y.: Mellen University Press, 1996.

Sugrue, Thomas. "Crabgrass-Roots Politics: Race, Rights, and the Reaction against Liberalism in the Urban North, 1940–1964." *Journal of American History* 82, no. 2 (1995): 551–78.

———. *The Origins of the Urban Crisis: Race and Inequality in Postwar Detroit*. Princeton: Princeton University Press, 1996.

———. "The Origins of the Urban Crisis: Race, Industrial Decline, and Housing in Detroit, 1940–1960." Ph.D. diss., Harvard University, Cambridge, Mass., 1992.

———. "The Structures of Urban Poverty: The Reorganization of Space and Work in Three Periods of American History." In *The "Underclass" Debate: Views from History*, ed. by Michael B. Katz. Princeton: Princeton University Press, 1993.

Sweeney, Ann. "Brewster 'Family' Returns to Projects." *Detroit News*, July 14, 1991, 1C.

Tait, Vanessa. "'Workers Just like Anyone Else': Organizing Welfare Unions in New York City." In *Still Lifting, Still Climbing: African American Women's Contemporary Activism*, ed. by Kimberly Springer. New York: New York University Press, 1999.

Tarrow, Sidney. *Power in Movement: Social Movements and Contentious Politics*, 2d ed. Cambridge: Cambridge University Press, 1998.

———. *Struggling to Reform: Collective Action, Social Movements, and Cycles of Protest*. Ithaca, N.Y.: Western Societies Program, Cornell University, 1983.

Tate, Katherine. *Black Faces in the Mirror: African Americans and Their Representatives in the U.S. Congress*. Princeton: Princeton University Press, 2003.

———. "Black Political Participation in the 1984 and 1988 Presidential Elections." *American Political Science Review* 85, no. 4 (1994): 1159–76.

———. *From Protest to Politics: The New Black Voters in American Elections*. Cambridge, Mass.: Russell Sage and Harvard University Press, 1993.

Teaford, Jon C. *The Rough Road to Renaissance: Urban Revitalization in America, 1940–1985*. Baltimore: John Hopkins University Press, 1990.

Teles, Steven M. *Whose Welfare? AFDC and Elite Politics*, 2d ed. Lawrence: University Press of Kansas, 1998.

Thomas, June M. "Applying for Empowerment Zone Designation: A Tale of Woe and Triumph." *Economic Development Quarterly* 9, no. 3 (1995): 212–24.

———. "Neighborhood Response to Redevelopment in Detroit." *Community Development Journal* 29 (1985): 79–90.

———. "Racial Crisis and the Fall of the Detroit Plan Commission." APA *Journal* (1988): 150–61.

———. *Redevelopment and Race: Planning A Finer City in Postwar Detroit*. Baltimore: Johns Hopkins University Press, 1997.

Thomas, Richard W. *Life for Us Is What We Make It: Building Black Community in Detroit, 1915–1945*. Bloomington: Indiana University Press, 1992.

Thompson, Heather Ann. "Rethinking the Collapse of Postwar Liberalism: The Rise of Mayor Coleman Young and the Politics of Race in Detroit." In *African-American Mayors: Race, Politics, and the American City*, ed. by David R. Colburn and Jeffrey S. Adler. Urbana: University of Illinois Press, 2001.

———. *Whose Detroit? Politics, Labor, and Race in a Modern American City*. Ithaca, N.Y.: Cornell University Press, 2001.

Thompson, J. Phillip, III. *Double Trouble: Black Mayors, Black Communities, and the Call for a Deep Democracy*. Oxford: Oxford University Press, 2006.

Tilly, Charles. *From Mobilization to Revolution*. Reading, Mass: Addison-Wesley, 1978.

Towns, Hollis. "Homeless Numbers Vary, Spur Debates." *Atlanta Journal-Constitution*, November 17, 1998, C1.

Toy, Vivian S. "City Council Approves Plan to Raze Parkside Homes." *Detroit News*, January 16, 1992, 3B.

———. "Mahaffey Wants to Shorten Wait for Federal Block Funds." *Detroit News*, March 19, 1991.

Trent, Kim. "HUD Chief Offers New Hope." *Detroit News*, December 7, 1993, 11B.

———. "HUD Official Scolds City for Not Meeting Public Housing Goals." *Detroit News*, December 6, 1991, 2A, 8A.

———. "HUD to City: Leave Parkside Residents Alone." *Detroit Free Press*, January 10, 1992, 2B.

———. "Low-Income Units Should Be Repaired, Not Razed, Some Council Members Say." *Detroit News*, December 3, 1991, 1B, 2B.

Tschirhart, Don. "Mrs. Henderson to Battle Mayor." *Detroit News*, September 14, 1983, 3A, 9A.

———. "Project Residents Raise Protest." *Detroit News*, August 23, 1987, 3B.

Tucker, William. *The Excluded Americans: Homelessness and Housing Policies*. Washington, D.C.: Regnery Gateway, 1990.

United Community Housing Coalition. "Detroit Urban League Detroit Wayne County Homeless Strategy Coalition: 24 Ways to Fight Homelessness Now!" *Housing Times*, Summer–Fall 1993, 5.

United New Orleans Plan, "Preliminary Report Updated: Community Congress III." United New Orleans Plan, New Orleans, 2007.

U.S. Bureau of the Census. "Current Housing Reports." *American Housing Survey for the Detroit Metropolitan Area in 1985*, U.S. Bureau of the Census, Washington, D.C., 1989.

———. "Emergency and Transitional Shelter Population: 2000." *Census 2000 Special Reports*. U.S. Bureau of the Census, Washington, D.C., 2001.

U.S. Bureau of the Census and U.S. Bureau of Labor Statistics. *Annual Demographic Survey, March Supplement*. Washington, D.C.: U.S. Department of Commerce, 1998.

U.S. Department of Housing and Urban Development. "American Housing Survey for the Detroit Metropolitan Area." In *Current Housing Reports H170/95-6*. Washington, D.C., 1995.

———. *Briefing on Detroit Public Housing*. Detroit, 1993.

———. *Coordinated Management Review: Detroit Housing Department*. Chicago: Office of Inspector General, Region V, 1990.

———. "HUD Assumes Control of Detroit Housing Commission to Restore Public Confidence in Agency." Press release, *HUD News*, no. 05-094, 2005.

———. *Low-Income Housing Program: Detroit Housing Department*. Chicago: Office of the Inspector General, Region V, 1983.

———. *Maintenance Review: Detroit Housing Department*. Chicago: Office of the Inspector General, Region V, 1992.

———. *Review. Detroit Housing Department, Findings and Corrective Actions, Comprehensive Assistance Improvements Program (CIAP)*. Chicago: Office of the Inspector General, Region V, 1992.

U.S. General Accounting Office. "Public Housing: Information on Receiverships at Public Housing Authorities." Report to the chairman, Subcommittee on Housing and Transportation, Committee on Banking, Housing, and Urban Affairs, U.S. Senate. Washington, D.C.: U.S. General Accounting Office, 2003.

———. "Public Housing: HUD's Oversight of HOPE VI Sites Needs to be More Consistent." Report to the ranking minority member, Subcommittee on Housing and Transportation, Committee on Banking, Housing, and Urban Affairs, U.S. Senate. Washington, D.C., 2003.

U.S. Government Accountability Office. *Empowerment Zones and Enterprise Community Program: Improvements Occurred in Communities, but the Effect of the Program Unclear*. Report to Congressional Committees. Washington, D.C.: U.S. Government, 2006.

"U.S. Housing Programs Overhauled: Bill Aimed to Increase Stock of Affordable Homes." *Congressional Quarterly Almanac*, 1990, 631–53.

U.S. President's Commission on Housing. *The Report of the President's Commission on Housing*. Washington, D.C.: Government Printing Office, 1982.

U.S. Senate. "Hearing on Homeless Situation in Michigan." Committee on Banking, Housing, and Urban Affairs, Washington, D.C., 1990.

Van DeBurg, William. *Modern Black Nationalism: From Marcus Garvey to Louis Farrakhan*. New York: New York University Press, 1997.

Vance, N. Scott. "Brewster Razing Bid Faulted." *Detroit News*, January 14, 1987, 3B.

———. "Mayor: Foes Happy over His Setback at Polls." *Detroit News*, November 10, 1988, 1A.

———. "Project Residents Protest Demolition." *Detroit News*, March 24, 1987, 1B, 7B.

———. "Young Fights Override Proposal: Calls Spending Curb Illegal Power Grab by Council." *Detroit News*, September 23, 1988, 1B.

———. "Young Wins Budget War with Council." *Detroit News*, June 3, 1987, 1B, 4B.

Vance, N. Scott, and Dave Farrell. "City Acts to Evict Woman, but She Has Moved." *Detroit News*, August 23, 1989, B3.

Vance, N. Scott, and Rob Zeiger. "Detroit Council Members Oppose Many Young Cuts." *Detroit News*, April 15, 1987, 4B.

Vardy, David P., Jeffrey A. Rafeel, Stephanie Sweeney, and Latina Denson. "Attracting Middle-Income Families in the HOPE VI Public Housing Revitalization Program." *Journal of Urban Affairs* 27, no. 2 (2005.): 149–64.

Velie, Lester. "Housing: Detroit's Time Bomb." *Collier* (1946): 14–15, 75–78.

Venkatesh, Sudhir Alladi. *American Project: The Rise and Fall of a Modern Ghetto*. Cambridge, Mass.: Harvard University Press, 2000.

Verba, Sidney, and Norman Nie. *Participation in America*. New York: Harper and Row, 1972.

Verba, Sidney, Kay Lehman Schlozman, and Henry E. Brady. *Voice and Equality: Civic Voluntarism in American Politics*. Cambridge, Mass.: Harvard University Press, 1995.

Verba, Sidney, Kay Lehman Schlozman, Henry Brady, and Norman Nie. "Citizen Activity: Who Participates? What Do They Say? *American Political Science Review* 87 (1993): 303–18.

Vidal, Avis C. "Rebuilding Communities: A National Study of Urban Community Development Corporations." Community Development Research Center, Graduate School of Management and Urban Policy. New School for Social Research, New York, 1992.

"Vote Totals—Results of Tuesday's Special Election." *Detroit Free Press*, April 25, 1991, 1B.

Wagner, David. *Checkerboard Square: Culture and Resistance in a Homeless Community*. Boulder, Colo.: Westview Press, 1993.

Wagner, David, and Marcia B. Cohen. "The Power of the People: Homeless Protesters in the Aftermath of Social Movement Participation." *Social Problems* 38, no. 4 (1991): 543–61.

Walker, Christopher. "Community Development Corporations and Their Changing Support Systems." Washington, D.C.: Urban Institute, 2002.

Walker, Jack L., Jr. *Mobilizing Interest Groups in America: Patrons, Professions, and Social Movements*. Ann Arbor: University of Michigan Press, 1991.

Walters, Ronald W. *Black Presidential Politics: A Strategic Approach*. Albany: State University of New York Press, 1988.

Walton, Hanes, Jr. 1997. *African American Power and Politics: The Political Context Variable*. New York, NY: Columbia University Press.

———. *Black Politics: A Theoretical and Structural Analysis*. Philadelphia: J. P. Lippincott, 1972.

Wang, Katie, and Jeffrey C Mays. "After Two Decades under James, Residents Heed Call for Change." *Star-Ledger*, May 10, 2006, 1–3.

Warren Connor Development Coalition. "Casino Gambling: Is It Worth It?" *Exchange* 11, no. 1 (1988): 1–5, 7.

"We Are Making Progress Now." *Michigan Chronicle*, July 31, 1965, 6B.

Weisman, Jonathan. "Bush Plans Sharp Cuts in HUD Community Efforts." *Washington Post*, January 14, 2005, A1.

Welch, Susan, Lee Sigelman, Timothy Bledsoe, and Michael Combs. *Race and Place: Race Relations in an American City*. Cambridge: Cambridge University Press, 2001.

West Central Organization. *By-Laws / West Central Organization*. Papers of the Office of Religious Affairs. Archive of Labor and Urban Affairs. West Central Organization, Box 26. Wayne State University, Detroit, 1965.

West, Cornel. "The Crisis of Black Leadership." In *Race Matters*. New York: Vintage Books, 1993.

West, Guida. *The National Welfare Rights Movement: The Social Protest of Poor Women*. New York: Praeger, 1981.

Westbrook, Robert B. *John Dewey and American Democracy*. Ithaca, N.Y.: Cornell University Press, 1991.

"When Life in the Projects Was Good." *New York Times*, July 31, 1991, A13.

White, Aaronette. "Talking Black, Talking Feminist: Gendered Micromobilization Processes in a Collective Protest against Rape." In *Still Lifting, Still Climbing: Contemporary African American Women Activism*, ed. by Kimberly Springer. New York: New York University Press, 1999.

Whoriskey, Peter. "Thousands Protest Blacks' Treatment: Six Students Who Were Prosecuted in Louisiana Garner National Wide Support." *Washington Post*, September 21, 2007, A1.

Widick, B. J. *Detroit: City of Race and Class Violence*, rev. ed. Detroit: Wayne State University Press, 1986.

Wilkes, Robert, Jr. "A Case Study of Homelessness in the City of Atlanta: Looking at the Impact of Urban Renewal. Paper read at National Conference of Black Political Scientists, at Atlanta. 1996.

Williams, Linda F. *The Constraint of Race: Legacies of White Skin Privilege in America*. University Park: Pennsylvania State University Press, 2003.

———. "Detroit Politics and Urban Theory: The More Things Change, the More They Stay the Same." Paper presented at the Annual Meeting of the National Conference of Black Political Scientists, Chicago, 1987.

Williams, Patricia J. *The Alchemy of Race and Rights: Diary of a Law Professor*. Cambridge, Mass.: Harvard University Press, 1991.

Williams, Rhonda Y. *The Politics of Public Housing*. Oxford: Oxford University Press, 2004.

Wilson, Carter. "Restructuring and the Growth of Concentrated Poverty in Detroit." *Urban Affairs Quarterly* 28, no. 2 (1992): 187–205.

Wilson, Danton. "Young Blasts Media Coverage." *Michigan Chronicle*, July 1, 1989, 1A, 5A.

Wilson, William Julius. *The Declining Significance of Race*. Chicago: University of Chicago Press, 1978.

———. *The Truly Disadvantaged: The Inner City, the Underclass, and Public Policy*. Chicago: University of Chicago Press, 1987.

Wimberley, Michael. "Leaders Blast Engler on Homelessness." *Michigan Chronicle*, January 17, 1992, 1A, 4A.

Wisler, Dominque, and Jose Barranco. "Validity and Systematicity of Newspaper Data in Event Analysis." *European Sociological Review* 3 (1999): 301–22.

Wolch, Jennifer, and Michael Dear. *Malign Neglect: Homelessness in an American City*. San Francisco: Jossey-Bass, 1993.

Wolcott, Victoria W. *Remaking Respectability: African American Women in Interwar Detroit*. Chapel Hill: University of North Carolina Press, 2001.

Wolf, Eleanor P., and Charles Leabeaux. *Change and Renewal in an Urban Community: Five Case Studies*. New York: Praeger, 1969.

Woliver, Laura. *From Outrage to Action: The Politics of Grass-Roots Dissent*. Urbana: University of Illinois Press, 1993.

Woliver, Laura, Angela D. Ledford, and Chris J. Dolan. "The South Carolina Confederate Flag: The Politics of Race and Citizenship." *Politics and Policy* 29, no. 4 (2001): 708–30.

Wood, Richard L. "Higher Power: Strategic Capacity for State and National Organizing." In *Transforming the City: Community Organizing and the Challenge of Political Change*, ed. by Marion Orr. Lawrence: University Press of Kansas, 2007.

Woody, Bette. *Managing Crisis Cities: The New Black Leadership and the Politics of Resource Allocation*. Westport, Conn.: Greenwood Press, 1982.

Wright, Talmadge. *Out of Place: Homeless Mobilizations, Subcities, and Contested Landscapes*. Albany: State University of New York Press, 1997.

Wylie, Jean. *Poletown: Community Betrayed*. Urbana: University of Illinois Press, 1989.

Young, Coleman. "From the Mayor. To: Honorable City Council." *Journal of the City Council*, 1989, 1222–23.

———. "Mayor's Message." City of Detroit Budget, 1986–87, presented to the Detroit City Council, 1986.

———. "Mayor's Message." City of Detroit Budget, 1991–92, presented to the Detroit City Council, 1991.

Young, Coleman, and Lonnie Wheeler. *Hard Stuff: The Autobiography of Mayor Coleman Young*. New York: Viking, 1994.

Zablit, Jocelyne. "Group Vows to be Advocate for Homeless." *Detroit Free Press*, January 29, 1988, 4A.

Zieger, Robert H. *John L. Lewis: Labor Leader*. Boston: Twayne Publishers, 1988.

Zorn, Christopher. "Comparing GEE and Robust Standard Errors for Conditionally Dependent Data." *Political Research Quarterly* 59, no. 3 (2006): 329–41.

# Index

Todd C. Shaw is an associate professor of political science and African American studies at the University of South Carolina, Columbia.

Library of Congress Cataloging-in-Publication Data
Shaw, Todd Cameron.
Now is the time! : Detroit black politics and grassroots activism / Todd C. Shaw.
p. cm.
Includes bibliographical references and index.
ISBN 978-0-8223-4495-7 (cloth : alk. paper)
ISBN 978-0-8223-4508-4 (pbk. : alk. paper)
1. African American political activists—Michigan—Detroit—History—20th century. 2. African Americans—Michigan—Detroit—Social conditions—History—20th century. 3. African Americans—Civil rights—Michigan—Detroit—History—20th century. 4. Community development—Michigan—Detroit. 5. African Americans—Housing—Michigan—Detroit. 6. Detroit (Mich.)—Race relations—History—20th century. I. Title.
F574.D49N48225 2009
977.4'34—dc22 2009012700